MICHAEL KULIKOWSKI i .... 'y
and Classics at Penn State .... g
ranges widely across ancient .... ır
contributor to the *London 1* .... 's
Gothic Wars, described by *B* .... l'
and by *Military History Review* ... breezy and animated, yet authoritative',
and *Imperial Triumph* (Profile, 2016).

PRAISE FOR *IMPERIAL TRIUMPH*:

'This is a wonderfully broad sweep of Roman history ... fascinating'
Mary Beard

'A genuinely bracing and innovative history of Rome for a general
audience' *TLS*

'This was an era of great change, and Mr Kulikowski is an excellent and
insightful guide to the process' *Wall Street Journal*

'Kulikowski's lively and engaging account brings clarity to the murky
world of the late Roman Empire. It lets us understand the endless
in-fighting between imperial hopefuls, the profound reforms of
Diocletian and the social transformation that expressed itself in
Christianity. It explains the many forces that led to the western empire's
disintegration and expertly guides us through a post-Roman world
which was eventually to give rise to modern Europe' Jerry Toner, author
of *Infamy*

'Kulikowski pairs his comprehensive understanding of late Roman
politics with an uncanny eye for spatial and material details as he
reconstructs an empire in a downward spiral of self-destruction.
Roman emperors and barbarian kings, pagan aristocrats and Christian
bishops, loyal soldiers and self-serving condottieri are woven into the
brilliantly dramatised story of *Imperial Tragedy*' Noel Lenski, author
of *Constantine and the Cities*

'Insightful, coherent and articulate' *BBC History Magazine*

'Demonstrates impressive mastery of a vast and complex field'
Australian Book Review

'A breezy and animated yet authorative look at this remarkable time
... sure to be of interest to anybody with a taste in character-driven
history' *Military History Review*

IMPERIAL TRAGEDY

FROM CONSTANTINE'S EMPIRE TO THE DESTRUCTION OF ROMAN ITALY (AD 363–568)

MICHAEL KULIKOWSKI

P

PROFILE BOOKS

This paperback edition published in 2021

First published in Great Britain in 2019 by
PROFILE BOOKS LTD
29 Cloth Fair
London ECIA 7JQ
www.profilebooks.com

1 3 5 7 9 10 8 6 4 2

Typeset in Garamond by MacGuru Ltd

Printed and bound in Great Britain by
CPI Group (UK) Ltd, Croydon, CR0 4YY

A CIP catalogue record for this book is available from the British Library.

ISBN 978 1 78125 633 6
eISBN 978 1 78283 246 1

CONTENTS

ACKNOWLEDGEMENTS

That the current world order is in crisis seems, as I write, to have become an article of faith. At all such moments, invocations of Rome's decline and fall are de rigueur, their vehemence in inverse proportion to their discernment. Professional historians can be forgiven the urge to contribute: a mistake. Historical analogy requires, by definition, simplification at odds with historical understanding. History neither repeats nor rhymes, and the only thing it should teach us is that, constrained by custom, by psychology, and by our always faulty memories, constrained most of all by circumstance not of our individual making, humans tend to make a mess of making their own fate. I hope I do justice to the mess and the muddle.

The acknowledgements to *Imperial Triumph*, this book's companion and predecessor, were very extensive. I remain deeply grateful to all the many people I thanked there, most of all to David and Ellen. (And, though not a person, to Melvin.)

As she steps down after almost three decades as dean of my college, Susan Welch requires a special note of thanks: watching her has taught me more about the workings of complex institutions and the meaning of leadership than any formal tuition could have done. Thanks to her support and mentoring, I have been able to continue with research and writing while also serving as head of department, something that, unfashionably, I will admit to enjoying.

The production teams at Profile and Harvard have, as always, been models of skill and efficiency, particularly my editors, Louisa Dunnigan and Penny Daniel, copyeditor Sally Holloway, and Sharmila Sen and Heather Hughes at Harvard. I deeply regret that John Davey, who commissioned this book and whose incisive but capacious vision underpins the Profile History of the Ancient World series, did not live to see its completion. Death and illness have silenced too many teachers and friends in the past three years, but they have left their mark on every page.

Just before this book was finished, the last of my grandparents died. From the Polish-Soviet War to the Blitz, from Siberia to the Anders army and Monte Cassino, from Broxbourne to Perón's Buenos Aires, they had survived the great imperial tragedies of the twentieth century. Piecing together their stories from the small stock they let slip or felt able to share, trying as a suburban schoolboy to imagine the unimaginable: long before I was conscious of it, they were helping me to become a historian. Their memory keeps me at it.

LIST OF
ILLUSTRATIONS

13. Honorius Cameo, depicting Emperor Honorius (395–423) and his wife, Maria (ivory and metal). Photo: Private Collection/ Bridgeman Images
14. Throne of Maximianus, Mainz Romano-Germanic Central Museum. Photo: akg-images
15. Dido making a sacrifice, from *The Vergilius Vaticanus* (Lat 3225 f.33v). Photo: Vatican Library, Vatican City/Bridgeman Images
16. Sarcophagus of Junius Bassus. Photo: De Agostini Picture Library/G. Cigolini/Bridgeman Images
17. The Istanbul Evangelist. Photo: De Agostini Picture Library/ Bridgeman Images
18. An Alkhan 'Hun'. Photo: Public domain
19. *Tessera* of Basilius. Photo: Public domain
20. The Taq-e Kesra, Ctesiphon. Photo: Library of Congress
21. The Castulo Paten. Photo: Wikipedia
22. Szilágysomlyó Medallion. Photo: KHM-Museumsverband
23. Bracteate from Funen. Photo: KHM-Museumsverband
24. São Cucufate, Portugal. Photo: Wikipedia
25. The Corbridge *Lanx*. Photo: with permission of the Trustees of the British Museum

While every effort has been made to contact copyright-holders of illustrations, the author and publishers would be grateful for information about any illustrations where they have been unable to trace them, and would be glad to make amendments in further editions.

Maps

The Roman Empire under Constantine

Atlantic Ocean

North Sea

Baltic Sea

BRITANNIAE

BRITANNIA II

FLAVIA CAESARIENSIS

MAXIMA CAESARIENSIS

BRITANNIA I

Rhine

GERMANIA INFERIOR

GALLIAE

II

BELGICA

II

LUGDUNENSIS

PANNONIAE

Danube

RAETIA II

NORICUM RIPENSE

NORICUM MEDITERRANEUM

PANNONIA

VALERIA

VIENNENSIS

II

AQUITANIA

I

GERMANIA SUPERIOR

RAETIA I

ALPES GRAIAE

VIENNENSIS

ALPES COTTIAE

ALPES MARITIMAE

LIGURIA

VENETIA ET HISTRIA

SAVIA

PANNONIA II

MOESIA

NOVEMPOPULANA

NARBONENSIS I

AEMILIA

FLAMINIA ET PICENUM

DALMATIA

MOESIA I

GALLAECIA

TARRACONENSIS

NARBONENSIS II

TUSCIA ET UMBRIA

PICENUM

PRAEVALITANA

DARDANIA

LUSITANIA

H I S P A N I A E

C A R T H A G I N E N S I S

CORSICA

Rome

SAMNIUM

CAMPANIA

ITALIA

APULIA ET CALABRIA

EPIRUS NOVA

MACEDO

BAETICA

SARDINIA

LUCANIA ET BRUTTIA

EPIRUS VETUS

THESS

ACHA

SICILIA

MACEDONIA

Mediterranean Sea

MAURETANIA TINGITANA

MAURETANIA CAESARIENSIS

MAURETANIA SITIFENSIS

NUMIDIA CIRTENSIS

PROCONSULARIS

Carthage

A

F

NUMIDIA MILITIANA

BYZACENA

R

I

C

A

Mediterranean Sea

N

TRIPOLITANA

LIBYA SUPERIO

ASIA Constantinian dioceses

0		1000		2000 kilometres
0	500		1000 miles	

THRACIA

Black Sea

SCYTHIA

Danube

MOESIA II

THRACIA

HAEMIMONTUS

Constantinople

RHODOPE

EUROPA

BITHYNIA ET PONTUS

PAPHLAGONIA

DIOSPONTUS

PONTUS POLEMONIACUS

ARMENIA MINOR

PONTICA

ARMENIA

HELLESPONTUS

GALATIA

LYDIA

PHRYGIA II

CAPPADOCIA

Tigris

MESOPOTAMIA

ASIA

CARIA

PISIDIA

ISAURIA

CILICIA

OSRHOENE

Euphrates

LYCIA ET PAMPHYLIA

ASIA

CRETA

CYPRUS

SYRIA COELE

EUPHRATENSIS

PHOENICIA

LIBANENSIS

S Y R I A

Aral Sea

Caspian Sea

LIBYA INFERIOR

IOVIA

Alexandria

O R I E N S

PALAESTINA

ARABIA

II

AEGYPTUS

HERCULIA

Nile

THEBAIS

Red Sea

The Roman Empire, *c.* 400

Atlantic Ocean

North Sea

Baltic Sea

BRITANNIAE

BRITANNIA II

VALENTIA

FLAVIA CAESARIENSIS

BRITANNIA I

MAXIMA CAESARIENSIS

GERMANIA II

Rhine

GALLIAE

BELGICA II

BELGICA I

ITALIA

ILLYRICUM

Danube

RAETIA II

NORICUM RIPENSE

NORICUM MEDITERRANEUM

PANNONIA I

VALERIA

DACIA

LUGDUNENSIS II

LUGDUNENSIS SENONIA

LUGDUNENSIS III

GERMANIA I

LUGDUNENSIS I

MAXIMA SEQUANORUM

RAETIA I

VENETIA ET HISTRIA

SAVIA

PANNONIA II

SEPTEM PROVINCIAE

II

AQUITANIA

I

AEMILIA

ALPES POENINAE

ALPES COTTIAE

ALPES MARITIMAE

LIGURIA

FLAMINIA ET PICENUM

DALMATIA

MOESIA I

VIENNENSIS

GALLAECIA

TARRACONENSIS

NOVEMPOPULI

NARBONENSIS I

NARBONENSIS II

TUSCIA ET UMBRIA

PICENUM SUBURBI-CARIUM

SAMNIUM

DARDANIA

PRAEVALITANA

HISPANIAE

LUSITANIA

CARTHAGINENSIS

CORSICA

Rome

CAMPANIA

APULIA ET CALABRIA

EPIRUS NOVA

MACED

BAETICA

BALEARES

SARDINIA

SUBURBICARIA

LUCANIA ET BRUTTIA

EPIRUS VETUS

THES

ACH

TINGITANA

MAURETANIA CAESARIENSIS

MAURETANIA SITIFENSIS

NUMIDIA

AFRICA

Carthage

SICILIA

MACEDONIA

Mediterranean Sea

A F R I C A

BYZACENA

TRIPOLITANA

LIBYA SUPERI

N

ASIA   Dioceses according to the Notitia Dignitatum

| 0 | 1000 | 2000 kilometres |
| 0 | 500 | 1000 miles |

The Roman Empire, *c.* 550

Atlantic Ocean

North Sea

Baltic Sea

Rhine

Danube

REGNA FRANCORUM

REGNUM SUEVORUM

VENETIA ET HISTRIA

AEMILIA

ALPES COTTIAE

LIGURIA

FLAMINIA

DALMATIA

PANNONIA

MOESIA I

REGNUM VISIGOTHORUM

TUSCIA ET UMBRIA

PICENUM

DARDANIA

CORSICA

SAMNIUM

Rome

CAMPANIA

PRAEVALITANA

APULIA ET CALABRIA

MACED II

SPANIA

SARDINIA

EPIRUS NOVA

EPIRUS VETUS

THES

ACH

BALEARES

LUCANIA ET BRUTTIA

SICILIA

Mediterranean Sea

MAURETANIA CAESARIENSIS

MAURETANIA SITIFENSIS

NUMIDIA

ZEUIGITANA

Carthage

BYZACENA

TRIPOLITANIA

LIBYA PENTAPO

N

| 0 | | 1000 | | 2000 kilometres |
| 0 | 500 | | 1000 miles | |

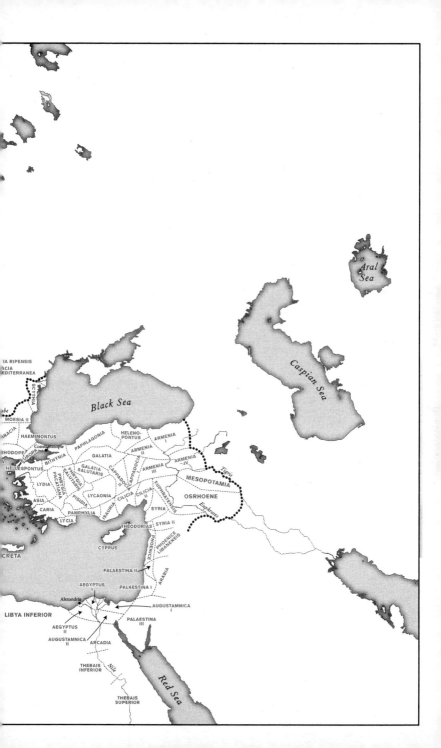

IA RIPENSIS
ACIA
EDITERRANEA

be

MOESIA II

RACIA

HAEMIMONTUS

INODOPE
Constantinople

EUROPA

BITHYNIA

PAPHLAGONIA

HELENO-
PONTUS

ARMENIA
I

HELLESPONTUS

GALATIA

ARMENIA
II

PHRYGIA
SALUTARIS

GALATIA
SALUTARIS

CAPPADOCIA

LYDIA

PHRYGIA
PACATIANA

PISIDIA

LYCAONIA

CAPPADOCIA
II

ARMENIA
III

ARMENIA
IV

ASIA

CARIA

ISAURIA

CILICIA

CILICIA
II

EUPHRATENSIS

MESOPOTAMIA

OSRHOENE

LYCIA

PAMPHYLIA

THEODORIAS

SYRIA I

SYRIA II

CRETA

CYPRUS

PHOENICE

PHOENICE
LIBANENSIS

Tigris

Euphrates

PALAESTINA II

AEGYPTUS

PALAESTINA I

ARABIA

Alexandria

LIBYA INFERIOR

AUGUSTAMNICA
I

AEGYPTUS
II

AUGUSTAMNICA
II

PALAESTINA
III

ARCADIA

THEBAIS
INFERIOR

Nile

Red Sea

THEBAIS
SUPERIOR

Black Sea

Caspian Sea

Aral
Sea

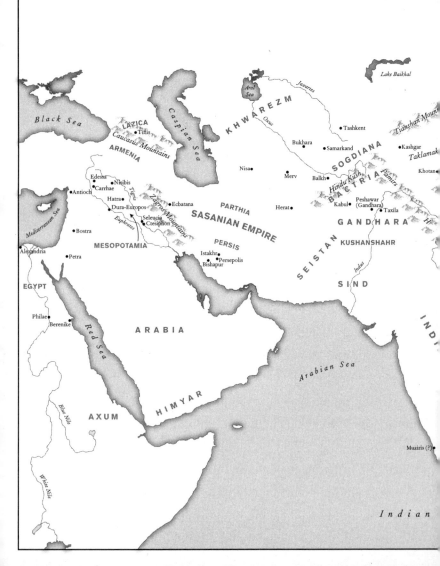

The Eurasian World

0   1000   2000 kilometres
0   500   1000 miles

The Sasanian Empire

Gaul and Spain

North Sea

Vetera
Colonia Agrippinensis
Bonna
Moguntiacum
Augusta Treverorum
Argentoratum

Londinium
Bononia

Aug. Suessionum
Durocortorum
Rotomagus
Lutetia

Vindonissa

Aventicum

English Channel

Augustodunum

Caesarodunum
Avaricum
Iuliomagus

Augusta Praetoria
Augusta Taurinorum
Susa

Lugdunum
Vienna

Civitas Arvernorum

Valentia

N

Bay of Biscay

Segodunum
Nemausus
Arelate

Nicaea
Antipolis

Massilia

Burdigala

Tolosa
Narbo

Emporion
Gerunda
Iluro
Barcino

Calagurris
Ilerda
Caesaraugusta

Tarraco

Legio VII Gemina
Asturica Augusta
Pallantia
Clunia
Uxama
Bilbilis

Dertosa

Aquae Flaviae
Bracara Augusta

Segobriga
Toletum

Valentia

Conimbriga

Emerita

Carthago Nova

Olisipo

Corduba
Illiberis

Hispalis
Malaca
Gades
Julia Traducta

Mediterranean Sea

Rhine

0   100   200 kilometres
0   100 miles

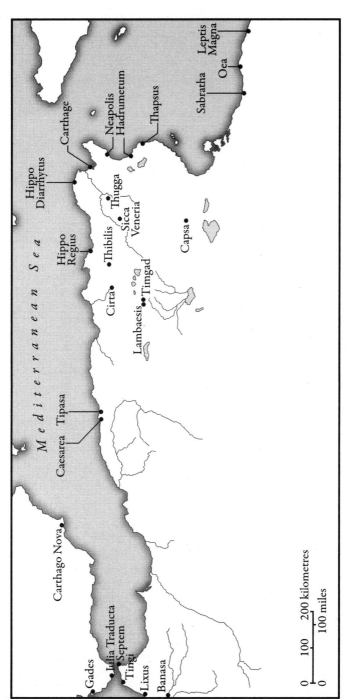

North Africa

Mediterranean Sea

Leptis Magna
Oea
Sabratha
Thapsus
Neapolis
Hadrumetum
Carthage
Hippo Diarrhytus
Thugga
Sicca Veneria
Hippo Regius
Thibilis
Capsa
Cirta
Timgad
Lambaesis
Tipasa
Caesarea
Carthago Nova
Gades
Julia Traducta
Septem
Tingi
Lixus
Banasa

0   100   200 kilometres
0   100 miles

Italy

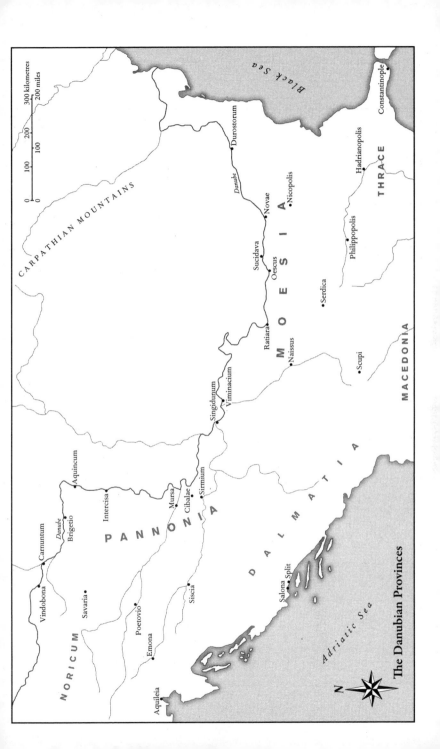

The Danubian Provinces

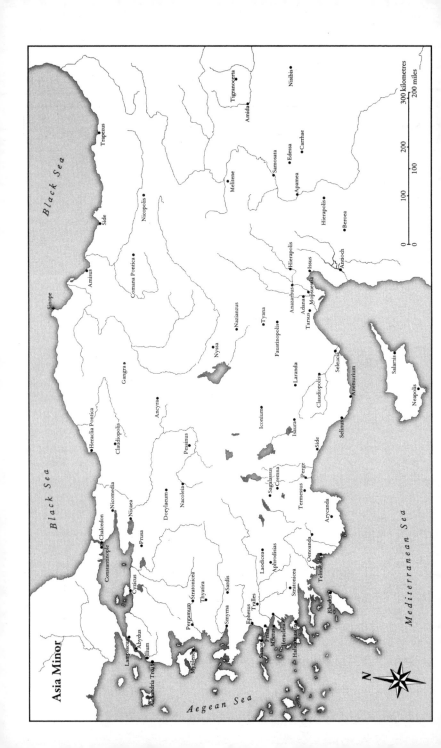

Asia Minor

Black Sea

Black Sea

Aegean Sea

Mediterranean Sea

Trapezus
Side
Amisus
Sinope
Nicopolis
Comana Pontica
Heraclia Pontica
Claudiopolis
Gangra
Ancyra
Pessinus
Nacoleia
Dorylaeum
Chalcedon
Nicomedia
Nicaea
Prusa
Constantinople
Cyzicus
Laodicea
Abydus
Ilium
Alexandria Troas
Mytilene
Pergamum
Thyatira
Stratonicea
Sardis
Smyrna
Ephesus
Tralles
Priene
Miletus
Heraclia
Halicarnassus
Rhodes
Laodicea
Aphrodisias
Stratonicea
Oenoanda
Telmessus
Arycanda
Termessus
Perge
Side
Sagalassus
Cremna
Selinus
Anemurium
Seleucia
Claudiopolis
Isaura
Iconium
Faustinopolis
Laranda
Tyana
Nazianzus
Nyssa
Adana
Tarsus
Anazarbus
Mopsuestia
Issus
Hierapolis
Antioch
Beroea
Hierapolis
Apamea
Samosata
Edessa
Carrhae
Melitene
Amida
Tigranocerta
Nisibis
Salamis
Neapolis

N

300 kilometres
200 miles

0   100   200
0   100

Syria

Tigris

Samosata

Bezabde

Edessa
Apamea
Zeugma
Batnae
Carrhae
Resaina
Nisibis

Cyrrhus

Singara

Antiochia
Seleucia Pieria
Beroea
Barbalissus
Nicephorium

Orontes

Laodicea
Apamea

Epiphaneia

Resafa

Raphanaea
Emesa

Mediterranean Sea

Tripolis

Palmyra

Dura-Europos

Circesium

Euphrates

Byblus
Berytus
Heliopolis

Sidon

Damascus

Tyre

Ptolemais

Lake Tiberias

Tiberias
Scythopolis
Gadara
Pella

Caesarea
Maritima

Gerasa

Bostra

Jordan

Jerusalem

Philadelphia

Gaza

Madaba
Dead Sea

Raphia

Elusa

Petra

Aila

N

0   100   200 kilometres
0   100 miles

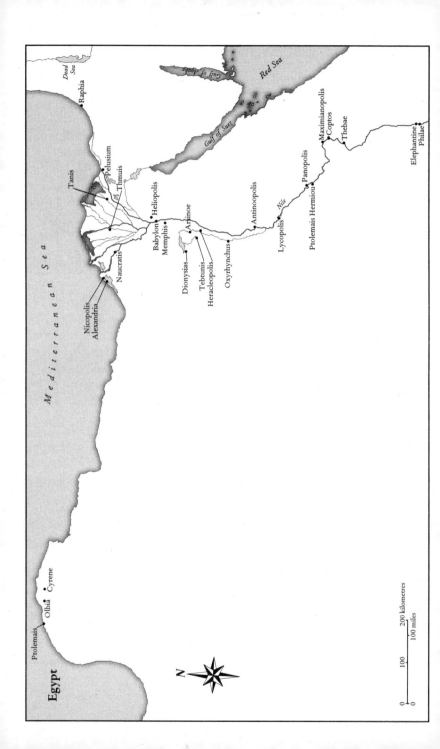

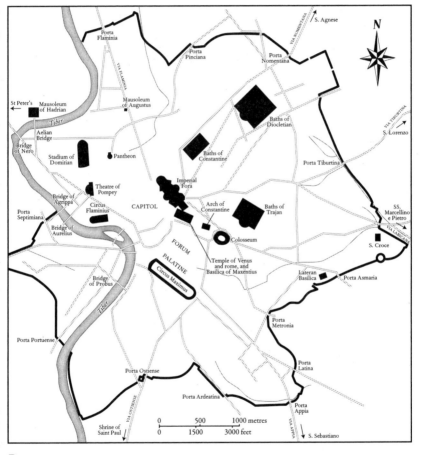

S. Agnese

Porta
Flaminia

VIA NUMENTANA

VIA FLAMINIA

Porta
Pinciana

Porta
Nomentana

VIA TIBURTINA

St Peter's

Mausoleum
of Hadrian

Mausoleum
of Augustus

S. Lorenzo

Tiber

Aelian
Bridge

Baths of
Diocletian

Bridge
of Nero

Pantheon

Baths of
Constantine

Porta Tiburtina

Stadium of
Domitian

Theatre of
Pompey

Imperial
Fora

SS.
Marcellino
e Pietro

Bridge of
Agrippa

Circus
Flaminius

CAPITOL

Arch of
Constantine

Baths of
Trajan

VIA LABICANA

Porta
Septimiana

Bridge of
Aurelius

Colosseum

S. Croce

FORUM

PALATINE

Bridge
of Probus

Circus Maximus

Temple of Venus
and rome, and
Basilica of Maxentius

Lateran
Basilica

Porta Asmaria

Tiber

Porta
Metronia

Porta Portuense

Porta
Latina

Porta Ostiense

Porta
Appia

VIA OSTIENSE

Porta Ardeatina

0	500	1000 metres
0	1500	3000 feet

VIA APPIA

S. Sebastiano

Shrine of
Saint Paul

Rome

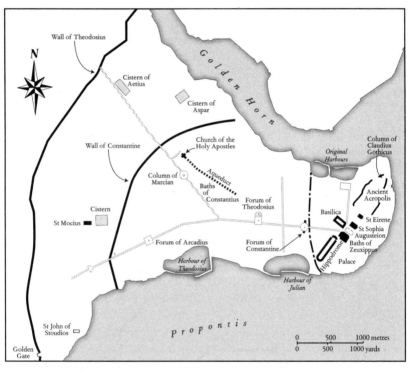

Constantinople

INTRODUCTION

In February or March 360, the senior Roman emperor, the augustus Constantius II, sent a perfectly reasonable command to his cousin and junior emperor, the caesar Julian. Rome was at war with Persia and the last time the two sides had clashed, just a year before, the Romans had suffered a disaster: the Persian king Shapur had assaulted the strategic city of Amida on the Tigris river (now Diyarbakır in south-eastern Turkey). After months of siege, the city's walls had been breached and the Persian forces had poured in, annihilating the garrison and slaughtering those civilians they did not take into captivity. The great king had only been prevented from pressing further into Roman territory by the coming of autumn and the end of the campaigning season, but he would surely strike again, and harder, as soon as winter was over.

Preparing to lead the next effort against Shapur in person, Constantius moved from his Balkan headquarters to Antioch, the metropolis – the provincial capital – of Roman Syria. Julian's task was to govern the Roman West, but whatever police actions he might need to undertake on the Rhine frontier were clearly a comparatively minor problem, and Constantius required him to send four whole infantry units, along with a levy of 300 men from every other unit in the Gallic field army. As senior emperor, Constantius was well within his rights to make this demand. His assessment of the respective threats was also entirely accurate. Julian's clear duty was to obey. He chose not to. Instead, he decided to usurp the title of 'Augustus', setting himself up as a senior emperor and his cousin's equal, knowing full well that civil war would follow.

Julian had been campaigning annually along the Roman frontier on the Rhine and upper Danube ever since his cousin had summoned him out of enforced leisure studying philosophy in Athens in 355. No love

1

was lost between the two men. Julian had been a very young child when his father and nearly all his male relatives had been slaughtered in 337 in a massacre that Constantius had engineered. As one of three sons of the emperor Constantine I, who had remade the empire in his image and defined its future, Constantius refused to countenance Constantine's half-brothers and their offspring sharing in the inheritance of empire. He had carried his full brothers (Constantine II – the elder, and Constans – the younger) with him, but it was Constantius who pruned the family's collateral branches so they could never challenge the sons of Constantine himself.

Julian had nurtured his revenge for a long, long time. All the while he expected a sudden blow to fall; assassination or execution if Constantius' notorious paranoia were to flare up. At no time had he expected so much as a glimpse at imperial power. But chance had played its part. Constantius' brothers had quarrelled and gone to war, Constantine II dying in battle. Constans, the survivor, shared Constantius' piety and assertiveness, but lacked his political insight and shrewd sense of self-advantage. He fell to a usurper in 350, whom Constantius suppressed three years later. Realising that he could not compel sufficient loyalty to govern his vast empire alone, Constantius hauled from retirement Julian's half-brother Gallus, the only other male relative to survive the 337 massacre (also on account of his extreme youth). Ruling by preference from the Balkans, Constantius sent Gallus to govern the East from Antioch, having made him caesar (junior emperor) and presumptive heir.

But Gallus proved unsuitable: as paranoid as his imperial cousin, he was also a braggart and a bully, and he made himself hated very quickly. His political ineptitude meant he lacked all defence against the seductive courtiers and plausible whisperers who fanned the senior emperor's suspicions. In 354, Gallus was summoned back to his cousin's court and summarily executed en route, at Pola (now Pula, in Croatian Istria). Unloved though he was, Gallus had served a function and Constantius could no more rule the empire alone in 354 than he could the year before. Julian was the solution, urged on Constantius by his wife Eusebia. The emperor was reluctant – he had wronged Julian badly and repeatedly, and must have suspected the younger man's hatred, even though it had never been vented in public. But he had no choice. Constantius sent officials to watch Julian and made every effort to keep the young caesar on a tight lead while he brought home military successes from Gaul that were real enough. And Julian inspired genuine affection in his officers and enthusiasm from his troops, having a charisma of which (by all contemporary accounts) Constantius was utterly devoid.

As with Gallus, so with Julian, and things were never likely to end happily. The caesar would undoubtedly have manufactured an excuse for usurpation regardless of the circumstances. Constantius' levy on the Gallic military establishment was a lucky gift, a fig leaf to cover naked ambition and well-tended resentment, but the coup had already been prepared. Since moving to Gaul, Julian had preferred to winter at Lutetia (now Paris), rather than at one of the traditional imperial residences at Treveri, Lugdunum or Arelate (Trier, Lyon and Arles, respectively). Lutetia was at some distance from the hotspots of the Gallic frontier, but, more importantly, it was also at a good distance from the civilian administration of the Gallic provinces, which was studded with men more loyal to the distant senior emperor than to the caesar close at hand.

No one had objected when Julian took himself and his personal guard units, the *scholae palatinae* and *protectores domestici*, to Lutetia in previous winters. But in the winter of 359, more confident of getting away with it, he had brought with him not just his guardsmen but four units of the field army as well. Anyone with eyes to see would have understood what that implied. For the rest of his life, Julian insisted on a most traditional denial: the soldiers had spontaneously demanded that he take the rank of augustus, and he had accepted only with the deepest reluctance. This was not true. Not just the units at hand in Lutetia but the whole Gallic army stood by him when they heard the news. They must have been waiting for it since moving into their winter quarters. This was how politics worked in the fourth-century empire. Gaul, its army and its bureaucracy, had become very used to conducting itself with real autonomy and in its own interests, whether or not those matched the will of the senior emperor. That had been true even in the reign of Constantine, but similar regional establishments were visible in the Balkans and the East by early in the reign of Constantius. While capable of working towards a common imperial goal, the regional factions none the less put their own priorities and those of their big men first. It was not in the Gallic interest to lose a substantial portion of the field army, so Julian became the natural choice for emperor and could be expected to act in the interests of the Gallic high command.

By his own intemperate standards, Constantius reacted to the news with circumspection. He rejected Julian's suggestion that he be permitted to hold the title of Augustus in the West, while remaining a mere caesar in the East, and did not immediately threaten Julian with Gallus' fate. Yet, deprived by Julian of his western levies, Constantius could only watch as Shapur's armies took Singara and Bezabde, fortress cities at the extreme eastern edge of Roman territory, razing the former (now Sinjar in Iraq) to the ground in the summer of 360. In winter 360–61, Roman armies retook Bezabde, but this back-and-forth presaged more fighting to come. Obeying an iron law of Roman history – that internal usurpation always trumps foreign threat – Constantius decided to confront his rebellious cousin, who had escalated his original offence in November 360. When celebrating the *quinquennalia* (fifth anniversary) of his accession as caesar at Vienna (modern Vienne in France), Julian not only decked himself in full augustal panoply, he also minted gold coins under the title of Augustus. Minting was a closely guarded privilege, the chief public medium through which emperors communicated their intentions to their troops, their officials and one another. For Julian to strike coins as Augustus was effectively to declare war.

As winter broke, early in 361, Julian manufactured a *casus belli* of his own. The Alamanni were a disparate group of barbarians who lived beside the imperial frontier on the upper Danube, in what is now south-western Germany. One of their kings, Vadomarius, was known to be a personal client of Constantius, and Julian now accused him of plotting to attack the Gallic provinces. Plausible or not, the charge was enough to justify mobilising the whole of the Gallic field army, ostensibly for a punitive expedition beyond the frontier, in reality for a much bolder move: a lightning invasion of the Balkans that would confine Constantius to the eastern provinces beyond the narrow gorge on the Danube known as the Iron Gates and the Succi pass between Serdica and Philippopolis (Sofia and Plovdiv in modern Bulgaria). Julian, with a field army under his personal command, marched down the Danube, transhipping part of his force down river in advance. His most trusted general, the *magister equitum* Flavius Nevitta, took the great military road along the Sava river, seizing Siscia and Sirmium (Sisak in Croatia and Sremska Mitrovica in Serbia). The Balkan garrison forces that had not gone east with Constantius to fight the Persians went over to Julian, who sent a handful of units back into Italy through Emona (Ljubljana in Slovenia) and over the Julian Alps, with the intention of taking the north Italian plain.

The success had been quite stunning, until two of Julian's legions rebelled on their way into Italy, switching their allegiance to Constantius and seizing control of the stronghold of Aquileia (nowadays a tiny town and major archaeological site in the Italian province of Udine, but then one of the empire's dozen or so largest cities). With these newly hostile forces behind him, Julian might need to contemplate war on two fronts and could no longer be sure of his supply lines to the loyal Gallic provinces. He halted at Sirmium, while trusted generals took part of the Gallic garrison through the Alps and seized the main cities of the Italian plain. From Sirmium, he began to pepper the eastern provinces with missives – he had been educated in Greek and fancied himself as a philosopher – in which he accused Constantius of serially wronging him; he hoped to turn elite public opinion his way, trusting that a shared vocabulary of Hellenistic high culture would count for more with them than did Constantius' dour Christian piety. Julian had not yet made public his apostasy from the Christianity in which he had been raised, but one can sense in his letters a visceral hostility to a religion of peace that had nevertheless countenanced the slaughter of his birth family.

Constantius, his vanity pricked, must surely have felt the psychological blow of Julian's taunting, while the military challenge he posed was real enough. There was no alternative now but to leave the eastern provinces to the mercy of the Persian king and set out against his rebel caesar. Constantius left Antioch at the head of his army in October 361, moving fast to get clear of the Anatolian highlands before winter. He had made it no further than Cilicia when sickness overtook him. Sensing that his illness was mortal, Constantius decided to die a statesman. Throughout his reign, since the massacre of 337 with which he inaugurated it, he had let *raison d'état* guide him, as well as a reptilian coldness that was strangely self-abnegating. On 3 November 361, he acknowledged Julian as his co-augustus and thus his legitimate successor, and died the same day. That, at any rate, was the official story and, though it might have been concocted by Constantius' high command to forestall further conflict, the gesture would not have been out of keeping with what we know of Constantius' character. Be that as it may, with his cousin's death, Julian began his sole reign as the last male survivor of the Constantinian dynasty, and one determined to dismantle the social and political revolution his great uncle Constantine had worked on the Roman world.

The conflict between Julian and Constantius illustrates many of the themes and structural features of late Roman history more generally. It shows the tensions inherent in the collegial rule of senior and junior emperors, but also its necessity for governing a sprawling territory with pre-modern communications. It shows the scale of the imperial state apparatus, military and civilian, and the demands made on it by continual warfare. It shows, too, how regional factions made up of interlocking networks of military and civilian families were in many ways more important than any individual emperor in determining the fortunes of the state. Finally, it reveals the social transformation of an empire that was not yet Christian but that had long since abandoned the religious *laisser-faire* of its first two and a half centuries. This distinctively late Roman empire, and the way its political economy developed and eventually disappeared, is the main subject of this book. For the reader to make sense of it, we need – very briefly – to jump back in time from the death of Constantius II to two emblematic moments: the year 324, when Constantine made himself sole ruler of the empire; and the year 284, when Diocletian seized the imperial purple.

I

THE MAKING OF THE CONSTANTINIAN EMPIRE

In the year 324, the western augustus Constantine decisively defeated in battle the eastern augustus Licinius, his sometime ally and brother-in-law, now turned deadly rival. With that victory, Constantine made himself sole ruler of the Roman empire. The pair of them had survived a series of bloody civil wars earlier in the century, when the governmental system that we know as the tetrarchy fell apart. This tetrarchy – 'rule by four men' – was created in the year 293 by the emperor Diocletian. Conceived as an attempt to resolve the persistent crises that plagued the Roman political elite and army during the third century, it had been largely successful. Diocletian had acknowledged that an empire stretching from the Atlantic to the Euphrates, and from the Rhine and the Tyne to the Sahara, could not be ruled effectively by a single man.

Having come to power in a military coup, after the reigning emperor was assassinated on campaign in Mesopotamia, Diocletian then defeated that emperor's son in the Balkans and received the grudging acceptance of the Roman Senate, a body that retained symbolic if not actual power. That kind of path to the throne had been the third-century norm, with rival armies proclaiming their own commanders emperor, each then fighting to impose control on the whole of the empire. The pattern had begun in the 230s, for a variety of reasons. One was the appearance of new, more powerful enemies on several frontiers, particularly new barbarian coalitions on the Rhine ('Franks') and the Rhine/upper Danube ('Alamanni'), and a new Persian dynasty that overthrew the Parthian rulers whom the Romans had long known.

This new dynasty, called Sasanian after its mythical founder, was less Hellenised and less familiar to the Romans than the Parthians had been, and also much more aggressive. The Sasanian shahanshahs ('kings of kings') were believers in the dualistic Zoroastrian religion and fervent supporters of its priesthood, and this faith gave a sense of mission to their wars of conquest, not least against the eastern provinces of the Roman empire. Repeatedly in the third century, and especially if the reigning emperor was far away, some kind of foreign threat would produce a usurpation, as a local commander was made emperor in order to confront the danger. And because usurpation was intrinsically worse for a ruling emperor's survival than any foreign invasion could be, usurpations always took priority over any other challenges. The consequence was continuous civil war.

That said, the existential crisis of the Roman ruling class was about more than just endemic civil war. It was also about social and dynastic transformation – something that civil war could exacerbate, but not cause all on its own. For the first hundred years of its history, the Roman imperial system founded by Augustus had rested on magistrates drawn from the ranks of the Roman Senate. What had once been the governing body of the old republic became a sort of incubator for provincial administrators and military commanders, though it was no longer meaningfully independent of the emperor. The ranks of this *ordo senatorius* (the Romans thought in terms of *ordines*, 'orders' distinguished by privileges and duties, rather than social classes) were swelled by the granting of Roman citizenship to more and more of the empire's population. When a provincial community was enfranchised, the richest of its local elites became eligible to join the Senate, and we find non-Italian senators emerging first from southern Gaul and southern and eastern Spain, then from the heart of the Hellenistic world in Greece, the islands and Asia Minor, and finally from Africa and a few urban patches in the northern provinces.

But however fast the Senate might grow, its numbers would never be sufficient to serve the many tasks for which magistrates were needed: tax collection, the administration of justice, maintaining public infrastructures, suppressing banditry, and so on. The vast expansion of the emperor's own wealth and lands, distinct from the land and property of the Roman state, meant that the slaves and freedmen of the imperial household were, for many decades, used for everything from estate management to taxation. Soon, however, the second tier of the Roman ruling class – known as the *ordo equester*, or equestrians – became the main actors in imperial administration. As the second and third centuries progressed, the government of the empire became more regularised, more bureaucratic and more professional, with the overwhelming majority of administrative posts filled by the equestrian order. At the same time, the army became more flexible in its system of promotions, so men who started as common soldiers could acquire equestrian rank and join the officer corps. Eventually, and certainly by the middle of the third century, such men had crowded senators out of most command positions.

By the time that Diocletian put an end to fifty years of civil war, no vestiges of the old senatorial aristocracy remained. In the fourth century, even the oldest and most esteemed families, even those in the city of Rome – with perhaps two exceptions – could trace their line back only to the crisis years of the third century. Diocletian was in many ways a revolutionary, but not in his treatment of the governing classes, which retained the old distinction of senatorial and equestrian ranks. It was Constantine who acknowledged that any meaningful distinction in the functions performed by each group had disappeared de facto, merging the equestrian order with the senatorial and ensuring that the senatorial aristocracy of the fourth century would be a very different thing from its early imperial counterpart. In most other respects, however, Constantine inherited an empire that had been fundamentally reshaped by Diocletian and this baseline structure is the stage on which this book's narrative plays out.

During the 290s, Diocletian had broken the very large provinces of the earlier empire into more than a hundred smaller ones, each with a civilian governor and many with some sort of military establishment. His goal had been to reduce the danger of usurpation by shrinking the resources available to any potential rebel and separating the function of commanding troops from that of supplying and paying them. The main evidence for the Diocletianic provinces is a bureaucratic document from around 312 known as the *Laterculus Veronensis* (*Verona List*). This names the more than one hundred provinces into which the empire was divided, each of which had its own governor. These officials had different titles – *proconsul, consularis, corrector* – and, as the fourth century progressed, a definite hierarchy of prestige emerged among the different provincial commands. Proconsuls governed Africa Proconsularis (roughly modern Tunisia), Asia (the north-western corner of modern Turkey) and Achaea (Greece and the Aegean islands), because those three provinces had been the most distinguished commands since the earliest days of the empire; in fact, later in the fourth century, the proconsuls would be given the special legal privilege of reporting directly to the emperor, rather than to any official of higher administrative rank. Unlike *proconsul*, the titles of *consularis* and *corrector* did not in themselves indicate higher or lower rank, but some provinces (usually the more urbanised ones in regions that had been part of the empire longer) were definitely better regarded than others. The tenure of a governorship in, say, southern Italy thus became a good indicator of future career success. Regardless of their title, however, the various governors all played the same role: overseeing the civilian administration of their province, including both the legal system and the province's obligation to the various financial bureaus of the state.

The hundred or so provinces, the number and borders of which were occasionally rearranged, were also grouped into larger units. Called dioceses, these groups of provinces tended to be quite stable and were in many ways the real building blocks of fourth-century government. Originally, under Diocletian and the tetrarchs, their main function was fiscal, joining together provinces that were subject to a particular hierarchy of tax officials. Constantine systematised diocesan governance under officials called *vicarii*, who had the authority to judge legal cases *vice sacra*, that is to say, in the imperial stead. His goal was not only to make the administration of justice more uniform, but also to ensure that different layers of provincial and diocesan jurisdiction would overlap, and potentially duplicate one another's work. That duplication, and an intentional lack of clarity about whose decisions could be appealed and to whom such appeals should be made, was meant to encourage the various officials to keep an eye on each other, surveillance and delation being good ways to hold officials in check at a distance from the imperial court.

The original Diocletianic dioceses (see map) remained largely intact until the empire began to fragment in the fifth century, though Constantine created two Balkan dioceses, Dacia and Macedonia, where there had previously been one. Later, Valens made Egypt its own diocese, separating it from the vast diocese of Oriens ('the East'), which stretched from Armenia and the Taurus to Arabia and Palestine. These two large dioceses were also distinguished by the odd titles of their *vicarii*, the *vicarius* of Egypt known as the *praefectus Augustalis* and that of the East as the *comes Orientis*. The diocese was in many ways the most critical level of imperial government, being the largest chunk of territory that could usefully be run as a single fiscal unit. Despite their importance, the *vicarii* never gained inappellate legal powers, because above them stood the most important civilian officials in late imperial government, the praetorian prefects.

These late imperial prefects were the direct descendants of an office that went right back to the foundation of the empire. Originally, a pair of prefects had commanded the praetorian guard, the privileged military force garrisoned in Rome itself. Very quickly, however, as the highest equestrian officers in the state and frequent surrogates for the emperor himself, they had come to exercise authority over many corners of the civilian government. Their function had begun to change in the third century, and their military function was definitively ended by Constantine, who also suppressed the praetorian guard after it supported a rival in a civil war.

Under the tetrarchy, each emperor had had his own praetorian prefect, and that practice continued under Constantine when he gave his children subordinate courts of their own. These prefects, whose number varied with the number of subordinate emperors ('caesars'), remained the most powerful officials in the imperial state. They could offer inappellable legal judgements in the emperor's stead; they supervised the collection and disbursement of revenues from the dioceses under their authority; and they heard appeals against lower ranking regional officials. Their financial responsibilities were enormous, because they were in charge of the *annona* – all the pay and rations of the imperial civil service and the army. The Roman empire was, at every stage of its existence, a machine for redistributing taxes in cash or in kind from the provinces to the army and the civilian administration (indeed, late Latin uses the same word, *militia*, to designate service in both the military and the civilian hierarchies). Private shipping networks hitched themselves to the official networks of the *annona* – one reason the late imperial state was essential to a functioning commercial economy. Along with control of that vast financial machine, the prefects saw to the imperial infrastructure, maintained the public postal system and levied taxes in cash, in kind or in conscription and *corvées* (unpaid labour), to ensure the upkeep of that infrastructure.

By the time of Constantine's death in 337, we can observe the de facto territorialisation of the praetorian prefecture. This became the de jure norm in the time of Constantine's sons, particularly after his middle son Constantius II became sole legitimate emperor in 350. Though the dioceses that pertained to particular prefectures might shift at times (and did so frequently in the later fourth and early fifth centuries, thanks to civil wars and invasions), four relatively stable prefectures grew up by around 350: Gallia, generally administered from Treveri and taking in the four dioceses of Britannia, Hispania, Gallia Narbonensis (Gaul south of the Loire) and Tres Galliae (Gaul and Germany north of the Loire and west of the Rhine); a prefecture of Italy and Africa, taking in the two Italian dioceses (Italia Annonaria north of Rome and Suburbicaria in the south), Latin-speaking Africa west of Cyrene, the Alpine provinces and sometimes Pannonia (Hungary, Austria and parts of Slovenia and Croatia); Illyricum, which was sometimes administered jointly with Italy and Africa and took in Macedonia, Dacia and often Pannonia as well; and finally a prefecture of the East, taking in Thrace, Asiana (Asia Minor), Oriens (the Taurus, the Levant and Mesopotamia), and Egypt. As marks of their privilege, the provinces of Achaea, Asia and Africa Proconsularis were exempted from their respective prefect's authority, though in practice they needed to work with his administration in financial matters. Rome itself was subject to the *praefectus urbi* ('urban prefect'), a highly prestigious senatorial post, and the *praefectus annonae*, generally a lower-ranking official with connections to the praetorian prefect. Constantine's new city of Constantinople, which became a second Rome in the course of the fourth century, was separated from Thrace and given its own independent *praefectus urbi* by Constantius in 359.

Each governor, *vicarius*, and prefect had a staff reaching into the dozens, sometimes into the hundreds, but even they were a relatively small element in the apparatus of imperial government. The palatine bureaus that operated in the imperial presence were known collectively as the *comitatus* (literally, 'the group of companions') and these travelled with the emperor between the various imperial residences. The household staff were known as *cubicularii* and they served under a *praepositus sacri cubiculi*, or 'head of the sacred bedchamber'; nearly all *praepositi* were eunuchs, generally from the borderlands between Rome and Persia where legal prohibitions on castrating Romans did not apply. They supervised the palace accounts, attended to the intimate needs of the emperor and his wife, and supervised a staff of teachers, clerks and servants collectively known as *ministeriales* or *curae palatiorum*.

The other bureaus of the *comitatus* dealt with the emperor's public functions. The *magister officiorum* ('master of the offices') was the most powerful of these bureau chiefs, in charge of the various *scrinia* ('departments') required to cover the emperor's public roles: his staff of three junior *magistri* – *memoriae, libellorum* and *epistularum* – handled imperial correspondence, received the appeals and petitions addressed to the emperor and the *relationes* ('official reports') of provincial administrators, and then drafted responses to them. The bureau maintained a corps of translators for diplomatic purposes, and the *magister officiorum* also controlled the confidential courier system of imperial government, which was staffed by roughly a thousand *agentes in rebus* ('doers of things'). These *agentes* started their careers as messengers, but very frequently ended up becoming highly confidential spies and assassins, doing the kind of dirty work that all governments need to have done with quiet expedition.

In another sign of his very extensive powers, the *magister officiorum* was the only civilian official in late Roman government with command of troops, as the titular head of the emperor's household forces, the *scholae palatinae*. Each *schola* (how many of these there were at any given time is disputed) consisted of 500 elite cavalry under the command of an officer known as a *tribunus* appointed personally by the emperor. The emperor drew his personal bodyguards, who were called *candidati* because of their white uniforms, from the *scholae*. Another palatine bureau, the corps of notaries, duplicated some of the functions also carried out by the bureau of the *magister officiorum*. The *notarii*, under the *primicerius notariorum*, kept track of official appointments across the length and breadth of the empire and drew up the imperial commissioning letters. The *primicerius notariorum* was responsible for maintaining the master list, the *laterculum maius*, of every imperial officeholder. But while *notarii* were technically mere clerks, they were often, like the *agentes in rebus*, seconded to more dubious special operations as spies and interrogators.

Though the praetorian prefects oversaw the largest sums of money circulating through the state system, Constantine had also inherited two palatine financial bureaus from the governmental reforms of Diocletian, each of them supervised by a *comes* (here translated as 'count' rather than 'companion'). The bureau of the *res privata*, whose *comes rei privatae* always travelled with the senior emperor, supervised five different *scrinia* handling various aspects of the emperor's personal properties, from taxation and rent to sale and forfeitures to the crown. These functions meant that agents of the *res privata* required large establishments in every province. The other financial bureau in the *comitatus* was the *sacrae largitiones* ('sacred largesses'), whose *comes sacrarum largitionum* controlled the imperial mints, the most important of which were at Rome, Treveri, Arelate, Sirmium, Serdica, Thessalonica, Antioch and Alexandria.

After years of financial instability, Constantine had refounded the Roman monetary system on the basis of a very pure gold coin, weighing 4.5 grams and known as the *solidus*. Silver and base metal coins continued to be minted for use in small transactions, but they were not pegged at a fixed rate to the *solidus*, and the fiscal side of the imperial economy was based entirely upon gold. The *sacrae largitiones* also ran the state's gold and silver mines and supervised the *fabricae*, or state factories, where weapons and armour for the officer corps were adorned with precious metals (the *magister officiorum* looked after the *fabricae* in which the unadorned versions were manufactured). Finally, the bureau was the destination for all taxes collected in silver or gold. These included various tolls and harbour taxes; the *aurum tironicum* (a tax that commuted a levy of military conscripts into gold); the *aurum coronarium* (the 'voluntary' donation that towns made to an emperor upon his accession and then at each fifth-year anniversary); the *aurum oblaticium* (paid by senators, on the same calendar); the *collatio glebalis* (an annual fee paid by senators); the *collatio lustralis*, or *chrysárgyron* in Greek (a tax on all tradespeople from shopkeepers to prostitutes, levied every five years, originally in gold or silver, later only in gold). There were fully ten *scrinia* in the bureau of the *comes sacrarum largitionum* and, as with the *res privata*, these operated everywhere at the provincial level as well as in the *comitatus*.

Apart from the bureau of the *magister officiorum*, with his *scholae palatinae*, Constantine had definitively separated the empire's military hierarchy from the civilian, formalising the very strong third-century trend towards that outcome. The field army, known as the *comitatenses*, was made up of numerous units of roughly a thousand men each. Many provinces, especially along the frontiers, also had their own garrison armies, known as *limitanei* or *ripenses*, many of which were units descended from the much larger Roman legions of the early empire. The field army was commanded by two generals who usually travelled with the emperor's *comitatus* and were thus known as *magistri militum praesentales* ('in the imperial presence'). The senior commander was called the *magister peditum praesentalis* while the junior commander was called the *magister equitum praesentalis*, which translate as 'commander of the infantry' and 'commander of the horse' respectively, even though both the *magister peditum* and the *magister equitum* led both infantry and cavalry and were generically known as *magistri militum*, 'masters of soldiers'. If several emperors were ruling in an imperial college, these commands would be duplicated in each *comitatus*, although over time – and in parallel to the development of regional prefectures – there came to be regional command establishments for the *comitatenses*: along with the praesental *magistri*, by the mid fourth century there tended to be a *magister per Gallias*, one *per Illyricum* and one *per Orientem*, each with a more or less stable core of *comitatenses* that might fluctuate depending upon military conditions in the region.

The permanent garrison armies on the frontiers were commanded by *comites* or *duces* with a variety of *limitanei* at their disposal, although these units were sometimes dispersed widely throughout a province and often functioned as much as policemen and customs officials as soldiers. Separately from the *comitatenses* and the *limitanei*, a corps of *protectores domestici* was recruited from the privileged and well-connected children of civil servants and the military hierarchy, and from high-born young men from client states on the frontiers. These soldiers attended the emperor's personal military commands and the *scholae domesticorum* served as a training corps for the men of very diverse backgrounds who joined the late imperial officer class. The *protectores domestici* served under a *comes domesticorum* who was a senior member of the *comitatus*. (Another group of 'regular' *protectores* were common soldiers promoted towards the end of their careers and assigned managerial posts, often in distant provinces, as a reward for long service.)

In later chapters we will see how the Constantinian governmental system, sketched out briefly here, functioned in practice, constraining what emperors and their subjects could and could not do. But important though they are, the structures of government were not the only way in which Constantine remade the empire. He also began the process, soon to become irreversible, by which it became Christian. Christianity had started out as a dissenting Jewish sect but had, by the second century, come to regard itself as a new religion worshipping the single, jealous God who had sent his son, Jesus, to redeem mankind. At first confined to small communities in rural Palestine and the cities of the Greek East, Christianity had, by the middle of the third century, spread widely. That is, at one level, quite surprising, because Christianity was a peculiar religion by ancient standards. Greeks and Romans had long understood the exclusive monotheism of the Jews, and their refusal to countenance other gods including those of the Roman state, as an exceptional phenomenon, tolerated because it was so clearly a minority faith and one confined to a restricted ethnic community. Christian exclusivity was different, though, both from Judaism and the other religions of the Graeco-Roman world, in that what made it efficacious was belief, not ritual actions.

Non-Christians might have very elaborate and philosophical beliefs about the true nature of the universe and the divine, or they might have little more than a jumble of unreflective superstitions, but all understood that acts of sacrifice were the duty that men owed the gods – whether at huge public festivals in which hundreds of animals were offered up or as an individual dropping a pinch of incense on an altar (for the Jews of this period, the correct observation of prayer and ritual behaviours served the same function). Christians could not take part in public festivals for fear of forfeiting their prospect of salvation, since their jealous God forbade them. Nor were they to honour the gods of the Roman state, or the cult of the divine emperors, in a taboo that could be interpreted as treasonable: refusal to sacrifice had led to several episodes of mass persecution by imperial authorities during the third century. After the second of these, the emperor Gallienus granted toleration to Christians and recognised the right of Christian churches to own property under Roman law, as a result of which the number of Christians increased rapidly in the latter half of the third century.

Despite many confident assertions to the contrary, we will never have any good sense of actual numbers, not even ballpark figures: our evidence is just not good enough. Still, by the year 300, Christians may have made up a majority of the population in parts of the Greek-speaking East, while being at most a substantial minority population in the Latin West. For the educated elites of both the Greek and Latin worlds, Christianity was just one option among many; indeed, just one monotheistic option among many, given the popularity of philosophico-religious systems like Neoplatonism that also had a strongly monotheist element to them. For the mass of the population, Christian worship existed alongside the public festivals of the gods and the pervasive folk beliefs of the countryside. Christianity was not yet a majority belief at any level of the social hierarchy, and there is no truth in the pious old idea that it appealed especially or exclusively to the poor and humble elements in society. Christian communities had become too varied, not to mention too wealthy and successful, for that to have been true.

By roughly the same point in the late third century, a clear hierarchy of clerical grades had developed within Christian communities, and their leaders, the bishops (*episcopi*), formed a network that reached right across the Roman world and indeed beyond it, into the Christian communities of Mesopotamia who lived under Persian rule. Certain bishops exercised greater authority than their neighbours, either from personal charisma, the antiquity of their city's episcopal see, or simply their city's size and importance in the grander scheme of things – or indeed for all three reasons, as at Carthage in Africa Proconsularis. A handful of sees (Rome, Alexandria and Antioch) claimed the right to speak for and to Christians, not just in their region or province but everywhere. They did so on the basis of their great antiquity and apostolic foundation (that is, their claim to have been founded by one of Jesus' companions and the first proselytes of his message). Christianity was thus an accepted part of the empire's religious landscape by 303, the year in which Diocletian launched the last persecution of Christians (the 'Great Persecution'), aimed at rooting out the religion altogether as a threat to public order and an affront to the gods who protected the Roman state. The grounds for this persecution and the events that sparked it are simply too complex to be discussed here, inextricably tied up as they were with the internal political machinations of the tetrarchs and their families. But from 303 to 305, Christians across the empire experienced some form of persecution, from the destruction of their churches and burning of Christian books in parts of the Latin West to extensive confiscations, torture and executions in Africa and the Greek East. In the West, persecution stopped in 305, but in the East it persisted in one shape or another up until 313. By then it had become a volatile factor in the civil wars that ended the tetrarchy, not least because of Constantine's own conversion to Christianity – which was to turn out to be one of the most momentous events in world history.

Constantine may well have been sympathetic to Christianity from a very early age. There were Christians in his family and his father, the caesar Constantius, had enforced Diocletian's persecuting edict as lightly as he could get away with in the parts of the empire he controlled. In fact, one of the many motives for the persecution may have been to knock Constantine out of the succession plan of the tetrarchs. But when Constantius died, his soldiers proclaimed his son emperor and Diocletian's successor Galerius, now the senior augustus, grudgingly recognised Constantine as a legitimate member of the imperial college. Between 306 and 312, the six years in which he ruled Gaul, Britain and Spain, Constantine tried to reverse as many of the consequences of the persecution as he could in those lands, and he did the same after he seized Italy and Africa from his rival Maxentius in the year 312. By that point, he had openly declared himself a Christian. Up till 312, he had had both the traditional priests of the state cults and Christian priests in his *comitatus*, among them bishop Hosius (or Ossius) of Corduba (Córdoba in modern Andalusia). They had provided him with rival explanations of a celestial vision he had seen, in the company of his campaign army, in the year 310.

What this was has been much debated, but it was perhaps an optical phenomenon known as a solar halo, in which light interacting with the ice crystals in clouds creates what look like circles or pillars in the sky. Be that as it may, everyone could agree that the heavens had sent Constantine a message, the only question was what they might have meant by it. Was it Apollo, god of the sun, promising Constantine victory? Or was it a sign from the one true and only God, as Hosius and his Christian fellows argued? Perhaps Constantine thought he could have it both ways, but then, when he invaded Italy in 312, decisively defeating Maxentius' field armies in the north Italian plain before marching on Rome, he had a dream on the night before the final battle. This directed him to paint a christogram (that is, the Greek letter *chi* superimposed on the letter *rho* and standing for *christus*) on his men's shields and march into battle under the protection of the Christian God. This he did, Maxentius' forces were duly vanquished and the usurper drowned in the Tiber. Constantine would return to this story of his conversion often in later life, and he clearly rewrote – or perhaps reinterpreted – what had happened many times over. But it is clear that from 312 onwards, he ruled as a consciously Christian emperor, and actively favoured Christian churches whenever he could.

He swiftly learned that this meant not just limitless successes, but daunting challenges as well. In 312, almost as soon as Maxentius was dead, the Christian emperor was asked to intervene in a dispute between Christians. Persecution had created a terrible schism in the north African church. Some maintained that priests and bishops had forfeited their legitimacy, and were no longer priests, if they had handed over Christian scriptures to the persecuting authorities (they were dubbed *traditores*, which means 'those who hand things over' and is the root of our English word 'traitor'). Not only could they themselves not be priests or bishops, but no one they had ordained or consecrated could be a priest or a bishop either. The immediate dispute centred on whether the newly elected bishop of Carthage, Caecilianus, could legitimately hold that office because the bishop who had consecrated him was alleged to have been a *traditor*. Caecilianus' opponents had elected a rival bishop, Donatus, and both sides now appealed to Constantine. The emperor sought advice from Miltiades, the bishop of Rome, who in 313 ruled against the Donatists (as Donatus' supporters came to be called). They again appealed the judgement, and Constantine summoned a council of western bishops to meet at Arelate in 314.

Episcopal councils had, for some time, been the favoured means of resolving disputes within the church, but their success depended on the willingness of the losing side to accept conciliar judgement, which was anything but a given. Thus when the bishops who had assembled at Arelate ruled against Donatus and supported the legitimacy of Caecilianus, the Donatists refused to comply with the order to depose their bishop, still insisting that he was the only true claimant to the see. Constantine, an autocrat by temperament as well as position, instructed his officials to suppress the recalcitrants by force. Some Donatists were martyred, some went into exile, but state violence merely drove the schism underground, resolving nothing. Donatus and his partisans continued to consecrate rival bishops in African towns and villages, and the conflict between Caecilianists and Donatists suppurated for more than a hundred years, long after Constantine's death. Yet stubbornly persistent though the Donatist schism would remain, the dispute was fundamentally a conflict over discipline and legitimacy, and its roots were firmly tied to their local context. By contrast, when Christians contested theological points, salvation and the life eternal were at stake, and the ramifications were consequently much greater. Constantine would discover this the hard way not long after he snatched the eastern empire from Licinius in 324.

The conflict between Constantine and Licinius could have been avoided had the former's lust for power not been insatiable. Licinius showed every sign of being content to rule the eastern empire while Constantine ruled the western, but Constantine provoked a conflict in 316, winning decisively and taking over most of the Balkans when the two sides reached a peace agreement. By the early 320s, Constantine was again deliberately provoking his fellow emperor and their final breach came in 323 when Constantine violated Licinius' territory while ostensibly prosecuting a war against the Sarmatians beyond the Danube. A final reckoning was inevitable, and Constantine's forces were again victorious. Routed, Licinius fled to Asia Minor and his army surrendered to Constantine. After being promised his life in return for unconditional surrender, Licinius was imprisoned at Thessalonica and executed not long afterwards, accused of plotting against a merciful emperor who had, so it was claimed, dearly wanted to spare his life.

Constantine had already fought his western war of conquest under a Christian banner twelve years earlier, but in 324 he could actually portray Licinius as a persecutor. The eastern emperor had, in fact, ordered measures against Christians in his territory as a means of retaliating against Constantine's aggressions, but that meant Constantine could spin his war of conquest as a Christian duty. In the aftermath of total victory, he made it clear that he was going to rule as a Christian, not merely favouring Christians as he did in the West, but actively attempting to impose Christianity on the non-Christian communities of the East and deliberately undermining the power of non-Christian cults. He also got himself deeply entangled in the theological politics of the Greek churches, fuelled by a supremely arrogant confidence in his ability to fix what was in reality unfixable.

The Christianity of the Greek East was rather different from the Latin Christianity of the West, and its ecclesiastical politics vastly more complicated. What is more, the East – where there had been a much larger Christian population to start with – had suffered much harsher persecution for a longer period of time than had the West, which had put all sorts of strains on eastern Christian communities. Differences inherent in the two languages were also significant. Greek is a much subtler language than Latin. Like modern German, it can produce infinite shades of meaning by coining new words out of existing morphological elements: for that reason, it can handle both deliberate (and deliberately irresolvable) ambiguity on the one hand, and minutely precise distinctions of meaning on the other. Latin is a simpler language, with a smaller vocabulary and no ancient tradition of new coinages, so one word nearly always had to be used for multiple concepts. It was for that reason poorly suited to the nuances of philosophy and theology, and there had arisen a long tradition of native Latin speakers using Greek in academic discussion and writing. But the sheer suitability of Greek for intellectual endeavour brought hazards when it came to theology.

The prospect of salvation in Christianity rested on belief, not on the careful performance of ritual acts. Believing the wrong thing about the Christian God meant putting one's salvation at risk. The kinds of philosophical hair-splitting that had long been the meat and drink of Greek intellectual life became a matter of life and death when placed in the Christian context of salvation. Much as ancient theologians (and pious modern scholars, for that matter) could pretend that right belief, or 'orthodoxy', was a single truth somewhere 'out there' awaiting the intellection of human minds to discover it, right belief was, and is, a construct forged in the contestation of rival theologians. Wrong belief might be condemned as heresy, but one churchman's heretic was another's guardian of true orthodoxy. Worse still, thanks to Greek's linguistic proteanism, the moment a theological formula had resolved one problem and established an uncontested agreement as to its orthodoxy (rare enough as that was), the fact of that agreement opened up new questions in need of resolution and the whole divisive cycle began again – and was, of course, vastly exacerbated by personal and political rivalries among churchmen, not least those bishops who claimed special spiritual authority for their sees.

In 324, the Greek church was in the midst of one such theological upheaval, disputing precisely how God the Father and God the Son were related to one another in the Christian trinity of Father, Son and Holy Spirit. We call this the Arian controversy, after the Egyptian priest Arius whose formulae were in dispute. Egypt's main episcopal see of Alexandria, which claimed apostolic foundation by Saint Mark the evangelist, had struggled with the same problem of *traditores* that had produced the Donatist schism in Africa, but in this dispute one side had hitched its claims to a genuine theological problem. Arius had been a student at Antioch, Alexandria's greatest rival, and had rejected the Alexandrian bishop's belief that God the Father and God the Son shared a single substance (*ousia* in Greek, *substantia* in Latin): since God the Father had 'begotten' God the Son, there was necessarily some moment at which God the Son had not existed and, if that were so, then God the Son could not share the same substance as God the Father, and must in fact be different from and subordinate to Him. For this critique, Arius found himself exiled by his bishop, and sought support elsewhere in the East. That immediately politicised the intellectual question and rival networks of bishops sought Constantine's support from the moment he had beaten Licinius.

The emperor turned to the same expedient he had tried in the West, calling a church council to resolve the dispute. This was held in 325 at Nicaea, a location in Asia Minor that could be reached fairly easily by most eastern bishops, while Constantine ensured that a smattering of Latin bishops attended as well. In the end, more than 300 bishops are said to have been in attendance, including bishops Eustathius of Antioch and Eusebius of Nicomedia, the city that housed the main imperial residence in Asia Minor. In a decision with far-reaching consequences, the bishop of Alexandria, pleading old age, sent in his stead his precociously brilliant deacon (and eventual successor) Athanasius. Supporters of Arius, led by Eusebius of Nicomedia, were in a clear minority, though they argued their case well. However, Athanasius was both a theological prodigy and a viciously shrewd politician. After long debate and much calling in of political favours, the council condemned Arius' teaching and mandated a theological formula by which God the Father and God the Son were *homoousios*, identical in being or substance (*homoousios* is a compound of the Greek words for sameness and being) despite God the Father's having begotten God the Son. The reader may suspect a paradox, but the Nicene formula was good enough to do the immediate work it had to: almost everyone was satisfied, at least for the moment, even those (like Eusebius of Nicomedia) who thought the homoousian solution intellectually indefensible. Only two bishops joined Arius in his refusal to relent, and the three were duly exiled.

The solution pleased the new emperor, a fact that should have benefitted everyone – and it would have if Christianity were better able to tolerate differences of belief. But it is not. Athanasius of Alexandria and his allies (including most of the Latin churchmen who may or may not have followed the details of what was really at stake) had a political as well as a theological investment in maintaining the Nicene formula against all comers. Athanasius succeeded to the episcopate of Alexandria in 328, which gave him a formidable power base to match his formidable argumentative skills, and he never hesitated in putting both to use. Many who thought Arius to be wrong (or at least partially wrong) also thought the homoousian solution to be equally, though differently, wrong. Eusebius of Nicomedia, for instance, favoured a solution by which Father and Son were alike in substance – *homoios* – but not identical in substance, as the Nicene *homoousios* would have it. Eusebius became a confidant of Constantine's as the emperor aged, eventually baptising him on his deathbed, and the bishop of Nicomedia used his position to fill eastern bishoprics with sympathetic homoians (or 'Arians', as they were caricatured by their Nicene opponents).

Athanasius, a tireless opponent of the homoians, was not above using dirty tricks to get his way and blocked as many such appointments as he could – with the result that he found himself exiled by the emperor at the time of Constantine's death. He would remain a disruptive force in Roman politics for decades, not least because Constantine's son Constantius was both an exceptionally pious Christian and an exceptionally convinced homoian. Constantius expended a great deal of energy, and huge amounts of cash and other resources, trying to find a variation on the homoian formula that could unify all the bishops of the empire, calling what he expected to be binding church councils half a dozen times: Antioch (341); Serdica (342); Sirmium (351); Arelate (353); Mediolanum (355); Ariminum and Seleucia (359); and Constantinople (360). Each time, he personally intervened in the drafting of creeds he intended to be universally acceptable, and therefore universally enforced. He failed in this ambition every time, in part because the theological differences he was trying to paper over were too wide, in part because partisan politics was deeply entrenched in the post-Nicene episcopate and in part because the imperial commitment to enforcing orthodoxy made compromise impossible. That is the structural point and it is a defining aspect of the later Roman empire: Nicaea and its aftermath made the emperor and his officials responsible for enforcing conformity to one form of Christian belief over another.

But while it is in theory possible to enforce conformity of practice, how does one go about enforcing conformity of belief? What Constantine had committed himself and his officials to enforcing was something not open to proof. Christian controversialists understood this, and seized upon it for its political utility. In the long run, the state was forced to expend vast resources on defining what people should profess to believe and then compelling them to do so. That created whole populations who were socially and politically marginalised, and at times even persecuted, for refusing to conform to whatever particular Christian formulae a given emperor endorsed. We shall see the negative consequences this had for imperial unity and the affairs of state time and again as the book progresses.

That said, the speed with which disputes about Christian orthodoxy became a central focus of imperial politics also demonstrates the speed with which the empire became Christian after Constantine. Within at most two generations, and probably much sooner, a majority of the imperial population was professing one or another form of Christian belief. Constantine took active measures to favour the church and signal his support for the Christian God, banning crucifixion as a punishment, changing marriage laws to reflect Christian moral teachings, and declaring that no public business apart from agricultural labour should be conducted on the day sacred to the sun (and on which God the Son had been resurrected after His crucifixion), thereby inventing the weekend. Favouring Christians in promotion to higher office was no doubt another important factor in encouraging self-interested conversions. Likewise, finally, the measures Constantine took against non-Christian religions must have had some impact. These were relatively minor, not to say benign, in the western provinces, but in the East the confiscation of temple treasuries would have a profound effect.

Temples had for over a millennium served the Greek world as a hybrid of banks and museums, and Constantine appropriated their gold and their treasures both to fund the new system of gold coinage based on the *solidus* (discussed above) and to pay for his magnificent new residence at Constantinople, whose public spaces would be adorned with the treasures of the whole eastern empire. The traditional centres of Hellenistic worship thus found themselves impoverished quite suddenly, which probably did more to undermine them than any other Constantinian measure, including one that has roused tremendous scholarly controversy: whether or not Constantine instituted a ban on pagan sacrifice. There is no iron-clad contemporary evidence for such a ban, but one of Constantine's sons issued a law banning sacrifice in 341 that states that his father had issued a similar ban in the past. There is other, perhaps less certain, evidence from a poem by Palladas, a contemporary. It is thus quite probable, if not absolutely proven, that Constantine banned pagan sacrifice in public, not just blood sacrifice but also the symbolic lighting of incense at the shrines of the gods. Rather as in Diocletian's persecution of Christians, enforcement must have depended largely on the attitudes of local officials, and any ban is likely to have done less long-term damage to the old non-Christian cults than the looting of their treasuries.

The destination for that loot was Constantinople, the new city on the Bosporus that Constantine founded on the site of ancient Byzantium, where Europe and Asia meet. He claimed to have had a vision directing him where to build his new city and that a divinity also helped him lay out its boundaries. Constantinople was a celebration of his victory over

Licinius and his new dominion over the whole Roman world, and it rapidly became a symbol of the Christian empire. The city was ceremonially founded and its ground broken on 8 November 324. Six years later, it was ready to be occupied, and the dedication took place on 11 May 330. Constantine wanted the city to be a second Rome and it deliberately echoed many aspects of the much older 'mother of empire'.

One of the most important aspects of fourth-century history is the way in which Constantine's city achieved the hopes he had for it, becoming by the end of that century the indisputable capital of the eastern empire. The emperor Constantius II, with whose death we began, did more than any other single person to put Constantinople on the track to dominance, giving it a proper senate and aggrandising its bishop at the expense of Antioch and Alexandria. Julian, his rebellious cousin and the furious antagonist of Christianity, might have been able to reverse some of the revolutionary impact of Constantine's reign. Certainly, he wanted to do so. But the brevity of his short reign, as the next chapter will show, ensured that he could not.

2

THE FAILURES
OF JULIAN

The emperor Julian is a source of endless fascination to scholars, not least because his brooding narcissicism speaks directly to many academics. But there is also the fact that he impressed himself vividly on some of the most eloquent authors whose works have come down to us: Ammianus Marcellinus, for whom Julian was the heroic centrepiece of history; the Antiochene orator Libanius, who lamented the failure of Julian's programmatic support of the old gods; John Chrysostom, the golden-mouthed Christian bishop who execrated Julian for his insistent paganism; and Ephraim, the Mesopotamian priest whose beautiful Syriac hymns revel in Julian's eventual failure and death. And then there are Julian's own writings, which so convey his personality that they flatter the historian into a sort of complicit intimacy. Julian brings out one's amateur psychoanalyst more than any ancient author save Saint Augustine, and only Augustus and Constantine rival him for the largest number of modern biographies of Roman emperors. All of this is more than a little ironic, because Julian's brief sole reign was a failure at every conceivable level. Indeed, even his staunchest admirers could not conceal the degree to which he alienated other people with his actions.

We can hardly explain Julian's failure except by recourse to his mental state. It is as if all his most dangerous impulses were set free when he stopped dissembling his reverence for the old gods and his hatred of

Christianity. In Gaul, when he still feared the wrath of his cousin Constantius, he had learned to be a good field commander and, as he himself tells us, he had read Caesar and Plutarch assiduously in order to improve further. The lightning campaign with which he seized control of the Balkans in the months before Constantius' death was a model of ancient strategic success. But once the threat of his cousin disappeared, he felt the Homeric lure he had absorbed in his happy youth with his eunuch tutor Mardonius, and the shade of Achilles began to whisper in Julian's ear, beckoning him to battle. He would win the Persian war his cousin had cut short, no matter that his preparations for it would soon turn the eastern cities against him. His religious convictions followed a similarly self-destructive path. Several strands of philosophical religion had converged in the Roman empire of the third century, when the mystical Neoplatonism of Plotinus had become dominant. In the fourth century, they diverged again into the dialectical and philosophical religiosity of Porphyry and the more spectacular mantic religion of Iamblichus. Julian had learned the first sort of Neoplatonism from Eusebius of Myndos and the latter from Maximus of Ephesus, but it was Maximus who had impressed himself more upon Julian's character. Now, unfettered by any constraint, Julian let loose his passion for theurgy and for divination. The costly excesses that he lavished on these pleasures repelled ordinary Greeks and Romans, and not just Christians but pagans as well.

Julian began from the moment he learned of Constantius' death, with Aquileia still up in arms against him. Sending his *magister equitum* (that is, his second-ranking general) Flavius Iovinus to convince the Aquileian legions to surrender, the new emperor launched a volley of open letters to the various cities of the East. In these, and in the ones he sent to close spiritual advisers like Maximus, he declared his intention of restoring the worship of the pagan gods. Travelling on via Philippopolis and Heraclea to Constantinople, he arrived in the imperial city on 11 December 361. There, one of his first concerns was to order the construction of a Mithraeum in honour of the heroic saviour god Mithras whose worship he approved – and to suppress insofar as he could the worship of the Christian saviour god whom he loathed. And, in ironic imitation of the metropolitan episcopal structure of the Christian church, he began to appoint his favourite philosophers as provincial priests of the old gods.

Julian's trusted adviser Salutius Secundus was made praetorian prefect of Oriens and put in charge of a series of high-profile treason trials. These were held in the city of Chalcedon, across the Bosporus from Constantinople and less prone to riot. The trials became a way for the new emperor's western high command to prosecute old feuds with those who had served Constantius. We find alongside Salutius some of the most powerful men in the western establishment: the *comes sacrarum largitionum* and newly appointed prefect of Illyricum, Claudius Mamertinus; the *magister peditum* Agilo; the *magister equitum* Nevitta; and the *magister equitum* Iovinus, who had served beside the caesar Julian in Gaul and then backed his winning bid against his cousin. Yet we also find Flavius Arbitio, a leading general in the 350s, now retired, and a long-standing enemy of Julian's, but too powerful a figure in the western establishment to ignore. The commission did the work expected of it: some of Constantius' officials – especially those thought to have been complicit in the fall of Julian's half-brother Gallus – were exiled; others were killed, including the *praepositus sacri cubiculi* Eusebius, widely hated as both a eunuch and a secret power-broker. The notorious *agentes in rebus* Apodemius and Paulus Catena ('Paul the Chain'), who had sown terror among senators and bureaucrats alike during Constantius' last decade, were burned alive. Other executions stirred up criticism, however, and some thought Julian had gone too far.

The new year of 362 opened with two of Julian's staunchest supporters, Mamertinus and Nevitta, taking up the consular fasces and giving their names to the year. (The Romans had no sequential system of numbering years, instead referring to 'the year when such and such were consuls'.) Flavius Iovinus returned to Gaul as *magister equitum*. Julian needed a trustworthy figure to hold the West for him, while he secured control of the Greek world and tried to impose his anti-Christian policies on the empire. From the very beginning of the year, his efforts to harm the church stepped up. Early in February, he issued a law ordering the return of all those bishops who had been exiled by Constantius for their Nicene beliefs, knowing that this was a sure recipe for disrupting Christian congregations across the empire. Only in May did he set out from Constantinople en route to Antioch and the war against Persia. This war would be for his glory and for the good of his loyal pagan subjects, but not for the Christians – he refused an embassy from the people of Nisibis (Nusabyn in modern Turkey), who were Christian, instead asking for their aid against Persia on the grounds that they were defying his orders to reopen the pagan temples: it is no mere coincidence that some of the most virulent attacks on Julian should come from a native of Nisibis, the Syrian Ephraim.

The route Julian took across Asia Minor was conceived, it is clear, as a pilgrimage of sorts. From Chalcedon and Nicomedia he went on to Nicaea, making a detour to worship at the shrine of the mother goddess Magna Mater at Pessinus. Then, via Ancyra (Ankara), he travelled east to Tyana, where he venerated the memory of the wonder worker Apollonius, whose third-century biographer Philostratus had portrayed him as a pagan counterpoint to Jesus. He arrived in Antioch early in June, and there he remained until March of the following year. He livened his days with monumental orgies of blood sacrifice, and by stirring up the rabid infighting of the city's Christians. Believing that the oracle of Apollo at Daphne had ceased to speak because the remains of the Christian martyr Babylas were revered nearby, he had the bones exhumed, sparking Christian protests and a grand procession demanding the saint's reinterment.

To further discomfit the faith that he hated, Julian offered imperial patronage to the Jews: the treasury would provide funds to restore the Temple in Jerusalem, where Jews had not been allowed to set foot since the time of Hadrian and the suppression of the Jewish revolt under Bar Kochba. That project would fail, as mysterious fires repeatedly halted construction. Though Christians took these as a sign of divine support, it is likely that Christian arsonists made their own luck. Another fire, which destroyed Apollo's shrine in Antioch itself, was eventually found to be an accident, though Julian initially blamed the Christians, who entirely reciprocated the hatred he felt for them. Yet Antioch's pagans were only marginally more pleased with their emperor now that they had a chance to see him up close: he avoided giving the circus games that provided holidays and entertainment for favoured cities, and he paid no attention to the action when he finally put some on; a food shortage caused in part by crop failure and in part by the needs of his campaign army angered others; and everyone could find an outlet for their resentment in the vast holocausts of cattle that he offered up to his various pagan gods – he was jokingly called the *victimarius*, or slaughterer, rather than priest, and his short height and devotion to his long philosopher's beard added to the ridicule, some calling him a dwarf and an ape.

His brittle ego wounded, Julian found the Antiochenes' resentment of him intolerable. In January or February 363, which he had opened with his fourth consulship in the company of the Gallic praetorian prefect Flavius Sallustius, he unleashed a ferocious satire on himself that was meant to terrify the citizens of Antioch. Read out like any other imperial pronouncement, it was then posted for public display on the Tetrapylon of the Elephants, a monumental triumphal arch in the centre of Antioch. This lacerating pamphlet, known as the *Misopogon*, or 'Beard-Hater', showers vitriol on Julian and on his Antiochene subjects, whose morality, frivolity and lack of respect are castigated without let-up. But while mocking himself, he also reveals the depth of his self-regard, and a firm conviction that everything he is doing is right. Given how few of his subjects, of any religious persuasion, shared that view, it is unsurprising that he gave up on trying to satisfy them and instead turned to the long-heralded invasion of Persia.

The previous December, Julian had refused an offer of peace put forward by ambassadors of the shahanshah Shapur II. The latter had troubles elsewhere in his empire with which he needed to deal. Persia's central Asian provinces of Sogdiana and Bactria, and perhaps also the so-called Kushanshahr in modern Pakistan, had been invaded by confederations of nomad aristocrats, disrupting royal administration. These nomads all claimed a sort of kinship with the ancient Xiongnu, a powerful steppe empire on the frontiers of China around the turn of the millennium. The Xiongnu legacy was a potent organising ideology on the steppe, and we shall come across many more such groups in the course of this volume, not least the steppe warriors we know best as the Huns. Whatever relationship the fourth-century invaders of Persia's eastern provinces had to the Huns we meet in Ukraine and the Danube basin in the later fourth century, they set up a dynamic that would plague the Persian kings for the rest of antiquity, constantly putting them on the defensive in one distant corner of the empire or another, and often at bad moments that the Romans were only too happy to exploit.

Late in 362, despite the favourable terms Shapur was offering, Julian knew that he held a trump card that made compromise unnecessary. Shapur's brother Ohrmazd had been in exile among the Romans since the mid 320s, and this Sasanian prince, whose royal lineage was impeccable, had long been a companion to Constantius, present even at that emperor's triumphal entry to Rome in 357. Julian's ambition was to put Ohrmazd on the Persian throne in place of his brother Shapur, and the military plan was both elaborate and plausible. One Roman force, under a distant relative of the Constantinian dynasty called Procopius, led an army north to the borders of Armenia, where he joined forces with the Armenian king Arsaces and constructed an elaborate feint against Persian territory. Meanwhile, Julian led the main army out of Antioch, via Carrhae, Callinicum and Circesium (where the historian Ammianus joined the expedition on 1 April, thereafter to narrate events as an eyewitness). From Circesium, the army reached Zaitha and half-derelict Dura Europus on the Euphrates, whence a fleet carried supplies downriver as the army marched on Ctesiphon. The northern feint worked, the larger part of the Persian army was despatched towards Armenia, and Julian got as far south as the Naarmalcha, the canal linking the Euphrates to the Tigris near Ctesiphon, with little opposition. Minor skirmishes, the surrender of several fortresses and the successful siege of Maiozamalcha by the commanders Dagalaifus and Nevitta, the former consul, spurred Julian onwards. Taken by surprise, Shapur's commanders cut the canal dikes and flooded the countryside, slowing the Roman advance at a critical juncture. When the Roman army reached the Persian capital in June, Ctesiphon had been heavily reinforced, and the flooded countryside made it impossible to feed a besieging force.

Ammianus, having seen it himself, portrays the unravelling of the invasion with a tragic inevitability. Realising that they could not safely return the way they had come, and perhaps deceived into thinking that the army could live off the land while marching north up the banks of the Tigris, Julian burned his transport ships on the Euphrates and with them many of his army's supplies. Abandoning Ctesiphon without a siege, the Roman army began to withdraw, but Shapur had recovered from the original deception and, marching south at speed, caught Julian's army just as its retreat was getting underway. Rather than fight an unnecessary pitched battle, he simply harassed the fringes of the Roman army as they made their laborious way out of Persian territory. Julian refused the offer of a treaty, finding the very thought humiliating. That was a mistake, for the beleaguered army was moving slowly. Every day brought more casualties, while Persian skirmishers made it difficult to gather fodder and food safely.

Then, on the morning of 26 June, one of the Persians' ceaseless raids had an unexpected denouement: taken by surprise, a section of the Roman army was scattered, and Julian rushed from his tent to rally the troops, neglecting to put on his armour. He and his bodyguard of *protectores* drove off the raid and went in pursuit, but a javelin, thrown by one of the Persians' Arab auxiliaries, struck Julian in the side. As he tried to pull it out he severed the tendons in his hand and fell from his horse, pouring with blood. In great pain, and obviously dying, he was carried back to camp. Ammianus clothes the deathbed scene in literary tropes drawn from the lives of the great Greek heroes: when the pain lessens, Julian demands his armour and weapons to once more rally his troops, just as the dying Theban hero Epaminondas had done at the battle of Mantinaea; when that proves impossible, he discourses on the sublimity of the human spirit with his closest companions, the philosophers Maximus and Priscus. Some suspect Ammianus of invention – as indeed one might – but Julian, a fantasist to the end, could well have performed just such a script from the classic books that had comforted him in his lonely adolescence.

He died that morning, as did many others, including Anatolius, the *magister officiorum*, although the prefect Salutius Secundus made a lucky escape. The soldiers, enraged by their losses, won a battlefield victory, and Ammianus' account records the number of senior Persian generals killed that day. But this small success was momentary. The camp fell into despair and rumours flew. Had it been an enemy spear or a Roman one that had killed the emperor, and was a vengeful Christian to be blamed? But worse, what to do next? Julian had no heir, either in the camp or elsewhere, and the campaign army had no natural leader, in part because it fused Constantius' eastern field army uneasily with the huge western force Julian had brought with him to conquer the East. The two officer corps did not trust each other and nor did they trust the palatine officials: senior members of Constantius' high command like Arinthaeus and Victor opposed the Julianic marshals Nevitta and Dagalaifus. A compromise choice might have been found in Salutius Secundus, old, steady, experienced and beholden to no faction. But he declined, and the possibility of marching out of Persia without an emperor remained impossible for most of the officer corps to imagine.

So it was that a junior guard officer, a *primicerius domesticorum* named Iovianus (Jovian, to us), was proclaimed emperor. The only explanation for his appointment is that the rival high commands could agree on nobody more senior, and thought that he would be safely beholden to those who had made him emperor. On the march again, battered by continual raids, the army continued slowly north. Almost a week after Julian's death, on 1 July, Shapur offered terms again – the army would be allowed to cross the Tigris unmolested if the Romans surrendered all the land Diocletian had taken from Persia in the time of Narseh, which is to say more than fifty years earlier, at the beginning of the fourth century. Moreover, the emperor would surrender Nisibis and Singara, fortified cities between the Tigris and the Euphrates that had been Roman for many centuries. Nisibis would be evacuated and its population forcibly transferred to Amida, which would remain in Roman hands, while Shapur would take without a battle the two cities that had long served to balance the power of the two empires in the region. It is impossible to exaggerate the scale of the Persian success and the Roman disaster. It is not that Julian himself was indispensable or that his death was itself a catastrophe: the competence he had shown as caesar in Gaul had abandoned him as augustus in Persia. The real catastrophe was Jovian.

A Christian, unlike Julian, he was also a weakling, entirely beholden to the high command, and it is here that his real significance lies. For us, as for his contemporaries, he seems no more than a sad epilogue to Julian and the dynasty founded by Constantine five decades before: his reign was short; he achieved little beyond the lamentable treaty with Persia; and our fullest source, Ammianus Marcellinus, goes out of his way to paint Jovian's reign in the most sombre of lights. And yet Jovian's brief reign actually prefigures much of the later fourth century's political history, which was dominated by the machinations of rival high commands in whose interest it was to make emperors of officers very junior indeed to the great marshals. That made for a politics in which rival cabals of senior officers and senior palatine officials contended with each other from different regional power bases – Gaul, Italy, the Balkans, the East – and thereby ensured that even the most individually imposing of emperors was too dependent on the high command to act freely. This power dynamic was a natural consequence of the late third-century reforms of Diocletian, and even more so of Constantinian governance, with its vastly expanded imperial administration and the consequent regionalism of its elites. It is a dynamic that will be a recurring theme henceforth, but what should be stressed here is Jovian's position in 363. He was augustus because the Gallic and eastern high commands could not accept as emperor anyone who had a significant power base of his own, and so compromised on a junior officer who would threaten no one. The more immediate question was whether he could inspire anyone's loyalty.

After the evacuation of Nisibis, Jovian made for Antioch. He allowed Julian's distant relation Procopius, who had been in command of the army that had initially drawn Shapur away to the north, to supervise the interment of the dead emperor at Tarsus in Cilicia, and then to retire quietly to family estates in Cappadocia; there he would develop plans to seize the purple in his own right as a member of the Constantinian dynasty. Jovian recalled to service his father-in-law Lucillianus, one of Constantius' more successful commanders on both the Balkan and Persian fronts. Lucillianus left retirement at Sirmium and went to secure the loyalty of the western provinces. Jovian tried to disguise the precariousness of his regime and his own role in the Persian debacle by minting coins with the legend VICTORIA ROMANORVM. That fooled no one, we can be sure, but he did at least win a revered place for himself in the memories of his Christian subjects: he quickly declared a 'peace of the church', decisively repudiating Julian's anti-Christian policy, while signalling that he would favour neither the Nicenes nor their homoian opponents, although he was a Nicene himself.

Rejecting Julian's legacy, however, did not require active measures against Julian's co-religionists: Ammianus Marcellinus is the only person that we know for sure left public life after Jovian's accession. It may be that, as a strongly pro-Julianic figure, he believed his career prospects would now be blighted for good, but it is also not impossible that he was cashiered either for his politics or for his paganism. Regardless, it was presumably now that he conceived his great project of writing a history of the Roman world since the reign of Trajan. If that is so, the death of Julian produced one thing for which posterity must be very grateful.

All of Jovian's early initiatives were undertaken before he reached Antioch in October, four months after Julian's death and the surrender of Nisibis and Singara to Shapur. A few weeks later he began to make his way north towards Constantinople, via Mopsuestia, Tarsus and Tyana. News from the West was bad. Lucillianus, having been so prominent in Constantius' Balkan high command, was not trusted by the Gallic establishment. That was headed by the *magister equitum* Iovinus, one of the key figures in the Julianic regime, and a very powerful man in Gaul, where his memory long endured and his role as a founder of churches was still celebrated in the Carolingian era. We soon catch a glimpse of the regional factionalism that had already been revealed in the later years of Constantius: the Pannonian Lucillianus tried to get his Frankish colleague Malarich, now in retirement, to replace Iovinus as *magister equitum*. Malarich wisely refused, which meant that Lucillianus decided to travel to Gaul and take command for himself. Iovinus acted first. At modern Reims, variously known as Durocortorum or *civitas Remorum/Remi*, where Iovinus was based, the rumour spread that Julian was still alive and the soldiery rose up against Lucillianus, lynching him and Seniauchus, one of the tribunes he had brought with him to enforce his position. Another tribune, a Pannonian named Valentinianus, was only saved by the timely intervention of Iovinus, who calmed the mutineers and openly declared himself in favour of Jovian's rule. Valentinianus was deputed to carry the news of Iovinus' loyalty to Jovian, whom he found at Aspona, a *mansio* on the road between Cappadocia and Galatia in Asia Minor.

Just before the end of the year, having promoted Valentinianus to the command of a guard unit, Jovian arrived at Ancyra with his court. He assumed the consulship there on the first day of the new year, in the company of his infant son Varronianus. But the portents were bad: the baby screamed and cried throughout the ceremony. A few weeks later, Jovian was dead, never having reached Constantinople: on 17 February 364, he died in the night, in the *mansio* at Dadastana, suffocated by toxic fumes from the fire in his sleeping chamber. As with Julian, rumours of foul play circulated and others spoke of suicide, but the official story may be true: it was in no one's clear interest to reopen the succession just as all were becoming reconciled to the new regime, so perhaps it was just a horrible accident. Be that as it may, the infant Varronianus, having bawled his way through the consular ceremonies just six weeks earlier, could hardly be made augustus, and none of Jovian's other relatives were suitable. The high command once again looked to Salutius Secundus, Julian's former praetorian prefect, and he again refused.

They settled instead on the tribune Valentinianus, who had brought the news of the Gallic mutiny and its suppression to Jovian at Aspona. Like Jovian, Valentinianus seems to have been a compromise candidate, someone junior enough to arouse no fears among the general staff or the key palatine officials. What is more, his conduct in Gaul and his lack of a personal power base might make the western establishment less distrustful. The decision was made to summon Valentinianus (whom we may now call Valentinian) from Ancyra to Nicaea, where the army acclaimed him augustus on 26 February 364, one week after Jovian had died. He rejected the soldiers' calls to appoint a colleague and instead made for Constantinople, arriving there in early March.

Valentinian, it would become clear, had an extremely forceful personality. Ammianus Marcellinus depicts him as a virtual savage, a half-literate Pannonian rustic, hardly better than a barbarian, but he was not all that different from any other late Roman officer of his age and rank – prone to bursts of sudden anger which he used to control those around him and aware that exemplary cruelty had a valuable place in management. His career had stalled under Julian, ostensibly because he was a Christian, but he had clearly been waiting to resume his position as soon as a change of regime allowed. A fast learner, he now worked out precisely how far he could challenge the high command. He had not let the soldiers chivvy him into picking a co-ruler at Nicaea, but nor did he imagine he could rule alone – the futility of trying had been demonstrated too many times since the death of Constantine, and the more recent growth of regional praetorian prefectures and regional high commands had simply exacerbated that trend. He would take a colleague, but the choice would be his, not the army's and not its officers'.

At Nicomedia, en route from Nicaea to Constantinople, he had already raised his younger brother Valens to the rank of *comes stabuli*, theoretically in charge of the transport and logistics for the imperial court, and also usefully honorific, for Valens had little experience of formal government. As a patronage appointment with plenty of opportunity for personal gain, it was not an unmistakable indication of future advance. Yet it may have been a trial balloon, to see whether further promotion of Valens would cause problems. Ammianus records that Dagalaifus publicly advised Valentinian not to choose a colleague from his own family, though perhaps his was the only cautionary voice, which would explain Ammianus' singling him out. Regardless, on 28 March 364, Valentinian presented his brother to the troops at the Constantinopolitan suburb of Hebdomon and he was acclaimed augustus. Both brothers soon fell seriously ill, and black magic or poisoning was suspected – not coincidentally, some of Julian's supporters were exiled at exactly this time and Procopius thought it prudent to flee from his Cappadocian retirement to distant Crimea. Both emperors recovered, however, and then travelled together to Naissus via Adrianople, Philippopolis and Serdica.

In the suburb of Mediana, the two augusti divided their palatine establishments and the praesental armies between themselves. Valens would govern the dioceses of Asiana and Oriens (which he would soon divide in two, into Oriental and Egyptian halves), along with Moesia and Thrace in Europe, while Valentinian would take the western dioceses: Spain, Britain and Gaul under the regional praetorian prefect for Gaul, with Africa, Italy and the Illyrian dioceses of Pannonia, Dacia and Macedonia under the praetorian prefect of Italy. Many units of the field army were split in half at this time to effect an equitable distribution of military manpower, which meant that, later in the century, units with the same name would appear in both the West and the East. Valentinian's role as the senior partner was emphasised by the much larger territory over which he would rule and the more troubled condition of the Rhine and upper Danube frontiers he would police. Humiliating as Jovian's peace treaty had been, its legacy would be more than forty years of peace on the eastern frontier.

It is important to understand the full significance of the 364 settlement between Valentinian and Valens. This was the first real recognition that the empire was not just too big to be ruled by one person, but that it was too big to be ruled in a unitary fashion. The division of responsibilities at Naissus really was a de facto division of the Roman world into two parallel empires, roughly along the line between native speakers of Greek and native speakers of Latin. Valentinian and Valens never saw each other again, and neither did much to help the other in their respective travails. Each *pars imperii* was meant to look after its own fate and the division at Naissus confirmed another structural change in the empire: the pattern set by Jovian's election was not a fluke or an accident. Factional rivalries within and among the regional high commands and prefectures would become the main drivers of imperial history, even when the emperor was as strong and competent as Valentinian.

After the great division of Naissus, Valens accompanied his brother as far as Sirmium. There, in August, the brothers parted company for good. Valens went East, though scholars are divided on how fast or how far he travelled. Valentinian's progress is much easier to follow, because it was he who issued most of the legislation from this period and the laws, more than anything, reveal imperial movements. By late August he was at Emona (modern Ljubljana) and he spent a large part of September in Aquileia. During the autumn he dealt with government and military business in the administrative centres of northern Italy, Verona and Mediolanum (now Milan).

The volume and breadth of Valentinianic legislation is impressive and shows a practical, hands-on approach to administration that harks back to the tetrarchs: the years 364 and 365 preserve an unprecedentedly large number of imperial constitutions, on all manner of subjects. But this is no accident of preservation: it seems clear that Valentinian (and perhaps Valens, too), used a barrage of legal measures to bolster his uncertain authority and project himself as the careful manager the empire needed. He did this by publishing constitutions that stated nothing new – one of the earliest Valentinianic laws lays out the favourable privileges of discharged veterans that had been in force for centuries, showing the emperor's concern for his fellow soldiers, while granting greater privileges to ex-*protectores* than to other ranks. Similar laws advertising the imperial concern for senators, for urban *curiales* (town councillors) and for the other major orders of society followed, all in the aid of advertising the new emperors' fitness to rule by making routine administrative matters into public legal events of general applicability.

Valentinian saw in the new year of 365 at Mediolanum, taking up his first consulate there. Valens did the same in Constantinople. From this point onwards, it becomes necessary to treat the history of the eastern and western empires in more or less separate narratives, adopting the approach already pioneered in the fourth century by Ammianus Marcellinus, who had recognised how tenuous the connections were between the affairs of Valentinian and those of his brother. Against most expectations, it was Valens not Valentinian who faced the hardest and most immediate challenge: a usurpation by the last claimant to the Constantinian dynastic succession, Procopius. The latter, as we saw, had fled to the Crimea shortly after the accession of Valentinian and Valens, and from here had sought support from the remaining partisans of the old dynasty. This was done quietly at first, and Valens seems not to have suspected the seriousness of the conspiracy because he left Constantinople for Syria in July. Within the month, Procopius had found his way to the eastern capital, there awaiting the perfect moment to strike.

It is remarkable how many men with connections to the old dynasty were willing to take up the Procopian cause – not just the direct partisans of Julian, but also senior generals of Constantius, men like Agilo and Gomoarius, who had by now gone into retirement. Constantius' widow Faustina rallied to Procopius as well and she and her young daughter Constantia took a prominent place in Procopius' entourage when he declared himself emperor. He did this publicly in another dynastic monument, the baths built by Constantine's half-sister Anastasia. Two infantry units destined for the Balkan field army, the Divitenses and the Tungricani Iuniores, also joined Procopius, and the seniority and authority of Constantius' old generals made it likely that other units could be suborned as well.

The coup took place on 28 September. Valens' praetorian prefect Nebridius was deposed. Salutius Secundus, that ancient product of the

Constantinian empire who had been thought *capax imperii* ('throne-worthy') and had declined the honour more than once, returned to his old post as prefect. The urban prefect of Constantinople was likewise deposed and replaced by a Gallic supporter of Julian named Phonimius. Another Gaul, Euphrasius, was made Procopius' *magister officiorum*. Taken together, it looks like the reconstitution of the old regime, but not every former Constantian came around: the still powerful Flavius Arbitio declined to support the rebellion, so the usurper confiscated his Constantinopolitan properties. The mint swiftly began striking coins in Procopius' image, in all three metals – gold, silver and bronze – with traditionalist legends like SECVRITAS REIPVBLICAE and REPARATIO FELIX TEMPORVM that recalled the Constantinian past. In contrast to the beardless imagery of Jovian, Valentinian and Valens, Procopius ostentatiously revived the bearded portrait favoured by Julian. Marking the dynastic connection like this was both obvious and necessary, and there can be no doubt that it made an impact.

Valens was certainly frightened. He could rally nowhere near the number of eminent supporters who had joined Procopius, he had less dynastic legitimacy and he had less experience of military command. And he would receive no help from Valentinian, who had left Mediolanum for Gaul shortly before hearing the news of Procopius' rising. The Gallic high command, still under the direction of Iovinus, was increasingly concerned at the potential threat of disturbances in Alamannia across the upper Rhine. Valentinian had to choose between alienating his generals, and perhaps provoking a usurpation in a region chronically prone to mutiny, and bringing aid to Valens. Really, there was no choice: his younger, less competent brother would be left to fend for himself. Valens was at Caesarea in Cappadocia when he learned about Procopius' rebellion and he moved from there into Galatia, where he rallied a campaign force. Arbitio, alienated by Procopius' vindictive seizure of his property, joined Valens and helped cement the wavering loyalty of the units that were accompanying him.

By late in the year, the main eastern field army had come up from Antioch and Valens felt bold enough to move. He marched into Bithynia, seizing Nicomedia and unsuccessfully laying siege to Chalcedon, across the Bosporus from Constantinople. When several of his units went over to Procopius, he followed the safest course of action and retreated to Ancyra for the winter, leaving all the major Bithynian cities in the hands of the usurper. Yet Procopius' power base was not growing any larger and he had little chance of expanding it: the Balkan high command, under Valentinian's former fellow tribune Equitius, blocked the most important passes from Thrace into the western Balkans so Procopius had no access to reinforcements from there.

Valentinian named both consuls of 366: his 7-year-old son Flavius Gratianus, named after the emperor's father and now styled *nobilissimus puer* ('most noble boy') to mark him as imperial heir, shared the consular fasces with Flavius Dagalaifus, Julian's great marshal, his reward for his key role in securing the succession for Valentinian. In the East, the forces of Procopius and Valens prepared for the inevitable resumption of hostilities, which began as soon as the campaign season opened in late March. From Pessinus in Galatia Valens took his army westwards and the two forces met at Thyatira (Akhisar) in Lydia. Old Arbitio addressed himself to the Procopian troops, which were under the command of his former subordinate Gomoarius. He denounced Procopius as a mere brigand and appealed to their personal loyalty to him, their former commander. They listened. Gomoarius and his troops came over to Arbitio and Procopius had little option but to retreat.

Valens pursued him to Nacolia in Phrygia, where, in May, the events at Thyatira repeated themselves: rather than fight his old comrades, Agilo went over to Valens. Procopius fled, but was betrayed by his remaining companions: he was handed over to Valens and immediately beheaded. As news spread, one of the dead usurper's relatives, a commander named Marcellus, tried to continue the rebellion at Nicaea and Chalcedon, but by then Valentinian had authorised Equitius to bring aid to Valens. Advancing through the Succi pass, Equitius besieged the remaining Procopian forces at Philippopolis. When he learned of the disturbances at Chalcedon, he sent a detachment of the Balkan army to suppress Marcellus, but at Philippopolis the defenders refused to surrender until they were shown the head of Procopius on a stake. In the purges that followed, they suffered great losses. The Constantinopolitans, by contrast, were asked to make an ostentatious show of sorrow and repentance for their treachery, but were otherwise left unmolested. More by luck than skill, and thanks to the efforts of generals left over from the prior regime, Valens had kept his throne.

While this was going on, Valentinian was engaged in a series of campaigns beyond the Rhine, in Alamannia, although most of these are hard to locate with any precision. He had reached Lutetia (modern Paris) by October 365 and for most of the next year he was based in Remi when not on campaign. That city was not in itself a key part of the imperial administrative structures, but it was the main residence of Iovinus, the *magister equitum per Gallias*. Having been appointed by Julian, whose loyal partisan he was, his power base was so deeply entrenched that he was nevertheless kept in his post throughout the following reigns. It is a reminder of the power wielded by the regional high commands and regional prefectures that a relatively stable group of very senior administrators – some of whom had served Julian loyally – held on to their posts throughout much of Valentinian's reign.

The emperor, for his part, made a great show of being an active soldier, since that was an essential component in imposing his authority, and in shoring up his legitimacy as a ruler. The European frontiers of the empire were simpler than those in Africa or the East. The Rhine and Danube rivers marked a clear line between inside and outside the empire, having done so since the Transdanubian provinces of Dacia were abandoned in the later third century. Yet neither the Rhine nor the Danube posed much in the way of actual physical barriers and, as a result, the peoples on the other sides of the rivers had a continuous experience of interaction with the empire. Indeed, interaction with the empire was the major catalyst for social change in the *barbaricum*, since it was Rome's complex state structure which exerted pressures for change on its neighbours. Romans not only provided aspirational models for those outside the provincial structure, they were also the conduits through which Roman goods flowed out into the wider continent.

Roman cultural influence can be envisaged as a series of bands or zones, running outwards from the imperial frontier. In the zone nearest to the frontier, the lives of the vast majority of people were little different from those of the provincials next door: the regular system of Roman taxation may have been all that set a peasant in Germania Prima apart from a peasant in Alamannia across the upper Rhine. Agriculture, a money economy – sometimes supplemented by local imitations of imperial coins – and even some elite fashions (Roman-style villas, for instance) were just smaller-scale versions of the imperial norm. In zones further out, the contrast would have been starker. Roman exports were rarer, confined to luxury and prestige goods rather than everyday items, while Roman coins circulated as bullion, not money, and there was no local minting.

Still further out, in Lithuania or Scandinavia, only the most portable of Roman goods were found – gold coins and medallions, rare weapons and armour – under the tight control of warrior elites who used them to symbolise their own prestige. These distant regions had commodities that the empire needed – Baltic amber, animal pelts, slaves – but little that has left a mark on the archaeological record, so we cannot even hazard a guess at the scale of this trade. Whatever the scale, it was not conducted by long-distance traders, but rather through stages of intermediate exchange. As a result, the continent's more distant people were, from the Roman perspective, half-legendary: early imperial geographies and ethnographies jumble the real and the fantastic together and Ammianus imports some of this fantasia into his fourth-century ethnographic digressions.

By contrast, there was a striking economic and political interdependence along the frontier, not least because of the army. Service in the Roman army brought with it not just regular pay and often a large discharge bonus, it also taught men from beyond the frontiers military skills that were of great use to them in prosecuting local conflicts. Many barbarians who served in the Roman army became entirely acclimatised to a Roman way of life, living out their lives inside the empire and dying there as Roman citizens after long years of service. Others, however, returned to their home communities beyond the frontier, bringing with them Roman habits and tastes, along with Roman money and products of different sorts. Their presence contributed to the demand for still more Roman goods beyond the frontiers, which helped increase trade between the empire and its neighbours. Roman installations on the frontiers found a ready market among barbarians close to the frontier, and Roman coins that found their way out into the *barbaricum* often found their way back to the empire through trade.

Lest we draw too harmonious a picture, the frontier was also deeply bound together by violence. Barbarian elites were warriors first and foremost, though some may have turned their hands to the plough from time to time. Constant low-level fighting – warfare, raiding, banditry, predation, call it what you will – was a fact of life on the frontier. The empire actually relied on that, absorbing losers and winners alike into its armies, settling refugees as farmers deep inside the empire. If anything, the empire cultivated frontier instability, subsidising some kings or chiefs over others, setting one against another, switching off the tap on the flow of goods with sufficient capriciousness to keep everyone guessing.

Not unexpectedly, the corollary of this constant low-level fighting was that it sometimes turned on the neighbouring Roman provinces, whose riches were a constant enticement, a sweet shop to be raided when imperial attentions were relaxed. But violence went both ways. Military victory was the essential guarantee of imperial legitimacy and the stockpile of victories needed regular replenishment. That meant periodic assaults upon the neighbours, scorching the earth, razing the villages, massacring some, enslaving others. Every frontier generation, at one point or another, was subject to this unkindly ministration. And, whatever it gained the emperor's reputation, it also gave barbarian leaders an incentive to become more militarily effective themselves.

That structural logic had operated on the frontier since early imperial times, but the third century saw a fundamental change, in that three major barbarian collectivities – there is no better word, since they were neither tribes nor 'peoples' nor cohesive polities – came on the scene in the course of just a few decades. The Alamanni, the Goths and the Franks became a permanent feature of late imperial politics, constant presences around which smaller barbarian groupings might come and go. Of the three, the Alamanni are in many ways the easiest to understand. In the course of the third century, the Romans started calling the barbarians along the upper Rhine Alamanni, and we occasionally see large numbers of these people taking collective action, raiding as far south as the north Italian plain during the chaotic years of the 270s. Presumably the many smaller groups of barbarians in the region had come to feel some sense of common identity or purpose. The reason may have been as simple as the fact that Rome did not trouble to differentiate among groups of people in the region, to the point that they began to feel less difference among themselves. (That phenomenon has been observed in more recent imperial relationships, on the north-west frontier of the British Raj, and in Russia's conquest of central Asia.)

In the fourth century, the Alamanni appear – mainly in the pages of Ammianus Marcellinus – as a loose confederacy of different kings who might unite their individual followings for major campaigns against the Romans, but who for the most part spent as much time at odds with one another as with the empire. We find different groups of Alamanni with different names (Lentienses, Brisigavi, etc.), each with their own king, and it seems likely that this was the level at which most political activity took place, and with which most people identified. Roughly the same process is detectable in the case of the Franks, who seem to have coalesced under that generic name from among the various tribes of the lower Rhineland. As with the Alamanni, the sense of kinship among various Franci, to the extent that it existed, was more than anything else a product of their facing an imperial Roman administration that lumped them all together.

If, as seems likely, most of the 'tribes' and 'peoples' along the empire's continental frontier had taken on the shape in which we find them because of their contact with Rome, then, working from west to east, we find first the various groups of Franci on the lower Rhine, then Alamanni on the middle and upper Rhine and upper Danube, then a variety of Quadi and Sarmatians above and at the Danube bend, where the river turns sharply south in modern Hungary before turning east again in modern Serbia and eventually debouching into the Black Sea. What 'Sarmatian' signified in the fourth century is quite difficult for us to parse, mainly because the name is so old, already used before the turn of the millennium to signify Iranian nomads north of the Black Sea. We know much less about the Quadi than about the Franks or the Alamanni further west, but they probably came into being in the third century in the same way: smaller groups of barbarians with different tribal identities coming to see themselves as being like one another because of the way they were treated in their relations with the Roman empire.

East of the Danube bend, we come to the Carpathian mountains and the broad strip of land between their southernmost edge and the river itself. By the fourth century, this entire region could be called the *ripa Gothica*, 'the Gothic river bank', and we will consider its relations with the eastern empire in the next chapter. Beyond these 'front line' barbarian groups, the Romans knew of scores of others, with some of whom they had relatively regular contact, while others remained mere names, hazily known and vaguely located. We should never overestimate the capacities of Roman intelligence gathering, and skilful handling of immediate neighbours did not translate into practical curiosity about the people of more distant lands. It was not until the seventh century that Roman emperors began to take a serious interest in understanding political events far beyond the imperial frontiers. Before that, it was the fifty kilometres or so beyond the *limes* (as Romans called a variety of boundaries, most especially the imperial frontier) that consistently experienced the impact of Rome, and Valentinian's aggressive approach is thoroughly characteristic.

In 366 and 367, he campaigned beyond the upper Rhine and took

Alamannicus as a victory title, before taking up residence in Trier by October of 367, at which point the imperial college had gained a new augustus. In spring 367, Valentinian had fallen seriously, perhaps mortally, ill and the Gallic high command went so far as to openly canvass the possibility of appointing a successor from among their own number if Valentinian were to die (without any reference to Valens). In the end, he recovered. Just as remarkably, he seems not to have blamed his staff for their contingency planning – and that despite his fearsome temper. But though he kept all his commanders in office, he also made sure to reaffirm his, and their, commitment to a dynastic succession: at Ambiani (modern Amiens), on 24 August 367, he raised his son Gratian to the rank of augustus. Gratian was still only a boy, but by having the 8-year-old raised in the purple, Valentinian ensured that the high command and the palatine bureaucracy would not be able to ignore the dynastic question were he to die suddenly.

For now, though, his health had returned and he was continuing his Gallic campaigns when distressing news arrived from Britain: groups of Attecotti, from what is now Ireland, as well as Frankish and Saxon pirates from the North Sea, were threatening the island's provinces, while Picts from beyond Hadrian's Wall had taken advantage of these disturbances to raid far into the south. Two senior generals had been captured and killed, the *dux Britanniarum* Fullofaudes, and the *comes litus Saxonici* Nectaridus, who had been in charge of the 'Saxon Shore', a series of coastal fortifications from the Wash to the Solent. A Spanish protégé of Iovinus, Flavius Theodosius, was sent to deal with the trouble as *comes rei militaris*, which is to say commander without portfolio. He campaigned throughout 368 and 369 and, as reward for his successes, he was promoted to the rank of *magister equitum* in succession to the ageing Iovinus. He held that rank until Valentinian's death and, along with Equitius in Sirmium and the Balkans, and the *quaestor* Eupraxius (in a recently created role, responsible for crafting the emperor's public pronouncements, especially laws), he was one of the three main bulwarks of the western emperor's regime.

While Theodosius campaigned in Britain, Valentinian invaded Alamannia, winning a striking victory at Solicinium in September 368 before returning to Treveri for the winter. In the meantime, there had been some major changes in his household. The mother of Gratian was Marina Severa, a woman of obscure parentage whom Valentinian had married while he was still a very junior officer, probably before he became a *tribunus*, the rank he held when he entered the light of history. Now, with his son publicly confirmed as legitimate heir to the purple, Valentinian could afford to pursue a more advantageous dynastic match. Severa was set aside and condemned to discreet exile on the excuse that she had engaged in fraudulent property transactions. In her place, Valentinian installed Justina, who came from a far more powerful Pannonian family than Valentinian's. During the reign of Constantius, when she was still a little girl, she had been married to the Gallic usurper Magnentius. After his defeat in 353, she and her brothers survived their father's execution by the victorious Constantius, and the family continued to prosper. It would now bring its network of patronage and support to the western emperor, and that would in turn give him greater independence from the Gallic high command. Iustina's brothers Constantianus and Cerealis were made *tribuni stabuli* in succession to one another, the same office that Valentinian had once bestowed on his brother Valens and thus a potential signal of promotions to come. For all its advantages, however, the marriage reintroduced into western imperial politics something that had been more or less absent since the death of Constantius: religious controversy among rival Christians.

Constantius had been a zealot, with a genuine commitment to the homoian position on the relationship of a supreme God the Father, and a subordinate and created God the Son. He had expended tremendous effort on enforcing this belief on the empire's bishops, both in the Greek East, where the homoian creed had considerable ecclesiastical support, and the Latin West, where, with a few Balkan exceptions, the opinion of churchmen was near universally hostile. Constantius' successor Julian had had no interest in which side emerged successfully from the Christians' internecine disputes. The mere fact that they were fighting was quite satisfying enough. And Jovian, as we have seen, was a Nicene who went out of his way to disclaim any interest in ecclesiastical faction fighting. Valentinian followed that same model. A Nicene himself, he was visibly indifferent to theological controversy. Some have regarded this as a statesmanlike even-handedness, others as further evidence of his brutishness and lack of wit. It might genuinely have been either. But we do know that Iustina was a deeply convinced homoian, not unusually so given her regional background: Pannonia and the western Balkans were the intellectual centre of anti-Nicene theology in the Latin-speaking world, by contrast with the vocally Nicene churches of Gaul and Italy. And it was not just Iustina: in the East, Valens aggressively promoted homoian beliefs over those of the Nicenes, which meant that Constantius' bête noire, the eternally oppositional Athanasius of Alexandria, endured yet another exile almost immediately upon Valens' accession. Valens' homoianism would be a major feature of his reign, as we shall see in the next chapter, while Justina's would become more and more prominent after the death of Valentinian in 375.

Here we should take some time to consider religious developments at mid century. The extent of Christian conversion prior to the age of Constantine is not known, because the evidence is simply lacking. In the fourth century, after Constantine and despite the theological battles of his sons' reigns, Christianity of one flavour or another spread inexorably through the population, at every level, in both the Greek and Latin worlds. Different people found different things to do with the faith. For the urban masses, Christian worship, religious processions and the elaboration of saints' cults with their strong admixture of local patriotism all provided a form of communal celebration. These civic festivities were analogous to those that had long been associated with the cults of the old gods, but also more participatory than those had been. In the villages and countryside, by contrast, the new religion could provide a release valve for social discontent that might otherwise have pushed people into brigandage. Thus, among the Donatist schismatics of Africa at odds with the official imperial church, fanatical Circumcellions looted the villages of rival Christians; in the eastern provinces, Christian mobs went about destroying non-Christian images and pulling down pagan shrines, representing a complex mixture of devotion and hooliganism familiar enough to us from modern sports culture.

For elites, both urban and rural, Christianity offered all the opportunities for public patronage and display as had the old cults in centuries past: we have seen how the powerful western marshal Iovinus was also a devoted church-founder at Remi and elsewhere, and archaeologists have been able to detect a boom in the construction of churches on aristocratic estates from the middle of the fourth century. Psychologically, Christianity offered believers a religious interiority and sense of being responsible for one's own spiritual health, but it did not make the intensive intellectual demands on its followers that philosophical paganism did. In other words, Christianity offered both liturgical ritual and a developed belief system that gave believers a powerful stake in their own salvation. The various strands of non-Christian monotheism had also offered plenty of scope for salvation, but the intellectual barrier to entry was much higher for a Neoplatonist than it was for an educated Christian. Ausonius of Burdigala (today's Bordeaux), the tutor of the young emperor Gratian, was indisputably a pious Christian, but his Christianity managed to be both profoundly felt and intellectually content-free. In other words, while Christianity left plenty of scope for abstruse intellectual questions of theology, it did not require its adherents to take an interest in them, and that no doubt contributed to its spread.

Indeed, by the time of Valentinian, at least at the level of the elite, it seems clear that most people were Christian by default; it now took more of a conscious choice to be a non-Christian than a Christian, a remarkably rapid transformation in the mere generation or so since Constantine. Just as remarkable was the consolidation of hierarchy within the church and the increasing power of the episcopate. The middle and later fourth century was the age of the great prelates, bishops whose power stemmed not just from their ability to act as interlocutors with imperial power, but also from their role as patrons for whole communities, finding in their congregations a base of support largely independent of familiar hierarchies of social status or imperial patronage. The sort of men who now became bishops demonstrate the scale of the change: when Constantine conquered the whole western empire in 312, and even when he conquered the East in 324, one would have been hard-pressed to find any church leaders with aristocratic or curial origins. Documents from the earliest church councils – for instance, the one held at Illiberis (Elvira in Spain) a few years before the turn of the fourth century – make clear that aristocrats and civic elites might well be Christian, but that church leaders were very rarely drawn from their ranks. By the time of Valentinian, by contrast, bishops came increasingly from the type of background in which they might just as easily have pursued high imperial office rather than an ecclesiastical position. Indeed, some bishops had already pursued an imperial career before their ordination.

Thus Ambrose, who became bishop of the great imperial city of Mediolanum in 374, was the son of a praetorian prefect of Gaul. He had himself started on the ladder of government as *consularis* (one of the grades of governor) of Aemilia and Liguria, when he was chosen by the people of Mediolanum to be their bishop and was advanced through all the clerical grades in the course of a week in order to take up his new office.

Other aristocrats, meanwhile, deliberately sought out episcopal office as a conscious alternative to other types of power: in 366, the episcopal election that followed the death of Liberius, bishop of Rome, led to the supporters of the two rival claimants – Damasus and Ursinus – fighting pitched battles and leaving 137 people dead in church. To no one's surprise, it was the better-born Damasus who prevailed, while Ursinus was banished after the urban prefect had restored order. But perhaps the greatest testimony to the increasing status of episcopal office comes in a famous taunt by the most aristocratic of Rome's pagans, Vettius Agorius Praetextatus, who said to that very same Damasus: 'Make me bishop of Rome and I will become a Christian.' And it was not just Rome. Although it is precisely in these years that we find the first explicit claims to the Roman bishop's possessing a greater authority than his fellow bishops as the successor to Peter and Paul, we are still a very long way from his having any real power to command them. Rather, just as Damasus was a formidable figure because of the wealth and prestige of his church and his personal capacity to channel those things productively, so could his counterparts be found in many great cities: Ambrose in Mediolanum, Felix in Treveri, Martin in *civitas Turonum* (modern Tours) and Basil in Cappadocian Caesarea.

The staunch anti-homoianism of Basil, whose ideas and insights were frequently Latinised by Ambrose in his own theological works, takes us from the increasingly aristocratic and politically engaged world of the western episcopate to an East where the much greater complexity of Christian politics produced a different landscape. As well as the complexity and hair-splitting potential of its Greek language, the East had also suffered longer from emperors who cared about theology: Constantine thought himself the religious peer of his bishops, while Constantius II subjected them to relentless theological micro-management. What is more, the East had at least three episcopal sees that could claim an apostolic foundation, and with it a primacy of power: Alexandria, Antioch and Jerusalem. But while their long-standing rivalry did not abate, all three were increasingly challenged by the growing power of Constantinople. It was an upstart of a city – a Constantinian, not an apostolic foundation – which grew inexorably more authoritative as more and more of the imperial administration was housed there. The barrage of conciliar decision-making by which Constantius had sought to regulate the church had, not unparadoxically, entrenched rivalries among episcopal factions that simmered beneath any momentary calm, waiting to explode given the opportunity. The accession of Valens and his personal preference for an extreme homoian theology provided just such an opportunity. And so it is to the conduct of politics in the East after the defeat of Procopius that we next turn.

3

THE VALENTINIANI

❦

The city of Rome, with its tempestuous Christian throngs and its super-rich senatorial aristocracy, was a challenging place to govern, but because Valentinian never once ventured there, he could keep some of its complexities at arm's length. And from the court's point of view, the politics of the western empire were difficult, but at least readily legible – Valentinian was a native of the Latin West, the factions within his court were mostly western, and the balance between the military high command, the palatine bureaucracy and the regional prefectures was one that could be maintained with careful management. In the East, Valens faced very much greater challenges, which were compounded by his lack of experience, an unimaginative character and a tendency to paranoia that was not always ill founded. He was also a Latin in a Greek-speaking world that was changing very fast. Those innate disadvantages were exposed still more cruelly by the need to divide his time between two large and highly charged urban settings, Antioch and Constantinople. By contrast, the frontier camps of the Rhineland and even major Gallic cities like Treveri were simple enough worlds to navigate.

Constantinople itself was one of the main reasons for the changing character of the eastern empire. In the course of just a generation, it had gone from existing solely in Constantine's imagination to a city that was increasingly the capital of the eastern empire; and unlike Rome, which was a city that had conquered an empire long before it was ruled by emperors, Constantinople was an imperial creation and an ongoing imperial project.

One of the new city's greatest impacts on the elites of the eastern provinces was its Senate. Constantine had brought many senators with him when he moved east and he created many more, both deliberately and by a natural expansion of the *ordo* after senatorial rank could be gained by holding imperial office. But Constantine's senators were Roman senators; they belonged to the city of Rome, even if they resided in the East. It was Constantius II who created the Constantinopolitan Senate, modelled on that of Rome – and it was this possession of its own Senate that would allow the eastern capital to alter the whole landscape of the Greek world.

As early as 340, the new city was where eastern senators were obliged to give the praetorian games that signalled entry into that rank. This was a sign of things to come. In 355, Constantius adlected the famed orator and philosopher Themistius to the Senate of Constantinople (that is, he 'read him into' the Senate, an imperial prerogative). Themistius was then tasked with recruiting new senators from around the East. According to Themistius himself, there were only three hundred senators of the city in 357, but that number rose to 2,000 over the next five years. Having functionally been a large but normal city council – like any Latin *curia* or Greek *boule* – when Themistius became a senator, the enlarged Constantinopolitan Senate now formed an eastern *ordo senatorius* that would be increasingly separate from that of the West. Its creation was an important step in inaugurating the Greek Roman empire that would flourish for many centuries longer than its western counterpart, and survive in one form or another to the dawn of the modern era.

It should come as no surprise, then, that already by the 360s there was mounting resentment of Constantine's city on the Bosporus. It drew the rich, the talented and some of the well-born away from their native cities. This mattered a great deal in the Greek world, where the sense of identification with the *polis* ('city-state', plural *poleis*, already the characteristic Greek polity a thousand years earlier) was deeply inculcated in urban elites, and where a renaissance of *polis* culture, lovingly cultivated by generations, had followed the Roman conquest of the Hellenistic East. The upstart metropolis, with its looming imperial palace complex and its convenient equidistance between the Danubian and the Syrian frontiers, was a threat to a world that had developed according to its own internal, city-centred logic over hundreds of years. One can sense the regret this caused in the words of Libanius, the Antiochene sophist whose voluminous writings are suffused with a sorrow for a world that was passing – not just the old gods, for whose prospects Julian's death was a final catastrophe, but also a world where young men still learned Greek oratory and philosophy instead of rushing off to law school and the forensic studies that would get them ahead in the capital.

The historian Eunapius of Sardis was likewise half aware that the world he inhabited was being changed for good by Christianity, and also by the new and ravenous city that Constantine had created. Like Ammianus Marcellinus and Libanius, Eunapius was a committed pagan and, like Ammianus, he wrote a history of the empire, though with a tiny fraction of the former's skill and narrative talent. That history, which survives only in fragments and in the heavy use made of it by the sixth-century historian Zosimus, usefully supplements our other evidence, but it is in his *Lives of the Sophists* that Eunapius' frame of mind leaps suddenly into view. Deliberately modelled on the work of the third-century sophist Philostratus, who had himself created the concept of the Second Sophistic and the renaissance of Greek learning and culture it was meant to signify, Eunapius' *Lives* depict a half-imaginary Polis-Land similar to that of Philostratus. For Eunapius, though, that Polis-Land was palpably under threat from hostile alternatives – the imperial court with its Latin legal culture, and a Christianity that rejected the god-filled world of a romanticised Greek past. Christians, too, hated the challenge posed by Constantine's new city, and none more so than the bishops of Alexandria and Antioch – the ceaseless religious controversy of the fourth century was fuelled as much by their mutual unwillingness to cede their authority to the bishops of upstart Constantinople as it was by their own rivalry.

Along with the construction of Constantinople, a subtler and less immediately visible change began to affect the ruling classes of the East, both pagan and Christian, in the middle and late fourth century. The Constantinopolitan Senate recruited by Themistius on Constantius' orders drew from both the age-old landed families of the *poleis* and an ambitious petty bourgeoisie whose powers, such as they were, depended on their role in imperial government. The arrivisme of this group was one reason Libanius could combine his lament for the decline of his world with an ugly sneer: ambitious men of the lower middle class no longer aspired to enter the *boule*, they wanted to go into the imperial civil service, which nowadays lent them a trumped-up prestige because so many imperial posts turned those who held them into senators. If it was only the oldest of the ancient families that stayed loyal to the identity of their *polis* – or worse, if even some of them succumbed to the vogue for imperial service – then the old ruling class would wither and slowly die, submerged in a sea of its social inferiors. Libanius was exaggerating for effect, but his analysis was precise and acute. If anything, he underestimated the scale of the change being wrought on the social world of the Greek East at mid century. Its cause was gold.

Constantine had displayed a missionary zeal to serve as apostle and bishop to those outside the empire. In far-flung regions like Arabia and Ethiopia, and among the Gothic kingdoms of the Danube and Black Sea steppe, he had sought to spread his new faith. He also ramped up imperial intervention in the Caucasus. This had diplomatic implications with Persia, in whose sphere of influence the states of the Caucasus had traditionally fallen. Constantine's sponsorship of Christian missionaries there meant competing with the Persian kings, though it also gave the two empires new opportunities to cooperate in managing the steppe nomad populations north of the mountains. Those two consequences had been predictable, but another consequence came as a surprise. Somewhere in the Caucasus, a new source of gold was discovered and the Romans could monopolise it because Persia's economy was wholly based on silver. A new source of Roman gold was hypothesised in the 1930s, when an economic historian postulated its existence in order to explain why the economy of the eastern empire was dramatically more robust than that of the West in the fourth, fifth and sixth centuries. Now, nearly a hundred years later, that deduction has been proved correct by the metrological study of surviving gold coins: ancient smelting techniques were incapable of refining platinum out of gold, so the platinum content in Roman gold coins is a foolproof way of discovering the origin of the gold. This analysis has begun to show three things: first, a major new source of gold was indeed discovered about this time, because from the mid fourth century onwards eastern *solidi* contain a hitherto unknown isotope in large quantities; second, this source produced gold that was purer than and unrelated to any previously known source; and third, gold from this new source barely entered the coinage in circulation in the West, staying confined, over many decades, to the eastern monetary system.

This is not just evidence for the growing political disconnect between the two halves of the empire, but also helps to explain a phenomenon that is attested in fiscal documents preserved in Egypt on papyrus: the disruption of old patterns of diverse and dispersed land ownership by urban *polis* elites who could trace their status back to the Hellenistic kingdoms, and their gradual replacement by a consolidated estate agriculture in the hands of men whose access to the gold economy was guaranteed by imperial service. Even if that pattern is unlikely to have been uniform across the Greek-speaking world, it would help account for the much greater attachment of fifth-century Greek elites to a centralised imperial government than their western counterparts demonstrated: their source of power was much more fundamentally predicated on an imperial structure than was that of western senators and warlords. It is not, then, actually a paradox if the eastern empire was in the end made stronger and more vibrant by the economic strangulation of the old elites and the rise of a new, court- and administration-centred aristocracy of service. What has been called 'later late antiquity' – a period between the sixth and eighth centuries – can only be a story of decline and fall in the Latin West, but it is one of spectacular cultural creativity in the East. That change had already taken root in the fourth century: 'later late antiquity' was no less different from the Severan or Constantinian empire in the East than it was from that in the West, but it was indisputably richer, healthier, more politically stable and artistically creative, and it remained so right through the early Arab conquests and the first Islamic caliphate of the Umayyads.

Even today, with all the new evidence at our disposal, the economic transformation slowly taking place in the Roman East can be glimpsed only in the occasional flash of illumination provided by our sources, so it must have been almost invisible to those living through it. But they would have experienced the pressure of political events far more vividly than we can even imagine. Valens had been lucky to survive the usurpation of Procopius, and it left him more aware than ever of how little room for independent action he possessed. He had been saved by the defection of the old establishment of Constantius' day to his side. They came not out of any regard for him, but because of loyalty to the greatest of their old marshals. His brother, busy winning uncomplicated victories over Franci and Alamanni in the West, had not lifted a finger to help him. Valens could not help but feel his deficit of authority, and so he tried to bolster it with vigorous military action. The Danube offered an opportunity, the Goths an excuse.

A series of campaigns by Constantine in the early 330s had led to a lasting peace on the lower Danube, but one that clearly gave the Gothic chieftains substantial power in the region. Glimpses of Gothic activity in the written sources are few, and it is hard to tell how precisely different Gothic groups related to one another ('Goth' being a generic term that takes in a number of polities and tribes, some with distinct names of their own). But the archaeological evidence reveals a productive agricultural world, heavily monetised up to a hundred kilometres from the Roman frontier, with aristocratic centres dotted across the landscape from the Carpathians to the Dnieper river. In 365, Procopius had called upon the leaders of the Gothic Tervingi to support his usurpation, relying upon his own connections to the Constantinian house and appealing to Gothic loyalty to their 30-year-old treaty with Constantine. The Tervingian response was dilatory and Procopius had already been defeated by the time 3,000 Gothic soldiers turned up in Thrace to offer support for the rebellion. Finding it over, they returned home.

Valens sent the *magister equitum* Flavius Victor, who had been an important figure in the eastern military establishment since the reign of Julian, to inquire of the Goths why they had decided to go to war even though they were bound by treaties of friendship to Rome. Representatives of the Gothic king Athanaric produced a letter from Procopius, asserting his legitimacy as the true heir of Constantine and calling for aid. The Goths now insisted that, although they had made a mistake, it was an understandable one, and unintentional. They fully acknowledged the legitimacy of Valens' rule. But Valens had no desire to let such excuses satisfy him. He saw an easy outlet for his ambition beyond the Danube and he decided to punish the Goths for their support of the usurper.

In 367, Valens launched the first of three annual campaigns along the Danube and beyond. By May of that year, he had moved with his palatine establishment and field army as far as Marcianopolis, a prime staging post for Danubian campaigns, and, in the course of the next month, he crossed the river at Daphne and began to lay waste to Gothic territory. He placed a bounty on captive Goths and sent the *magister militum* Flavius Arinthaeus to capture as many locals as he could. But most of the Gothic population fled into the mountains, the Gothic kings refused to give battle, and by September Valens was back on Roman territory at Durostorum, having failed to win the victory he was hoping for. Wintering at Marcianopolis, he tried again the following year. This time, his main base was a place known only as *vicus Carporum*, 'the village of the Carpi', a reference to the tribal population that had once lived across the Danube and that Diocletian had admitted to the empire under treaty, settling them as farmers in the

Balkans. Heavy rains made campaigning impossible, the Danube and its marshes overflowed and became impassable.

Valens' third invasion was launched the following year, 369. This time he went via Noviodunum, penetrating north and east towards the Black Sea steppe rather than into Transylvania and the Carpathians, as previously. The Tervingian king Athanaric lost a confrontation in the field, as frontier peoples usually did when a Roman army forced them into a set-piece battle, but Valens did not press his advantage, perhaps because of the lateness of the season. It did not matter. He had the victory he wanted and, after retiring back to the imperial frontiers, he sent Victor and Arinthaeus to negotiate with Athanaric.

Valens entered his third consulship at Marcianopolis on 1 January 370, and in late January or February he met the Tervingian king on a boat in the middle of the Danube. It was a symbolic gesture on both sides, Valens acknowledging Athanaric's autonomy, the latter able to present his submission as a treaty between equals. This left the king free to reassert his authority over his more bellicose followers by persecuting Gothic Christians, whom he had come to think of as a Roman fifth column. But the peace also threw the Gothic population a lifeline, for the three years of war had badly affected trade and access to Roman imports, and this, Ammianus tells us, more even than the military defeat, was what convinced Athanaric to make peace. Valens' three years of fighting on the Danube frontier had achieved a return to the status quo of the Constantinian period, and might have led to lasting stability in the region. That it failed to do so was, as we shall see, the result of several historical accidents.

From the Danube, Valens returned to Constantinople in time for Easter 370. There Themistius, the faithful mouthpiece of official sentiment, talked up the humanitarianism that had led Valens to resolve the war so peacefully. Why destroy your enemy when you could turn him to peace and make him love and honour you, and when his men would later provide soldiers for your armies? The oration in which those sentiments are expressed is one of Themistius' real bravura performances, but what he failed to say was that another war was now brewing, this time against a far more dangerous enemy: the Persia of the ageing Shapur II.

Shapur's peace treaty with Jovian had left him little to fear from the Romans on his western frontier: the trans-Euphratean cities that had long been the bulwark of the Roman East were in his hands. But Armenia remained, as it had been for centuries, a bone of contention. King Arsaces

IV had long been a loyal ally of Rome, a staunch supporter of Constantius II, and a willing abettor of Julian's invasion – it was he who had helped Procopius organise the feint that drew Shapur northwards as Julian fell upon Ctesiphon. Jovian's peace treaty did not explicitly mention Armenia, but the Romans had in fact neglected the kingdom's affairs since 364, as Valens dealt first with Procopius and then with the Goths.

Shapur, now in his seventies but still vigorous, took the opportunity to avenge himself on Arsaces. The Armenian king was invited to negotiations with Persian envoys, but then was seized, imprisoned and blinded before being immured at the Sasanian fortress of Agabana and tortured to death. Shapur now planned to rule Armenia as a Persian province, rather than as a client kingdom. Armenian nobles who had earlier seceded from Arsaces would be installed as governors, while Persia's buffer zone of client kingdoms would be pushed northwards to Iberia (modern Azerbaijan), where Shapur deposed the Roman ally Sauromaces and installed his own client Aspacures, Sauromaces' cousin.

All this took place while Valens was still fighting the Goths, but once that war was over, he felt he had to do something about Persian actions in Armenia. The emperor began his journey to Antioch in April 370, and arrived there by the end of the month. In the meantime, he had welcomed to his court Pap, son of the murdered Arsaces, and promised him aid. With Roman backing, Pap returned to Armenia, where he was well received by a section of the nobility. Shapur himself then led an army into Armenia and forced Pap to retreat. He spent months hiding in the mountains of Lazica, but when Shapur retired for the winter, Pap re-entered his capital, executed Shapur's governors and sent their severed heads back to the Persian king. It was a provocation that could only mean war, but not one that Pap could fight on his own. He needed Roman support, and Valens was willing to oblige. He put Flavius Arinthaeus in command of a large field army, sending him to protect Armenia and to reinstall Sauromaces on the Iberian throne. The latter agreed to divide the kingdom with his cousin Aspacures, each taking the part nearer to their imperial patron. Shapur, however, regarded the deal Arinthaeus had brokered as an unacceptable encroachment on Persian rights. He severed diplomatic ties with Valens and prepared to launch a full-scale war against the empire. It would detain Valens for most of the next decade, and Antioch would become his primary residence.

Before that, though, he needed to settle the ecclesiastical politics of Constantinople, where Eudoxius, Constantius' long-serving homoian bishop, had died. Valens had to make sure that this offered no opportunity for a Nicene resurgence, and he spent the winter of 370–71 on the Bosporus. Then, from the late summer of 371 until his final Gothic campaign in 378, Valens was engaged continuously on his eastern front. The Persians threatened war annually, though no full-scale invasion ever came. It is likely that old Shapur was having too difficult a time controlling the rivalry among his aspiring heirs, while also containing Hunnic state-building in Bactria, Transoxiana (the lands between the present day Amu Darya and Syr Darya rivers in central Asia) and the old Kushanshahr (much of modern Afghanistan and north-western Pakistan), to prosecute a Roman war as he would have liked. A small Persian assault was deflected by the *magistri* Traianus and Vadomarius, the latter an Alamannic king who had been an ally of Constantius and an enemy of Julian, and who was now a senior officer in the eastern army. This skirmishing ended with yet another truce, but the ongoing threat was such that Valens could not leave Antioch: if he did, Shapur might decide to invade. After his decidedly mixed performance against Procopius and in three successive Gothic wars, Valens could not afford another less than decisive military outcome. He was effectively stranded in a large and fractious Greek city, with the complexity of which he was ill equipped to cope.

Antioch had and would challenge more imaginative emperors than Valens. It was the only city in the empire that served as the seat of so many different administrators, each with his own powerful set of interests, and all constrained by the frequent presence of the emperor within its walls: the praetorian prefect of the East; the *comes Orientis*, which was the unusual name given to the *vicarius* of the diocese of Oriens, who administered fifteen provincial governments from Cilicia in the north to Arabia; and the *consularis Syriae*, which is to say the provincial governor. The city was likewise the diocesan headquarters for the staff of the two main financial bureaus, the *res privata* and the *sacrae largitiones*. Finally, there was the military. The *dux Syriae*, the standing military commander for the region, was based at Antioch, though his troops were dispersed at *castella* (small forts) throughout the province. But either a *magister militum* or a *magister equitum* was also usually resident in the city, managing the eastern *comitatenses*. Each of these officials had a substantial staff, but their overlapping jurisdictions were hard for contemporaries to disentangle, providing almost limitless scope for the playing-off of one section of the government against another.

Antioch also had a particularly large and vigorous *boule*, whose traditional authority and economic hegemony was being threatened by the new class of imperial officials, a rivalry evoked in the bitterly resentful letters of Libanius. There were also the inevitable religious divisions. A homoian line of succession in the church of Antioch, represented by a bishop named Euzoeus, had been powerful since the reign of Constantius, if not before. But it was not the sole rival of the Nicene succession, which was itself in schism: supporters of Meletius, who was willing to accommodate some of the views of the homoian clergy, were opposed by Paulinus, a radical Nicene supported by many bishops in the Latin West and also, predictably, by Athanasius of Alexandria. While Valens was in Antioch, he repeatedly sent Meletius into exile, from which he kept creeping back, though the emperor tolerated Paulinus as too weak to bother with.

Valens was easily spooked at the best of times, and these overlapping religious and political intrigues kept him suspended in a watchful anxiety that would end with a bloodbath. Yet even those, like Ammianus Marcellinus, who thought Valens a dreadfully bad emperor, conceded that some of his paranoia was justified. Ancient people could all agree that magic and divination were dangerous outside official contexts, although drawing the line between the licit and the illicit was much harder. Illicit magic could unlock occult knowledge about the future of the state, and that was necessarily dangerous in the hands of private individuals. For this reason, illicit magic had long been punishable as *maiestas* – treason or *lèse majesté*. Constantius, a more statesmanlike figure than Valens, had pursued rumours of magic and illegal divination mercilessly, and black magic had been suspected at the very start of Valentinian and Valens' reigns, when they fell ill simultaneously.

At Antioch, it was fear of divinatory conspiracy that set Valens and the citizenry against one another. In the winter of 371, word reached his ears of secret divinatory games being played among the Antiochene nobility and members of his own court. The discovery of minor peculation by junior fiscal officers unravelled a chain of revelations that implicated former governors and *vicarii*, members of the *protectores domestici* and other well-placed courtiers, confirming Valens' worst fears. A magic tripod, modelled on the famous oracular stool of Delphi, had been used to reveal the name of the man who would succeed Valens on the throne. The game had spelled out the Greek letters for THEOD, at which point all those present concluded that a senior *notarius* named Theodorus, a well-liked palatine official of Gallic birth, was meant. This revelation, reported to us in the history of Ammianus, has the look of an *ex post facto* rationalisation, insofar as the four Greek letters are in fact those of Valens' actual successor, Theodosius.

What is clearly true is that the divinatory game set off a massive purge of the palatine hierarchy, in which many probably loyal supporters of the emperor were killed in a single sweeping condemnation. It provided an excuse for further bloodletting as well, and for the settling of old scores – thus the philosopher Maximus, Julian's old confidant and friend, was accused of having heard the oracle about Theodorus, admitted to having heard it but also dismissing it as obviously false. He was none the less executed in his home city of Ephesus. Ammianus names dozens more specific examples and it is clear that he was himself present in Antioch at the time and that he knew personally many of those executed. He does not deny that Valens faced genuine conspiracies, but condemns him vehemently for being unable to tell the true from the false, and for the slaughter of the innocent that resulted. It is no wonder that most Antiochenes, pagan and Christian alike, welcomed Valens' eventual death on the battlefield as a proof of divine vengeance.

Valens was not the only paranoiac in his family, however. Valentinian was equally prone to fits of rage and deliberately terrorising his own officials. He pursued accusations of magic with just as much rigour as Valens, but he did a much better job of insulating himself from direct blame. Indeed, like Constantius II before him, he had a talent for appointing men to do his dirty work while preserving deniability for himself, sometimes punishing officials for doing precisely what he had asked of them. When we last saw him in 368, Valentinian had just won a victory over the Alamanni at Solicinium. This sort of everyday success was the foundation of imperial propaganda, and it is hard to gauge the actual scale of the victory or what such campaigns accomplished in the grander scheme of things. What seems clear is that the administrative framework of northern Gaul had been permanently damaged in the 350s by the usurpation of Magnentius and its aftermath. It would appear that the defensive infrastructure had never been fully restored. As both archaeological and literary sources confirm, Valentinian spent a great deal of time repairing old fortifications and building new ones along the northern frontiers. But his campaigns into the agricultural lands beyond the *limes* were mainly raids against civilian populations, designed to sow terror and manufacture ostentatious victories that would convince his subjects of the emperor's care. With less fighting and fewer grandiose claims, he rebuilt the Saxon Shore fortifications in Britain and on the Channel and North Sea coasts of the continent. It was also in this period that Valentinian brought civilian and military hierarchies of the empire into more parallel career paths, creating parity of rank at equivalent stages of seniority in each.

In 369, while the *comes* Theodosius continued his campaigns in Britain and the *magister peditum* Severus suppressed Saxon pirates in Armorica, Valentinian launched another punitive campaign, this time against the Alamanni, one of whose chieftains had attacked Moguntiacum (modern Mainz) and seized a considerable number of captives there. Leading the campaign personally, the emperor crossed the river at Altaripa and pushed deep into the lands beyond, reaching the Neckar river and provoking the admiration of Roman senatorial grandees like Quintus Aurelius Symmachus, then prefect of the city of Rome, and one of the great epistolographers in an age full of letter writers. The army returned to imperial territory via the Breisgau, and Valentinian, as was now his habit, wintered at Treveri. There, the young augustus Gratian continued his education in letters with the Gallic aristocrat Ausonius and in military matters with his father's general staff. The account of Ammianus smooths the contours of Valentinian's reign into a series of barely differentiated frontier battles: in 370, Theodosius was promoted to the rank of *magister equitum* and campaigned beyond the upper Danube opposite Raetia (in present-day Switzerland), while the emperor raided across the Rhine. The campaigns of 371 appear to have been similarly unremarkable.

Events in Rome, however, were less satisfactory. It was in 368–9 that the *praefectus annonae* Maximinus, a Pannonian close to Valentinian's private circle, waged what can only be understood as a deliberate persecution of the nobility of the city of Rome. He was the son of a minor official, born at Sopianae in the Pannonian province of Valeria, supposedly a descendant of the Carpi settled there by Diocletian – though that may simply be a convenient aspersion cast on a low-born man by the snobbish Ammianus. Maximinus studied law, his father's rank giving him an entrée to the profession, and worked the networks of patronage efficiently enough to win a series of (admittedly not very prestigious) provincial governorships, in Corsica, Sardinia and Tuscia. It was from that office that he was recruited to the role of *praefectus annonae*, in charge of the grain supply to the city of Rome, which depended heavily upon the annual arrival of the grain fleet from Africa. In that office, which was not responsible for the administration of justice in any regular manner, he was well placed to observe – and if necessary attack – the Roman elite.

Although our sources make it seem as if the initiative was that of Maximinus personally, inviting us to root it in his personal class resentment, the campaign was actually systemic: it was an attempt by the military high command and the provincial aristocrats who staffed Valentinian's palatine bureaus and regional administration to weaken the hold of the senators of Rome and Italy on the most prestigious offices. Only a much wider base of tacit support, disguised by the surviving sources, can account for the career of Maximinus: despite being hated by seemingly every side, he was promoted repeatedly, first to the extraordinary and irregular position of *vicarius* of Rome (the city was normally governed by the urban prefect, over whom there was no external jurisdiction), then to the prefecture of the Gauls in 371. An older school of scholarship liked to see Maximinus – and by extension Valentinian – as a sort vengeance taken by a proletarian soldiery on its social betters, but to do so is to fall into a trap laid by Ammianus, writing with Antiochene disdain.

The inquisition visited on the Roman Senate by Maximinus was in fact the metastasis of the regional factionalism that had grown up under Constantius along with the regional prefectures and high commands. There was now, however, one vital difference: for all that Constantius was easily misled by malicious whispers, his own capacity for ruthless intrigue and his prestige as Constantine's son gave him a control over his administration that Valentinian could not match, despite his personal valour and his reputation for feral brutality. The persecution at Rome was not the work of a malignant official exceeding his orders, but a collective endeavour by the Gallic and Balkan high commands – Pannonians and Spaniards, Gauls and Africans – all of whom understood that the Italian super-nobility was indispensable to the prestige of empire, but all of whom were equally happy to see its wings clipped whenever possible. Where convenient, scions of the ancient nobility were useful; the Balkan general staff was hand in glove with the Italian Petronius Probus, who sprang from the clan of the Anicii, the oldest among the great Christian senatorial families (Probus was paternal grandfather of two fifth-century emperors, and he spent the decade between 367 and 376 in sequential tenure of one or another praetorian prefecture).

But Probus, whom we shall meet again, was unusually agile and ambitious for a man of his class. Most of the great senatorial families of Rome and Italy followed a model of service that had been inculcated in them since the third-century reign of Gallienus, when a concerted effort had been made to keep the control of military and administrative office out of the hands of senators. The Roman clans that were considered old in the fourth century almost all had their roots in the Severan empire. Any claims of still older, early imperial pedigree were almost completely manufactured. These Romans of Rome were nevertheless very different from the wider, provincialised senatorial aristocracy that had come into being during the very long reign of Constantine. For the most part, their governing careers were highly traditional, not to say symbolic, and interspersed with many years of retirement from government into the *otium* – stately leisure – of the well-born: first a minor magistracy at Rome, as *corrector* of aqueducts, say, then a good Italian governorship, and from there one of the customarily senatorial provinces of Asia or Achaea, or with luck the proconsulate of Africa and then, at the apex of their *cursus*, the urban prefecture of Rome. Men of their background had neither the need nor the desire for the hard graft it took to prosper in the service bureaucracy of the Constantinian empire, but their decorative value was real, and neither the provincial aristocracies nor the bureaucratic parvenus of Valentinian's court and general staff could ignore them or deny them access to power. For all these reasons, Maximinus was lavishly rewarded for menacing the complacent Roman senators, by joint agreement of the regional factions on whom Valentinian's regime depended. Their dominance, and the balance between their Gallic and Balkan poles, would be revealed in the aftermath of Valentinian's death, which claimed some very distinguished victims, among them the *magister equitum* Theodosius, father of the future emperor.

This elder Theodosius, having conducted several successful British campaigns, was sent to Africa to deal with a complicated situation the intricacies of which are very hard for modern scholars to disentangle. This is in part because we have only one continuous narrative, in the history of Ammianus Marcellinus, and he recounts African events in these years as a separate, monographic storyline, only obscurely connected to his chronology of events elsewhere in the empire. The social complexity of the African provinces simply adds to our difficulties, because they were very different from one another. Africa Proconsularis, centred on the magnificent city of Carthage, was one of Rome's oldest overseas conquests, but much of the African diocese had been subject to client kings or left to its native chieftains well into the first century AD. Roman military colonies dating back to the Republic had grown into flourishing cities, but around them was a patchwork of imperial estates, native villages and indigenous municipalities that only gained access to Roman citizenship after AD 212, when the emperor Caracalla extended the franchise to every free inhabitant of the empire. As important to the exceptionalism of the African diocese was how much of its land and its agricultural wealth – a majority in some provinces – was owned either by one of the rich senatorial families of the city of Rome or by the *res privata* of the emperor. But nowhere else in the empire were the great landowners so physically removed from their largest estates.

The varying jurisdictions and social hierarchies – civic, imperial and private – were complicated still further by an earlier and wider Christianisation than we see in much of the Latin West. This had led to the proliferation of numerous tiny bishoprics in very minor places, barely hamlets by most standards. That most of these episcopal sees had both Caecilianist (that is, anti-Donatist, named for an original opponent of Donatus early in the fourth century) and Donatist hierarchies, each with genuine support among the populace, added another layer of potential conflicts. Finally, although densely urban and very populous, large parts of urban Africa backed on to impenetrable mountain or semi-desert steppeland. The inhabitants of these regions were not fully integrated into settled imperial society, but they were often clients of local big men who did play a role in the Roman order. The access that some African aristocrats had to reserves of manpower and loyalty that were not tied to imperial structures meant that the regional factionalism so characteristic of fourth-century politics had a uniquely centrifugal potential in the diocese.

This was the landscape into which the *magister* Theodosius was sent to suppress what became a revolt against imperial authority, though it had not begun as one. In fact, it had started out as a fairly typical example of petty intrigue between minor provincial officials and the palatine bureaucracy. Tripolitania – now western Libya – was the land from which the Severan dynasty had emerged two centuries earlier, and which marked the easternmost outpost of Latin Africa before one came to the Greek cities of Cyrene. Tripolitania was also the province in which the steppe and desert came closest to the settled zones of the coast. For that reason, its Romanised cities and agricultural zones were in closer continual contact with the pastoralist tribesmen of the Libyan desert, both as trading partners and as victims of their raids and harassment. Even Leptis Magna, the provincial capital with its resident bureaucracy, was in easy reach of tribal raiders. It was the central government's inadequate response to one such raid that sparked the problems.

The commander of the African diocese's small standing army, the *comes Africae* Romanus, was said to have refused to bring military aid to the inhabitants of Leptis unless he was bribed to do so. This may well have been true, peculation being an endemic characteristic of late antique governance. That said, the *comes* had an establishment of, at best, 20,000 men stretched across a frontier zone that ran for nearly 2,000 kilometres, from Mauretania Sitifensis to Tripolitania. It is likely, too, that Romanus had other demands on his resources, no matter how desperate the situation of the Leptines. One way or another, he also had strong connections at court. When the provincial council of Tripolitania sent an embassy to Valentinian at Trier to complain about Romanus, it was rebuffed by the *magister officiorum* Remigius, who was related to the *comes Africae* by marriage. Back at Leptis, there was another raid, and then another complaint, but Romanus bribed the *notarius* sent to investigate and even succeeded in having his accusers prosecuted. A couple of years after this, however, Romanus fell into a dispute with a powerful local noble in Mauretania named Firmus, and that led to war.

Firmus came from the sort of family common on the Roman frontiers, in Europe and the East as well as in Africa. His father, Nubel, was both a grandee in Roman provincial society and a 'king' who derived his authority from hereditary succession over certain groups of Mauri. A good parallel is Vadomarius, king of the Alamanni, who, after a long career as both ally and enemy of Constantius and Julian, became a distinguished Roman general, serving on the eastern frontier. When Nubel died, he left many sons, some by his wife, others by concubines, all of them well connected. Firmus, for instance, was a strong supporter of Donatist clergy, while his half-brother Zammac was a close friend of the *comes* Romanus. Firmus and Zammac quarrelled over their father's property, and the latter was killed, whereupon Romanus denounced Firmus to the imperial court. The latter relied upon his connections to protest his innocence, but Romanus' kinsman Remigius suppressed any discussion of the case and Firmus felt more and more menaced. Finally, probably in 371, he revolted with the support of two of Romanus' own units, the *pedites Constantiani* and the fourth cohort of the *equites sagittarii*. He also called up soldiers from the frontier Mauri, and his rule was widely recognised in the two Mauretanian provinces and even in Africa Proconsularis. He minted no coins, however, which means he was making no claim on the imperial purple, despite his sometimes having been portrayed as a usurper by modern scholars. Fighting was widespread, and Caesarea, the capital of Mauretania Caesariensis, was badly damaged by fire. Valentinian's court sent the *magister equitum* Theodosius to Africa to suppress the rebellion and Ammianus gives us an intricate account of the raids and counterraids that followed.

One of Theodosius' first acts was to supersede Romanus, whom he blamed for fomenting the disturbance. Thanks to the intervention of Valentinian's senior *magister militum*, Flavius Merobaudes, Romanus escaped further censure or punishment, but his relative, the *magister officiorum* Remigius, was dismissed from office in disgrace and hanged himself at his home in Moguntiacum shortly thereafter. The war with Firmus that Romanus had provoked lasted for years, and took in not just the urban centres of Caesariensis and Sitifensis but the tribal zones of the Aurès and Rif mountains, right into southern Tingitania, the Roman province in modern Morocco so poorly connected to the rest of Roman Africa that it was assigned to the diocese of Hispania and subject to the *vicarius* at Emerita Augusta (modern-day Mérida). Theodosius suppressed the rebellious army units fairly early, and Firmus' brother Gildo took the side of Theodosius and the emperor, seeking his own advantage and probably serving under one of Theodosius' subordinates, the future usurper Magnus Maximus. Ammianus' long account of the war's minor engagements pays literary homage to the Republican historian Sallust, whose history of the war against Jugurtha in the second century BC has a similar African setting. But there is no need to rehearse the details of ambush, betrayals, murder and rapine here. In 375, faced with defeat on all sides, Firmus committed suicide. His brother Gildo would go on to wield a similar amount of power more successfully and for longer. With Firmus dead, Theodosius set about restoring the finances of the ravaged Mauretanian provinces.

He was still there when Valentinian died suddenly in 375. By that point, the emperor had moved his base of operations from Gaul to the Balkans, leaving his son Gratian, now in his early teens, at Treveri, his court stocked with able men of proven loyalty. Valentinian's final Gallic campaigns, between 372 and 374, were all against Macrianus, an Alamannic king who had first emerged as a powerful frontier figure during Julian's reign. Ultimately, Valentinian gave Macrianus favourable peace terms so he could instead deal with a new crisis in the Balkans: the Quadic followers of a certain king Gabinius had risen up and invaded Pannonia Prima and Valeria, the two provinces at the top of the Danube bend. During Valentinian's long residency in Trier, the Balkan high command had largely been left to its own devices, safe in the hands of Equitius, the *magister militum per Illyricum* and one of Valentinian's oldest allies, and of Petronius Probus, the Roman senator of the Anicii and a long-serving praetorian prefect. They kept the peace quite effectively and we have no record of trouble in the regions policed from the diocesan capital of Sirmium during the whole of the late 360s and early 370s.

It was a change in the balance of power between the regional prefectures that started the problems on the Danube frontier. We have already seen that Maximinus was rewarded for his service at Rome with promotion from prefect of the *annona* in Italy to the praetorian prefecture of the Gauls. From that power base, he immediately began to intrigue against his counterparts in the Balkans, accusing Equitius of laxness in dealing with the barbarians and managing to have his own son Marcellianus appointed *dux Valeriae*, commander of the frontier troops in north-eastern Pannonia. Maximinus claimed that this appointment would allow the emperor to carry his programme of frontier fortification from Gaul to Illyricum, since Equitius was not being efficient enough in doing so. The Quadi had been at peace with the empire under the client king Gabinius since the time of Constantius II, so when Marcellianus ordered imperial troops to build a large fortress on the left bank of the Danube, Gabinius believed him to be breaking a treaty of long standing. When the king protested in autumn 374, Marcellianus invited him to a banquet to discuss the issue, and then had him murdered.

The outraged Quadi invaded Valeria just as the peasants were taking in the harvest, devastating the year's crops and sweeping south. At a *mansio* named Pristensis, they very nearly captured Constantia, the posthumous daughter of the emperor Constantius: she had been dining there en route to the West, where she was to marry the young Gratian. The provincial governor, who was accompanying the imperial princess on her journey through his territory, barely got her back to Sirmium, more than thirty kilometres way, rushing ahead of the Quadic raiders. These latter, having now been joined by their Sarmatian neighbours, found Sirmium itself too well fortified to besiege, and contented themselves with laying the countryside to waste. Two legions of the field army – the Pannoniaca and the Moesiaca – sent by Equitius against the invaders suffered severe losses, and the invasion was the worst the region had experienced in several generations. Constantia did indeed make it to Gaul, and her marriage to Gratian was concluded late in 374 or early in 375, but Valentinian headed to the Balkans as soon as spring broke.

The new year had opened with Gratian consul for the third time and Equitius as his colleague – a necessary sign of imperial confidence in a Balkan high command whose prestige had been bruised by the invasion. Valentinian arrived at Carnuntum, in Pannonia Prima, in May 375 and made ready for a major campaign. Merobaudes and the *comes rei militaris* Sebastianus were sent to attack one part of the Quadi's territory, and in August the emperor marched downriver to Aquincum, within the city limits of modern Budapest, where he left his palatine establishment and crossed the river into Quadic lands. The two imperial armies devastated swathes of territory beyond the river for nearly two months before returning to Aquincum to disperse to winter quarters.

Valentinian took some of his forces with him to Brigetio (now Szőny on Hungary's border with Slovakia), situating himself strategically between Carnuntum and Aquincum. At Brigetio, in November, he received an embassy from the Quadi, begging for peace and a treaty by which they would commit to providing soldiers for the imperial army. Because the campaign season was effectively over and the army had largely dispersed, Valentinian, Equitius and the general staff had already decided to grant the Quadi terms. Equitius decided that, as a token of imperial forgiveness, the envoys should be honoured by an audience with the emperor himself. Having been admitted to the imperial presence, the suppliant ambassadors admitted their own fault but also protested that the injustice of Marcellianus and other Roman officials had provoked them into revolt. Prone as ever to strategic bursts of anger, useful in cowing friends and enemies alike, Valentinian, according to Ammianus, 'became more and more enraged as he replied, railing against the whole Quadic people in loud and abusive language'; and then, as he worked to calm himself, he became 'speechless and suffocating, as if struck by a bolt of lightning from the sky, his face burning fiery and red'. The servants of the imperial bedchamber rushed to pull him to a more private place, but a few hours later he died – seemingly from a stroke brought on by fury. It was the end for the 55-year-old ruler whose personal courage and military competence had been plain to all.

It was also fitting that so choleric a temper should have been burned up by its own heat.

Although it surprised everyone, Valentinian's sudden death did not cause widespread chaos: western government had become so corporate, so completely in the hands of the palatine and prefectural bureaus and the general staff, that mere imperial thrombosis could not undermine the basic stability of the system. But imperial transitions did not pass without casualties and this time was no exception. At Brigetio, the high command moved quickly, without reference to either Valens or Gratian. Valentinian's brother-in-law Cerealis was sent to fetch his sister, the empress Justina, and her very young son Valentinian, from the imperial residence of Murocincta, the precise location of which is unknown. At Aquincum, the Balkan army's main winter quarters, the 4-year-old child was acclaimed emperor by the assembled troops. The Balkan general staff under Equitius, and the regional bureaucracy under Petronius Probus, had managed the Illyrian prefecture effectively without imperial supervision for a decade, so it is little wonder they were willing to act so decisively now. Working with the senior *magister militum* Merobaudes, they had to make sure Valentinian II was safely established as a recognised emperor before the Gallic bureaucracy under Maximinus and Gratian's palatine guardians could take action.

Mistrust ran deep between Treveri and Sirmium: as *praefectus annonae* Maximinus had clashed with Probus, while the whole Balkan command had resented the imposition of Maximinus' son Marcellianus on them in the previous year. But when news of the elder Valentinian's death and the younger's acclamation reached Gaul, the western establishment was furious at having been taken so completely off guard. They delayed recognising the new augustus, working out how to assert Gratian's authority, while both sides sought the support of their uncle Valens in Antioch. The eastern emperor, whose seniority had been most clearly ignored, began the new year as sole consul, thereby refusing to take sides between the courts of his nephews, but he did send an embassy to Gaul early in the new year. This was led by the philosopher Themistius and joined by senators from Rome as well, who helped broker a deal between the Gallic and Balkan high commands. Several prominent careers were ended, either by retirement, trial or execution. Maximinus was deposed as praetorian prefect and would be tried and executed later in the year, along with Simplicius and Doryphorianus, his equally hated successors as *vicarii* of

Rome. Maximinus' colleague at Treveri, the *magister officiorum* Leo, also resigned. In Illyricum, Petronius Probus retired from his long tenure as praetorian prefect, while the *magistri* Equitius and Sebastianus disappear altogether from the historical record. At Carthage, the *magister equitum* Theodosius was executed early in 376, while his son Theodosius resigned as *dux Moesiae*, prudently taking refuge on the family's estates in Spain. The regional commands had each forced the other's worst enemies out of public life, and had the elder Theodosius, the only real wild card, put to death. It was a solution that suited everyone who survived it.

Themistius, serving now as the joint representative of Gratian and Valens, brought news of Valentinian II's recognition to Rome in April 376, delivering an oration in praise of the settlement. By then, Gratian's regime had begun to patch up its relations with the Roman Senate and to dissociate itself from the fall of Theodosius. Though Maximinus had already fallen from power when Theodosius was killed, that death was now blamed on the former prefect's tyrannical malignancy, and Maximinus' trial and execution in summer 376 was a major concession to senatorial sentiment. The young Valentinian was in effect powerless, sent to Treveri to be raised at the court of his elder half-brother. Gratian's appointees governed all the western prefectures, despite Valentinian having notional responsibility for Italy, Africa and Illyricum. Valens, having helped broker the deal that stabilised the western provinces, now acquiesced in his nephew's aggrandisement. In that, he had little choice, given the challenges he faced both in the East and, quite suddenly, along the lower Danube. Those challenges take us away from the minutiae of court politics and back to the larger Eurasian currents that were working their effects on the fourth-century empire.

4

ADRIANOPLE AND
THE COUP OF
THEODOSIUS

⬥⬥⬥⬥⬥⬥⬥

Among numerous misfortunes confronting the eastern emperor, the
360s witnessed serious social disruption in both the Eurasian steppe
and the Arabian desert, and these converged on Valens in the last two
years of his reign. One of the problems faced jointly by the emperors and
the Persian shahanshahs was controlling the predations of nomads into
the settled empires that lay to the south of the steppe world. Rome had
not always been so exposed to that threat, which is very much a phenomenon of late antiquity. For the entire period in which the Romans were
conquering first a Mediterranean and then a European and near Eastern
empire, from roughly 250 BC to AD 100 or so, the problems they faced
were primarily the product of local circumstances – local histories and
geographies, and the impact of the Romans themselves. In the third century AD, however, the vast Roman empire was exposed to the currents of
a much wider Eurasian world, both directly and indirectly.

When the Parthian empire was taken over by the far more bellicose
Persian dynasty of the Sasanians, events in central Asia, the Hindu Kush
and south Asia affected Rome through its relations with Persia. But events
in the steppe world also affected Rome directly, at the terminus of the
Eurasian steppe corridor just north of the Danube. To understand the

buffeting both the Roman and the Persian empires experienced in the later fourth and fifth centuries, it is necessary to understand Eurasian geography and geopolitics at the time, which allowed political and social change as far away as north-western China to have consequences on Rome's and Persia's frontiers.

Northern Eurasia is made up of four broad climatic zones, which become more and more noticeable as one moves from west to east, but especially east of the Urals which arrest the prevailing western winds and the precipitation they bring in from the Atlantic. North of the Arctic Circle, there is tundra, then, further south, there is the taiga (northern forest). The taiga shades into wooded steppelands, which themselves shade into grasslands that are too arid to sustain sedentary agriculture. South of the grassland steppe runs a series of deserts, with their occasional oases fed by rivers that spring up in the mountain ranges along the deserts' southern edges. From the jagged mountain uplands of Anatolia, Armenia and the Caucasus, mountains line the Caspian coast of northern Iran before reaching the Kopet Dag that separates Iran and Turkmenistan. From there, the Hindu Kush and Pamirs give way to the Tian Shan and Kun Lun, north and south of the Taklamakan desert, and to the Himalayas along the southern edge of the Tibetan plateau.

As the zones of mountain and desert broaden in the east, so the band of grassland steppe narrows, but from the Carpathians to Mongolia, the Eurasian steppes bind the continent together. Except at the Altai and Sayan mountains in southern Siberia, the steppe runs without interruption for almost 8,000 kilometres, from the Pacific to the Danube basin. Beginning at the Yumen pass (what the ancient Chinese called the Jade Gate) west of Dunhuang, the steppe runs along the so-called Hexi corridor on the Chinese frontier, around what is now the autonomous region of Xinjiang and its enormous Taklamakan desert, then around the Tian Shan, Pamirs and Hindu Kush. There in inner Asia, the deserts of modern Kazakhstan separate the steppe from pockets of arable land fed by the Murghab, Syr Darya and Amu Darya rivers in modern Turkmenistan, Uzbekistan and Afghanistan.

These regions – ancient Margiana, Sogdiana and Bactria – had once marked the outer limits of Hellenistic civilisation, but in the third century they fell under Persian hegemony and sometimes political control. So, too, did the Hindu Kush and the large part of modern Pakistan (Gandhara, Swat, parts of Sind) that had previously been subject to the Kushan emperors, originally a steppe nomadic dynasty from the north, but who for centuries ruled over a diverse kingdom that mingled Greek, south Asian and central Asian religions and cultures in a rich syncretism – it was in the Kushan empire that Buddhism evolved in opposition to the Zoroastrianism of Persia, and from which Buddhist monks and their texts spread to China. The Sasanians took over much of the Kushan empire in the third century, considering it part of Persia and its nobility Persians, and calling it Kushan-shahr in the same way they called Persia Eranshahr. In the fourth century, this Kushanshahr was an intermittently rebellious shadow of its former self, ruled by a cadet dynasty of the Sasanian kings. In that same period, Sogdiana, Bactria and Margiana were subject to new steppe nomadic pressures, as we saw in our discussion of Shapur II's foreign adventures.

Other nomads made their impact felt further west. South of the Ural mountains and north of the Caspian Sea, the grass and forested steppe zone narrows into a thinner strip of grassland north of the Caucasus and the Black Sea into present-day Ukraine and Moldova. The steppe then tapers into a small gap between the eastern edge of the Carpathians and the Black Sea coast that funnels travel south towards the Danube basin and the Rumanian region of Dobrogea. A similar strip of steppeland continues south along the Caspian into the steppes of modern Azerbaijan and Iran. The Hungarian plains (the Puszta or Alföld) between the Danube bend and the southern Carpathians are the furthermost limit of the Eurasian steppe, which is why the losers in steppe warfare have so often ended up there over the millennia, but it is too small to support the number of animals needed to support the kind of nomadism that flourished on the steppe. What is important is the way that politics and warfare on the steppe played out across thousands of kilometres in a way that they did not in less open landscapes.

That said, it can be very difficult – indeed, frequently impossible – to follow the history of the steppe world. Only when Eurasia's literate cultures were affected by steppe polities do we get a sense of the busy, febrile life of the continental interior. Chinese, Indian, Persian and Mediterranean texts, coins and inscriptions all shed periodic light, but these settled and literate polities were often not entirely sure who they were dealing with, and for good reason. For millennia, the cultural exchanges on the steppe meant that very different peoples could share the same technologies, arts, political structures and symbols of rulership, and these things had a way of transcending such niceties as linguistic differences.

For the outside observer, steppe nomads all seemed the same, and so it made a certain sense to keep using the same generic names for them over many centuries, even when any original ethnic connotations had become meaningless. It was the Greek historian Herodotus, writing in the fifth century BC, who first described the Scythians north of the Black Sea, but for more than a millennium thereafter 'Scythians' (*Skythai*) were what Greeks saw when they looked out at the Eurasian steppe. For them, it did not matter that these various generations of Scythians came from different places, spoke different languages and recognised no similarity to one another. The Chinese and the Persians had their own, analogous traditions of seeing something eternal about the threat and the promise from the steppe. The horse warriors, with their lances and compound bows, and their fearsome mobility, were always a potential danger, always ready to pounce when their imperial neighbours lost their vigilance, but they were also useful clients and allies, recruited to fight civil wars and battles between the empires, and a ready market for the industrial and craft products of the settled civilisations. Either way, the world of the steppe, from the third century AD onwards, impinged continuously upon the Roman, Persian and indeed Chinese empires.

In the fourth century AD, a very old ethnic name reappears on the Eurasian steppe, that of the Huns. Linguistically, our word Hun goes back to the name of the Xiongnu (sometimes written Hsiung-nu), an extremely powerful nomadic empire that was the paradigmatic example of a steppe empire for the Chinese sources, patterning their understanding of steppe nomadic culture for hundreds of years in the same way the Scythians of Herodotus did for the Greeks. China's Han dynasty had destroyed the Xiongnu empire in the first century BC, though a rump of the former ruling elites survived in the Altai region. In the fourth century, people styling themselves as Xiongnu began to make a reappearance. We find them described as Hunnoi (Latin and Greek, and their modern derivatives) or Chionitae (the Latin and Greek word for the central Asian subjects of the Persian empire), Huna (Sanskrit) and Xwn (Sogdian). These are almost certainly all different ways of writing the same indigenous word and that indigenous word is almost certainly what the people called themselves. But does that mean that all these people were 'really' Xiongnu in some authentic existential sense?

That gets us straight to one of the great debates of modern scholarship on this period, about ancient ethnic continuity, mass migration and how we can best detect either of those phenomena historically. Substantial migrations took place in antiquity just as they do now. The only species as mobile as humans are the rats and dogs that accompany us everywhere, and the parasites that live in and on us. The movement of whole populations is attested on occasion in ancient sources, and 'barbarian migration' is one of the oldest scholarly tropes, inextricably linked to ideas about the fall of Rome, and superimposed by European scholars on the world's other cultures during the early modern centuries in which Europe discovered and tried to conquer the rest of the world.

In the popular imagination, for sure, there is an abiding belief in the idea that barbarian invasions bring down empires. But much recent scholarship has sought to bring nuance to discussions of historical migration, whether from the darkest north or in wave after wave of steppe barbarians. It is not just that these traditional narratives understate the diversity of ancient steppe empires, but that they conflate the migration of peoples with the hostile invasion of settled empires, ignoring the fact that devastating invasions do not actually require the movement of very many individual people at any one time. What's more, they ignore how complex and variable identities can be – while people cannot simply shed their backgrounds and take up others at will, neither is any one aspect of identity, any single sense of belonging or difference, immutable.

People know this from their own lived experience, but even scholars find it hard to import that knowledge into their studies, to remember that a person's primary sense of identification can change in the course of a lifetime and that, even more, a group's identity does not stay the same over generations just because its name does. In other words, neither the name Hun nor cultural parallels in decorative arts or fighting styles can demonstrate that a single ethnic or political community – the Xiongnu, the Huns – travelled over four centuries and thousands of miles, with its identity – still less its genes – intact. Cultural behaviours, names with a prestigious history, attitudes towards rulership – all these are transferable and adoptable. Very few biological descendants of the Han's Xiongnu enemies need to have found themselves among the Chionitae of Persia or the Huns of Europe for the name to have stayed the same. That is to say, there is no way of establishing the 'truth' about the connection between Xiongnu and Huns because there was not one. But there was a half-real, half-imaginary sense of continuity and perhaps of kinship.

It is important to dwell on these things in order to counteract the more hysterical modern accounts of Rome's fourth-century history, whether in popular literature, scholarly narratives or the maps and graphics of television history shows. All of these portray a floodtide of Huns (a *Hunnensturm*, as the Germans call it) streaming from the frontiers of China to the edge of Europe in the course of a year or two, gathering up and destroying other nomads along the way until, arriving north of the Black Sea, they set all the settled barbarians of eastern and central Europe in motion rather like a breakshot in pool. One need not look very far to find outsized claims that make the Huns responsible for the fall of the Roman empire. An equally hyperbolic tendency applies to the size of the territory they are said to have controlled: some have imagined a coherent Hunnic empire eventually stretching from modern Bohemia all the way to the Altai mountains. The ancient sources provide precious little support for that view – indeed, none at all. Greek and Roman writers knew that by the 370s the Huns had conquered and defeated various Alanic and Sarmatian polities north of the Caucasus and the Black Sea, and that afterwards they badly disrupted the settled communities of Goths from the Dnieper river west. Beyond that, they had little certain knowledge, save that the Huns seemed very different from, and much more frightening than, the Alans, hitherto the archetypal steppe nomad horse warriors in the Roman imagination.

It is difficult for us to glean much more than that ourselves, because the 'Huns' of the Caspian and European steppe did not swiftly begin to strike their own coinage, whereas the Huna or Xwn of central Asia, the Kushanshahr, and eastern Iran did, and in great quantity. In fact, the fourth-century history of these eastern 'Huns' is marginally clearer than that of the western groups who shared their ethnic name. The Persian king Shapur II had grown old by the 370s, though without much slackening of his warlike vigour. His anger at Valens' interference in Armenia had him preparing to invade the eastern Roman provinces early in the decade, when Hunnic disturbances deflected those intentions. Although the nature of the threat goes unspecified in the written sources, the evidence of the coinage has grown much clearer recently – a consequence of the huge number of new coin types uncovered during the past two decades of warfare and looting in Afghanistan and its neighbours.

On the basis of where major quantities of coins were being minted in order to pay troops, it looks as if Shapur was attempting to reimpose direct rule on Bactria and perhaps also Kabulistan, the Hindu Kush and even Gandhara, though it is impossible to know whether this was part of an ambitious plan or merely a response to new threats. For at the same time we begin to find the first coins minted in Bactria and Gandhara in the name of a new 'Hunnic' ruler, Kidara. This Kidara gives his name to the Kidarites, a people from the central Asian steppe regions who were now attempting to impose their rule on the sedentary populations between Bactria and Gandhara. In doing so, they clearly adapted to local traditions, with coin legends in Middle Persian, Brahmi, and occasionally also in Bactrian scripts. They adopted Zoroastrian imagery from Sasanian coinage, and they called themselves kings of the Kushans, the rulers whom they had in fact displaced, although the Buddhist monasteries of Gandhara and Swat continued to flourish under their rule. We have coins minted in the names of various Kidarite rulers, some of whom sport old Sasanian names (Varahran, Peroz), others Indian (Buddhamitra), and that sheer variety suggests that – whatever language these 'Hunnic' conquerors spoke among themselves, and whatever names they used in that context – they were primarily interested in presenting a reassuringly familiar picture of stability to those they had conquered.

From the places at which these Kidarite rulers minted silver coins, it seems that the effective centre of their power was beyond the Hindu Kush, in Gandhara and Swat (the distribution of copper coinage, which imitates the silver and was probably struck semi-officially for small and local transactions, follows the same pattern). Then, when at the very end of the fourth century they conquered the region of Taxila to the east of the Indus river, they started issuing coins in gold, as the Kushans had done, and spelling names like Peroz in the Brahmi, rendering that Iranian name as Perosa.

At the same time, and just as clearly, Kidarite control of central Asia and the old Kushanshahr was far from complete. They were challenged there not just by Shapur, but by another group from the steppe: these Alkhan (or Alkhan Huns) are first met during the mid to late fourth century in control of Kabulistan, where they made use of the Sasanian mint at Kabul and minted coins describing their ruler as the king of Balkh in Bactria. By the fifth century, they were driving eastwards across the Khyber pass into the Kidarite territories in the old Gandharan heart of the Kushanshahr. We do not know whether Shapur actually suffered a defeat by either Kidarites or Alkhan, or whether he merely failed to stop them consolidating their power, but the sometime Sasanian provinces of central Asia and the Kushanshahr were never again properly under the control of a Persian king.

That is a minimalist reading of the new numismatic evidence. Reconstructing steppe history is a matter of guesswork much of the time and, with historical guesswork, it is always better to err on the side of minimalism. If that methodological maxim holds true for the history of the Kidarites and Alkhan, it does so still more for Hunnic history in the western part of the Eurasian steppe, where the sources are more shadowy, the guesswork still less informed by evidence. Assuming that western Hunnic groups, whose names and claims we cannot discern in the absence of coins, did in fact follow the sort of patterns we can detect on the eastern edges of Persia, it is possible that during the 350s and 360s rival clans of Hun warriors developed an overlapping hegemony on the western reaches of the Eurasian steppe. These brought previous steppe polities, most prominently those of the Alans, into a tributary relationship. Perhaps one clan, or one family, dominated all others, or tried to, as Kidara did in Gandhara and the Alkhan did at Balkh, though we have no evidence for any such dynastic claims among the western Huns until well into the fifth century. Probably, we should imagine western Hun clans developing the same sort of semi-predatory, semi-dependent relationships with the Roman and Persian empires as other nomadic groups had done in the past – relationships that changed and grew more ambitious only when they moved to conquer the sedentary barbarians of the Dnieper and Danube regions, which is to say the various kingdoms of the Goths.

The catastrophic defeat of one Gothic polity, and the ripples of disturbance this spread between the Dnieper and the Carpathians, would eventually end with a major Gothic rebellion breaking out inside the Roman empire and Valens' death on the battlefield. Yet, despite that fateful outcome, it remains important not to give in to the old apocalyptic narrative of the *Hunnensturm*, the sudden eruption of the steppe nomads driving all before them, barbarian tribes toppling on to one another like dominoes until the Roman frontier was breached. For one thing, the evidence from central Asia and easternmost Persia documents a much less dramatic pace of historical change, and for another, it is only hindsight that makes the events of the 370s in the European provinces of the Roman empire seem unusual, even unique.

The vast majority of Roman encounters with the people beyond its frontiers fell into very familiar patterns. We have seen this in north Africa already, where the revolt of Firmus wavered between a Roman civil war and a war between the imperial army and Moorish tribespeople. We see it, too, on another desert frontier, the fringes of Arabia that fell alternately under Roman and Sasanian influence. And we see it, finally, on the Rhine and upper Danube, where Gratian faced problems that had nothing to do with events on the Eurasian steppe. It is important to emphasise this point early and often, because the imperial failure to treat the advent of the Huns in Europe as the extraordinary event it became looks at best near-sighted, at worst negligent, until one realises that, at the time, the empire's Hunnic troubles of the 370s did not look so unusual at all. Indeed, the military career of the young emperor Gratian, such as it was, illustrates that point quite precisely, and needs to be considered before we return to the catastrophe that engulfed his unhappy uncle Valens.

Gratian's problems were the usual homegrown problems of policing the imperial frontier, inherited from his father Valentinian. As we have seen, Gratian's reign as western augustus had begun suddenly, with the news of his father's death and the palatine coup that elevated his half-brother Valentinian II to the rank of augustus. Fraught as they had been, negotiations eventually left Gratian unambiguously the senior emperor in the West, with his father now commemorated as *divus Valentinianus* in the traditional way. Gratian's childhood tutor Ausonius became his *quaestor*. Along with the senior *magister militum* Merobaudes, Ausonius was the main power behind the throne. Gratian and Valentinian II travelled little and showed themselves to their subjects only infrequently – their youth might encourage thoughts of usurpation if it were too widely displayed. For that reason, a promised visit to Rome by Gratian never took place, even though it would have helped repair relations between the Gallic court and the Roman aristocracy, which had been severely damaged by Valentinian I's indifference and the active hostility of Maximinus. Still, measures could be taken even at a distance: senators still awaiting trial for magic and treason were released, exiled senators recalled, confiscated property returned, and tax arrears cancelled.

Quintus Aurelius Symmachus, who had known Ausonius since the days of Valentinian I, now served as interlocutor between the Gallic court and the Senate in Rome. He was well rewarded for this, given the privilege of reading out to the Senate the imperial letter announcing the execution of the hated Maximinus, and having his aged father designated consul for the year 376: that was an increasingly rare honour for someone who was a *privatus*, not a member of the imperial family. The old man died before he could assume the honour, but the reconciliatory point had been well made. Others were in need of similar conciliation. Gratian's new Gallic praetorian prefect, Antonius, was a relative of the executed *magister equitum* Theodosius and, within the year, his brother Eucherius was made *comes sacrarum largitionum*. The rehabilitation of damaged reputations had begun and by late in 376 the regime had stabilised.

It has long been customary to view the events of Gratian's reign through the eyes of Decimus Magnus Ausonius, the rhetor from Burdigala (Bordeaux) whose preponderant role in western politics began with the death of his pupil's father. Already *quaestor*, he then became praetorian prefect in succession to Antonius. As was quite normal for a man in his position, Ausonius used the opportunity to aggrandise his family. His son Hesperius was made proconsul of Africa in 376, and his elderly father, Julius Ausonius, was made praetorian prefect of Illyricum in the following year, but probably died soon afterwards. Hesperius, meanwhile, was associated with his father in the praetorian prefecture of the Gauls, to which the two jointly added the combined prefecture of Italy, Africa and Illyricum in 378. Ausonius' son-in-law Thalassius was made first *vicarius* of Macedonia and then proconsul of Africa in succession to Hesperius. Finally, when Ausonius was designated for the consulship of 380, he gave up his prefectures, leaving Hesperius in charge of Italy and Illyricum and promoting another Bordelais relative, Siburius, to the prefecture of the Gauls. Flavius Merobaudes shared with Ausonius in this domination of the western government, his importance going back to Julian's days. Now he became the only person outside the imperial family to twice hold the consulship in the later fourth century. These great men, with deep regional followings, could have tied the hands of even a powerful emperor, but they made it nearly impossible for Gratian to go from being a cloistered child emperor to an effective sovereign.

Unlike his father, whose indifference to religious controversy was proverbial, Gratian was a Nicene who let himself be guided by the powerful Nicene bishops of Gaul, Italy and the West. (He did, wisely, tolerate homoian Christians in their Illyrian strongholds, but through weakness not conviction.) In Africa, because the Donatist party had evinced support for the revolt of Firmus in the last years of Valentinian, Gratian now renewed imperial prohibitions on their conventicles and approved a synod to be held in Rome to judge the Donatist bishops. But he himself never went to Rome, nor even as far as Italy. Indeed, in the first years of his reign as augustus, he rarely left the immediate vicinity of Treveri, save for brief campaigns via Moguntiacum and Confluentes (modern Koblenz) in the early autumn of 377.

News from the East was bad, as we shall soon see in more detail: in 377, a rebellion of Gothic settlers had broken out in Moesia and Thrace and Valens had been slow to react. Gratian responded to his uncle's request for reinforcements by sending some Gallic units to the western Balkans, hoping to campaign against the Goths himself in the subsequent year. As it was, however, the departure of those troops offered an opportunity to the Alamannic group known as the Lentienses to raid Roman territory in Raetia, probably late in 377. The punitive campaign began in April 378 under the command of the two *comites rei militaris*, Mallobaudes and Nannienus. Both were experienced commanders, inherited by Gratian from his father, and they won a decisive victory at Argentaria (Strasbourg) in which Priarius, king of the Lentienses, was killed. The episode, strategically quite trivial, reminds us of an important political reality: the Gallic high command had their young emperor so firmly under control that they could ensure a local police action was completed before any aid was despatched to the flailing eastern regime – and this despite Gratian's personal enthusiasm for bringing aid to his uncle. It is yet another demonstration of the regional blocs into which the empire had at this point coalesced, and so it was only in May 378 that Gratian could proceed to the Balkans.

There, the situation had become very dire indeed. Valens had not left Antioch for any length of time between 371 and the latter part of 378, guarding against a possible invasion from Persia. As so often in Roman history, Armenia would provide the *casus belli*. Shapur remained furious at the aid Valens had given to Pap of Armenia, son of the murdered Arsaces, and continued to plan an invasion, though campaigns against Kidarites and Alkhan kept him occupied in the early years of the decade.

The timing of the next confrontation over Armenia is hard to work out. Ammianus' Roman account is chronologically imprecise, while the detailed narrative offered by the fifth-century Armenian historian Faustus of Byzantium is filled with a great deal of legendary content that is difficult to disengage from fact. From what we can tell, although it had been Roman troops who had restored him to his throne, Pap came to resent the imperial garrison commanded by the *dux Armeniae* Terentius, and so he opened friendly correspondence with Shapur. It was the eternal

Armenian story: caught between the two empires and resenting both, the Armenians were culturally closer to Persia but more comfortable politically with the Romans, and always pining for the other when under the tutelage of the one.

Terentius began to suspect Pap of treachery and reported as much to Valens, who summoned the Armenian king to Tarsus. He was interrogated and imprisoned, but after a time allowed to return to his kingdom, where he promptly resumed making friendly gestures to Persia. In 374, the Roman *comes* Traianus had Pap murdered and set his young sons up in his place. They exercised no practical authority, and Roman high-handedness fuelled the resentment of even well-disposed Armenian nobles. Meanwhile, Shapur had settled his central Asian affairs insofar as he was able, and could now engage freely on the Armenian front. Both the Romans and the Persians spent 376 and 377 mustering campaign armies, while a small Persian expedition into Iberia ended with the massacre of its Roman garrison.

Valens, like every Roman, could not help but see Persia as the primary threat to Roman interests, though by 377 the danger in Thrace was in fact considerably greater. It was only with great reluctance that he had begun to detach troops from the eastern front. Their absence seems to have contributed to the Roman losses in Iberia, but worse was to come. More has been written on the disastrous years between 376 and 379 than on almost any other topic in late Roman history. This literary outpouring began in the immediate aftermath of the battle of Adrianople, where Valens was killed. Ammianus Marcellinus' Book 31 is a monographic account of the battle itself. His Greek contemporary Eunapius of Sardis brought out the first edition of his history as a response to Adrianople, conceiving it as a continuation of the work of the third-century Athenian historian Dexippus, who had personally commanded the defence of Attica against an earlier generation of 'Scythian' invaders. Eunapius argued that the Roman defeat was the malign consequence of the empire's conversion to Christianity, and Nicene Christians likewise saw a divine message – God's chastisement of their homoian persecutor Valens. For modern scholars, Adrianople has long been a decisive marker of Rome's decline and fall, and perhaps the emblematic starting point of a *Völkerwanderung*, an imagined 'migration of peoples' out of the 'Germanic' north into the empire. Or, in a Victorian interpretation that has returned to favour thanks to contemporary fears about immigration, the Asiatic Huns are made responsible for shattering the stability of the frontier world and driving violent migrants into an empire they would soon destroy. The real story is much more complicated, and cannot be painted in simple black and white.

As Valens' Transdanubian campaigns had demonstrated in the 360s, the Gothic polities between the Dnieper and Danube rivers and between the Black Sea littoral and the Carpathians were strong and well-organised, capable of at least holding their own against the emperor's armies. In fact, even long before the reign of Constantine, the empire had encouraged stability on the lower Danube frontier, with the result that the Gothic periphery had become wealthier, more socially stratified and politically better organised. That strength was the reason Valens had put so much stock in punishing Athanaric for sending aid to the usurper Procopius. It also accounts for Athanaric's ability to conclude a binding peace with Valens and to impose it on his diverse subjects. None of that recent history, however, prepared the emperor for the size of the Gothic forces that appeared on the empire's doorstep in 376.

Ammianus believed that these Goths had been driven to the frontier by the pressure of the Huns. Having given us a heavily clichéd ethnography of northern Europe and expatiated on the extreme savagery of the bestial Huns, he explains that they subdued some of the Alans north of the Caucasus and east of the river Don (the ancient Tanaïs), incorporated the survivors into their own army and then attacked the kingdom of the Goth Ermenrichus (or Ermanaric), leader of the Greuthungi. His kingdom lay in modern-day Ukraine and probably centred on the Dnieper and its tributaries. A later, sixth-century account by a Byzantine writer named Jordanes, who claimed Gothic descent, is purely imaginary, building fiction on to the scaffolding of Ammianus. The latter, in a few short sentences, claims that the fearsome and warlike Ermenrichus was defeated by the Huns after a very long struggle and then killed himself. He was succeeded by one Vithimer (not necessarily a kinsman), who allied himself with some of the Huns against the rest but eventually died in battle.

Vithimer left a young son, Viderich, in the charge of two generals, Alatheus and Saphrax. They assumed leadership of the Greuthungi and sought refuge closer to the empire, in the lands of Athanaric and his Tervingi. Athanaric, too, decided to face the Huns, and he, too, was defeated – after making a stand on the Dniester river. He retreated behind the line of the Prut, which today forms the border between Moldova and Rumania. There Athanaric faced a mutiny, led by one Alavivus, who marched the larger part of Athanaric's following to the imperial frontier. Athanaric and those loyal to him fled into the Carpathian foothills, perhaps planning to reconstitute his authority along the old Roman *limes transalutanus*, a string of third-century fortifications along the river Olt built when the empire still controlled the Transdanubian provinces of Dacia. Alavivus and his part of the Tervingi then petitioned Valens for admission to the empire and settlement in Thrace.

Up to this point, the story is not that of an unprecedented cataclysm, a barbarian tempest like no other. Instead, it looks more like the sort of political upheaval that happened several times a generation beyond Rome's continental frontiers. Barbarian leaders came and went along the periphery of empire. Dynasties and polities lasted for a short time or a long time, but then they disappeared suddenly in the aftermath of a military defeat, and the losers usually needed Roman help: the empire's military bureaucracy was used to dealing with large-scale resettlement of displaced barbarians and had been doing so since the first century AD. The Gothic request for resettlement was far from unique or unprecedented. Its unintended consequences certainly were.

We do not know how many Goths followed Alavivus in 376, with their families and their portable wealth, in the hope of finding a new home inside the empire, but both sides understood what they were doing. Seasoned bureaucrats and soldiers knew how to manage these transfers, while frontier peoples understood that migrations undertaken in circumstances like these meant submitting to the Roman emperor and giving up autonomy in return for safety. Although the Huns had shattered the Gothic leadership, we need to put out of our minds modern images of Stukas strafing the fleeing crowds of 1939. There was no chaos or confusion. Alavivus kept tight control of the Tervingi, while several months of negotiations ferried information between the local commanders and Valens at Antioch. Valens was delighted to accept the Tervingi's petition: he could use all those recruits for the ever-looming war with Persia. Once Valens had granted his permission for resettlement in Thrace, the actual process of moving the Tervingi and their families across the river began in the high summer of 376. The site of the crossing was probably Durostorum, with its good road route down to the major city of Marcianopolis (now Devnya in Bulgaria). On the Gothic side, Alavivus' colleague was a commander named Fritigern, known to the Romans since Valens' war against Athanaric and a convert to Christianity in its aftermath. Perhaps for that reason,

Fritigern became the main interlocutor with the local Roman administrators in charge of the resettlement.

Two of these administrators, a *comes rei militaris* named Lupicinus and Maximus, probably a *dux* without portfolio, soon proved to be a major problem. Many of the Goths had come to the Danube with their weapons – the same combination of sword, spear and round buckler used by the vast majority of Roman infantry. Unusually, the Roman commanders failed to disarm many of the migrants. Perhaps the scale of the operation took the Roman administration by surprise; perhaps there was negligence or even a deliberate decision to let men who would soon be shipped to Antioch for the Persian war keep their own weapons, sparing imperial *fabricae* the expense of rearming them. But allowing many Goths to keep their arms made the customary profiteering of local administrators more dangerous. Roman officials were expected to make money from their office, through bribes, fees for services and the possibilities for arbitrage between markets that their high mobility gave them. The Gothic migrants now faced the sort of extortion that was the common lot of provincial peasants across the empire when times were hard – restricting the amount of food available to the refugees, officials created an artificial food crisis in order to sell rations that should have been distributed as part of the resettlement. They offered (so we are told) dogmeat at the price of one dog for every Gothic child enslaved. This exploitation made the Gothic migrants restive and resentful, and circumstances conspired to bring them re-enforcements.

By the time the river crossing had actually begun, word had spread beyond the frontier that the emperor was welcoming recruits for his coming war with Persia. As a result, in autumn 376, the Greuthungi led by Alatheus and Saphrax arrived on the Danube and also petitioned the emperor for admission and resettlement. So, too, did old Athanaric with his remaining Tervingian followers. This time, Valens rejected the petitions, in a deliberate display of arbitrariness designed to show who was in charge and make clear that would-be migrants could not expect a positive response as a matter of course. Athanaric got the message – he returned with his followers to 'Caucalanda' (perhaps the Buzau range of the eastern Carpathians). Alatheus and Saphrax, however, bided their time. The Tervingi of Alavivus and Fritigern were relocated to Marcianopolis, well south of the river and on the main highway across the Haemus mountain range into Thrace. But organising this transfer took attention away from affairs on the left bank of the river, where Alatheus and Saphrax seized the moment and crossed into the empire in makeshift transports. Hoping the emperor would accept a fait accompli, they encamped near the Tervingi, who were being shepherded to Marcianopolis.

The situation was not yet out of control, but Lupicinus began to grow worried. He housed the main body of the Tervingi in temporary quarters around Marcianopolis, seconding units from the Roman field army there with them to keep order. Since Alavivus, Fritigern and their immediate retainers were soon to become officers in that same field army, they were treated with due respect and allowed to reside inside the city. One night, when Lupicinus had invited them to a banquet at his residence, a brawl erupted between some *comitatenses* and some Gothic soldiers whom they refused to allow into the city to buy extra supplies. There were casualties on both sides and Lupicinus panicked, ordering Fritigern's bodyguards to be killed. Word got out and the Tervingi, fearing that their commander was dead, threatened to storm the city gates. Lupicinus released Fritigern to reassure the Gothic soldiery of his safety, but we never hear of Alavivus again. Fritigern presumably betrayed him to Lupicinus in order to consolidate his own power. Safely back among his followers, Fritigern decided that the fiasco he had survived had been an act of deliberate treachery, though mismanagement and incompetence are just as likely explanations. He began to withdraw into the countryside, an action that Lupicinus correctly interpreted as an act of open rebellion. Fourteen kilometres from Marcianopolis, Lupicinus brought Fritigern to battle and died there alongside all his junior officers.

Collecting the arms of their fallen enemies, Fritigern and his followers began to raid the region systematically, some pushing as far south as Adrianople in Thrace. They found sympathisers among some of the local population. Slaves, many of them Goths themselves, flocked to join Fritigern, as did many of the region's miners, rejecting backbreaking work in the mines in favour of freebooting – and all using their local knowledge to aid the rebels. Other Balkan Goths soon found their way into Fritigern's army as well. Two Gothic officers named Sueridas and Colias had been stationed with their units at Adrianople, and had hitherto taken no interest in Fritigern's plight. But in 377, they got their marching orders for the Persian front and requested supplies for their march from the *curia* of Adrianople, presumably because the imperial officials who should have fitted them out for the journey had been called away to Marcianopolis. The *curiales* stood on their legal right to refuse supplies for the march, inasmuch as they had already done their legal duty under the laws of military billeting. When Sueridas and Colias refused to set out without adequate rations, the *curiales* asked the *fabricenses* – workers in the city's imperial arms factory – to help them force the soldiers to depart. That was a mistake. Provoked by the makeshift missiles hurled at them, Sueridas and Colias let their troops loose on their tormentors to massacre any they got hold of. After that, they marched off to join Fritigern.

That episode, itself quite minor, reminds us that the Gothic war in the Balkans was neither a planned nor a unified uprising, still less a mass invasion and conquest; rather, it was a series of small revolts, each with a different trigger, that eventually converged into a threat to the whole region. The combined forces of Fritigern, Sueridas, Colias and others, joined by provincial malcontents of various stripes and well-equipped from the imperial *fabricae*, welded their diverse followings into a competent fighting force. They were even able to manage a supply train as complex as that of an imperial field army, because so many of the rebels had served as Roman soldiers at one or another time in their lives. Thus, by the summer of 377, this was not the same group of people who had crossed the Danube a year before but rather a new, more heterogeneous field army, the diversity of which was recognised by a contemporary like Ammianus: he ceases to use the word Tervingi to describe them and instead starts to call them *Gothi*, 'Goths' in a generic sense.

Although Fritigern clearly had the ability to despatch troops wherever he liked in the provinces of Moesia and most of Thrace, he seems to have moved the main body of his followers into Scythia, the modern Dobrogea, where the Danube bends north and east to empty into the Black Sea. His motives remain unclear, but he may have been contemplating a return to Gothia at the head of his new and imposing army. However, the gravity of the situation finally impressed itself upon both imperial courts. Valens determined to buy off Shapur, sending his long-serving *magister militum*, Flavius Victor, to patch up a peace agreement. In the meantime, he sent two *comites rei militaris*, Profuturus and Traianus (the murderer of king Pap of Armenia) to try to contain Fritigern. In the West, Gratian sent two good generals, the *comes rei militaris* Frigeridus and the *comes domes-ticorum* Richomeres, to observe the situation, offer help if they could and – most importantly – seal off access to the western Balkans and Illyricum. Meanwhile, the old guard who had been displaced in the aftermath of Valentinian II's proclamation saw an opportunity to recoup their position in the Balkans. The son of the executed *magister equitum* Theodosius came out of retirement and resumed his career.

Late in 377, Profuturus and Traianus fought a major battle with Fritigern '*Ad Salices*' ('At the Willows'), an unknown location between the coastal city of Tomi and the Danube mouth. Fritigern won a comprehensive victory and Profuturus died on the battlefield. While Richomeres guarded the routes westwards, his counterpart Frigeridus fortified Beroea, inside Valens' imperial territory, and wiped out the forces of a certain Farnobius, one of Fritigern's subordinates, sending the Gothic survivors to Italy to be resettled as farmers. By now, Valens had sent his second-ranking commander, the *magister equitum* Saturninus, to contain the rebellion over the winter of 377–8. The emperor would then take personal charge of the war during the next campaigning season. In late summer 377, Saturninus and Traianus attempted to blockade Fritigern's followers in the Haemus for the winter, but they failed and Fritigern led his main force to winter in the open country south of the Haemus, where they could supply themselves from the autumn harvest and launch raids as far as Constantinople itself. By the end of winter, Fritigern's army had the free run of Thrace, while both eastern and western emperors were preparing to take the field personally.

Valens arrived at Constantinople in April or May 378 and immediately faced food riots from a discontented populace. Gratian and his court set out from Treveri in late April and arrived at Sirmium in Pannonia in early August. Valens had by then reorganised his officer corps, cashiering Traianus and bringing back old Sebastianus, who had been forced into retirement in Italy by the coup of 375, but who had served successfully under Constantius, on Julian's Persian campaign, and in many of Valentinian's Alamannic campaigns. As with the sudden return of the younger Theodosius, this demonstrates how sidelined factions could seize on crises to restore their lost positions. Sebastianus quickly won some small successes against Fritigern's dispersed forces and, while that offered a badly needed boost to Balkan morale, it also convinced Fritigern to concentrate his forces so they could operate as a single unit. They rendezvoused at Cabyle, in the valley between the Rhodope and Haemus mountain chains, and then marched south-east towards Adrianople, where Sebastianus was headquartered. Meanwhile, Valens left Constantinople on 11 June for Melanthias, just far enough from the city to escape the rioting. Early in August, word came that Gratian had reached Sirmium and was preparing to march eastwards to help catch the Goths in a pincer manoeuvre. Valens, supposedly jealous of the successes Sebastianus had won, made quickly for the city of Adrianople and encamped in its suburbs to await his nephew.

Fritigern was now based at Nike, an imperial road station near Adrianople, and Valens' scouts reported that the force he commanded was quite small. Despite this, when Richomeres arrived with the vanguard of the western army, he advised Valens to wait the short time it would take for Gratian to arrive with the main western field army. Valens disagreed, but his high command was not so sure, and Ammianus records a furious debate between proponents of swift action, like Sebastianus, and those, like Victor, who favoured more cautious preparation. In the end, Valens chose immediate engagement, urged by his palatine officials not to share the certain victory with his nephew. Now Fritigern was worried. His forces were indeed not at full strength, and his cavalry units, commanded by Alatheus and Saphrax, had not yet arrived at Nike. On 8 August, he sent an embassy of homoian priests to convey to the emperor terms for a proposed peace, but Valens rejected their overtures. The following morning, he prepared his army for battle in the plain between Nike and Adrianople. Fritigern held his forces back, despatching more envoys, while the Roman troops languished in the sun and the Goths lit fires that sent choking clouds of smoke towards their lines. The battle's tactical details cannot be reconstructed with any precision from Ammianus' account, despite modern attempts to claim otherwise. We do know that fighting started accidentally, when two Roman units advanced prematurely on the right wing. Then, with the Roman line of battle disordered, Fritigern's cavalry arrived under Alatheus and Saphrax and took the Roman left by surprise. The force of that flank attack compressed the whole Roman infantry line upon itself, hampering its ability to fight, and the rout began in the afternoon, when the centre ranks broke and began to retreat in disorder. Valens was forced to seek shelter with the Mattiarii, a senior unit of the field army, because his palatine guards had been totally wiped out. When the reserve forces declined to rally and try to turn the tide, Richomeres, Victor and Saturninus – the only surviving members of the high command – surrendered the field. The butchery lasted until dark.

Even at the time, no one knew how Valens died. The prosaic version had him struck by an arrow and killed amid the common soldiery as evening fell. A more romantic account claimed that the mortally wounded emperor was carried from the field by a handful of loyal retainers who hid him in a deserted farmhouse. As he lay dying, a Gothic unit surrounded the house and set it on fire, rather than pause in their plundering. Only one man escaped to tell the enemy how close they had come to capturing a Roman emperor. Whatever the case, Valens' body was never found. Thirty-five senior officers, including Sebastianus and Traianus, died along with him, as did fully two-thirds of the field army he had led into battle that morning. It was a military disaster that, if not quite unprecedented, had not been experienced since the emperor Valerian had been defeated and captured by the Persian king Shapur I more than a hundred years before.

The aftermath of the battle was ugly. The military and administrative structure of Moesia and Thrace lay in tatters, and Gratian returned to Sirmium, where he met with the generals who had survived the slaughter. The victorious Fritigern laid siege to Adrianople but could not penetrate its walls and so made for Constantinople instead. There, Valens' widow Domnica became the public face of imperial resistence, although Ammianus implies that the effective defence lay with auxiliary troops from Arabia, sent by the Arab queen Mavia on whom Valens had imposed peace before leaving Antioch. In the eastern provinces, the first task was to ensure that the chaos in the Balkans did not spread further. In Oriens, the *magister militum* decided to purge Gothic soldiers from the army, and there were pogroms against Goths in the cities of Asia Minor and Oriens that carried on into 379. In the western Balkans, meanwhile, indecision reigned. No coherent plan for dealing with Fritigern could be put together before winter fell and Gratian may have wanted to return to Gaul, the threat of the Alamanni as always providing a ready-made excuse. But to leave Sirmium now would invite a usurpation, and that would serve no one's interests, so he wintered there, perhaps contemplating a renewed offensive in Thrace in the spring.

Events overtook him. The younger Theodosius, a former *dux Moesiae*, had returned to service in the Balkans early in 378, though an edifying but implausible story claims that Gratian called on him to save the day only after Adrianople. When 379 opened, both consuls were western, Gratian's praetorian prefect Ausonius and Quintus Clodius Hermogenianus Olybrius, a member of the great clan of the Anicii, thereby providing evidence that Gratian was attempting to conciliate the Roman Senate. The first significant event recorded in the new year was an imperial proclamation: at Sirmium, on 19 January, Theodosius was elevated to the imperial purple by Gratian, who had become senior emperor upon his uncle's death. The background to this proclamation was deliberately consigned to obscurity, but we can probably infer a barracks coup by soldiers of the Pannonian and Balkan armies.

At the end of 378, Gratian was in command of the whole empire's surviving field armies, save the few distant units that Valens had left on the eastern front. But his own trusted high command and most of his civilian establishment had come with him to Sirmium from Gaul, which meant that the Pannonian general staff, and what few remnants of the eastern command survived the debacle at Adrianople, were now in a position of relative political weakness. They perceived the personal impotence of Gratian, and reckoned that his demonstrable unwillingness to act force-fully east of the Succi pass made a rival proclamation viable. Theodosius was an ideal candidate: the son of a great military hero, he was young and not yet very distinguished, thus likely to be biddable and reliant upon his general staff. And so a 'spontaneous' proclamation of Theodosius was engineered by the Pannonian and eastern establishments and presented to Gratian as a fait accompli.

Rather than ask his Gallic power base to suppress a dangerous and perhaps quite popular coup, Gratian acquiesced, if with no great enthusi-asm. He gave his new colleague his reluctant blessing and returned to the West before the start of summer, providing Theodosius with no material support for the pacification of Thrace and Moesia, which he transferred formally to eastern jurisdiction. Gratian may very well have hoped that Theodosius would embarrass himself, as in the event he rapidly did, but his decision reminds us how, structurally, the two *partes imperii* had become very distant from each other since the time of Constantius and Julian. It is also a reminder of how difficult it is to write a single narrative for both halves of the empire after 364, so we will turn first to Gratian and his western court before moving back to Theodosius and the Gothic war he inherited.

The story of Gratian's reign is usually told as that of his high officials, and still more of the interactions among such powerful bishops as Damasus of Rome and Ambrose of Milan, or great senators like Virius Nicoma-chus Flavianus and Vettius Agorius Praetextatus and many others whose names pepper one of our best sources for the reign, the correspondence of Quintus Aurelius Symmachus. In these narratives, the story is all about religious crises: the ongoing fight over homoian congregations in the western cities; the controversial removal of the altar of Victory from the

Senate House in Rome; a new crisis over heresy and clerical discipline arising in Spain. It is never about Gratian as ruler, still less the young Valentinian II, whose court resided in Mediolanum, where his mother Justina, the second wife of Valentinian I, was a powerful supporter of the homoian party. But if Gratian was as subject to the pressures of his establishments as were all the emperors of this period, he was certainly not the do-nothing ruler he is sometimes made out to be. He returned to northern Italy in the summer of 379, travelling to the imperial residence of Mediolanum for the first time in order to ensure that his younger half-brother's court would continue to hew to its subordinate path. The year before, just prior to heading east, Gratian had demanded a statement of faith from Ambrose, the new Nicene bishop of Mediolanum, who had replaced the homoian Auxentius in that year. As a sop to the homoians in his close entourage, and to the establishment of his step-mother Justina, Gratian restored one of Mediolanum's churches to its homoian congregation, and so Ambrose – in the first of the confrontational behaviours for which he would soon become famous – refused to meet Gratian when he stopped there en route back to Gaul. From Mediolanum, in late summer, the emperor travelled through Raetia, perhaps conducting a short raid against the local Alamanni. Then, from the head of the Rhine valley he marched up to Treveri, where he would remain for well over a year.

It was during this period that Gratian conceived of the need to reimpose some sort of uniformity upon the Christian churches of the West, where the homoian and Nicene factions were quite evenly balanced in their support, the Nicenes dominant in Gaul, Spain and Italy, homoians in most of Illyricum. Theodosius, as we shall see, had issued a unilateral order in favour of the Nicenes and condemning among many other heresies the homoian interpretation of Christology in 381; he then called a council solely of eastern bishops, ostensibly to regulate the succession to the bishopric of Constantinople, but equally implying the independence of the Greek church from the Latin and his own independence from the senior augustus Gratian. Embarrassing though this was, there was little Gratian could do save convoke his own council to rule on the same matters in 381, at Aquileia on the cusp of Italy and Illyricum. The city's bishop, Valerianus, presided but Ambrose was the leading force among the several dozen bishops who attended, all from the Latin West. Ambrose's goal was to assert his own dominance over the churches of the Italian and Illyrian prefectures by securing the condemnation of the bishops of Ratiaria and

Singidunum as homoians. He did this by outrightly underhand methods, and the council reasserted the Nicene interpretation of the relationship between God the Father and God the Son. In the process, Ambrose became the leading figure in the Latin church and earned the lasting hostility of both the eastern bishops to whom he presumed to dictate and bishop Damasus of Rome, whose primacy Ambrose was clearly challenging.

The wrangling that surrounded the council and the rival ecclesiastical blocs we can discern in this period are a precise parallel of the political dynamic we have seen among the empire's civilian and military establishments. In contrast to Constantine and his sons, an emperor like Gratian was buffeted and managed by the rival episcopal factions around his court, rather than dominating their bishops in favour of his own cherished theological line. This reflects not just the youth of Gratian and Valentinian II, but also the increasing institutional power of church structures in the cities of the empire – particularly in the great imperial cities, where the bishops wielded tremendous influence over the local populations, and where their access to economic power was a match for all but the wealthiest of senators. The confirmation of this new dynamic would come in the reign of Theodosius, as formidable an individual as the first Valentinian, but even less able to escape the dominance of either the ecclesiastical or the secular factions that surrounded him.

In 381, Gratian decided to move his court to Mediolanum and take control of affairs from his young half-brother. The city was much better placed to mediate between Pannonia, Rome and Treveri than was the Gallic capital, but the next two years of western history are very poorly documented and we know little of what happened. In June 383, Gratian left Mediolanum on campaign against the Alamanni. Theodosius, as we will see below, had finally resolved his Balkan problems in what could be portrayed – however arguably – as a victory over the Goths. He had also elevated his eldest son, Arcadius, to the rank of augustus and named him consul for the year 383, a dynastic move Gratian chose not to recognise. While still in Raetia, Gratian learned of a coup d'état in Britain, led by a senior army officer named Magnus Maximus, a Spaniard and a distant relative of Theodosius who had served under the latter's father in Africa, although the precise nature of their familial relationship remains unclear. Maximus had recently won some signal victories against the Picts north of Hadrian's Wall, but quite why he seized the purple has never been adequately explained. Regardless, Gratian diverted his field army from the

Alamannic campaign to deal with the usurper, who had made with all haste for the continent and won the allegiance of the troops in northern Gaul.

Gratian and Maximus faced each other near Lutetia (modern Paris), and the field army abandoned the legitimate emperor for his rival, starting with the cavalry units of Mauri who may have remembered Maximus from the African campaigns. It was later said that Gratian had alienated his regular troops by doting too heavily on his favourites, a bodyguard of Alan cavalrymen. He and 300 supporters fled the battlefield, but he was caught and executed at Lugdunum by the *magister equitum* Andragathius on 15 August 383. Theodosius perhaps had no chance, or perhaps had not bothered, to assist his colleague; nor would he make any move to interfere in western affairs for quite some time. Despite his resolution of the Gothic wars in the Balkans, he still had a great deal to occupy him in the East.

5

THE REIGN OF
THEODOSIUS I

Theodosius had returned to favour in the worst possible circumstances. The Gothic crisis had given him and other victims of 375 a chance to re-enter public life, but it left them with few resources that could be translated into effective power. The eastern army had been functionally annihilated at Adrianople, and Gratian was content to leave his unwelcome new colleague to flounder along as best he could. How precisely Theodosius went about reconstituting government in the Balkans is hard for us to determine. Much has been made of the Spanish core of his supporters, not least in modern Spanish scholarship, but the one Spaniard clearly attested in his entourage is the future praetorian prefect Maternus Cynegius, and the evidence for Theodosius' distinctively Iberian outlook evaporates on close inspection.

Rather than a Spanish country gentleman, the new emperor was a typical child of the camps, the son of one of the great Valentinianic marshals, bred to follow his father's path into the *schola* of the *protectores* and then on to a precocious command. His connections will have been developed during his father's period of military pre-eminence, as he was making his way through his junior career, in the 360s and earlier 370s. The resemblance to the milieu from which Valentinian and Valens had emerged is no coincidence, and Theodosius, it would soon become clear, resembled Valens more than either his own father or Valentinian. Competent enough, he lacked the strategic vision of the great commanders and had none of the tactical brilliance that some of his own generals would demonstrate. Indeed, had the ecclesiastical faction that he came to favour not emerged to write the era's history, and consecrate him 'Theodosius the Great' and the champion of orthodoxy, he would probably have been remembered as a second Constantius, lucky in civil wars but otherwise disappointed and disappointing.

When Theodosius became emperor in 379, he was peculiarly ill equipped to deal with the challenges he faced. He had been restored by a faction of Balkan and north African officers loyal to the memory of his father, few of whom had support networks in the eastern provinces to which fortune had consigned their futures. Growing up in the Latin military culture of Valentinian's army, Nicene in faith but deeply incurious about what that meant in practice, Theodosius was unprepared for the complexities of religious politics among the Greek churchmen on whom he would have to rely for public legitimacy: his regime had neither dynastic cachet nor much prospect of the military success that would provide its own legitimation.

The first order of business was to reconstitute a field army large enough to take on Fritigern's Goths. There were no troops to be had from further east: Valens had stripped the diocese of Oriens of its field army for the Gothic campaign, and the troops that remained in Syria were needed to deter a Persian offensive. That became less likely when Shapur II died in 379. His son, the weak Shapur III, faced constant opposition from his own nobles, as well as the final loss of Bactria, the Kabul region and Gandhara as far as the Punjab to the rulers of the Kidarites and the Alkhan. He therefore gave up disputing the Armenian succession, but that did nothing to help Theodosius find the resources he needed to restore the Balkans.

To rally the scattered remnants of Valens' field army was essential, but not nearly enough. Only new conscription would suffice. In June 379, Theodosius made Thessalonica his base. It provided better access to the Balkan theatres on both sides of the Succi pass than did Constantinople, and it could be supplied by sea, as bases further inland could not. Largely impervious to land-based attacks, Thessalonica was therefore a viable residence even if Fritigern maintained control of the interior. Thessalonica was also a Latin cultural island in the Greek-speaking southern Balkans, and so Theodosius' time there did nothing to prepare him for the politics of Constantinople when he finally got there, almost two years later, in November 380.

Meanwhile, there was heavy fighting to be done. By July and August 379, the new emperor was issuing laws from distant Balkan sites like Scupi and Vicus Augusti, which suggests that he had rustled up enough troops to start campaigning. In the *Notitia Dignitatum*, a fifth-century document that lists the empire's military establishment, there appear many units known as *pseudocomitatenses* that seem to date to these years; their title implies that they were 'false' or 'ersatz' units of the field army, promoted from garrison units to make up for the units lost on the field at Adrianople. Laws from this period talk of calling up bakers and cooks, and the speeches of Themistius and Libanius imply that farmers and miners were being conscripted as well. Still other troops were recruited from client barbarians from beyond the Danube, and also from Armenia and Iberia in the Caucasus. None of them were especially effective, save as cannon fodder, and served mostly to keep battlefields shifting from place to place without resolution. A victory was announced in November 379, but its significance was small. Early in 380, Theodosius suffered a major defeat in Macedonia, some of his new recruits going over to the Goths, others deserting *en masse*. By now, the Goths had begun to impose 'tribute' on parts of the Balkans, presumably arrogating to themselves the tax revenues of the Roman state. Gratian, despite maintaining control of the western Balkans, did nothing to help with matters further east.

Confident slogans on the coinage, victory titles and the careful praise of orators, both pagan and Christian, did little to disguise the paucity of the achievement. Theodosius himself, meanwhile, had fallen very ill, and seemed likely to die. In September or perhaps October 380, on what all took to be his deathbed, he was baptised in Thessalonica by bishop Ascholius, a western appointee in whose debt he would soon find himself. But, to the surprise of all involved, the emperor recovered and finally made his way to Constantinople, where he was immediately drawn into the ecclesiastical conflicts with which that city was riven. The extent of Gratian's determination to leave Theodosius to his own devices was demonstrated early in 381, when the western generals Bauto and Arbogastes halted a Gothic army on the frontier between the Pannonian and Dacian dioceses and drove it back into the eastern empire without taking any further action.

Theodosius at last drew the inevitable conclusion. Every battle he had fought had been lost and the Gothic war was just bleeding on. Not only did he lack his father's native talents, but his troops were of marginal quality and his high command boasted no one with the tactical ability of a Richomeres or an Arbogastes. A negotiated peace with the Goths would have to be arrived at eventually, so he might as well put the best possible face on it. He opened negotiations in 381 and peace was finally concluded on 3 October 382. It took so long to work out because the Gothic leadership had never been consolidated, and may in fact have become more dispersed. Theodosius welcomed Valens' old foe, the Tervingian king Athanaric, to a peaceful retirement in Constantinople, having him buried with the highest of honours when he died of old age on 25 January 381. But otherwise, not one of the leaders associated with the Danube crossing and the uprising of 376–8 is still attested in 382: Fritigern, Alatheus, Saphrax, Videric, all have disappeared from the records.

That means we do not really know how, or with whom precisely, the Gothic peace was negotiated. However, we do have a good record of changing imperial propaganda over time. Ever since 378, the reliable mouthpiece Themistius had been confidently predicting triumphs that failed to materialise. In 382, his tune changed and it was suddenly much better to fill Thrace's fields with Gothic farmers than with Gothic dead. In his thirty-fourth oration, the great masterpiece of his political oratory, he rewrote the entire history of the preceding half decade to cast its dismal record of military failure as careful preparation for a peace from which all involved had benefitted, the Goths celebrating a triumph over themselves and their transformation into productive farmers.

The terms of Theodosius' treaty are the subject of endless scholarly dispute, most of it arguing not from the minimal evidence, but from scholars' preconceptions about the nature of Gothic history. The panegyrics of Themistius and Pacatus both say that the Goths became farmers, while a polemical treatise by the philosopher Synesius, written two decades later, claims that the Goths were ceded land. The Goths may have been expected to pay taxes like Roman provincials or they may have been allowed to live according to their own customs – the sources tell us both things. All we can say with certainty is that Roman contemporaries now agreed that the Gothic threat was over. Some of the Goths, perhaps the vast majority, sank into the rural mass of the Balkan population where they long remained. Others continued to be recruited to fight for the emperor. No doubt many aspired to roles in the regular army, but most were recruited into 'native' auxiliary units under their own officers. Simultaneously, the normal process of recruiting frontier barbarians into the regular army continued. This created two different classes of officer: those in the comitatensian units who could look forward to a traditional military career within the officer corps; and those in command of native units whose career prospects were badly constrained. This new state of affairs would have momentous consequences a quarter of a century later.

For the moment, in the early 380s, however, Theodosius had other things to worry about: the parlous state of the eastern church and, presently, the usurpation of Magnus Maximus in the West. Theodosius' illness in autumn 380 had led to his baptism by bishop Ascholius of Thessalonica. Ascholius was a client of the staunchly Nicene bishop of Rome, Damasus, and an ally of Peter of Alexandria. Peter was the hand-picked successor of the fanatical Nicene patriarch Athanasius, whose chequered career had dominated the middle years of the fourth century and caused much grief for a whole series of emperors going back to Constantine. Athanasius had, on his deathbed, consecrated Peter, leaving him to continue the old man's hardline intransigence on matters of theology. Unlike Nicene Thessalonica, however, the main churches of Constantinople were governed by Valens' appointee, the homoian bishop Demophilus, while the dissenting Nicene minority was led by bishop Gregory of Nazianzus, second only to the late Basil of Caesarea for his intellectual authority among Greek-speaking Nicenes. Early in 380, Theodosius issued an edict affirming the sole legitimacy of the Nicene church of Constantinople, possibly thanks to lobbying by Gregory's followers. But it had had no impact in the intervening nine months and Demophilus remained firmly in control of the Constantinopolitan church until Theodosius himself arrived in the city towards the end of the year.

It remains uncertain just how vigorously Nicene Theodosius had been prior to his arrival in the East, or whether, like Valentinian and many other officers in this period, his sincere piety was compatible with an indifference to theological niceties. In 380, however, he was inclined to take seriously the implications of his baptism and his obligation to defend the Nicene faith into which he had been baptised. Thus, when he entered the capital in late November 380, he immediately offered Demophilus a choice: assent to the truth of the Nicene faith and keep his episcopate, or be deposed in favour of someone else. When the bishop demurred, his congregation followed him out of the cathedral, establishing a schismatic homoian episcopate that would endure for decades. In January 381, the emperor made over all the churches of Constantinople to the Nicene party. It made no difference to Theodosius that majority opinion in Constantinople was probably against him and in favour of Demophilus, or that enforcing the transfers required the deployment of military force. Indeed, the use of soldiers to manage doctrinal partisanship would be a general feature of the next few decades, as it had been intermittently since the time of Constantine. Since Theodosius had yet to win any military victories worth the name, he needed to rely more heavily on Christian ceremony to buttress his legitimacy, and that made him more politically dependent on episcopal support than any of his predecessors.

Perhaps the most important long-term consequence of this was the great imperial church council that Theodosius was convinced to call, in Constantinople itself, pre-emptively forestalling the plans Gratian was laying in the West. It opened in May 381, with at first only the bishops of Thrace and the province of Asia in attendance. The council's first order of business was to elevate Gregory of Nazianzus to the episcopate of the city, to establish the Nicene faith as the only acceptable formulation and to expel from their sees more than thirty bishops who would not give up one or another part of their homoian confession. The council also tried to regulate the disputed bishopric of Antioch, where there were two rival Nicene bishops as well as a homoian challenger. One of the Nicenes, Meletius, died while the council was in session, and so the council recognised his surviving rival Paulinus. But at this stage a delegation of Egyptian bishops, including Peter of Alexandria's brother and successor Timothy, arrived to join the council, along with a few bishops from Macedonia. This provoked more trouble, for Timothy and his followers objected to the elevation of Gregory as improper – a bishop should not, according to some canonical rulings, be transferred from one see to another. This was a view shared by the Roman church and, although no representatives of the Latin church were present, Timothy – the Alexandrian successor of Athanasius whose relations with western bishops had been so good – could set himself up as the champion of canonical propriety.

In the face of this challenge, Gregory took the magnanimous (or perhaps merely pusillanimous) step of giving up his new see and returning to Nazianzus, where he spent the next decade writing countless learned theological treatises, as well as iambic poetry that combined great classical elegance with much venting of spleen at clerical rivals. Likewise after

Timothy's arrival, the succession of Paulinus at Antioch was reversed and the priest Flavianus was made bishop. The council then elected the Constantinopolitan senator Nectarius to the bishopric of Constantinople, advancing him directly from lay status to the episcopal throne. It took a number of other measures of long-standing consequence as well. For the first time, the council placed the bishop of Constantinople second only to the bishop of Rome in authority, on the grounds that Constantinople was a second Rome. This was a bitter blow to Timothy of Alexandria, who had seemed in the ascendant since his arrival, and would raise to a new pitch the existing rivalry among the oriental sees of Alexandria, Antioch and Constantinople. The Roman church never recognised this declaration of Constantinopolitan parity, even though the Council of Constantinople is regarded as the second of the great 'ecumenical' – that is, universally binding – councils of the Christian church, Constantine's epoch-making council of Nicaea having been the first. The council ended on 9 July 381, and marks an important symbolic stage in the transformation of Constantinople from an imperial residence into the capital of the Greek-speaking world.

Yet controversy refused to die down, with new faultlines opening between West and East, Latin and Greek. When Gratian's council of Aquileia met in September 381 with Ambrose of Milan presiding, it refused to recognise key parts of the Constantinopolitan settlement, including the elections of Nectarius of Constantinople and Flavianus of Antioch, and insisted that Paulinus was the only legitimate bishop of the latter city. The eastern bishops in turn refused to recognise the legitimacy of these Latin pronouncements. Theodosius responded by calling new councils in Constantinople in both 382 and 383 to affirm the decisions of his original council of 381, though Alexandria now sided with the westerners against the election of Flavianus at Antioch and in favour of Paulinus. This Antiochene schism would go on for another quarter century and colour the outcomes of church councils for many decades thereafter.

Along with these ecclesiastical ructions, and the western usurpation of Maximus in 383, Theodosius faced a financial crisis, inasmuch as Thrace had suffered too badly during the Gothic war to sustain its tax burden and had to be given repeated tax concessions. For reasons that are less clear, parts of Asia Minor – particularly the diocese of Pontus – required similar tax relief. The deficit in imperial finances this created meant that relatively prosperous provinces faced heavier fiscal exactions, which created painful discontent in the cities of Oriens. Theodosius was determined to buttress his dynastic credentials, however, and to that end proclaimed his son Arcadius augustus on 19 January 383, at the age of six.

While that compromised his relations with the western regime of Gratian, the usurpation of Maximus soon rendered the question moot. And, despite these various challenges, and the bankruptcy of Thrace, the Danube region itself had quieted down a great deal, although the situation beyond the river was still disturbed. In 386, a number of Goths, led by one Odotheus, crossed the river, but were met and defeated by the Theodosian general Promotus: their defeated remnant was transferred to Phrygia and settled there, presumably as farmers, never to be heard from again. That is significant because it shows the extent to which imperial authority over the Danube frontier had been restored since the peace of 382. Frontier management was functioning normally again, handling such incursions with the combination of military action and carefully timed leniency that had characterised imperial responses to barbarian activity throughout Roman history.

The eastern dioceses, bereft of an imperial presence for the better part of a decade, suddenly reminded Theodosius of their unique set of problems in 387. Antioch, always fractious – if not as much as Alexandria – erupted in rioting that touched on the imperial dignity. The trials for sorcery and treason that punctuated Valens' years in the city show just how complicated Antioch's politics could be, overlaid as they were with so many different officials with good claims to jurisdiction. Rival Christian groups, with their own competing episcopal successions, only exacerbated political rivalries. In the 380s, moreover, Antioch was home to one of the most extraordinary orators of late antiquity, the Christian cleric John whose nickname Chrysostom (Golden Mouth) conveys as much as any description. A native Antiochene, he had been a pupil of the pagan sophist Libanius, but was baptised in his twenties and became a priest and a charismatic preacher of unparalleled skill. Although sophisticated in his own theological thinking, he preached a relatively straightforward understanding of Christian scripture and Christian duties that was far easier to follow in everyday life than were the more philosophical or allegorical readings popular with many of his contemporaries. In 387, still no higher up in the ecclesiastical hierarchy than a mere *presbyter* or priest, he found himself at the centre of a violent controversy that might have had even more painful consequences than it did.

The city had suffered periodic food shortages during the 380s, a consequence not just of drought, and of the fiscal exactions made necessary by the aftermath of Adrianople, but of the pressures put on its infrastructure and finances by the huge imperial establishment in the city, with its prefect, vicar (the *comes Orientis*) and various provincial authorities. When, in February 387, the imperial government announced an increase in the *aurum coronarium* and the *aurum oblaticium* (the accession and quinquennial anniversary taxes on cities and senators, respectively), the city council demanded that the governor and the bishop resist these increases. When that produced no result, a mob marched on the governor's residence, and tried to batter its way in; thwarted, it descended upon the official portraits of the emperor and his family – which were legally as sacrosanct as the emperor himself – and smashed them to pieces. Worse, the crowd pulled down and dismembered the bronze statues of Theodosius and Arcadius – the former about to celebrate is *decennalia* and the latter having just celebrated his *quinquennalia* – and threatened to burn down the city's imperial palace. The incipient arson was suppressed overnight, and the next morning the *comes Orientis* began to round up and arrest rioters, punishing many summarily and cruelly, as the evidence of Libanius tells us.

But the real fear was what the emperor would do. Theodosius would have been within his rights to execute the whole *boule*, and it is no wonder that so many of the city's well-born fled to the countryside to await the outcome of the imperial wrath. The bishop, Flavianus, travelled to Constantinople to intercede for his flock, and the imperial commission of inquiry was provisionally authorised to downgrade the city from its treasured status of metropolis and subordinate it to its hated neighbour Laodicea; to close the baths, circus and theatres; and to cancel the free distribution of bread to the poor. Chrysostom made his name with 'On the Statues', a series of homilies in which he set out the lessons the Antiochenes should learn from the coming afflictions, as well as urging them not to give up hope. That advice turned out to be justified. The commissioners who met in the court of the *magister militum* Hellebichus counselled leniency and Flavianus' intervention likewise paid off. Theodosius and his consistory decided that the suffering imposed during the investigation was punishment enough.

The Antiochenes were lucky to have got off as lightly as they had, given the severity of their crime: the destruction of the imperial image was as damning in its collective significance as usurpation was in an individual.

Chrysostom's intervention had not been direct, but his conduct secured his reputation permanently, which would in turn eventually lead to his being called upon to serve as bishop of the imperial city itself. In 387, however, it was not merely the intervention of Flavianus, or the generosity of Hellebichus' commission, but luck that spared Antioch the worst that its citizens might have expected: by late in the year, Theodosius had become convinced of the need to intervene in the West. He had been able to ignore the overthrow and murder of Gratian, with whom he had been on poor terms. But when Magnus Maximus decided to overthrow the regime of Valentinian II in Italy and Pannonia, the situation was changed dramatically.

Maximus had done a remarkably effective job of consolidating his authority in the West. When the news of Gratian's death arrived at Mediolanum in 383, the junta that ruled for the young Valentinian II – who had now, in theory, succeeded Gratian as the senior augustus in the imperial college – barred the Alpine passes and cordoned Maximus off in the western prefecture of Gaul. Britain, largely denuded of troops, remained under Maximus' control, and it is likely that he began the process of enrolling mercenary Saxons from the North Sea coast to garrison Britain. It is also possible that he reorganised the British frontier, abandoning the whole highland zone and withdrawing Roman administration to the more fertile lowlands, on a line running from the Dorset coast, through the Severn estuary, to the east Yorkshire wolds.

The Spanish diocese also went over to Maximus. The *magister equitum*, Andragathius, who had ordered Gratian's execution, remained the key military figure in Maximus' regime, ensuring the support of the Gallic high command. Very few of Gratian's supporters were purged and every effort was made to project a sense of normality, as if no usurpation had taken place. Valentinian II's notional subjects seemed willing to collude in that pretence and to do business with the new emperor in Treveri. The deliberate curtailment of Valentinian's actual authority, which had been the tacit policy of Gratian and Theodosius, now continued under Maximus. We find both churchmen and senators accepting Maximus as the senior western emperor – bishop Ambrose, for instance, made fully two journeys to Treveri, seeing in the Nicene Maximus a more congenial interlocutor than any at the court of Valentinian's homoian mother Justina. Theodosius, for his part, allowed images of Maximus to be displayed in eastern cities, clearly acknowledging the Gallic emperor as a legitimate member of the imperial college. And while it used to be thought – and is still alleged in some works of reference – that in 384 Theodosius travelled as far as Verona in Italy to make clear his support for Valentinian II and his regime, that represents a copyist's mistake in the fifth-century compilation of imperial laws. On the contrary, an orator like Themistius could trumpet Theodosius' intention of restoring order on the Rhine, while in reality the emperor never left the Balkans and may not even have met Valentinian when the latter's court travelled to Aquileia in September of that year.

Like that of Gratian a decade earlier, the court of Valentinian found itself more dependent than it would have liked on the senatorial aristocracy of the city of Rome. Petronius Probus, who had haunted the highest reaches of imperial office for decades under many different regimes, had returned to power as the praetorian prefect of Italy, Illyricum and Africa at the same time that Maximus revolted. Probus was the grand old man of the Christian Anicii, but the government at Mediolanum courted his pagan fellow senators just as assiduously: Quintus Aurelius Symmachus assumed the urban prefecture in Rome and Vettius Agorius Praetextatus – the same man who had joked with pope Damasus about becoming a Christian if he could be bishop of Rome – replaced Probus as praetorian prefect of Italy and Illyricum in 384 and was designated western consul for 385, although he died before he could take up the honour. Much has been made of the efforts of the unsuccessful request by Symmachus, in his role as praetorian prefect, to have the altar of the goddess Victory restored to the Senate House in Rome, a move objected to by Christian senators who found a champion in Ambrose: he ominously threatened excommunication if Valentinian were to commit an act of such great apostasy. The episode, which was not a major one, has often been blown wildly out of proportion as a sign of a 'pagan revival' among the senatorial aristocracy of Rome, a picture woven out of various pieces of disparate evidence that do not in fact make a single whole. That a few tremendously powerful senators were ostentatiously non-Christian is evidence of neither a pagan 'party' nor a senatorial hostility to the Christianity of the court; rather, it represents the sentimental nostalgia for a dying world that one finds in *Brideshead Revisited* or *The Leopard*.

Far more significant were the struggles between different ecclesiastical factions, and here Ambrose proved himself a master of spiritual flummery that could check any opposition he might face. Valentinian and Justina's palatine troops, many of whom seem to have been Goths (or at least to have been slandered as such by our hostile witnesses), were homoians like Justina. When, in 385, the court decided to concede some extramural churches to homoians so that they could worship in one another's company, Ambrose led his congregants in a riot. The bishop's response was even more outraged after the imperial court issued a law in January 386 conceding many rights to the homoians, and the court actually backed down in April in the face of his agitation. Finally, in June, Ambrose appropriated to himself the dividends that holiness paid: he was directed by divine inspiration to discover the remains of two hitherto unknown protomartyrs, a certain Gervasius and Protasius, whose relics duly proceeded to perform miracles for his enthusiastic congregation.

It is important for us to place this display in the context of Roman aristocratic showmanship. Ambrose came from that world – he may have been a distant relative of Symmachus, in fact, though from a family that had suffered confiscations in 340 after picking the wrong side in the civil war between Constantine's sons – and he had governed a province before he became bishop. He knew how to work a crowd, and how to leverage the patronage of a vast clientele to his political advantage. The bishop's humbling of the court, in much the same way that he would later control Theodosius, is a reminder of how different the ecclesiastical landscape of Italy was in comparison to the East. The Italian homoians were a small group, mostly of Balkan origin, and easily isolated by a large congregation of Nicenes vociferously supporting their charismatic bishop; in Constantinople, by contrast, Theodosius had found himself supporting a Nicene party that lacked the support of the majority of the populace, and found it a challenge to impose his will on the church.

Ambrose, as he staged his propaganda victories over Valentinian, had one eye on the court of Maximus. The latter had been making a big show of Nicene orthodoxy – easy enough in Gaul where there was not even a minority population of powerful homoians. Right back to the reign of Constans, the youngest of Constantine's sons and successors, who had sheltered Athanasius of Alexandria in the many exiles to which Constantius had consigned him, the Gallic episcopate had been consistent in its theological position and constitutionally disinclined to the subtleties that its Greek counterpart would insist upon bringing into theological talks. Maximus, like his rivals a product of the camps but with no real experience outside the West, was unlikely to break from the western norm. The staunchness with which he pursued a Nicene line came naturally enough, and also helped nicely to distinguish him from his Italian rival. In only one respect would his policy backfire on him. In Spain, a diocese that has rarely concerned us in this book because it rarely concerned imperial politics, a dispute had broken out in the late 370s among various bishops in the diocese about what approach should be taken to the teaching of a pious aristocrat named Priscillianus.

This Priscillian (as he is called in English) was a highly educated layman whose spiritual conversion led him to embrace a form of Christianity characterised by an extreme asceticism, but one that did not also require an eremitical existence away from the common crowd. In fact, Priscillian's appeal to people of his own social rank was precisely what set off the fears of the Spanish church hierarchy, for this entrepreneurial holy man was encouraging his peers to private worship in their country villas and rural estates, rather than in the towns, where the bishops could keep an eye on them. Bishops Hyginus of Corduba and Hydatius of Emerita Augusta, respectively the capitals of Baetica and Lusitania, ranged themselves against Priscillian and in 380 called a council at Caesaraugusta (Zaragoza) to consider his views.

The small number of bishops they assembled, mainly from Spain but with some outliers from Aquitania across the Pyrenees, condemned various practices in which Priscillian and his followers were believed to engage, though Priscillian himself did not attend. Instead, a couple of his episcopal supporters – obscure clerics of much lower rank than his enemies – ordained Priscillian bishop of Abila (now Ávila, famous for its much later saint Teresa, but then an obscure country village, deliberately chosen as Priscillian's see for just that reason). The provocation was too great for his enemies. They wrote to Gratian, still alive at the time, accusing Priscillian of being a Manichee – a charge that could prove deadly were it to stick, because pagans and Christians of all persuasions could agree that Mani's dualist religion, brought from Persia to Rome in the third century, was an abomination. Gratian had replied with a generic condemnation of Manichees, reaffirming the anti-Manichaean laws already in place, but failing to address the specifics.

Priscillian understood the threat facing him and sailed for Rome, seeking an audience first with Damasus, and then with Ambrose at Mediolanum, and being admitted to the presence of neither. His supporters did, however, secure a hearing with Gratian's *magister officiorum* Macedonius, a personal enemy of Ambrose, who persuaded the emperor in favour of

Priscillian. He and his allies returned to Spain and their petty sees and the matter might well have rested there, or at least faded into the provincial shadows, had Maximus not staged his coup. Priscillian's enemies seized the opportunity to bring the case to the new emperor, a Spaniard himself and ostentatiously Nicene; he duly commanded that a council be held at Burdigala, surely knowing that its outcome would be appealed, and Priscillian was then tried by the emperor himself at Treveri, despite the protestations of several powerful bishops, including the saintly Martin of Turonum (Tours). The trial, as it happened, was not for heresy (that was a matter for churchmen and their councils), but for sorcery. Found guilty, Priscillian was put to death along with several followers, which opened a nasty schism between those bishops who had accused Priscillian and those who, though thinking him a heretic, could not countenance the interference of a secular judge in an ecclesiastical case.

Ambrose, like the more charismatic but politically less canny Martin, was among those who protested Maximus' presumption, but while Martin kept as much distance from the usurper as he could, Ambrose's hunger for factional advantage kept him in communication with the usurper's court at Treveri, even as he continued to deal with the court of Justina and Valentinian at Mediolanum. But there is no real question that it was the former that most Italian bishops would have favoured, given a choice. This influenced Maximus' next move, a lightning assault across the Alps early in 387. As had very often previously been the case, the rest of Italy collapsed swiftly following the capture of the northern plain. Justina and her son fled with their court to Aquileia, and thence to seek shelter with Theodosius in the East, so that Valentinian would now become the pawn of the eastern rather than the western emperor. Thessalonica became the exiles' new residence and a dynastic connection was swiftly arranged: Theodosius married Galla, the daughter of Valentinian I and Justina, and the offspring of that union would keep the Valentinianic line alive for another two generations. In Italy, Maximus took up residence in Mediolanum, claiming the consulship for the next year and receiving a delegation from the Roman Senate welcoming him enthusiastically. The eastern emperor moved to secure the Balkan provinces and claimed nominal control of all Illyricum, although the northern diocese of Pannonia clearly remained in the hands of Maximus' supporters.

The plan of attack was simple: Theodosius would march with an army along the main invasion route across the Balkans and through the Julian

Alps, while Valentinian and Justina would sail from Thessalonica to Rome. The eastern emperor would thereby restore his new brother-in-law to his rightful throne. Early in 388, Theodosius' four senior generals, Timasius, Promotus, Arbogastes and Richomeres, routed Maximus' forces first at Siscia, where the Kupa and Sava rivers meet. They did so again at Poetovio (Ptuj, on the Drava in Slovenia), where Maximus' brother Marcellinus was killed on the battlefield. Maximus attempted to hold Aquileia on the other side of the Julian Alps, but he had too few troops to withstand a siege. He surrendered to Flavius Arbogastes and was promptly executed. While the fighting was still ongoing, Justina died, relieving Theodosius of any rival for control of Valentinian.

When he arrived in northern Italy, Theodosius stripped his new subjects of any honours they had received from Maximus' regime and declared the usurper's laws null and void. He also reformed the western administration, installing his eastern supporter Trifolius – formerly his *comes sacrarum largitionum* – as praetorian prefect of Italy and Illyricum. This made very clear where the real authority in the empire was going to lie, regardless of Valentinian's technical status as senior augustus. But, as always happened in this phase of Roman history, the regional factions were stronger and more enduring than any individual, even the emperor. Trifolius might hold the prefecture, but the old Gratianic high command began to reconstitute itself, led by a close relative of Gratian's staunch supporter Flavius Bauto, Flavius Arbogastes, who was given the senior *magisterium* in the west.

Never a natural campaigner, Theodosius ceded control of mopping-up operations to Arbogastes while himself remaining in Italy. The general invaded Gaul in the later part of 388 and met little resistance from the surviving supporters of Maximus. At Treveri, Maximus' son Victor, theoretically co-augustus with his father even though he was only five years old, was strangled to death on Arbogastes' orders. Arbogastes then launched a punitive strike against some Franks who had used the distraction of the civil war to raid the provinces of Belgica. Even with that, however, the river defences in northern Gaul, weakened by the withdrawal of troops for Maximus' invasion of Italy, were not now fully restored. The western field army was also reduced in size, with Theodosius commandeering several crack units of its *comitatenses* to incorporate into the still weakened eastern field army.

When the year 389 began, both living augusti were residing at

Mediolanum. The consuls of the year were two of the eastern generals, Timasius and Promotus, who had helped Theodosius to victory. The emperor continued to seed the Italian government with his supporters and, in June, Valentinian was sent to Treveri, where he would be out of the way. Only then did Theodosius travel to Rome, where he made his *adventus* (ceremonial entry) on 13 July. He remained there for over a month amid much public reconciliation of senators who had sided with Maximus – as indeed most had. Symmachus, who had delivered a panegyric to Maximus only a year before, was magnanimously pardoned. The way for these gestures had been prepared by the appointment of Ceionius Rufius Albinus as urban prefect. Albinus came from one of the great senatorial families: his great-grandfather had held a consulate under Maxentius in the early fourth century, and had survived to become urban prefect under Constantine; his grandfather and namesake was urban prefect in 335, the year he shared the consulship with Constantine's half-brother; and his father had been prefect of Gaul under Constantius, before going on to be the first of Valentinian's urban prefects at Rome. Even if most of them had supported a usurper, Theodosius needed to conciliate the Roman aristocracy as a group, and it was men like Albinus, a fourth-generation urban prefect, who could swing the rest of the Senate behind them.

The emperor formally presented his 4-year-old son Honorius to the Senate and people of Rome. Forming part of the ceremony was one of the longest Latin panegyrics preserved from the fourth century, delivered by a Gallic orator called Drepanius Pacatus, a friend and client of Gratian's old tutor and prefect Ausonius. This won Pacatus enough favour to gain him the proconsulate of Africa, the most coveted post in a senator's career apart from the urban prefecture itself. The speech was quite typical of its genre, fulsome in praising Theodosius for restoring liberty after the tyrant's defeat, and stressing the emperor's paternal care for his new brother-in-law Valentinian – although throughout it there is not the slightest doubt that Theodosius was the only emperor that mattered, very much as he would have wanted it.

While Theodosius remained in the West, government of the East was largely in the hands of Eutolmius Tatianus, a man whose career had begun under Constantius and who had seen service under every emperor since then. Theodosius had made Tatianus praetorian prefect before departing to the West, and kept him in that post as long as he was away. A native of Lycia, Tatianus is a good illustration of another growing distinction between East and West: unlike the great senators with whom Theodosius was treating at Rome, Tatianus came from a family of no real account, entered the service of a provincial governor as his *assessor*, or chief clerk, from which position he was able to rise to a provincial governorship and become *praefectus Augustalis* (the eccentric name given to the *vicarius* of Egypt). From that post, he became *comes sacrarum largitionum*, one of the two senior financial officials in the East. Through all of these posts he accumulated wealth, connections and clients, but the independent power base that an aristocrat like Ceionius Albinus could take for granted as prefect of Rome simply did not exist for a man like Tatianus. That fact bound him and others like him much more closely to the structures of imperial government, and gave them greater incentives to sustain them than western senators tended to have. This relative strength of elites' investment in government is another striking difference between East and West, and one that would increase in significance in the coming century.

Having honoured Rome with his presence, Theodosius had no intention of remaining. He left the city on 30 August and returned to Mediolanum, which was his main residence for the rest of 389 and most of 390, in which year the otherwise powerless Valentinian shared the consulate with Flavius Neoterius, one of the trusted civilian administrators whom Theodosius had brought with him from the East. Whatever Theodosius' plans had been before he set out westwards, the difficulty of governing the entire empire, particularly its more restive regions, from a north Italian base was brought forcibly home to him in April 390.

In Thessalonica, as in most substantial cities of the empire, circus racing was at the very centre of public social life, and popular charioteers were the footballers and pop stars of their day. Early in 390, Flavius Buthericus, the *magister militum per Illyricum*, had arrested a charioteer who had attempted to rape a servant belonging to Buthericus. The mob in the circus demanded the charioteer's release and, when Buthericus refused, they started a violent riot in which the general and many of his troops were lynched. Theodosius got word of this not long afterwards and flew into a rage, ordering the execution of the offending citizenry. Units of the Illyrian army carried out the order with gusto. One source – the church historian Theoderet, not terribly reliable – puts the number of dead, trapped in the circus and systematically massacred, at 7,000.

Ambrose, no doubt genuinely shocked, chose this moment to demonstrate his dominance over yet another emperor. He had already publicly remonstrated with Theodosius once, over an imperial decision in the previous year. In the eastern frontier town of Callinicum (now the devastated city of Raqqa in Syria), Nicene zealots had rioted and torn down a Jewish synagogue and a church of rival Christians. Theodosius had commanded the Nicene bishop of the town to repair the buildings at his own expense and to punish the offending members of his flock; it did not matter that Jews and heretics had been targeted, the rioting was an offence against public order. To protest this decision, Ambrose preached a sermon in the imperial presence: the emperor's favour and protection was owed only to the orthodox; heretics and Jews neither deserved nor should expect it. On that occasion, Theodosius gave way with good grace and allowed the Nicene vandals of Callinicum to go unpunished. But after the slaughter at Thessalonica, Ambrose flexed his muscles far more vigorously. He publicly rebuked the emperor in an open letter and closed the doors of Mediolanum's churches to him, refusing him communion. Theodosius was thus constrained to undertake a penance of eight months, a part of which he spent in Verona, the other great military centre of the north Italian plains, and mercifully lacking an overweening bishop. In August, still at Verona, he issued a law to the effect that capital judgements should entail an automatic 30-day stay of execution, so that the events of Thessalonica could not be repeated. Not until December was he welcomed back into the communion of the church of Mediolanum, with a public reconciliation of emperor and bishop on Christmas Day.

We should not underestimate the extent to which the theatrics of Ambrose, once begun, were ultimately welcomed by the emperor as well: far from the abject humiliation of secular authority which the episode came to represent for posterity, this was an opportunity for the emperor to publicly show himself a pious Christian who had won the full support of an Italian church that had much preferred the fallen usurper to the young emperor whose side Theodosius had taken in the recent civil war. At the same time, it shows how central the episcopate had become to political life. Constantine and Constantius had felt entirely free to do as they pleased with their bishops, although they often chose not to. By the 380s, the respect and popular support commanded by a bishop like Ambrose meant that there was no possibility of ignoring or evading his wishes.

The following year, 391, opened with the loyal Tatianus becoming consul prior (the one whose name came first in the annual dating formula) and Symmachus, in token of his reconciliation, consul posterior. That honour had its own bitter sting, however, for Theodosius had already two years earlier refused to permit the restoration of the altar of Victory in the Roman Senate House. Now, in February 391, he took a step that went much further than any emperor had yet done in confirming the empire's essential Christianity: on 23 February the emperor banned all pagan cult, in a law addressed to none other than Ceionius Albinus, still prefect of Rome and a member of the same social circle as Symmachus. The ban was extended later in the year to include private households, and penalties were laid down for those who persisted in honouring their household gods, the *lares* and the *penates*. It is tempting to see this as the inevitable culmination of a process that had begun with Constantine's (probable) ban on temple cult in the East. More likely, however, it marks Theodosius' personal journey from a relative indifference to theology to becoming a convinced Nicene.

Ambrose, as we shall see, went from strength to strength, and ever since Damasus of Rome had died in 384, he no longer had any serious rival as the most senior and important bishop in Italy. In the larger trajectory of Christian history, he is something of a transitional figure. No longer beholden to the emperor in the same way that the imperial bishops of the Constantinian period had been, he nevertheless relied upon his reputation for learning, his deeply authoritative voice and his class-based right to command as the basis of his power. What he did not particularly have was the reputation for ostentatious personal sanctity that was an alternative source of spiritual authority growing in significance in this period.

Across the Alps in Gaul, for instance, Martin, bishop of Turonum, was, if not the most powerful, then certainly the most famous of the Gallic bishops. Turonum was not a major administrative centre or closely linked to imperial authority, so the power inherent in its bishopric was less than that of cities like Treveri or Arelate, where the presence of imperial administrators had a magnifying effect on the status of local bishops, even those who were themselves mediocrities. But, despite this, Martin was one of the celebrities of his age: the son of an officer in the *comitatenses*, he had been born early in the century in Pannonia and raised in Ticinum (modern Pavia), one of northern Italy's garrison towns, where he entered military service as soon as he was old enough, After years in the army, he had some sort of conversion experience while serving in Gaul: the famous hagiographic legend is that Christ appeared to him in the form of a suffering, unclothed beggar, and Martin drew his sword and cut his own military cloak in half to clothe the beggar. After this, he realised that military service was incompatible with his Christian belief, and was discharged from the army, surviving a period of exile to establish a monastery near Pictavium (Poitiers) from which he was later called to become bishop of Turonum. Unlike Ambrose, who had demonstrated his sanctity by discovering the relics of Protasius and Gervasius, Martin's reputation for personal asceticism generated the belief that he himself was capable of working miracles. Martin's sanctity was not always enough, though – as we have seen, his intervention promoting leniency towards the Priscillianists met with no success. Yet Martin also represents an alternative model of Christian leadership that had not really existed when Constantine became emperor, a model that would long outlast the structures of the empire itself.

Ambrose's model of Christian leadership, as we noted, was transitional, and not just in contrast to ascetic masters like Martin. Ambrose also represented a level of Roman cosmopolitanism that was beginning to fade during his lifetime. He came from a social background that had meant education in Greek language and literature. This high cultural ideal of bilingualism went back to the Republic and early empire, when Latin elites continued to learn Greek even when, as often, Greek elites failed to reciprocate by learning Latin. Ambrose was not a deeply original thinker, but his aristocratic education made him a powerful reader of Greek theological texts, and one who could translate them meaningfully into a Latin context, not in the sense of literal translation but by repurposing Greek ideas for a new audience. It is through Ambrose that the theological ideas of the Cappadocian fathers – Gregory of Nyssa, Gregory of Nazianzus and, in particular, Basil of Caesarea – were diffused into the discourse of Latin churchmen and continued to have an influence into the Middle Ages.

But Ambrose's level of Greek literacy was becoming rarer among Latin speakers. It survived among the great senators of Rome, some of whom made a lot of antiquarian fuss out of their love for the classics of Greek and Latin literature. Among the general run of the Latin West's well-connected *honestiores*, however, the need to learn Greek had largely disappeared, and so the mechanisms for teaching it became more limited. In the early empire, and even under the Antonines, when imperial offices were relatively few in number and senatorial status meant residing in Italy, it was much easier to sustain a single, normative ruling culture, requiring fluency in the classic works of both the Greek and Latin worlds. But with the expansion of imperial government down to the provincial and municipal levels, a man could join the imperial government without uprooting himself from his home, and so there was less call for such a universally shared high culture reaching from one end of the empire to the other.

The language of Roman government had always been Latin, and that never changed, even if official communications were usually made available in Greek form in the eastern provinces so that the *bouletai* and other local worthies had no need to learn the western language. The universal extension of Roman law across the third century, however, had meant a much deeper penetration of Latin into the local government of the eastern provinces. Greek speakers ambitious of imperial service even near to home needed to learn Latin, something loudly lamented by learned fourth-century Hellenes like Libanius of Antioch. There was not, any longer, a corresponding need for Latin speakers to do the reverse, and so many did not.

We may take as our example of this phenomenon a much younger contemporary of Ambrose, Aurelius Augustinus, known to posterity as Saint Augustine. Perhaps the best known of all the fathers of the church, still the subject of pious reverence among Catholics and Anglicans, and arguably the author of the first true autobiography in western history, Augustine came from the minor town of Thagaste in Numidia. He was born to a Christian mother named Monica and a pagan father, Patricius, a modestly connected member of the town's governing class. The family was well enough off that Augustine could expect a decent education, and so he was sent to study with a grammarian in Madaurus, a municipality not far from Thagaste. The boy proved talented, and a wealthier citizen of Thagaste sponsored the teenaged Augustine's journey to Carthage, where he studied rhetoric – and was exposed to all the cultural diversions of the big city. Though he had been raised a Christian – his pagan father had been sympathetic enough to the religion to accept conversion on his deathbed – he found the racy, illicit esotericism of the Manichees deeply seductive. At Carthage he carried raffishly on, as a young man will when living on someone else's penny, but he still proved exceptionally good at his studies. He took a concubine, whose name we never learn, but who would in time bear him a son named Adeodatus.

A typical member of the municipal class, Augustine returned to Thagaste in the mid 370s to teach grammar, and then went on to open a school of rhetoric in Carthage, where he remained for the better part of a decade. In 383, he moved to Rome, where he won the patronage of Symmachus thanks to an introduction from his Manichean friends. Symmachus got the young teacher an endowed chair of rhetoric in the imperial city of Mediolanum, and there he found that ascetic Christianity attracted him nearly as much as his Manichean enthusiasms had previously done. He had brought his mother Monica with him and, as a provincial matron on the make, she brokered him a good marriage for which he abandoned his concubine of many years in 385. But before his betrothed could come of age, he experienced a moment of conversion: as he was walking contemplatively in a garden, so he tells us, he heard a voice urging him to pick up and read the Bible. Opening the book to Paul's Letter to the Ephesians, he saw the revealed truth, and there and then decided to devote himself to the Christian God and His orthodoxy. He broke off his engagement, was baptised by Ambrose in 387, and prepared to return to Africa with his mother and his son.

Monica died before their ship sailed from Ostia, but Augustine returned to his home, sold off the family property to serve the poor, and founded a monastic community for which he wrote a communal ascetic rule. Before long, his fame as a preacher against Manichees, Donatists and heretics led him first to the priesthood, and then to the bishopric of Hippo Regius, a coastal city in Africa Proconsularis. It was here, for nearly forty years, that he became indisputably the most important churchman in the Latin West, and perhaps the most prolific and influential Latin author in history.

And yet he had no Greek (or so basic a level as to barely count) and his career was entirely western in its focus and influence. For all that Augustine's ecclesiastical fame would eventually reach far and wide, his impact on the development of the Greek church was minimal, and many of his ideas were ignored or dismissed altogether in the Greek world, when they were known at all. And for all that he was deeply involved in the politics of the African church, and in lobbying for imperial support in ending the schism between Caecilianists and Donatists, he was never a political force in the same way that Ambrose was. To put it somewhat differently, Ambrose was a man of the Constantinian empire, whose power was simultaneously his own, that of his class position, and that conferred by the imperial stature of his bishopric. Augustine, by contrast, was an early manifestation of a future world, one in which the genuinely independent powers of bishops rested on foundations of their own making.

Greek bishops never developed quite the same independence of action that their Latin peers did, in much the same way that the service aristocracy of the eastern empire could exercise much less independence than the senatorial *rentiers* of the West. This sort of east–west distinction widened in the last years of Theodosius' reign. When Theodosius left Mediolanum for the East in 391, there were three reigning augusti – Valentinian II, Theodosius and Arcadius, in decreasing order of seniority – but there was no question but that Theodosius himself was the sole ruling emperor. In part for that reason, it has long been scholarly practice to call Theodosius the ruler of a united Roman empire – indeed, the last of such rulers. At best a simplification, that is really a fundamental distortion. We have already seen how, since the time of the Valentiniani, the two halves of the empire had been fundamentally separate spheres of action that influenced events in the other from time to time. This pattern was intensified by the dominance of the regional palatine and military establishments, and by the increasingly ambiguous position of the central Balkan dioceses: Pannonia was clearly part of the western empire, and Thrace just as clearly part of the East, but the status of the Dacian and Macedonian dioceses – between them taking in some of the empire's worst trouble spots as well as the dividing line between Greek and Latin speakers – would remain a problem for decades.

Theodosius left Mediolanum in late April or May 391, and spent all of the next month in Aquileia, addressing a whole series of laws to his eastern officials in preparation for his own return. He arrived in Constantinople in July, and in early autumn he travelled to Thessalonica, from which base he campaigned against 'bandits', who may have been mutinous soldiers or possibly some of the Goths settled in 382 – or indeed both.

He returned again to Constantinople in early November and spent the next two years there. Much of the legislation that survives from this period concerns the church, and we can perhaps see in that pattern a foreshadowing of later Byzantine emperors, with their dual focus on the city of Constantinople and its church, as well as other churches across the eastern empire. The ceremonial life of Constantinople was ever more elaborately Christianised in this period, never more so than when Theodosius received a most precious relic, the head of John the Baptist: wrapping its reliquary in his own purple cloak, he led the 7-mile-long procession from the city to the mustering field at the Hebdomon, where a new church had recently been built on his orders to honour the sacred relic. The health of the emperor, the health of the empire, and the health of the Christian community were increasingly indistinguishable under Theodosius, and it was during this period, too, that Rufinus, formerly *magister officiorum*, replaced old Tatianus in the emperor's favour, becoming praetorian prefect of the East in late 392.

In the West, meanwhile, effective rulership was in the hands of the *magister militum* for Gaul, Flavius Arbogastes, and the praetorian prefect of Italy and Illyricum, Virius Nicomachus Flavianus, a member of the highest senatorial aristocracy of Rome. These grandees of military and civilian life did not much care for each other but, by keeping the Alps between them, they were able to rub along well enough, and the West was relatively quiet in the year between Theodosius' departure and early 392.

Valentinian II, now resident in Vienne, is a figure all but invisible to us, aged eighteen but as powerless in the hands of others as he had always been. It was a grim and humiliating position to be in for a child all but born in the purple. Anxious to take control of his own affairs, he attempted to dismiss Arbogastes from his command, personally handing the *magister militum* an order depriving him of his office. The *magister* laughed in the emperor's face and tore up the document – Valentinian had not appointed him, he said, and Valentinian could not dismiss him. That reveals the true extent of Theodosius' control, but also the degree to which the military and civilian high commands were able to dictate their own terms. In frustration and despair, Valentinian killed himself: his body was found in the palace at Vienne on 15 May 392. Rumours of murder immediately surfaced, as they were bound to, but the probable truth is that Arbogastes drove over the edge a young man who had never experienced autonomy, and had suddenly realised that he never would.

Be that as it may, the imperial suicide put Arbogastes in a difficult position. He was himself far too senior an officer to contemplate seizing the throne: as we have seen, only officers of middling rank could safely don the purple. One had to be well-connected, but neither senior nor powerful enough to threaten the high command or the palatine establishments. If he seized the purple, there was little chance of Flavianus' Italian regime accepting him, and Theodosius would not tolerate as distinguished and independent an officer as Arbogastes as a colleague. So the general temporised, asking Theodosius to send his elder son Arcadius to serve as the western emperor, with nothing else changed. He demonstrated the seriousness of his proposal and the extent of his loyalty by minting new coins in the name of just the two augusti, Theodosius and Arcadius. But when Theodosius was unmoved, Arbogastes turned to Eugenius, a teacher of rhetoric at the court, declaring him emperor on 22 August. He continued to hope for the best. Though he had a new emperor of his own, he continued to recognise Theodosius and Arcadius and to mint coins in the name of three augusti. Valentinian's remains were sent back to Mediolanum with due solemnity and bishop Ambrose was asked to mediate between the regimes of Eugenius and Theodosius.

Those efforts came to nothing. Theodosius refused to recognise the new western emperor, taking the consulate of 393 for himself, alongside the eastern general Flavius Abundantius, and promoting his younger son Honorius to the rank of augustus on 23 January of that year. This implied a decision to go to war; the only question was the timing. Theodosian laws of 393 suggest preparations for a substantial campaign and, as consuls for the coming year, Theodosius designated Arcadius for the third time and Honorius for the second, though they went unrecognised in the West. The death of the empress Galla in childbirth at Constantinople on 29 April had made it less important for Theodosius to honour the memory of the Valentinianic dynasty, but that fact did not make him any more hospitable to Eugenius and his patron Arbogastes. The latter, seeing that the eastern regime was now implacable, had patched up an alliance with Nicomachus Flavianus in Italy. The Roman Senate recognised Eugenius, and so Flavianus continued his praetorian prefecture as the representative of a new emperor. It was a curious alliance between the townhouses of Rome and the barracks of the camps, reminiscent of that between Petronius Probus and the Pannonian general Equitius twenty years before.

It was not, however, an alliance in aid of a 'pagan revival', the defiant uprising and last stand of aristocratic pagan opposition to the stifling Christian orthodoxy of Theodosius. That interpretation, of long standing in the scholarship, has now been comprehensively exploded. It is true that Eugenius and Arbogastes were both non-Christians, but that was not uncommon among the military high command or teachers of rhetoric. It is also true that Flavianus was one of the more flamboyant among the pagan senators of Rome. But this was not a cohesive alliance of like-minded pagans. It was an old-fashioned civil war between regimes that could find no path to reconciliation or cooperation. When it came, despite being well prepared, Arbogastes and Flavianus lost. Lacking the troops to meet an invasion in Pannonia, and mindful of the failure of Maximus that he had helped to engineer, Arbogastes concentrated on defending the Julian Alps against Theodosius' invasion, which began in August 394. The emperor left his elder son, the adolescent (though legally adult) Arcadius, in the charge of Rufinus, the prefect who had succeeded Tatianus as Theodosius' most trusted civilian official. With Persia still neutered by the disputes among Shapur's successors, the emperor felt able to take almost the whole of the eastern field army with him against Eugenius and his supporters. This force was still smaller than it had been before Valens' debacle at Adrianople and, as in the campaign against Maximus, additional units were recruited from the Gothic settlers of 382: they fought under their own native officers, without being incorporated into the *comitatenses*, something that would have as yet unforeseeable consequences.

The Theodosian armies passed through the Balkans without opposition, as Arbogastes had planned that they should, but the battle that proved decisive was joined at the Frigidus on 5 and 6 September 394. The precise location of the battle remains unknown: Frigidus just means 'Cold River', of which there is no shortage between Emona (modern Ljubljana) and Aquileia. While some have argued for a battle on the river Soča (Isonzo), a site along the Vipava or one of its tributaries like the Hubelj or the Bela, all now in Slovenia, is much more likely. It was a bloody and close-fought affair. On the first day, Theodosius allowed his Gothic auxiliaries to absorb the brunt of the casualties, but night still fell on a Theodosian defeat. But then, on the second day, a massive wind – the Bora, for which the region is well known – blew up into the faces of Arbogastes' men, making it hard for them to fight, and rendering barrages of arrows ineffectual. In the end, they collapsed in a rout. Eugenius was captured and immediately executed. Arbogastes and Flavianus fled the field, both then taking their own lives rather than face the victor's certain wrath. There was no further resistance, and from the field of the Frigidus, Theodosius moved on to Mediolanum. He swiftly reconciled himself to the Roman Senate yet again, declining to conduct purges despite the blatant disloyalty that so many senators had shown by siding with Eugenius so very soon after the defeat of Maximus. As if to illustrate this signal leniency, the consulship of Olybrius and Probinus, offspring of the Anicii, the Senate's most illustrious family, inaugurated the new year of 395.

Before he could celebrate his *dies imperii* at the end of January 395, Theodosius suddenly fell ill and died, leaving the 10-year old Honorius and the teenaged Arcadius as his heirs; but Arcadius was back in Constantinople, under the thumb of the prefect Rufinus, which left Honorius as the only descendant on the spot. Control of the western government was therefore seized by an altogether more senior member of the dynasty, Flavius Stilicho, the husband of Theodosius' niece Serena. Ambrose gave a bravura performance in his funerary speech for the dead emperor, one that cautiously recognised this political fait accompli – as well it might, for Stilicho held all the cards. He had been one of the senior *magistri militum* on the campaign against Eugenius, and remained as the *magister militum praesentalis* while Theodosius was reestablishing his authority in Italy. With the emperor dead, he announced himself as guardian of both remaining augusti, Arcadius and Honorius. That had an entirely predictable effect: the eastern and western high commands, having managed to wage two hot wars against each other twice in less than a decade, now descended into a long cold war between Stilicho in the West and a succession of Arcadius' would-be puppet-masters in the East. As a result, the three decades between 395 and 425 were among the most disturbed in Roman imperial history.

6

STILICHO AND
HIS RIVALS

Theodosius left two heirs, one a child, one a teenager. In an earlier century, this would almost have guaranteed a usurpation, but no longer. Effective control of government was in the hands of the military high command and its allies in the prefectural and palatine bureaucracies. These needed an emperor to give a face to the government, and to provide symbolic legitimacy. But they no longer needed an emperor who could actually lead them. Arcadius and Honorius, the sons of a respected and intermittently effective ruler, were perfectly acceptable to the men who were really in charge and who could now strike deals among themselves to parcel out the prime commands. Stilicho and Rufinus, the most powerful men in the West and the East respectively, are an interesting study in similarities.

Rufinus was a Gaul, from the minor province of Novempopulana (today the French Basque country north of the Pyrenees). His rise to power is almost invisible to us, but Theodosius appointed him *magister officiorum* in 388, in time for the campaign against Maximus, and he aggressively extended the powers of that office, raising its formal rank above that of formerly senior palatine officials like the *quaestor*. He was on good terms with powerful and well-connected men in both halves of the empire, appearing in the letter collections of both the Antiochene sophist Libanius and the Roman senator Symmachus. Rufinus was with

Theodosius throughout the Maximus campaign, accompanying him on his Roman journey of 389 and urging him to do penance and reconcile with Ambrose after the massacre at Thessalonica. When the emperor returned to Constantinople, Rufinus engineered the demotion of two long-serving generals, Timasius and Promotus, the victors of the Maximus campaign, both with careers stretching back to the reigns of the Valentiniani. Not long thereafter, he replaced the similarly long-serving praetorian prefect Tatianus, driving him into prudent exile.

Stilicho, who replaced Promotus after the latter's fall from grace, was the son of a cavalry officer from the time of Valens whom later hostile sources identify as a Vandal. Well-connected in the military establishment of the eastern empire, Stilicho's father married a Roman woman, presumably also of a military family, and was able to get his son a prized tribunate and service on a prestigious embassy to Persia in the early 380s. After that, the young officer married Theodosius' niece Serena, and was given the office of *comes stabuli*, a high-profile palatine appointment that marked him out for higher things. By 385 or so he had become *comes domesticorum*, which meant he commanded the imperial bodyguard during the Maximus campaign. He then won promotion to *magisterium militum* at the same time that Rufinus was promoted to the rank of praetorian prefect. All of this suggests that by the latter part of the 380s, and even more so after the war with Maximus, Theodosius was systematically promoting men whose rise to power was associated primarily with his own reign, and not that of his predecessors or rivals. When the Eugenius campaign began, Arcadius was left behind in the charge of Rufinus, who was to look after the affairs of the East, while Stilicho was one of the two chief commanders in the war against Arbogastes and Eugenius.

Since the empress Galla had died in 394, just before her husband, Stilicho and Serena were now the young emperors' only living adult relatives. No one disputed that Honorius was commended to their care by their dying relative. But Stilicho claimed – perhaps quite truthfully – that Theodosius had commended both Arcadius and Honorius to his guardianship, and the same thing was publicly stated in Ambrose's funerary speech for the dead emperor. Yet Stilicho's claim could not fail to provoke the hostility of Rufinus. Our extant eastern sources, none contemporary, report that Rufinus was guardian of the 17-year-old Arcadius (though he was legally an adult and did not actually need a guardian), just as Stilicho was for the much younger Honorius, which suggests that this was the line put about by Rufinus and his palatine establishment. In January 395, Stilicho held most of the good cards: he had the emperor's body; he had one of the emperor's sons; and he had both the empire's field armies, though of course these had just recently fought a war against each other. He also had an excuse to intervene in eastern affairs.

Early in 395, possibly shortly after Theodosius' death, the native officer Alaric mutinied, along with the auxiliary unit of Goths he commanded. Not only had his men suffered extraordinary casualties at the battle of the Frigidus – seemingly as a result of the emperor's deliberate tactical choice – but he was refused the reward he had expected for his service, promotion to a *magisterium* and the command of regular units. That was a consequence of the strange status of the 382 settlers: unlike commanders of barbarian origin recruited directly into the elite units of the *comitatenses* or the palatine *domestici*, the settlers of 382 were trapped permanently in the inferior status of auxiliary troops (what were not yet, but would soon be, called *foederati*, 'federates'). The mutinous Alaric now marched on Constantinople under arms, and began to negotiate with Rufinus, who may have intended to use him as a counter against Stilicho. Our sources blame Rufinus for authorising Alaric to plunder the Balkan provinces, but this canard is certainly a retrospective blackening of Rufinus' memory (similar things were alleged about Stilicho after the latter's fall). More likely, Rufinus refused to negotiate because Constantinople itself was basically impregnable, and so Alaric's followers were forced to live on plunder. Stilicho used that as an excuse to march into the Balkans, ostensibly to suppress Alaric but no doubt also to threaten Rufinus.

Rufinus' response was a clever one. He had Arcadius issue an order recalling the eastern field army (which was needed, not least because of a raid by Huns across the Caucasus and into Asia Minor in July) and he may perhaps have commanded Stilicho himself to retire from Illyricum. Stilicho made a show of compliance, returning to Italy himself, and sending a large number of eastern units back under the command of Flavius Gainas. That was a pragmatic decision, acknowledging that the eastern and western field armies, so recently at war with each other, could not operate effectively together side by side. Gainas marched the eastern units back via the main Balkan highway, arriving two weeks after the body of Theodosius had been returned to Constantinople accompanied by Stilicho's wife Serena and their son Eucherius.

When, on 27 November, Arcadius and Rufinus came out of the city to review the returning troops, Gainas cut Rufinus down in public as a traitor. Whether or not the killing was ordered by Stilicho, it was done with the connivance of the eastern *praepositus sacri cubiculi* Eutropius, the eunuch chief of the emperor's domestic staff, who was very close to Arcadius. It was he who received the vast bulk of Rufinus' confiscated estates, though he allowed Rufinus' wife and daughter to keep some of their property in Jerusalem and retire there. Eutropius hoped to secure his own dominance by marrying Arcadius to Aelia Eudoxia, the daughter of the late Flavius Bauto and thus a cousin of Arbogastes, and a ward of the general Promotus whose destruction Rufinus had engineered. Eudoxia's connection to the great military families would help Eutropius counter the dominance of Stilicho.

To the latter, Eutropius was no more congenial than Rufinus had been. In any case, Stilicho had dynastic plans of his own. As early as 395, he had married Honorius to his elder daughter, Maria, which helped to cement his own role as a member of the imperial dynasty. He then spent 396 in Gaul, attending to the frontier defences, until Alaric gave him another excuse to intervene in the East. Early in 396, Alaric and his supporters invaded mainland Greece via the pass at Thermopylae and plundered as far south as the Peloponnese over the course of the next year or so. They were only deterred when Stilicho arrived in the Peloponnese with part of the western field army. Having sailed across from Italy, he caught Alaric by surprise and drove him north into mountainous Epirus. Eutropius and his regime were outraged by this intervention. Deciding that a menacing but controllable Alaric was infinitely preferable to the fearsome western *magister*, Eutropius conferred on Alaric the *magisterium militum* he had craved for so long. This neatly outflanked Stilicho, who was transformed by this flick of the stylus from the saviour of Greece to a combatant in a civil war against another lawfully commissioned general. To drive that point home, Arcadius' court declared Stilicho *hostis publicus*, a public enemy.

Stilicho knew that he had lost this round and withdrew to Italy. The threat from Alaric remained in abeyance for several years, so it is worth taking a step back from the details of politics and taking a broader view. The larger part of the empire's population – even its elite population – was unaffected by the difficulties at court and on the general staffs. In fact, in many parts of the Latin empire, the second half of the fourth century was one of the richest and most prosperous moments in history. Regions that are today sparsely inhabited and relatively poor were rich, their agricultural wealth exploited by a wealthy landowning elite: the Portuguese Alentejo, for instance – now one of the modern country's least populous and poorest regions, with limited agriculture and even less tourism – was then peppered with hundreds of rural sites, some of them true palaces, set among diverse croplands and vineyards. Sicily, perennially among modern Italy's poorest and least tractable provinces, was at the end of the fourth century a paradise of senatorial wealth. The villa of Casale at Piazza Armerina, built earlier in the century and flourishing at this time, contains some of the most spectacular mosaics to survive from antiquity – amazingly detailed hunting scenes, erotic depictions of sporting women, and so on, across dozens of public and private rooms, covering thousands of square metres. Sites of elaborate rural display are found in many other unlikely places as well – Herefordshire and Gloucestershire in western England, the Cantabrian coast along the Bay of Biscay, the fertile plains around Lake Balaton in Hungary. Only in northern Gaul is there evidence for a decline in prosperity.

There was a close connection between government activity and this rural prosperity. The Roman empire remained, in the fourth century, a machine for transferring food and other primary materials from their places of production to the granaries and warehouses that supplied the state and its armies. All other state activity was subordinate to the working of the *annona*, the supply system for government and army. Most of the empire's capitalist economy was thus linked to and dependent upon the main *annona* routes in one way or another. Commercial goods that flowed alongside the *annona* were then distributed internally and sold on into remoter areas, as were more regional and local products. In Spain, Italy, much of southern Gaul and lowland Britain, the infrastructure of storehouses, way stations and record-keeping fuelled the engines of the local economies. But in northern Gaul, possibly as early as the war against Magnentius and certainly after the reign of Maximus, this system was beginning to fracture, losing the region some of the economic and cultural links to the Mediterranean parts of the empire.

Social change in the countryside took other forms as well, and the later fourth century is when we begin to see a dramatic upsurge of rural Christian sites. Although the peasantry of the Latin West would maintain many non-Christian practices for centuries after the fall of the empire – to the horror of churchmen right down to the eighth century – the great estates of the western elites begin to take on a noticeably Christian aspect from the 370s onwards. We see this in small rural basilicas and cult sites on the lands of western *possessores*, though whether we should interpret these as mainly for the use of the great families themselves or as part of a concerted effort to bring Christianity to the labouring population is unclear. Probably that varied with the intensity of an individual landowner's beliefs, though it seems clear that, outside the very narrow bounds of the Roman Senate itself, western aristocracies had now become overwhelmingly Christian in their outlook, switching their patronage from traditional urban amenities like baths and public entertainments to churches, both urban and rural.

In the East, there seems to have been both a greater Christianisation of the rural population of the villages and a greater survival of Hellenism in the cities at a social level below that of the highest elites. Nevertheless, one dramatic consequence of the Christianisation of eastern society was the development of whole new literary cultures in languages other than Greek. The most striking of these is Syriac, the literary form of Aramaic that flourished in the cities of the imperial hinterland, from the Arabian borders of Egypt up to the headwaters of the Tigris and Euphrates rivers. While literary Syriac began mainly as a vehicle for translating Greek theological works, it was very soon being used to write poetry, history and original works of Christian theology and devotion – for instance, the hymns of Ephrem of Nisibis, attacking Julian and lamenting the loss of his native city to Shapur in the wake of Jovian's humiliating peace. Even fifty years ago, the worlds of Greek and Syriac Christianity tended to be treated in relative isolation, but recent research has made it clear that Greek and Syriac cultures intermingled with one another in a process of constant dialogue. Graeco-Syriac culture in turn influenced neighbouring cultural zones further east, and it is in this way that first the Armenian and then the Georgian languages came to be written and to produce their own texts in a Christian context, Armenian by the early fifth century and Georgian by the later fifth century.

In the sixth century, Arabic began to take shape as a literary language in the zone between the Persian and Roman empires, all to one extent or another part of the cultural efflorescence of the region that began with the Christian Syriac writers of the fourth century. Further south, in the lands surrounding the Red and the Arabian seas, Ge'ez (classical Ethiopian) began to be written as a liturgical language in this same period, as did the Coptic language promoted by the native Egyptian church and its most famous representative, bishop Shenoute of the White Monastery in Upper Egypt. It is all an interesting contrast to the shrinking horizons of the Latin West, and part of the reason that late antiquity is at one and the same time a period of enormous creative growth and also of political decline and fall.

It is the political disruptions of the years after 395 that so contribute to the vision of decline, for, with the exception of the few years between 397 and 401, there was near constant civil war or frontier disturbance until the middle of the 410s. Much, but not all, of the chaos fell on the West, with Gaul, Italy and Pannonia among the worst affected regions. In 397, as we have seen, after the two campaigns of Stilicho, the government of Eutropius had successfully pacified Alaric by giving him the command he so badly desired. Eutropius was busily entrenching his own position, replacing generals of the Theodosian period like Timasius with more pliable creatures of his own.

Unusually for an official in his palatine position, Eutropius took active command of troops, and fought a campaign against a group of Transcaucasian Huns who had got as far as Armenia. This would prove to have momentous consequences, for the raiders whom he defeated retreated through Persian territory, where they were attacked by the shahanshah's troops and most of their booty taken from them. The Roman prisoners of war who thus passed into Persian hands were resettled in Ctesiphon, but the episode sparked an unprecedented period of cooperation between the two empires to safeguard the Caucasian passes against raids from the Eurasian steppe.

The relationship between Ctesiphon and Constantinople was helped by the murder in 399 of Varahran IV, and the succession of Yazdgerd I in that year. Yazdgerd began his reign with a persecution of Christians in his territory, but a Roman embassy led by the *comes sacrarum largitionum* Anthemius (the grandson of Flavius Philippus, praetorian prefect under Constantius II) and Marutha, the bishop of Armenian Sophanene, gained a favourable audience with the king, during which Marutha worked a healing cure that relieved Yazdgerd of his chronic headaches. The king became personally convinced that peace was in the best interests of what were coming to be known among Persians as 'the two eyes of the world', Constantinople and Ctesiphon. Yazdgerd returned many of the Roman prisoners seized from the Hun raiders by Varahran's troops, and the rulers agreed to share the costs of defending the so-called Caspian Gates, chiefly the Dariel and Derbend passes in the centre of the Caucasus mountains.

The hegemony of Eutropius was thus, in many ways, considerably more effective than had been that of Rufinus, and the alliance with Yazdgerd – remembered as a vicious tyrant in the Persian tradition, but with universal respect in the Greek – would last beyond the reign of Arcadius and well into that of his son. Arcadius himself, though fully of an age at which he might have taken a personal role in governing, seems to have lacked any interest in doing so and was not encouraged to develop one. Instead, he occupied himself with the same pious activities favoured by his young wife Eudoxia, though it was she who seems to have had the more public presence, overseeing the transfer of relics to Constantinople and actively suppressing homoian congregations in the city – probably much to the dismay of the many troops of Gothic descent who were homoians and increasingly deprived of places to worship.

Shortly before his successes on the eastern frontier, Eutropius had also intervened in the conflict between Stilicho and the *comes Africae* Gildo. The latter came from the family of Nubel whom we first met during the reign of Valentinian I. Like Nubel, and like his own elder brother Firmus, Gildo effectively straddled the line between Moorish chieftain and Roman aristocrat – his daughter Salvina, for instance, was married to Nebridius, a nephew of Theodosius' first wife Aelia Flacilla. At the same time that he successfully pursued office and power in the Roman system, Gildo maintained a vast private clientele that included tribal frontier peoples whose connections to the empire were tenuous at best. Having been rewarded with a wide-ranging *comitiva Africae*, as well as a *magisterium*, for having betrayed his brother Firmus, Gildo was, along with Stilicho and Rufinus, one of the most powerful men in the empire when Theodosius died.

When Constantinople broke definitively with the regime of Stilicho in 397, Gildo sensed an opportunity to improve his own position, offering to divert the African grain supply away from the city of Rome and to the eastern capital instead. He kept back the grain ships in 398 so that Stilicho had to divert *annona* from Spain and Gaul to supply Rome. The Italian general now plotted his revenge. He commissioned Gildo's brother Mascezel, whose children Gildo had executed in obscure circumstances, to lead an army against him and, in the summer of 398, Mascezel and units of the Gallic *comitatenses* defeated Gildo, who was executed on 31 July. Mascezel died soon afterwards, perhaps at Stilicho's instigation. The vast estates of Gildo and his family were confiscated to the imperial treasury, but proved to be so large and complex that a separate financial bureau had to be created to deal with them. Stilicho's control of western affairs was thus further consolidated, while in Italy ecclesiastical politics had become more manageable since the death of Ambrose in April 397.

Eutropius, too, had been angling to place a churchman of his liking on Constantinople's episcopal throne, and had done so by arranging for John Chrysostom, the charismatic and immensely popular Antiochene preacher, to be installed in 397. Chrysostom's episcopate proved a stormy one, however, for his own sense of pious propriety led him to spurn the lavish social calendar that the wealthy senators of the imperial city expected of him. His loyalty to Eutropius was quite real, though, as for that matter was Arcadius': when Eutropius fell, it was despite the objections of the emperor at whose side he had so long served. His downfall was a stroke of luck from which Stilicho would benefit, but which he had done nothing to engineer. Late in 398, Eutropius was designated consul for 399, a step too far for public opinion to tolerate. It was one thing for a eunuch to command an army – Eutropius had been ridiculed, but proved an able general – and he might even, as the most favoured official in the imperial court, be granted the honorific title of *patricius*. But a eunuch consul was beyond the pale, and not only did Stilicho's court propagandist Claudius Claudianus have a field day with this shocking innovation, but the eastern establishment recoiled in horror as well.

A minor uprising in Phrygia became the excuse for a palace coup. An officer named Tribigild mutinied in 399, and it was Flavius Gainas who led the praesental field army to suppress it. The details of what happened are difficult to disentangle, because much of our understanding depends on a bizarre allegorical drama written by the philosopher Synesius, later the bishop of Cyrene. As baffling an example of rococco excess as anything the late Second Sophistic could throw up, Synesius' *De Providentia* addresses contemporary court politics through a fantastic tale of two Egyptian brothers at war with one another; his polemical *De Regno*, which deals with an earlier stage of the affair, is only marginally less convoluted. Nevertheless, of several narratives that can be extracted from these sources, the most plausible is that Gainas saw in the mutiny an opportunity to engineer the fall of Eutropius and replace him as the main power behind Arcadius' throne. He represented Tribigild's main demand as the deposition of the eunuch *patricius*, and by so doing gained the support of Eutropius' court rivals.

As Eudoxia was also fixedly hostile to Eutropius, Arcadius finally acceded to the chorus of denunciations, and Eutropius fled to the church of Saint Sophia to seek refuge with his ally Chrysostom. Securing a promise that his life would be spared, Eutropius agreed to leave the sanctuary of the church and, having been stripped of his property, went into exile in Cyprus. A new praetorian prefect, Flavius Aurelianus, soon recalled Eutropius to court and had him executed on entirely spurious charges of conspiracy. It was thus Aurelianus, not Gainas, who became the chief beneficiary of the coup, taking the eastern consulship of 400 as his reward, and sharing it with the western *consul prior*, none other than Stilicho.

Gainas was furious. In April, he marched to Chalcedon, on the Asian side of the Bosporus opposite Constantinople, and demanded a praesental *magisterium* for himself and the deposition of Aurelianus as the price of his loyalty. Both wishes were granted. Aurelianus went into exile, and so did John Chrysostom, while Flavius Caesarius, a former ally of Eutropius, became the new prefect. For a change, the interests of the empress Eudoxia, since early January named augusta, and those of Gainas seemed to coincide. The latter no doubt hoped to run the government in the same sort of condominium as Stilicho enjoyed in the West, but, despite appearances, he had incurred the permanent enmity of Eudoxia. They shared their hostility towards the exiled Chrysostom and the dead Eutropius, but that was all, and Gainas and his troops continued to be denied access to churches in which they could worship according to their homoian liturgy. (The regions from which barbarian soldiers, not least Gothic ones, tended to be recruited had been evangelised by homoian bishops and their devotion to that theology was sometimes a cause of friction with Nicene congregations in cities like Constantinople and Mediolanum.) Lacking the political insight, let alone the political connections, of Stilicho, Gainas was unable to master the intricacies of the Constantinopolitan court, and moved his own bodyguard out into Thrace, joined by those units of the *comitatenses* that were personally loyal to him. There he was within striking range of the imperial city, but did not have to suffer daily reminders that he possessed a rank far in advance of his actual power.

His departure made other homoian soldiers in the city more vulnerable, and the citizenry unleashed a pogrom targeting 'Gothic' troops while the palatine guard units stood by and watched. Even so, Gainas hesitated – and that hesitation proved fatal. In September, Aurelianus and his allies were recalled from their brief exile and the deposed prefect restarted the consular games his exile had interrupted. Gainas was declared a public enemy and the distinguished general Flavius Fravitta, also of Gothic origin, was sent to bring him to heel. Somewhere in the Thracian Chersonnesus, during the winter of 400–401, Fravitta won a decisive victory over Gainas; when Gainas sought to flee as far away as he could across the Danube and into the *barbaricum*, he was captured and killed by a Hunnic chieftain called Uldin. Tribigild's sputtering rebellion was suppressed in Phrygia at the same time. The victorious Fravitta took up the consulate of 401, with Stilicho's close ally Flavius Vincentius, praetorian prefect of Gaul, as the western *consul prior*.

Thanks in part to our dependence on Synesius' bizarre pamphletry, the whole sequence of events from Tribigild's revolt to the death of Gainas has been read since the nineteenth century as a simple story of 'Romans' like Aurelianus against 'Germans' like Gainas, or, still more schematically, of pro- and anti-German parties at the eastern court. That analysis has more to do with modern nationalism than the way fourth-century contemporaries understood their own politics; the idea of a Germanic and barbarian northern world confronting a monolithic Roman world is ours, not theirs. People of the fourth century recognised ethnic identities; some of them, like Ammianus, disliked Pannonians, while others, like Synesius, hated Goths. But neither they, nor any of their contemporaries, would have lumped Alaric, Gainas, Tribigild and Fravitta together into any category save 'soldier', even though they were all Goths and thus all 'Germanic' in nineteenth-century terms. That is why both Victorian and more recent narratives that analyse the respective fates of the eastern and western empires in terms of the East successfully purging itself of 'Germanic control' while the West tolerated the 'German' Stilicho's power have been so strongly challenged by the best recent scholarship.

Furthermore, the distinction between the political dynamics of the two *partes imperii* was actually even simpler: the East was dominated by a ruling elite that needed its imperial government to function, because it was functioning government that gave the elites their individual power. Flavius Caesarius and the brothers Eutychianus and Aurelianus between them held the praetorian prefecture six separate times in less than two decades after the fall of Rufinus, cycling in and out of power as factional discord dictated; but none of them commanded resources sufficient to challenge, ignore or withdraw from the actual structures of government. Politics and power were different in the West: the old senatorial families, even those below the level of the super rich, needed to renew their connections to imperial office and its regnant bureaucrats, in each generation and in each branch of the family tree – it was how men like the urban prefect Ceionius Rufius Albinus could be the son, grandson and great-grandson of previous urban prefects. But these same men could always disengage entirely if things went badly and fall back on their own resources, withdrawing to the rich, small worlds of their own estates. That fundamental divergence in the class structures of East and West, rather than anything in the ethnic backgrounds of the governing elites, is what explains their different trajectories in the fifth century. There were plenty of men like Aurelianus in the West, but they had to function among others who would, in the last analysis, prosper with or without access to the apparatus of imperial government. Men who could do that simply did not exist in the East.

The differences in class structures between East and West had economic consequences as well as administrative ones. The richest western elites were also those most likely to dabble in government, but their landed estates generated income whether or not their patrons had access to the greased wheels of provincial office-holding – senators were just as likely to keep their income out of imperial hands as not. In the East, by contrast, properties on a comparable scale did not exist, and so wealth was much more reliably recirculated through the imperial fisc. When those contrasting economic rhythms were combined with the vastly greater access to new bullion enjoyed by the government in Constantinople, the diverging viability of the eastern and western administrations begins to make sense.

One key consequence was the eastern government's ability to choose its battles. As early as the year 401, and throughout the fifth century, Constantinople could choose to bribe potential threats into oblivion, or at least shunt them westwards – a luxury that the western government did not have. Alaric, as it happens, proved the test case. Since 397, he and his followers had been content to draw wages as a legally constituted standing army in the diocese of Macedonia. But in 401, with Gainas dead, there was something new to wish for, a praesental *magisterium* in the imperial capital. Fravitta, the victor over Gainas, had quarrelled with Aurelianus and lost, paying a fatal price when he was executed halfway through the year. This whetted Alaric's appetite, but what happened next is baffling. Rather than take Fravitta's place, and seemingly encouraged by the eastern government, Alaric attacked northern Italy late in 401 while Stilicho was fighting Alamanni on the Raetian frontier.

Alaric would, over the next decade, demonstrate his capacity for terminal indecision, and now he hovered on the frontier of Italy, threatening Stilicho with invasion to no obvious purpose: the sources do not tell us what he was actually asking for. In spring 402, he did in fact invade the north Italian plain, thereby forcing Stilicho to act. But the campaign was a distraction and an annoyance for Stilicho, who – correctly, as events would show – understood the frontier situation in Raetia and Noricum to be more dangerous than anything Alaric could contrive. Returning to Italy, he forced Alaric away from Mediolanum and brought him to battle twice. At Pollentia, on Easter Sunday, Stilicho not only took Alaric's wife and children prisoner, but also commandeered the treasure that Alaric had amassed in half a decade's plundering. Stilicho then pursued the retreating enemy, offering to return the prisoners he had taken, and, when that was refused, he won another victory at Verona and again offered Alaric a truce.

Holding the upper hand, not least because many of Alaric's followers had come over to him, Stilicho allowed Alaric to withdraw from Italy – given Stilicho's cold war with Constantinople, it would have been foolish to destroy as biddable and violent a potential weapon as Alaric might well prove to be. For the next two years, until late 404 or early 405, Alaric remained in one of the four Pannonian provinces. That diocese had become a sort of no man's land between East and West ever since Theodosius' campaign against Eugenius and, by basing himself there, Alaric could effectively play East off against West while potentially threatening both.

Another consequence of the 402 campaigns in northern Italy was that the court of Honorius gave up Mediolanum as its primary residence and instead settled in Ravenna on the Adriatic coast, where the emperor remained during the winter of 402–3 and throughout the whole of the next year. We know very little about precise events in either the East or the West during that time, but the fact that Arcadius and Honorius shared the consulship of 402 is a sign of easing tensions, as are the consuls appointed for 403: Theodosius II, the infant son of Arcadius, born in April 401 and made augustus in January 402, and the aged western general Flavius Rumoridus, who had otherwise faded from view nearly twenty years earlier, when he served Valentinian II. While Honorius remained childless, the family of his elder brother continued to grow, with another daughter, Marina, born in February 403. Her mother, the empress Aelia Eudoxia, remained the dominant figure at the eastern court. Indeed, a recurring feature of the coming decades would be the central role of the women of the Theodosian household, among them Arcadius' daughters Pulcheria, Flacilla and Marina, and later Licinia Eudoxia, the youngest daughter of Theodosius II. In the West, as we shall soon see, Stilicho's wife Serena, herself a Theodosian princess, would discover a formidable rival in the youngest child of Galla and Theodosius I, Galla Placidia, just now entering adulthood. Another pattern typical of fifth-century politics also becomes visible in these very earliest years of the century: the daughters of Arcadius were kept unmarried and exercised their power through privileged access to the emperor and conspicuous acts of Christian piety. They might be named Augusta or *nobilissima*, but they would not be given the opportunity to bear children: that was reserved for the wives of the reigning Theodosian emperor, and would prevent the creation of too many potential heirs. It was a less violent way of achieving what Constantine's sons had effected in the summer of blood in 337.

The relative peace between East and West broke down in 404 and 405. The first sign was a refusal to recognise each other's nominees for the consulship of 404, when Honorius was western consul and Aristaenetus, who was a distant relative of the Antiochene rhetor Libanius and had held the prefecture of Constantinople in 392, served in the East. In 404, the praetorian prefecture was again in the hands of Eutychianus, while John Chrysostom was once again bishop of Constantinople, having returned from exile a couple of years earlier. But the fiery preacher never really did reconcile himself to life in the imperial capital, and Eudoxia remained implacable towards him. His final exile came in June 404, even though there were massive riots in his support which left many of his supporters dead in the streets. He died in exile three years later, but his persecutor Eudoxia preceded him to the grave, suffering a bloody miscarriage and dying of an infection on 6 October 404. Her position as the leading Theodosian empress would in time be assumed by her daughter Pulcheria.

Modern scholars have a hard time explaining why every single constellation of Arcadius' advisers was equivalently opposed to the western regime of Stilicho. Perhaps they genuinely believed him to have had designs on the Balkan provinces now under eastern administration, though he had given no evidence of acting on such ambitions in the half decade since he had first quarrelled with the regimes of Rufinus and Eutropius. He instead concentrated on strengthening the military defences of Italy. The Pollentia and Verona campaigns against Alaric had tested their effectiveness and highlighted just how critical the defence of the north Italian plain remained. One reforming measure was to transfer fighting units from the Rhine and upper Danube frontiers to reinforce the praesental field armies in northern Italy, which may also have brought other administrative changes in Gaul. But in 404, faced with the eastern regime's ongoing unwillingness to recognise western appointees or promulgate western legislation, Stilicho responded, granting Alaric the same sort of appointment that Eutropius had given him five years before.

Early in 405, Alaric's followers returned to Epirus, their leader once again bearing the codicils of office appointing him *magister militum*, this time issued in the West. At the same time, Stilicho named a hitherto unknown official called Iovius as the praetorian prefect for Illyricum. It was as close as Stilicho ever came to lending credibility to eastern propaganda, though it was really a purely symbolic action: it reasserted a hegemony over eastern appointments that Stilicho had always claimed to possess and, given that Alaric was already in Illyricum, he might as well be used to torment an uncooperative eastern court. At Constantinople, Anthemius became praetorian prefect, the office his grandfather had held under Constantius, and was also the eastern consul of 405. He would soon be named *patricius*, the honorific title now regularly taken by the senior figure at each imperial court. Anthemius would hold his new office for nearly a decade, an astonishingly long tenure of office at a court not known for the stability of its leading personnel. Events soon overtook all the parties involved, however, in a most unexpected way.

Late in 405, a Gothic army under one Radagaisus, hitherto completely unknown to history, marched through Raetia, crossed the Alps and invaded Italy. Who Radagaisus was, or how he came to be where he was with his following, has produced much speculation. This mainly consists of grand theories about Hunnic expansion into central Europe setting off mass migrations, of which Radagaisus' actions were the latest in a series of Hun-triggered catastrophes that had begun with the Danube crossing of 376. The limited evidence means that such speculation can never be excluded, and simple narratives that join dots together in causal patterns are comforting. But just because something satisfies our aesthetic sense of storytelling does not make it true: Radagaisus' invasion, and an equally serious attack on Gaul just over a year later, look more like continuations of the massive raids of the late third century than anything new. Grander alternative theories ignore an inconvenient fact – as soon as Radagaisus' forces hit the north Italian plain and won their initial victory, they split into three armies, two of which disappear from history, presumably because they had collected the booty they wanted and gone home. Only the group personally led by Radagaisus remained in Italy, though that was alarming enough in itself – in a virtually unprecedented sign of crisis, the government in Ravenna was frightened into allowing landlords to arm their slaves. Throughout the winter of 405–6 and into the new year, Stilicho gradually harried Radagaisus into the Appenines, until he attempted to break away with an assault on the small city of Florentia. Instead, he found himself besieged by Stilicho's forces in the hill town of Faesulae (today the pretty Florentine suburb of Fiesole), where he was taken prisoner on 23 August and immediately executed. His surviving followers were pardoned and enrolled in Stilicho's praesental field army.

The general did not enjoy the fruits of this victory for long, however. On the last day of 406, a large band of Vandals, Alans and Suevi defeated a Frankish army on the eastern side of the Rhine and then crossed the river near Moguntiacum, spreading devastation in the northern provinces of Gaul. As with Radagaisus' invasion, there have been attempts to modernise old stories of mass migration caused by the Huns, but the evidence is again lacking. We seem to be looking at highly organised warbands intent upon plunder and concessions from the imperial government, not least incorporation into its military: word of Alaric's successful bid for high Roman military command over what was in effect a private army had by now spread far and wide in the European *barbaricum* and it was a model others were keen to imitate. That is to say, stable polities of the *barbaricum* were certainly facing new pressures: we should not minimise the 'churn' caused by Huns and their vassals north of the Caucasus any more than we should the parallel evidence in Sogdiana, Bactria, Gandhara and Swat, where the extensive numismatic evidence is more eloquent of actual Hunnic hegemony than anything we have in the West. And yet, at the same time, we must also recognise the striking opportunities for profit that political instability between the eastern and western empires offered, and the potential attraction Alaric's relatively successful model of leadership could exercise.

The Rhine crossing of 406–7 ultimately proved far more dangerous to the government in Ravenna than had Radagaisus' invasion of northern Italy, because it sparked off a new cycle of usurpations. As we have seen, the administration and defences of northern Gaul had not been fully restored after the fall of Maximus, and when Stilicho reinforced his Italian *comitatenses* early in the 400s, he would no doubt have stripped away the best of the available troops. That would explain why no *comitatenses* were available to repel the invasion at Moguntiacum. Instead, as the invaders fanned out across Belgica Prima and Secunda and Germania Prima, the army in Britain mutinied. First, a certain Marcus and then a Gratian were proclaimed emperor and killed in turn, and we know nothing about the prior careers of either. Thereupon the army chose a common soldier named Constantine, supposedly because of his auspicious name, and raised him to the purple. The new augustus led what seems to have been the whole British field army across the Channel and very rapidly took control of Gaul as well: the legitimate praetorian prefect at Treveri (which would never again be a major administrative centre) retreated first to Lugdunum and then to Arelate.

The Spanish diocese followed Gaul into the usurper's camp. Constantine plucked one of his sons from monastic retreat and named him caesar, marrying him off to produce heirs. His *magistri militum*, Iustinus and Nebiogastes, seized Arelate in either late 407 or early 408, and Honorius' prefect Limenius and his *magister militum per Gallias* Chariobaudes both retreated across the Alps. Stilicho sent his subordinate Sarus, a Gothic commander who had been in the service of the western emperor since at least the time of Radagaisus' defeat, to drive the usurpation back out of Gallia Narbonensis. Sarus defeated and killed Constantine's general Iustinus, then besieged the usurper in Valentia (modern Valence), murdering Nebiogastes when the latter attempted to negotiate. In response, Constantine promoted two of his colleagues in the British command, Gerontius and Edobich, to the rank of *magistri* and they chased Sarus back into Italy. Arelate now became the usurper's de facto capital. He made a treaty with the various invaders of 406, which effectively confined them to the northern Belgicas: even two years later they had not made any impact south of the Seine river. Constantine's coins declare him the *Restitutor Rei Publicae* ('Restorer of the State'), and he reopened the mint at Treveri and regarrisoned the city. All that remained was to convert himself into a legitimate member of the imperial college.

Italian politics made it plausible that he might do so. Intrigue at Honorius' court now becomes harder for us to trace because the letter collections of Ambrose and Symmachus, who died in 397 and 402 respectively, disappear, as does the poetry of Stilicho's panegyrist Claudian, who was also dead by 404. That means that we cannot really follow the development of a great conspiracy against Stilicho until the trap was finally sprung. We may infer that, so long as the court resided at Mediolanum, Stilicho had been able to dominate his rivals, civilian and military, but that after the move to Ravenna members of the palatine staff were increasingly in control of the feckless Honorius. They naturally played on the same sort of resentments that the young Valentinian had felt towards Arbogastes.

In the second half of 407, when the emperor resided at Rome, he was in much closer contact with his sister Galla Placidia, who had long been the most visible representative of the Theodosian house there. She was now, like Honorius, coming to an age when she could expect to play a role in politics, as her cousin Serena had been doing for two decades. That there was hostility between the two seems certain. The raw dynastic calculations of Serena and Stilicho cannot have helped, marrying each of their daughters in turn to Honorius. The elder, Maria, died in 407, and the wedding of the younger one, Thermantia, took place early in 408. If either marriage produced an heir, it would guarantee Placidia's future exclusion from power. We should not be surprised if Placidia plotted against her cousin and her cousin's husband and, given that the Roman Senate – for whom Placidia had been the face of the dynasty – played an active part in Stilicho's downfall, we may suspect, if not prove, her influence at work.

As the usurpation of Constantine was taking shape in Gaul, Stilicho again found himself confronted by Alaric, who had spent the quiet years in Illyricum and Epirus rebuilding what he had lost at Pollentia and Verona. As a legitimate *magister militum*, he could call on the network of imperial supply depots at will, though it is genuinely unclear to what degree normal government was functioning in some of these provinces, or to whom their civilian officials reported. As always, usurpations took priority over other threats, and Stilicho no doubt planned to deal with Constantine first of all. Alaric was as serviceable in that role as he was in the Balkans but, unfortunately for Stilicho, his price was high. Having moved his forces to Noricum for the winter of 407–8, he demanded their wages, which were apparently in arrears.

For reasons that are not entirely clear – perhaps opposition to his plans from rivals at court – Stilicho asked the Senate in Rome to rule on the matter, pointing out that if Alaric were not paid, he would surely invade Italy again rather than go and fight Constantine. The Senate was deeply divided, seemingly between an old guard who, like Stilicho, had already served under the first Theodosius, and a younger generation that had known only the hegemony of the great patrician. The emperor himself joined Stilicho and the great men of the city in their debate. Against strident opposition, Stilicho was in the end able to force through a decision to pay Alaric the 4,000 pounds of gold he was demanding as back pay for his men's expenses for the journey from Emona to Epirus. 'Not peace but a pact of servitude' was the epigrammatic judgement of a senator called Lampadius, but, for all the opposition it aroused, paying off the lesser evil to fight the greater was standard imperial policy.

As the emperor and his immediate entourage prepared to return to Ravenna from Rome, rumour reached him that Arcadius had died in Constantinople. It proved to be true. On 1 May, Honorius' elder brother was succeeded by the 6-year-old Theodosius II. The regency was effectively in the hands of the prefect Anthemius, whose hold on office was thereby secured for more than half a decade longer. Both Honorius and Stilicho saw an opportunity to assert authority over the East, Honorius as the (now very) senior augustus, and Stilicho as the emperor's father-in-law and potentially the grandfather of the next heir. But the threats from Alaric and Constantine were made no less real by the promise of eastern opportunities, and there was unrest among the soldiery in the praesental field army. The emperor's personal presence was needed at Bononia (modern Bologna) to quell the whispers of mutiny. At Bononia, Stilicho convinced Honorius that he would endanger the dynasty fatally if he left Italy to go to Constantinople, as he was planning to do. Alaric might invade despite having been bribed to behave and Constantine would certainly do so.

His arguments were good ones, and Stilicho got his way. It was decided that he alone should go to Constantinople, welcome the new emperor to his secondary role in the imperial college and reassert the predominance of the senior generation of Theodosiani. It was that tactical victory that gave Stilicho's enemies their chance. A certain Olympius, who held some sort of court position that we cannot pinpoint, triggered a coup that now unfolded at great speed. It was widely rumoured that Stilicho planned to set his son Eucherius on the eastern throne, since he was no less a Theodosian than was the infant Theodosius II. Olympius convinced Honorius that the rumour was true. In August, the emperor journeyed to Ticinum, where the army was mustering for its campaign against Constantine. Most of Stilicho's trusted supporters were there in the city: Chariobaudes, *magister militum per Gallias* now awaiting his restoration; Limenius, the praetorian prefect of Gaul driven out by Constantine the previous year; and others like them. When Honorius arrived with his entourage, the campaign army mutinied in a riot that was carefully staged to cause the maximum confusion with the least possible destruction. It lasted for four days, and the Stilichonian officers were singled out and killed in the first flare of rioting on 13 August. Over the next three days, the *magister officiorum* Naemorius, the *comes sacrarum largitionum* Patruinus, the *quaestor* Salvius, and Macrobius Longinianus, the praetorian prefect of Italy, were all killed as well.

Stilicho was at Bononia when he received the news and, as the plotters intended, neither he nor anyone else knew whether Honorius himself was among the dead – the attempted coup had been staged in such a way as to leave open the question of whether the emperor or his father-in-law Stilicho was the true target. Puzzled but wary, Stilicho decided to set the mercenary warband of his lieutenant Sarus upon the regular army if it turned out that the emperor had been killed, but when news arrived that Honorius was alive and returning to Ravenna from Ticinum, Stilicho, too, made for Ravenna. He had lost almost his entire network of support in the coup, but even so his personal authority was enormous. It might have been enough to restore his position, had he been able to see the emperor himself. He never got the chance.

On 21 August, just before he arrived at Ravenna, word reached Stilicho that the emperor had ordered his arrest as a public enemy. While his household armed itself in fear, he sought shelter in a church. The next morning, a squad of *domestici* arrived in the company of the bishop of Ravenna, swearing under oath that they had orders to arrest Stilicho and conduct him to his emperor, nothing more. Pious Christian that he was, Stilicho accepted these oaths as binding and left the church, whereupon his guards read out a second order from the emperor commanding the immediate execution of his father-in-law. The account of Olympiodorus, the most realistic and pragmatic of the fifth-century historians, tells us that as Stilicho's bodyguard prepared to 'rescue him from his fate, Stilicho cut short their attempt with terrible threats and submitted his neck to the sword'. It was a tragic end to one of the late empire's most extraordinary careers.

7

GALLA PLACIDIA
AND FLAVIUS
CONSTANTIUS

S tilicho's executioner outside the sanctuary of the church was a junior officer named Heraclianus. He was rewarded with the post of *comes Africae*, but his victim's death proved to be an unmitigated disaster for the western empire. Stilicho's retainers, whom he had forbidden to defend him at the last, spirited his son Eucherius off to Rome, where he was soon hunted down and killed. His supporters were purged from the armies and in cities around Italy. The wives and children of his barbarian auxiliaries – mainly remnants of Radagaisus' army – were murdered in their thousands. Those that survived fled to Noricum and joined Alaric. Stilicho's property was confiscated for the state, while the court continued its orgy of political intrigue. Olympius replaced the murdered Naemorius as *magister officiorum*. Theodorus, the nephew of the senator Lampadius who had denounced Stilicho's proposal to pay Alaric, now became praetorian prefect of Italy and Illyricum. His appointment signalled that, while Stilicho might be dead, the West was not ready to give up its claims on the Balkan dioceses.

Alaric was now denied the 4,000 pounds of gold he had been promised. He gave Honorius' government one last chance, demanding an unspecified sum of gold and an exchange of hostages, presumably the surviving families of his new supporters. Olympius and Theodorus rebuffed this overture with the full support of Honorius and, in October 408, when the mountain passes from Noricum into Italy were still open, Alaric marched his entire army straight down the Italian peninsula to Rome. The campaign army in Ticinum, which had neither set off on its journey after the riots of August nor been disbanded or otherwise disciplined for its mutiny, did nothing to stop him.

During the winter of 408–9 Alaric besieged Rome – the first of three sieges – and blockaded the route up the Tiber river from the artificial harbour of Portus, near Ostia, thereby threatening the Romans with starvation. Panic gripped the city and scapegoats were sought. Galla Placidia seized the opportunity to eliminate a rival, having Stilicho's widow Serena strangled by order of the Senate. Collectively, though, the Senate dithered and Alaric's support grew as slaves and field hands joined him from across Italy. Ravenna made no effort to deal with the siege, Olympius concentrating instead on the systematic purge of potential Stilichonians and revoking legal measures that had annoyed the eastern government and could now be conveniently blamed on the dead Stilicho. That was one of Olympius' few astute moves, for it would lead to a reconciliation with the regime of Theodosius II at a crucial moment a year hence. At the same time, in response to an embassy from Constantine, Honorius sent him a purple robe and imperial regalia, acknowledging him as his colleague. It was a sign of the Italian regime's weakness that it was no longer contemplating a campaign against the usurper. As a result of this gesture, Constantine could advertise the year 409 as the consulship of Honorius for the eighth time and Constantine for the first, although, needless to say, the usurper was never recognised in the East, where Theodosius II was made consul for the third time.

As the new year opened, Honorius' government remained in crisis. In besieged Rome, the Senate finally gave in to Alaric and begged him for a truce. In exchange for his letting food into the city, a senatorial embassy would go to Ravenna to negotiate on his behalf. Led by Caecilianus, Priscus Attalus and Maximianus, it received a gracious welcome at court. Olympius, ever conspiring, seized the opportunity to damage a rival and conferred the praetorian prefecture on Caecilianus, evicting Theodorus from that post, while Attalus was made *comes sacrarum largitionum*. Alaric was invited to a parley at Ariminum (modern Rimini), between Rome and Ravenna, some months thereafter. Caecilianus did not hold his prefecture for long – by the time the negotiations with Alaric began in spring 409, Iovius, the old ally of Stilicho and rival of Olympius, had become prefect and now led the embassy to Ariminum. Alaric knew the strength of his position, and set his demands high. He wanted money and grain, and also the highest generalship, the *magisterium utriusque militiae*, or command of both services, which Stilicho had held before him. Iovius favoured this arrangement, but either the emperor or Olympius balked. They conceded as much grain and money as Alaric might want, but not a position in the imperial hierarchy. Outraged, Alaric turned away from Ariminum and began to march down the via Flaminia towards Rome, intending to renew his siege. Olympius' hold on Honorius soon collapsed, and he was forced to flee to Dalmatia, but the change brought Alaric no comfort: Iovius had lost face in failing to manage the negotiations, and he now swore an oath (or so we are told) never to make peace with the Gothic general. Allying himself with the *comes domesticorum* Flavius Allobichus, he engineered a mutiny against Olympius' appointees, and Allobichus now took over the praesental *magisterium* in Ravenna.

The time ought to have been ripe for Constantine III, as he could now legitimately claim to be, to profit from the total discomfiture of the Italian regime, but his own fortunes began to look shaky at just the same moment. In the summer of 408, as the coup against Stilicho was unfolding in Italy, Constantine was faced by an uprising in Spain. Although the Spanish administration had uniformly acquiesced in his usurpation, not all the Spanish aristocracy did the same. In the dynasty's native province there were still relatives of the Theodosian house, in the shape of some distant cousins of Honorius named Didymus, Verinianus, Theodosiolus and Lagodius. The first two of these put aside a family feud to organise an army with their personal funds, mobilising their private bodyguards and the workers on their estates. In response to this news, Constantine despatched his son (now his caesar) Constans along with the *magister militum* Gerontius and a praetorian prefect, Apollinaris (the latter the grandfather of the poet, prefect of Rome and bishop Sidonius Apollinaris, whom we will meet later in the book). Deep in the Iberian peninsula, the armies met and, though Didymus and Verinianus were victorious in their first major engagement, in the next one, in Lusitania, they suffered a total defeat. The brothers were captured and taken by Constans and Apollinaris back to Arelate, where they were executed. The surviving brothers, Theodosiolus and Lagodius, who had taken no part in the rebellion, now fled to their relatives, the former to Rome, the latter to Constantinople. Gerontius remained behind in Spain, and it was his rebellion early in 409, rather than the Theodosian uprising, that really tore the Gallic prefecture apart.

Constantine had won recognition from Ravenna before Honorius learned of his cousins' execution. Arguably now the legitimate emperor in the Gallic prefecture, Constantine was determined to suppress Gerontius. He again sent Constans to Spain with a new *magister militum*, Iustus. Gerontius set up one of his dependants as augustus, an otherwise unknown Maximus. There were thus now four emperors in the Roman world: Honorius, Theodosius II, Constantine III and Maximus. The last is thoroughly obscure, though coins were minted in his name at Barcino and he and Gerontius established their regime firmly in the provincial capital at Tarraco (Tarragona). There is no record of whether the other Spanish provinces remained loyal to Constantine or sided with Gerontius, but the latter decided that the best way to ensure the success of his fledgling regime was to stir up the barbarian warbands of northern Gaul to open up a second flank against Constantine and Constans.

The literary sources for what followed paint an unrelievedly black picture: 'all Gaul smoked as if a funeral pyre,' writes the poet Orientius. With Gerontius' encouragement, in the high summer of 409 the Vandals, Alans and Sueves left the Belgicas and invaded Aquitania and Novempop- ulana, raiding far and wide before crossing the Pyrenees into Spain in late September. The damage they caused in southern Gaul was spectacular but not lasting, whereas their presence would alter the dynamic of the Spanish provinces for ever. Their passage had been eased, perhaps unintentionally, by Gerontius' having left the passes ungarrisoned. He had decided to confront Constans in Gallia Narbonensis, and their armies circled one another indecisively there for the rest of the year. Despite the threat to his west, Constantine developed designs upon Italy, having formed an alliance with Allobichus, Honorius' *magister militum*. The latter, like his ally Iovius, was staunchly opposed to negotiations with Alaric, who now had no supporters at all at court.

After the debacle at Ariminum, Alaric calmed down enough to offer reasonable terms – a modest amount of grain and a couple of unimport- ant provinces like Noricum in which to dwell. Perhaps this was a ruse, or perhaps he was actually contemplating retirement, following a decade of freebooting that had won him so little. But these new demands were twice rejected and he briefly reopened the siege of Rome before deciding that something more dramatic was needed to force the Honorian regime to heel. He cannot have missed how much more effective Constantine had been at extracting concessions from Ravenna than he himself had been.

Usurpation, as always, had concentrated the imperial mind. Alaric decided that what he had been missing was a usurper of his own, and so he set out to find one. He allied himself to a faction in the Roman Senate that was as displeased with Ravenna as he was, a faction represented by at least one of the men who had gone to Honorius earlier in the year to try to negotiate on the city's behalf. This was Priscus Attalus, one of the Senate's leading lights. His family was from the East, he had held office already under Theodosius I, and by December 409 the regime of Iovius at Ravenna had named him urban prefect, presumably to retain his loyalty. It did not work.

Attalus was proclaimed emperor at Rome in December and, while it is customary to portray him as a stooge of Alaric, he in fact took his own independence very seriously. He had the approval of other Romans who wanted some relief from the stultifying incompetence of Honorius and his ministers and he clearly believed that the alliance with Alaric would serve his faction's interests. He gave the top military commands to Alaric and the latter's brother-in-law Athaulf, but the rest of his nascent regime was plucked from the upper echelons of the Senate. Attalus tried to set his own policies, but that wilfully ignored just how contingent his position was on the good will of Alaric and the latter's superior military skills.

Against his general's advice, Attalus hesitated to seize Carthage and its vital grain supply for Rome. Then, when it became clear that the *comes Africae* Heraclianus would stay loyal to Ravenna, he sent a general of his own choosing to Africa, where he was defeated and killed. Despite that failure, he refused to let Alaric send a handful of Goths to seize Africa, perhaps mistrusting the latter's intentions. Instead, Attalus marched on Ravenna, stopping at Ariminum to open negotiations. Honorius, in a sign of his regime's abjection, offered to share the throne with Attalus, who, in a sign of his blind arrogance, declined, insisting that Honorius should be deposed and go into exile on an island. The delay caused by this haggling proved fatal because Ravenna suddenly had an unanticipated stroke of luck. Nearly 4,000 soldiers, sent by the eastern regime of Anthemius, arrived; they had been requested during the time of Stilicho, and no one had dared hope they would actually materialise as they now did. Ravenna was by no means the impregnable site that it has sometimes been claimed, but it was much harder to besiege than was Rome because of the marshiness of the surrounding territory. Thus reinforced, Honorius could afford to be just as intransigent as his rival.

Alaric had had enough. Both Honorius and Attalus had now proved equally hopeless at governing, and neither was prepared to give him what he wanted. At least Honorius belonged to the legitimate dynasty. Early in 410, Alaric deposed Attalus but allowed him to retire comfortably to his townhouse in Rome. But if he thought that would win him credit in Ravenna, he had failed to reckon with the regime's wonted incompetence. Iovius and Allobichus were now at odds with one another, and the latter sent an invitation to Constantine III to invade Italy. The Gallic emperor did so as soon as the mountain passes opened early in 410, but by the time he got to Liberona in the Po valley, word arrived that Allobichus had been executed on suspicion of the treason of which he was undoubtedly guilty. Deprived of his Italian ally, Constantine returned to Arelate, where he met his son Constans, whom Gerontius had finally defeated in western Gaul. Constantine's praesental *magister militum* Edobich went north to recruit new troops in the Rhineland, while Constans led the surviving units of the British field army to halt Gerontius.

Alaric, meanwhile, needed a conclusion, and almost any one would do. His authority with his troops was deteriorating as it became harder and harder to keep them supplied. He left Rome well garrisoned, and took up a defensible spot near Ravenna from which to reopen negotiations. Chance again intervened. Sarus, the powerful Gothic warlord who had served with Stilicho since the Pollentia and Verona campaigns, had returned to the service of Ravenna after Stilicho's execution without ever receiving a regular military command. Why Sarus turned up and attacked Alaric at precisely this moment is unclear, though one source tells us he thought his own position would be damaged if Alaric made peace, and later events suggest he had a long-standing grievance against Alaric's brother-in-law Athaulf. He certainly acted without the knowledge of the bumbling court at Ravenna, once again led by Olympius, back in office as *magister officiorum*.

Alaric interpreted the unprovoked attack as evidence of Honorius' continuing bad faith. There would be no more attempts at peace. Marching back to Rome for the third and last time, Alaric put the eternal city to the sack. For three days, beginning on 24 August 410, his followers stripped the city of the wealth of centuries. The treasure seized was on a staggering scale: five years later, Alaric's successor Athaulf gave his imperial bride 'fifty handsome young men dressed in silk, each bearing aloft two very large dishes, one full of gold, the other full of precious – nay, priceless – gems, which the Goths had seized in the sack of Rome'. Supposedly out of reverence for Saint Peter, Alaric left untouched the church on the Vatican hill that housed his tomb, and in general the Goths made an effort not to violate churches. But however much some might take comfort in that slight forbearance, the verdict of the world was shock and horror: Rome, the mother of the world, had been killed.

A hundred years later, Honorius' stupidity was so proverbial that a legend circulated about his response to the sacking: when he received the news that Rome had fallen, he was immensely relieved to learn the messenger meant the imperial city; he had been frightened that his favourite chicken, Roma, had died. The story inspired John James Waterhouse's masterpiece of high Victorian kitsch, *The Favourites of the Emperor Honorius*, in which he is depicted feeding his birds as his counsellors try to attract his attention. But the sacking was as bad for Alaric as it was for the city, and the ruin of everything he had worked for. It solved none of his problems, guaranteed no better future for his soldiers and left them all on a permanent war footing with no prospect of a happy conclusion. His followers might have seized more wealth than they could imagine, but food would still run short, and there were few places left on the peninsula that could feed them.

Alaric decided to make for the south of Italy and attempt to cross from Rhegium to Sicily. The island's still undepleted grain fields, among the richest in the empire, might sustain his supporters for a long time, perhaps long enough to find transport to Africa. But he could not get to Sicily, never mind any further: the sea proved too stormy to make the crossing, although in one story it is a magic statue that thwarts his passage. There was nothing for it but to make for the north. Beginning the march back towards Rome, he fell ill with fever. Not far from Consentia (modern Cosenza), he died, within a month or so of the debacle at Rome for which he is best remembered. He was buried in secret and command of his followers was taken by his brother-in-law Athaulf, whose task it became to extricate the army and its camp followers from Italy.

Disease had rid Honorius of one of his chief tormentors, but it was a new arrival in the regime who delivered him from the still more pressing challenge of Constantine in Gaul. Flavius Constantius, who would dominate the next decade of western Roman history in much the same way that Stilicho had the last, was a native of Naissus (now Niš in Serbia). We know nothing about his career path, though he was already a serving soldier during the reign of Theodosius I. Presumably he had come west during the Eugenius campaign and remained there under Stilicho. He played no documented role in the chaos before and after Stilicho's execution, and emerges on the scene only in 410, perhaps as *comes domesticorum*, when he orchestrated the second fall of Olympius and had him clubbed to death. Constantius was then elevated to the *magisterium utriusque militiae*, senior commander of the praesental army.

The fractured remains of Alaric's following interested him much less than did Constantine. Early in 411, shortly after Honorius celebrated his *vicennalia* in Rome (despite its having been merely nineteen years since he became augustus, not twenty), Constantius and his *magister equitum* Ulfilas led a field army over the Alps. They arrived at Arelate at the same time as Gerontius. The latter had again defeated Constans, this time at Vienne, and was now planning to overthrow his father Constantine. Gerontius fled before the advance of the army of Constantius and Ulfilas, but most of his troops shifted their loyalty to them, as they continued the siege that Gerontius had begun. They also intercepted Constantine's loyal *magister* Edobich as he marched to Arelate from the Rhineland along the main highway down the Rhône valley. Trapped between the forces of Constantius and Ulfilas, Edobich sought asylum with an old friend, a Gallic nobleman called Ecdicius, but his new troops were routed. Ecdicius chose the winning side over the duties of friendship and murdered Edobich, sending his head as a gift to Constantius.

At Arelate, Constantine realised that his cause had become hopeless. He took refuge in a church and got himself ordained as a priest. The relieved populace opened the city gates to Constantius, who took Constantine and his surviving son Julian prisoner and sent them back to Honorius in Italy. They were executed beside the river Mincio early in September 411, and on 18 September their heads were displayed on spikes at Ravenna, before being sent to Carthago Nova in Spain to convince supporters there that the cause was well and truly finished.

Spain, like northern Gaul and Britain, remained quite lost to the government of Honorius. We know this because of the extraordinary and detailed account of Hydatius, a later fifth-century bishop from Aquae Flaviae, now Chaves in modern Portugal. Although his literary pretensions sometimes get the better of him, Hydatius had access to good sources of local history, and he had lived through much of what he chronicles. He tells us that after the Vandals, Alans and Sueves broke through the unguarded passes of the western Pyrenees, they looted far and wide in the Spanish diocese, holding well-protected cities hostage to their rampages and inducing widespread famine. As we have seen, the only effective military forces in the Spanish diocese were those led by Constans and Gerontius, initially together, then locked in a bloody civil war. When the campaign shifted from Spain to Gaul, that only further denuded the Spanish provinces of troops, and it was years before the government of Honorius was able to give any attention to Spain. Both these circumstances meant that the countryside – and sometimes the cities, too – was criss-crossed by well-armed warbands, the invaders pitted against the militias and private armies of the senatorial landowners and the urban *curiales*. The initial impact of the invasion had passed by 411, and the different ethnic warbands staked out their spheres of influence: the Alans took Lusitania and Carthaginiensis; one group of Vandals, known as the Silings, took Baetica; while some other Vandals and the Suevi split the province of Gallaecia between them. This division has occasioned a great deal of scholarly controversy, and there is no obvious logic behind it (Hydatius says the groups' leaders drew lots for the provinces, which is highly improbable but about as good an explanation as any).

One way or another, we should not envisage the Alans, Vandals and Sueves taking over the governing apparatus of the provinces they inhabited, but alternately raiding and allying themselves to provincial elites as was useful. That becomes an ongoing dynamic in the fifth-century western provinces where new populations came to settle: not so much conquest and replacement of Roman by barbarian government, but rather the arrival of new military forces who could be both dangerous and useful for the locals, weakening ties between province and imperial centre.

We can find parallels to the relatively well documented Spanish situation all over the western empire. Analogous forces had been at work in the north of Gaul ever since the time of Magnus Maximus, as is suggested in the material evidence. In the late fourth century and the early fifth century, a new culture developed in the countryside of the lower and middle Rhineland, inside the old Roman frontiers, characterised by new forms of burial in large cemeteries arranged in neat rows (*Reihengräber-felder* is the German word for these, and has entered the English language scholarship as well). These were once interpreted as evidence for mass migrations from elsewhere, but we now understand that the change in fashion began in the region itself and was later exported into what had previously been non-Roman territory. These new burial habits reflected changing settlement patterns and, more importantly, new forms of social authority: as the populations of northern and north-western Gaul increasingly lost touch with the formal structures of the Roman state, control devolved to a more local level that was not validated by the distant claims of imperial legitimacy and which therefore required far more lavish public displays of wealth and power.

Even more dramatic – though less immediately visible in the material evidence – is the change that took place in Britain, where we are told that, in 409 or 410, the population threw out their Roman officials and, to all intents and purposes, seceded from the empire. What that might mean has occasioned even more debate than has the Gallic or Spanish evidence, not least because it is the disappearance of Roman government in Britain that ushers in the 'Age of King Arthur', a miasmic swamp of speculation that sober scholars enter at their peril.

What actually took place in Britain remains exceptionally obscure. Probably, the units of *comitatenses* taken to the European mainland by Magnus Maximus in the 380s were never restored to full strength, and the revolt of Constantine III stripped the province of all but very local garrisons. As a result, the day-to-day tasks for which the empire needed soldiers – guarding the *annona*, policing banditry, intercepting raiders – no longer got done. Raiding from Ireland increased dramatically, and probably also from the Pictish north. In 409 or so, the frustrated Britons sent a provincial delegation to Ravenna to request aid from Honorius' embattled central government, but they were instructed to look to their own resources. That response prompted rioting in the main administrative centres and was remembered in the sources as the Britons throwing out their Roman magistrates – a congenial fable enshrined not just in such patriotic tomes as H. E. Marshall's *Our Island Story* (1905) and its modern descendants, but in respectable scholarship as well.

In fact, the British evidence coheres with the Gallic and Spanish, but reports it in a different way: faced with insoluble crisis in the imperial centre, provincials were forced into local self-defence and self-government, whether they liked it or not. In places where the imperial superstructure was restored, as it was in much of Gaul and Spain, the period of local autonomy looked like an unfortunate interlude; in places where it was not, it was remembered as a popular revolt against Rome. And even where imperial government was restored, the process was slow and not always greeted with enthusiasm, as the aftermath of Constantine III makes clear.

We have seen the way that Constantius and Ulfilas put an end to that usurpation. Gerontius died soon after his one-time comrade: having fled back to Spain and the court of his client Maximus, he faced the revolt of his remaining followers, who set ablaze the house in which he had taken refuge. His situation hopeless, he killed his wife and last faithful servant, and then fell on his own dagger. Maximus fled to the Vandals in Gallaecia, whence he would later make a second ill-omened attempt at usurpation.

But these Honorian victories did not mean that Gaul was pacified. Just at the moment when Constantine's regime was collapsing, another Gallic revolt erupted in the Rhineland. It is hard not to imagine some continuity between the revolts, although none is explicitly attested in the sources. Clearly, though, some substantial portion of the Gallic elites was displeased with the prospect of renewed control from south of the Alps. This new revolt centred on a man called Jovinus and his brothers Sebastianus and Sallustius, who were members of a noble clan that may have been connected to the regime of Constantine. It may be that the family of Jovinus, based in Germania Secunda, had helped hold the north for the usurper, and they certainly had strong connections with nearby frontier warlords: Guntiarius, a Burgundian chieftain, and Goar, an Alan, are named as key supporters. More explicitly than in Britain and Spain, where similar alliances were no doubt being contracted, we see in the Jovinus revolt the willingness of local elites to make peace with new regional powers in order to enhance their own local positions. And Jovinus' proclamation was no futile gesture, but actually serious enough for Constantius and Ulfilas to flee south of the Alps late in 411.

There, in Italy, Alaric's successor Athaulf was facing difficult choices. He was a powerful nobleman in his own right and an enemy of the Gothic general Sarus who had scuppered the last set of peace talks between Alaric and Honorius. Although Athaulf and his followers had been left unmolested for most of 411, Italy was not a sustainable long-term residence for them. If for no other reason, this was because Athaulf had with him both the former usurper Priscus Attalus and the emperor's sister Galla Placidia, with whom he would soon contract a marriage alliance as an alternative focus of Theodosian dynasticism. And so, very late in 411 or early in 412,

Athaulf and his followers marched into Gaul by the coastal road with all the riches they had captured in the sack of Rome. That was surely enough to buy them supplies as they went, and it is worth noting that their passage into Gaul was an orderly troop transfer, not a destructive invasion.

Once into Gallia Narbonensis, and following the advice of Attalus, whose political ineptitude showed no signs of abatement, Athaulf flirted with the idea of supporting Jovinus against the clearly hostile Constantius. Whatever attraction that course of action might have had, the discovery that Sarus had joined the Rhineland usurpation ended any further thoughts of alliance. Athaulf hunted down and killed Sarus, declared himself for Jovinus, and then changed his mind when the latter made his brother Sebastianus co-emperor. He instead brought down the regime: Sebastianus was killed and his head sent to Ravenna, while Jovinus was despatched to Honorius alive, only to be executed en route, perhaps early in 413. A massive purge of his supporters, and probably also those of Constantine, was now orchestrated by officials loyal to Ravenna, until an amnesty was granted in June 413. Despite this and other efforts to reconcile the Gallic nobility, the warm relationship between the two regions' senatorial elites had been broken for ever, and each increasingly saw the other as a bunch of foreigners with whom they shared few, if any interests.

The Gallic revolts were not the only threats facing the Italian regime in that year. In Carthage, the *comes Africae* Heraclianus was restive. He had won his position by betraying Stilicho and had long been an ally of Olympius, contributing to the defeats of Attalus and Alaric by keeping Africa's grain out of their hands. The sudden ascendancy of Constantius aroused his envy, and gave him a goal to aim for. Ravenna tried at first to conciliate him and he was designated as western consul of 413. But this was not enough, and early in his putative consulship he revolted openly and cut off the grain supply to Italy. Though it is sometimes said that he declared himself emperor, the fact that he minted no coins disproves this; he wanted not to replace the Honorian regime but to control it in succession to Stilicho, Olympius and the incumbent Constantius.

Once the seas opened for the year in spring 413, Heraclianus sailed a fleet to Italy but was defeated by Constantius' lieutenant Marinus, who pursued him back to Carthage when the rebel *comes* fled. Seeing no realistic path to success, Heraclianus' own supporters murdered him shortly thereafter, and Marinus conducted a major purge in the city of Carthage. He, too, now fell foul of powerful, if shadowy, figures in the African church and aristocracy. In September, he was recalled to Italy and dismissed. The consulate of Heraclianus was abolished, and his goods were confiscated and bestowed upon Constantius as a reward for his loyalty. For a very brief moment, Honorius was the sole person claiming the western throne. That was in itself a triumph at this point, but the successive proclamations in most of the western dioceses revealed a pattern of entrenched warlordism that would characterise the rest of the fifth century.

The violent suppression of Jovinus had done little to soothe the Gallic aristocracy or reconcile it to Ravenna, and some of the Gallic elites now struck up a friendly alliance with Galla Placidia and Athaulf. These two decided that the time had come to provide an alternative Theodosian house, to oppose the erratic and ineffectual court of the still childless Honorius. Gallia Narbonensis had long been the richest and most densely urban part of Gaul, and it had also been the least damaged by the civil wars and invasions of the previous decade. It would be the new regime's base. In September of 413, Athaulf and Placidia took up residence in Narbo (modern Narbonne), while Tolosa (Toulouse) in Aquitania also sided with them. The city council of Massilia (Marseille), by contrast, stayed loyal to Ravenna and repelled the forces Athaulf sent to occupy it, while Arelate remained firmly in the hands of its Honorian government. A territorial base was merely the first step, however: on 1 January 414, as Constantius was celebrating his first consulship in Italy, Placidia and Athaulf were married with great ceremony at Narbo, with Priscus Attalus declaiming the *epithalamium* or wedding oration. Placidia was either already, or soon became, pregnant, and she had every intention of being the mother of an emperor. Lest there be any doubt, the child would be named Theodosius.

The alliance of an indisputably legitimate member of the ruling dynasty with one of the best generals operating in the Roman West was a direct threat to Flavius Constantius, whose relations with the eastern regime of Theodosius II were likewise souring – the eastern consul for the year was never recognised in the West. Indeed, Placidia and Athaulf were far more dangerous than any of the usurpers Honorius had yet faced. Entirely lacking in other qualities, Honorius' sole merit was his legitimacy. Placidia, particularly Placidia with a male heir, would almost certainly attract the loyalty of many people who supported Honorius only for want of anything better.

Constantius acted fast, marching to Arelate and focusing all his efforts on the new regime's greatest weakness, an inability to adequately supply its army. A naval blockade prevented supplies reaching Narbo by ship, and Athaulf could neither disperse his followers widely enough to allow them to feed themselves, nor secure enough food to keep them concentrated in one place and stay effective militarily. Seeing his support wavering, he put up his own emperor – Priscus Attalus once again – knowing that he could be discarded if Placidia's child was a boy. The hapless aristocrat, who had now been baptised a homoian Christian by the Gothic bishop Sigesarius, proved just as incapable of arousing loyalty this second time around. It was Placidia, not Athaulf, who was the natural focus of Gallic support. Any harsh measure to secure supplies would immediately negate that support, so the pair abandoned Narbo and crossed into Spain, the birthplace of the Theodosian dynasty. Attalus was again deposed and left behind in Gaul for Constantius to deal with – he spent the next two years a prisoner in Ravenna before being displayed in triumph, mutilated and exiled to the island of Lipari in the Tyrrhenian Sea. This was the last serious usurpation Honorius faced in a reign that toddled on for nearly another full decade.

In the East, Honorius' nephew Theodosius II would prove equally long-lived and personally ineffectual, but he was blessed with a vastly more competent regime to support him. When his father died in 408, Theodosius was only seven years old, and the regency devolved upon the palatine bureaucracy. The child had been the tool of others even when Arcadius was still alive: on the day of his baptism, in a carefully rehearsed move orchestrated by his mother, the empress Eudoxia, the bishop of Gaza presented the infant Theodosius with a petition, asking him to close the temple of Zeus Marnas in that city. The official carrying the baby rocked his head in a gesture of assent, and so the petition was granted (unless, as has been argued, the whole story is a sixth-century invention – if so, it is a very plausible one).

From the week of his birth to the day of his death, most of Theo-dosius' decisions were made for him by someone else. The praetorian prefect Anthemius, in power when Arcadius died, remained there for years, his long ascendancy a sharp contrast to the kaleidoscopic turnover of power in the West. The care of young Theodosius lay in the hands of the Persian eunuch Antiochus, who had been the boy's tutor for some time already, and the eastern empire had been more or less at peace since Arcadius' death. Financially secure, Constantinople could ignore the occasional rumbling on the frontier, or at least buy it off, and the Danube was patrolled by a large new fleet. Relations with the Persians were also

quite good and the ecclesiastical disruption that had characterised Chrysostom's episcopate was a thing of the past. Indeed, so much better were
the eastern state's finances than those of the West that in April 414, late
in Anthemius' prefecture, he was able to waive forty years of tax arrears
throughout the prefecture of Oriens.

Perhaps even more than under Theodosius I and Arcadius, it was now,
during the minority of Theodosius II, that Constantinople became the
true capital of the eastern empire, surpassing Antioch and Alexandria both
in size and in the lavishness of its townscape. This was a remarkable feat
considering how much younger a foundation it was. Its defences were also
increasingly formidable: huge new walls, to this day called Anthemian in
honour of the prefect who ordered their construction, blocked off the
peninsula that housed the city centre. Although they are nowadays in a
part of the city that tourists enter at their peril, the walls are still enor-
mously impressive and they effectively rendered the city impenetrable to
whatever violence was afflicting the rest of Thrace and the Balkans. That
became still more true after sea walls were put up later in the century,
followed shortly thereafter by the Long Walls, sixty kilometres west of the
Anthemian walls in Thrace, where even a truly enormous army approaching the city would be forced to break up and risk dispersal.

Beneath this surface calm, there was a quiet revolution in the eastern
government in 414: Anthemius died, the old tutors and staff of Theodosius
were dismissed, and his care and education were taken over by his elder
sister Pulcheria, a princess every bit as ambitious as her aunt Placidia in the
West. On 4 July 414, Pulcheria was proclaimed augusta and, in order to
establish continuity with the regime of her father Arcadius, she recalled the
former prefect Aurelianus from retirement to his old post. Aurelianus did
not hold his restored office for long, but another of Pulcheria's appointees,
the *magister officiorum* Helion, kept that position for more than a decade,
until 427. Unlike Placidia, whose strategy relied upon marriage and the
potential of producing an heir, Pulcheria pledged herself to virginity and
persuaded her sisters to do so as well: one year before becoming augusta,
she had dedicated an altar in the Hagia Sophia 'for her own virginity and
her brother's sovereignty'. This sums up her political programme nicely.
Her brother Theodosius would be the sole carrier of dynastic destiny, but
she could influence affairs from a position ostentatiously free of personal
ambition. She would neither be used by a husband's faction to pursue
rival interests, nor herself become a focus for resistance, but would instead

maintain her powerful influence by retaining personal control over her brother behind the scenes.

The fifth-century church historian Sozomenus already recognised this as a deliberate political strategy, and Pulcheria was one of his favourite figures. She had a genuine interest in fostering orthodoxy, and she filled the palace in Constantinople with monks and holy men while encouraging her brother to similar theological enthusiasms. In part because of Pulcheria, and in part because she was successful in awakening Theodosius' own interest, his reign is notable for the scale of religious investment in Constantinople, and the dominance of the imperial family in its cityscape, to the point that whole quarters of the city were named for the princesses Marina and Pulcheria. This religious patronage was a novel way for imperial women to exercise political ambitions, one that opened up in part by accident, after the emperor and his court had become more or less permanent residents of a single location. Pulcheria would manage her brother's affairs throughout the later 410s, before helping arrange his marriage to Aelia Eudocia, after which she set up her own separate household.

Meanwhile, as one admiring author put it, the city of Constantinople became as it were one giant church, enwrapped in the piety of its rulers. The intensity of this piety would bear mixed fruits over time – as in earlier reigns, orthodoxy and imperial politics could be a toxic mix. As Constantinople became ever more dominant, Alexandria and Antioch became ever more jealous, and nurtured their schismatic populations. Relations with Persia were also strained, directly and indirectly, by the pious rigour of the Constantinopolitan regime. We will look at these issues at the start of the next chapter, after tracing the lingering end of Honorius' reign.

The execution of Heraclianus and the exile of Priscus Attalus had marked the end of significant western usurpations for years to come – Gerontius' short-lived imperial protégé Maximus made another attempt at usurpation towards the end of the reign, but that, like the Spanish diocese in which it was launched, was basically a sideshow. Gaul would always be a greater worry, given how hostile parts of the Gallic aristocracy remained. But by forcing the nascent regime of Athaulf and Placidia into Spain in 414, Constantius had effectively marginalised them. The birth of their child might have counted for a great deal, but the infant boy – named Theodosius with high hopes – died shortly after birth and was buried in a silver coffin in Barcino. Athaulf's enemies had kept themselves in check just as long as his imperial dream remained plausible, but soon after the infant Theodosius died, Placidia's husband fell victim to the assassin's knife. He was murdered while inspecting his stables, at an unknown date, though the news had reached Constantinople by 24 September 415. The killer was a servant who had once been loyal to Athaulf's personal enemy, long conjectured to be the freebooting general Sarus whom Athaulf had killed two years before. The conjecture is strengthened by the fact that Sigeric, the brother of Sarus, now claimed leadership of Athaulf's bereft following. It was not a consensus choice, and Sigeric was in turn assassinated within the week. A new leader, Wallia, took military control of the tattered army that had once sacked Rome.

Placidia, though she had suffered deliberate public humiliation during the very brief ascendancy of Sigeric, remained the single most significant figure in this particular political constellation, not because of the scant resources she at the time commanded, but because of who she was. Though she would never again have the chance to establish a dynastic base that could really threaten her brother, her alliance with Athaulf had left her a permanent foundation of Gothic supporters on whom she could rely to guarantee her personal independence. She therefore allowed herself to become the chief prize in negotiations between Wallia and Constantius, the latter determined to use Placidia to his advantage and not merely to neutralise the threat she posed. The *magister militum* offered to supply Wallia and his men with the food they needed if they gave up Placidia and thereby paved a route for Constantius into the imperial family.

After several tense months of negotiations, during which Wallia's Goths were forced to buy up food at exorbitant prices from Vandal warlords elsewhere in Spain, they found themselves bountifully provided for by the Roman state, and also given a clear charge: rid the peninsula of the Alan, Vandal and Suevic bands that had made themselves at home there since 411. The salaried cooptation of semi-dependent warlords would become the main lifeline of western emperors over the coming generations – but with ever diminishing returns. In the campaign seasons of 416 and 417, Wallia's men set about their task with a real gusto. Their campaigns were a wild success, effectively destroying the independent Alan warbands and the Siling Vandals who had made Baetica their main sphere of activity. These Silings disappear from history, while the surviving Alans sought refuge in Gallaecia with other Vandals, called Asdings, which meant that later Vandal leaders would call themselves 'kings of the Vandals and Alans'.

Placidia was returned to the court of her brother in Italy. On 1 January 417, Constantius took the consulship for the second time and on the same day married Placidia – with her brother's consent but not her own. To play a supporting role in the ambitions of Constantius had never been part of her plan, and her privileged access to the Goths would always give her more freedom of movement than most late ancient women, even most late ancient princesses, possessed.

Gaul, meanwhile, remained quiescent, though there is no evidence that the Rhineland was reinforced in any meaningful way or that regularised provincial government returned to the northern Belgic provinces or lower Germany; indeed, it seems quite likely that the de facto abandonment of much of northern Gaul – particularly those parts that now lie beyond Amiens north of the Somme and west of the Rhine – was an accomplished fact by 415 or so. Traditional narratives of Frankish conquest or infiltration are exaggerated, but government across the whole region appears to have devolved to the level of the *civitas* or city territory, with surviving municipal elites and warlords of varying origins competing for local power. Having written off its ability to control those northern territories save by way of periodic military incursions, the Italian regime made real efforts to restore its prestige and authority elsewhere in Gaul. The regional government in Treveri and its immediate environs was reestablished, though not at full strength. Even so, it was an essential element for monitoring, if not always controlling, events on both sides of the middle Rhine frontier. The seat of the Gallic prefecture was not moved back to Treveri, however, but kept at Arelate, deep in the south, which suggests the limitations faced by the central government.

Our sources go from bad to much worse as the century wears on, but one potentially useful text is a document known as the *Notitia Dignitatum*. We have this in the form of a Renaissance copy of an early medieval copy of a late Roman deluxe manuscript, purporting to describe the administrative establishments of both the western and the eastern empires. A series of chancery documents underlie the deluxe illustrated volume that we see today, and that functional document was, in its western portions, updated sporadically right through the mid 420s. In these updatings, we witness both the shrinkage of the praesental field army into the sole professional force available to Constantius and his subordinates, and the parcelling-out of commands along the Rhine and upper Danube to regional commanders in charge of small local forces that could monitor and police, but not really control or administer, their territories. The creation of a separate command at Argentoratum (modern Strasbourg), for instance, is evidence for precisely this model, and there was a similarly isolated command at Moguntiacum. In the late 410s, and for several decades to come, this approach to governing the lands around the main frontier towns provided the framework of both military administration and such limited civil government as survived; as time went on, these garrisoned cities came to resemble islands of imperial governance in a chaotic landscape full of warlords – Italian, Gallic, Gothic, Frankish, Alan, Alamannic and Burgundian – and then finally became themselves alternative centres of warlordism.

The south of Gaul presented Constantius and the Italians with a different set of challenges – it had suffered much less from the invasions and civil warfare of the past decade or more, and had never ceased to be administered by one imperial regime or another. From the perspective of the central government, the restoration of order was therefore a matter of insuring against future usurpations among the southern Gallic aristocracy, much of which had every reason to remain disaffected after the purges that accompanied the suppression of Constantine III and Jovinus.

To assure himself of the support and loyalty of the south, Constantius therefore oversaw the creation of a new regional consultative body called the *Concilium Septem Provinciae*, or the Council of the Seven Provinces. This was established by an imperial edict in 417, and was to meet annually in Arelate, allowing the elites of southern Gaul to have a formal venue in which to air their interests, vent their grievances and communicate their concerns to the central authority. The Council would represent only the southern provinces: Novempopulana up against the Pyrenees, the two Aquitanias in the west, the two Narbonenses in the south, Viennensis in the south-east and Alpes Maritimae on the border of the Italian diocese.

In tandem with the devolution to military government in the north, the Council of the Seven Provinces was a sure sign of the central government's diminished authority. The Italian regime was in effect acknowledging that full-blown civilian government could be maintained only in Africa, Italy, southern Gaul, parts of Spain and perhaps a few corners of Illyricum. The consequences of this for the daily lives of the inhabitants of the other western provinces are largely opaque to us, but must at the very least have meant that the administration of justice broke down, taking on an increasingly semi-official character, or otherwise that it fell to local clerics and strongmen. For the imperial government, the outcome of these territorial retrenchments was a failure to restore the previously existing tax base, and that, as much as anything, would set the western empire on a fatal course completely different from that of the East, where neither the tax base nor the money supply were ever imperilled.

Perhaps the worst of it, from the Italian perspective, was a suspicion that the Gauls could never really prove themselves trustworthy again, and it may be that renewed Gallic grumbling greeted the establishment of the new governmental order. That would explain why, in 418, Constantius availed himself of a potential weapon: Wallia's Goths. By that time, Wallia had effectively cleared Tarraconensis, Baetica, Lusitania and Carthaginiensis (four of the Iberian peninsula's five provinces) of their warlords and opened the way for the restoration of imperial government. In the main provincial cities, we find renewed evidence of the imperial civilian administration. Vandals and Suevi remained in control of parts of Gallaecia, but, along with Britain and north-western Gaul, the province lay at the very edge of the Roman world and possessed neither sufficient strategic nor economic value to make its recovery crucial. By contrast, controlling problematical Gallic aspirations was essential, and so Wallia was told to cease his campaigning and instead to settle down to garrison Aquitania Secunda (now the French regions of Aquitaine and Poitou-Charentes to the west of the Limousin), where his men could be mobilised quickly to suppress murmurs of usurpation anywhere in the Seven Provinces.

Thirty years later, this settlement had grown into a semi-dependent kingdom on imperial soil, with a de facto capital at Tolosa, but in 418 no such outcome was intended. In effect, Alaric's dream of regularising his followers' association with the imperial government was finally realised by Wallia – who himself died before the settlement took place. His successor as the head of these Goths – whom we may now for convenience call Visigoths, though the name is anachronistic – was one Theoderic, said to have been the grandson of Alaric. He would prove a towering figure in the politics of the next few decades, but in 418, and as long as Honorius lived, he was as loyal to the Ravenna regime as the *comites* and *duces* of the Rhine frontier. The Gallic nobility, cowed by the formidable garrison in their midst, remained quiescent for the best part of a generation.

Constantius had every reason to be well pleased. He was now clearly the dominant power in the state, and the fact that we know so little about the court factions surrounding him suggests that there was none that could challenge his predominance. The generation of commanders that emerges into the light in the 420s – Asterius, Bonifatius, Aëtius, Castinus – was now rising through the ranks, though career paths are hard to trace in the limited sources we have available.

Constantius also seemed likely to achieve what Athaulf had not, father an heir to the throne. Late in 417 or early in 418, Placidia gave birth to a daughter, Iusta Grata Honoria, who would one day play the game of imperial politics as deftly as her mother. Somewhat over a year later, on 2 July 419, Galla gave birth to a son, Valentinian. The palace intrigues that followed these births are invisible to us, but intrigues there must have been: on 8 February 421, Constantius was raised to the imperial purple as augustus, Placidia was elevated to the rank of augusta, and their infant son Valentinian became *nobilissimus puer*. Honorius, we are told, was hostile to this arrangement and accepted Constantius' elevation much against his will. It would not be recogniaed in the East while Constantius lived.

One reason Honorius may have been more willing to tolerate Constantius than the sources suggest, however, was his own obvious failure to inspire loyalty. In 418, the usurper Maximus, who had briefly reigned in Tarraconensis before the collapse of his sponsor Gerontius, and who had then taken refuge in the camp of one of Spain's barbarian warlords, now reappeared, again claiming the purple, this time in Gallaecia. A Spanish aristocrat named Asterius was appointed *comes Hispaniarum* and sent to Tarraco, where we have a long account of his involvement in a baroque ecclesiastical scandal involving magic books and accusations of clandestine Priscillianism. Asterius' main task was to suppress Maximus, but he also campaigned against the Vandals and the Sueves, who had come to blows with one another. The effect of the latter campaign was ambiguous: the Vandal army turned away from its Suevic foes, attacked Asterius, and then marched into Baetica, which had so recently been cleared of its warlords. By contrast, the former campaign was a stunning success. Maximus was captured and sent back to Italy. Asterius was honoured with the title of *patricius* in succession to Constantius, who died on 2 September 421, not long after his successor's victory in Spain. Honorius had not needed to endure his unwelcome co-emperor very long, while Maximus now joined the *catalogus tyrannorum*, 'catalogue of usurpers', that Honorius had suppressed. He was displayed in the festivities that, on 23 January 422, marked the *tricennalia* of Honorius, in the year that he held his thirteenth consulship while Theodosius held his tenth in the East.

If Honorius was unmoved by his colleague's death, the military high command was in ferment. Constantius' dominance had prevented the rise of any clear successor, but succession to the *magisterium utriusque militiae* was by now just as important to the stability of the western empire as was the succession to the imperial throne. Asterius had died shortly after becoming *patricius*, possibly even before Constantius himself, so Flavius Castinus was appointed to the office. He was opposed by Placidia, who favoured her own supporter Bonifatius, and Castinus' position was weakened almost at once by failure. He personally led a campaign against the Vandals in Baetica in 422 and lost it disastrously; he may have been sabotaged by Visigothic auxiliaries supplied by Theoderic and personally allied to Placidia.

Castinus nevertheless remained powerful enough to drive Bonifatius out of his praesental command and force him into exile in Africa. Once he was there, however, Placidia got this fait accompli regularised, and Bonifatius was made *comes Africae*, in which role he would have as much authority – and as much power to make mischief – as had Gildo and Heraclianus before him. Yet the fragility of Placidia's position after the death of Constantius and the exile of Bonifatius became clear in 423, when her supporters – many of them Goths who had formed her private bodyguard since the days of her ascendancy in Narbo and Barcino – fought pitched street battles against supporters of her brother, from whom she was increasingly estranged. The damage that did to her standing in Ravenna convinced Placidia to flee to Constantinople, where she might find support against her brother from the regime of her niece Pulcheria and nephew Theodosius. She and her children, Honoria and Valentinian, were imbibing the pious atmosphere of the eastern capital when news came that Honorius had died on 15 August 423. He had been an emperor of abiding uselessness, and the aftermath of his death was no happier. The contrast with the strength of the eastern court could not be much starker.

8

THE REIGN OF
THEODOSIUS II

✦✦✦✦✦✦

The reign of Theodosius II provides more than a few of the stereotypes that moderns have come to associate with Byzantine history – an initially pejorative eighteenth-century designation for the eastern, Greek Roman empire after Constantinople was founded on the site of ancient Byzantium. The epithet was meant to qualify the period and its people as different from, and inferior to, the Roman empire that preceded it – and also different from the supposedly more dynamic culture of its contemporary Latin Middle Ages, the imagined basis of European modernity. Old Graeco-Roman stereotypes of Near Eastern cultures – culturally static autocracy, slavish dispositions, irrational and barbarous religiosity – came by elision to apply to the Greek Roman empire, orientalising it in a deliberately deprecatory way.

Nowadays, by contrast, the forty-year boom in the study of late antiquity as a site of boundless diversity and creativity has (of necessity) focused more on eastern developments than the politically riven and rapidly disintegrating West. None the less, the alert reader will have noticed – perhaps with relief – that in the last chapter, as in this one and those that follow, the barrage of names of various palatine and military officials has grown smaller. That smoothing effect is not an illusion, but an artefact of the sources: while we have some relatively detailed narrative accounts – mostly church histories, along with fragments of classicising histories and disjointed notices in chronicles – we have fewer and fewer of the inscriptions that fleshed out the workings of politics in the second half of the fourth century. The evidence of the law codes narrows as well, and then peters out after a flurry of legislation at the end of the 430s.

Fortunately, triangulating the evidence of laws, letters and inscriptions with the narrative evidence was what allowed scholars to reconstruct in detail the connections by which men rose to prominence during the later fourth century, and thus also the way that government worked. In their relative absence, our grasp of the fifth century is poorer, notably in the West, but in the East as well: the court, consistory and military high command who had long controlled the political life of the empire become more opaque. The extraordinary level of detailed information about court politics that lurks in the massive dossiers of three great church councils (at Ephesus in 431 and 449, and then at Chalcedon in 451) give unprecedented insight into the day-to-day workings of petition and reply, judgement and dissent, and scheming for influence within household and *consistorium*, but they cover less than five years of a 50-year reign. We can extrapolate from the style of government they reveal, and also get a synchronic sense of law-making at Constantinople from the contents of the great Theodosian Code and the new laws (*novellae*) that supplemented it, but change over time becomes harder to detect and account for.

In part because of this evidentiary lacuna, it remains difficult even for scholars to escape old stereotypes of Byzantium – 'monuments of unageing intellect', as Yeats once had it, but not a great deal of action. Political instability is much easier for the historian to write about than political stability, and stability is exactly what characterised the court of the younger Theodosius. Things look static in part because, even after he came of age, the emperor both lacked a consistent vision of his empire and also was not subject to the kind of sudden enthusiasm that might wildly skew imperial activity. But this lack of imperial interest did not – as it had, for instance, under Honorius in the West, or the minority of Arcadius in the East – lead to the open warfare of factions, the dominance of a particular favourite, or the succession of rival strongmen – and that despite the fact that contemporaries could at various times detect the hand of the empresses Pulcheria and Eudocia, and for a time the eunuch *praepositus* Chrysaphius, in imperial decisions.

But what looks like the greatest paradox of the reign – how a personally very weak emperor reigned unchallenged, unthreatened by usurpation or dynastic rivalry, for the better part of half a century – can in fact be explained by the remarkable degree of harmony that existed within the palatine bureaucracy and the senior civilian members of the *consistorium*. Many of them could trace the rise of their families back to the reign of Constantius II. Also, most had not developed the interlocking marital connections to the military and senatorial aristocracies of the wider empire, preserving an essentially civilian and Constantinopolitan perspective that meant individual rivalries did little to deflect them from essentially common interests in orderly, stable government along consistent and consolidated lines. A similarly shared interest lay in keeping prospective military dynasts – generals like Ardaburius, Aspar, Plintha and Procopius – further from the reins of power than proved possible in the West; it helped that none of those had the tactical genius and flair for command of a Flavius Constantius or a Stilicho and that, with very rare exceptions, none had the opportunity to win victories on a scale that might stoke their ambitions for greater things. We can, in other words, recognise that the stability of the reign was quite real, even if we cannot always trace the individuals responsible for it.

As we saw in the last chapter, the year 414 had been a turning point of sorts, with the death of the long-serving praetorian prefect Anthemius, the recall of the aged Aurelian to the same position, the dismissal of the eunuch *cubicularius* Antiochus from the emperor's tutorship, the appointment of Helion as *magister officiorum*, and the rise to prominence of Pulcheria, Theodosius' elder sister, who in that year took control of his education and pushed it in the direction of the theological studies she herself favoured. She, and later her rival empress Aelia Eudocia, Theodosius' wife, would both take similar levels of interest in questions of orthodoxy and church authority, and the reign would be a period of many great church councils. But the religious ferment of these years, though no doubt encouraged by the enthusiasms of the imperial court, was spontaneously at work elsewhere in the eastern world as well.

To modern eyes, the most shocking ecclesisatical events of the early part of the reign came not from the court or even the imperial city, but rather from Alexandria. The city had always been prone to rioting and, during the high imperial period, several emperors had found it salutary to discipline the Alexandrians with great violence. This level of general turbulence meant that the city never developed the same sort of strong *polis* government that characterised Antioch and many of the East's other large cities – imperial officials were far more important to the administration and the textures of urban life in Alexandria than was the case anywhere else. This mattered, because it made Alexandria the only eastern city apart from Constantinople itself where few alternative networks of authority intervened between imperial officialdom and the episcopal establishment. The upshot was that – from before the time of Athanasius of Alexandria, even – the bishops of Alexandria possessed a local dominance that no other bishop, not even the bishop of Rome, could imagine.

At the start of Theodosius II's reign, the Alexandrian episcopate was in the hands of bishop Cyril, one of antiquity's least savoury churchmen, as vicious an ecclesiastical pit fighter as Athanasius, but at the head of a church that had grown much stronger and very much richer. In the north African church of the middle fourth century, Christian piety and the enforcement of orthodoxy could serve as a cover for sheer hooligan-ism – the Donatist circumcellions were as interested in brawling and fighting pitched street battles as in their supposed vocation as monks. Cyril exploited similar rowdies in Egypt, but on a greater scale, creating what was in essence a paramilitary force of his *parabalani*. These able-bodied 'lay brothers' were recruited from among the urban poor and employed to collect the sick and the indigent from the streets and bring them care and comfort, but they were at the same time the jihadist terrorists of their day, as the Maccabees had been of theirs. The *parabalani* could be brought out on to the streets to thump those whom Cyril considered enemies of the faith – Jews, pagans, Christians of opposing theological opinion.

For Alexandria, huge as it was, was not yet a fully Christian city. Along with its many Jews, it had a thriving pagan community – a community with whose philosophers a Christian might study, and which naturally gravitated towards various forms of non-Christian monotheism. The most inspiring teacher of the age was, most unusually, a woman. Her name was Hypatia and she was the daughter of an earlier philosopher and mathematician called Theon. Her teaching, which has not been preserved in writing, is generally assumed to have been of the Neoplatonic variety, descended from the traditions of another Egyptian, the great Plotinus, but she and her father seem to have devoted much of their time to establish-ing the text of scientific classics like the astronomical tables of Ptolemy, as well as bringing them up to date. She was a powerful and influential figure in Alexandria, on the list of local grandees whom new imperial officials made a point of visiting early and often. It was not just other pagans who studied with her, and she remained a figure of pious virtue in later Christian sources as well (it was said that she remained a virgin, and rejected a potential husband by hurling her menstrual rag at him to demonstrate the carnal reality with which he claimed to be in love). A powerfully symbolic figure – a pagan, a woman and an intellectual authority – she became embroiled, perhaps accidentally, in the sort of violence to which Alexandria was always prone.

The imperial governor, the *praefectus Augustalis* Orestes, was a baptised Christian, but a Constantinopolitan and a foreigner to Alexandria. When he arrived in that city in 415, he found it overcome by strife over bishop Cyril's decision to round up and banish the city's Jews in what can only be described as a pogrom. When Orestes interfered to quell the disturbances this inevitably provoked, Cyril's *parabalani* and monastic allies from the hills of Nitria descended upon the city and, in the ensuing rioting, Orestes was himself wounded and nearly lynched. He responded with relative restraint, putting to death only the worst of the perpetrators, but this only enraged Cyril further. The two proved irreconcilable, and Orestes sent word to the court in Constantinople, angling to have the impossible bishop removed from his see.

In the midst of this stand-off, rumour spread that it was Hypatia who had the ear of the *praefectus*, and that it was she who was preventing his reconciliation with the bishop. The rumour is highly unlikely to be true: a 60-year-old pagan philosopher, schooled over many years in the city's deadly politics, would have had the sense to stay out of a fight between Christians about the treatment of Jews. All the same, truth is no barrier to fundamentalist conviction, and the *parabalani* were delighted with an excuse to attack a figure who went against their entire worldview: she was a pagan who taught many Christians who should know better, and she was a woman with power among men when female submission was a Christian duty.

A mob of Cyril's supporters gathered, inflamed by a reader in the church of Alexandria named Peter, and kidnapped Hypatia, taking her to one of the city's numerous churches. Here they exposed her to the humiliation of being stripped naked, and then stoned her to death with roof tiles. From the church historians of her own day to Charles Kingsley's stodgy, fictionalised triple-decker novel to a recent film called *Agora*, the murdered woman philosopher has attracted ongoing fascination, as much for her uniqueness as for the appalling manner of her death. For some a proto-feminist idol, for others the *exemplum* of a righteous pagan, she has also been taken as a symbol of the passing of the old world of Greek philosophy.

In fact, the teaching of Neoplatonic scholars continued in Alexandria down to the reign of Justinian in the sixth century, but the ever-increasing marginalisation of Hellenes within the mass of the Greek population is laid bare by the brutal murder of Hypatia: her intellect and her sex rendered her unusually transgressive, but all those who believed as she did were becoming outsiders in their own countries. A hundred years earlier, philosophers and bishops competed to impose their own narratives on, and interpretations of, events before the ruler, but that had all changed. The discourse of the empire was Christian, and there was not yet any vision that could reconcile the old philosophical teaching, deeply imbued with a pagan monotheism, and the militant Christianity of the Theodosian empire. The old philosophical schools, attractive still to the studious, were marginalised at both the level of public, civic devotion and within an intellectual milieu that was more and more concerned with the nuances of Christian theology.

Indeed, if Hypatia is a symbol of an old world ending, then Eudocia, the wife of that most Christian of emperors, Theodosius, was an opposite and equal symbol of the future. As in other things, Pulcheria was a motivating force here. She had intervened in the affairs at Alexandria as far as she could, but Cyril's great plausibility played on the piety of the court, and the initial order to punish his *parabalani* was retracted and their number in fact increased. Aurelian, old at the time of his appointment, was out of office by 416, perhaps dead, and his successor Monaxius managed affairs at court until 420. Though Theodosius had come of age by 417, the government clearly rested in the hands of Pulcheria within the palace, and of Monaxius and the consistory in the larger administration. It was through Pulcheria that the emperor was found a suitable bride, who would alone of the imperial family be permitted to produce heirs.

In 421, the daughter of an Athenian sophist named Leontius came to Constantinople to prosecute a dispute with her brothers over their inheritance. Her aunt was married to Theodosius' *comes sacrarum largitionum* Asclepiodotus, and was able to secure her an audience with Pulcheria, who took up her case. Named Athenaïs at birth, and educated in Greek literature by her father, she was presumably an attractive companion for the bookish young emperor – while her social status, honourable but not aristocratic, would ensure she posed no challenge to Pulcheria. Converted to Christianity, she took the name Aelia Eudocia, and married the emperor on 7 July 421. Pulcheria established a separate household for herself, but it is not clear that her influence waned to any great extent.

Eudocia – who was given the rank of augusta in 422 – brought a different sort of learning to the palace, one that was friendlier to things not purely theological, though still clearly Christian: one of her own verse productions was a cento of Homeric verse that retold stories from Genesis and the Gospels in twinned half-lines from Homer. The cento form – taking half lines from Homer in Greek or from Virgil in Latin and using them to tell a very different story – was a popular one in late antiquity, a form of clever sport for aristocrats to show off their erudition, and it is telling that this should have been one of the ways in which Eudocia stamped her presence on the court.

If the mental and social worlds of the eastern empire were changing, one thing that remained the same was the way Roman imperial history could be intermittently and sometimes violently affected by events taking place on the other side of the world. Disturbances between the Caspian Gates and the Pamir mountains inevitably affected the Persian empire, as did the propensity of the east Iranian frontier zones – from Bactria, through the Hindu Kush, to the Kushanshahr – for rebellion and secession, whether ruled by a Kushano-Sasanian cadet dynasty or one of the Hunnic clans. That in turn affected Persian attitudes towards and relations with the Roman empire. When the aggressive nomadic coalitions that rose and fell in shifting configurations on the Eurasian steppe impinged upon the Caucasus, that could directly affect both Roman and Persian core territories. It was why Eutropius, the much-reviled eunuch minister of Arcadius, had personally campaigned against Huns in Armenia, and why Rome and Persia may actually have decided to share the expense of garrisoning the main passes through the Caucasus. The evidence for this is late, but it is consistent with the generally very good relations between the court of Yazdgerd I and those of both Arcadius and Theodosius II, and it seems possible that the emperors agreed to subsidise the maintenance of the large Persian fortress called Biraparakh, in either the Dariel or Derbend pass through the mountains.

The ongoing focus on the steppe world to the north affected not just the political activity of the Persian kings, but also the ideology and the self-projection of the Sasanian state. Put simply, the ideology of the Persian monarchy became more thoroughly Iranised in the course of the fifth century, while retaining some of the Mesopotamian and Hellenistic tinges of earlier periods. The royal and dynastic mission was increasingly cast in terms of heroic Iranians fighting against implacably opposed 'Turanians' – a term for the steppe nomads derived from the *Avesta*, the great epic poem of ancient Iran, originally transmitted orally but taking canonical written shape precisely in the middle and late Sasanian period. Also drawn from the Avestan tradition was a new royal epithet, *kay* or 'hero', which was added to official titulature in this period, claiming legitimacy by descent from the mythical Iranians of the epic past.

The renewed persecution of Christians and other non-Zoroastrians under Yazdgerd II in the mid fifth century may likewise have stemmed from this more explicitly religious conception of the king's authority and duty, though that is inference. Regardless, it is worth noticing that while Roman imperial ideology never ceased to place Persia at the centre of its ideological universe, identifying the eastern neighbour as its chief adversary right until it ceased to exist, later Sasanian ideology really did see Rome and Persia as 'two eyes of the world', civilised forces ranged against the chaos of the barbarous steppe, that is to say, the forces of Turan.

In practical terms, Yazdgerd I had brought considerable stability to the Persian throne after the troubled reigns of Shapur II's immediate successors, Shapur III and Varahran IV, neither of whom could maintain a secure hold on his throne. The death of Arcadius had not threatened the peace that Rome and Persia had sustained for decades, and it is reported in a much later source that the regents of Theodosius II went so far as to seek a pledge of support from Yazdgerd to help secure the child emperor on his throne. What is more, Yazdgerd allowed for considerably greater freedom of Christian worship inside the Persian empire, with a new bishop, Isaac of Ctesiphon and Seleucia, becoming the head of the Persian church. Indeed, the Syriac culture that was flourishing in this period needs to be understood as the cross-border phenomenon that it was, creative and increasingly independent of the Greek culture in whose shadow it had developed during the fourth century.

One consequence of the growth of communities of Christians outside the Roman empire would become clear later in the century, when the increasingly bitter theological disputes within the church of Roman Syria would be solved in part by the exile of many members of the losing party to Persia and points east. Lest one paint too rosy a picture of Romano-Persian relations, however, we should remember that, in an empire whose rulers' Zoroastrianism was every bit as exclusive as imperial Christianity, other religions always existed on sufferance. That was especially true of Christianity, vulnerable to persecution both when relations with Rome soured and whenever Christians inside Persia threatened the dominance of the Mazdean priesthood (so-called for Ahura Mazda, the supreme good deity in the dualistic Zoroastrian cosmology). This happened late in Yazdgerd's reign, when Christians – perhaps encouraged by the suppression of non-Christian religions in Egypt and parts of the Roman East – tore down a fire temple. That brought a period of repression that lasted past the death of Yazdgerd in 420 and well into the reign of his successor Varahran V. The persecution, in turn, provoked the first war between the two empires in decades.

In 421, a Roman field army entered Persian Mesopotamia via the northern Armenian route, and attacked Nisibis, before being defeated by an army under Varahran's personal command. Nevertheless, a victory was celebrated in Constantinople on 6 September, and another campaign was launched in the following year. This too went badly for the Romans, at least at first, but then the Persian 'Immortals', as the Shah's elite troops were called, were ambushed and beaten back in a surprise attack by a junior officer named Procopius, perhaps a mere *dux* or a *comes* without portfolio. That reversal, combined with bad news from the Danube and the Caucasus, meant both sides chose peace. Seemingly one condition of this was the breaking-off of relations between the Christians of Persia and those of the empire, an action taken in 424 at a council held in Seleucia-Ctesiphon and presided over by the bishop Dadisho.

The Procopius whose victory helped bring about the peace was a distant descendant of the usurper of the same name in the reign of Valens, and he was married to a daughter of the long-serving praetorian prefect Anthemius. His reward for his success was now to become the *magister utriusque militiae* of the eastern field army and receive the honorific title of patrician. He would go on to be the father of an emperor. Meanwhile, peace with Persia lasted more or less unbroken until the death of Theodosius in 450, save for a brief episode of fighting in 440 as the Persian kings reoriented their attentions to their north-eastern frontiers and the steppe nomads of Turan.

The motive that had drawn Theodosius' ministers into deciding on peace in 422 was an incursion into the Balkans by the Huns. This reached as far as Thrace, and was threatening enough to provoke the recall of some Mesopotamian troops. The Hun king responsible for the invasion of 422 was probably Rua (or Rugila, as he is sometimes called), and it seems likely that, under his leadership, a small warrior Hun elite had established a wide-ranging hegemony over the various barbarian polities of the Carpathian basin and the westernmost fringe of the Eurasian steppes along the lower Danube and the Black Sea. These European Huns, like the Kidarites and the Alkhan whose hegemony in eastern Iran and central Asia was being challenged at this time by another group of Huns called the Hepthalites, all claimed the legacy of the old Xiongnu tradition. With it, they laid claim to an imperial ideal stretching back centuries, whether or not any of them could really trace their descent back to the Ordos or the Altai.

Calling Rua's hegemony a Hunnic empire, as many do, goes too far in attributing to him or his peers a consistent ability to exercise control over or mobilise their subjects. More often, it was a matter of preying upon some of them, extracting tribute or protection money, while creating strategic alliances with, or strategic opportunities for, the more powerful clients. At various times, Rua and his successors were able to mobilise other steppe nomads – various Alani are the most prominent – and more settled military aristocracies of Goths, Rugi, Heruli, Sciri and Gepids, though the mechanisms by which they did so are unclear in most cases; so, too, is the question of quite where Rua's own core of support lay – the Hungarian Puszta at the Danube bend is most likely – and how far east his control really extended. The confidence with which modern scholars sometimes postulate a coherent Hunnic hierarchy, capable of coordinating strategies on the Danube, the Black Sea and the Caucasus (and sometimes even eastern Iran) is not borne out in the sources. We are more likely to be looking at a form of shared hegemony, common among steppe nomadic cultures into early modern times. Be that as it may, Rua's Huns would cost the court at Constantinople monumental sums during the 430s and 440s, and permanently subvert the high imperial structure of the Balkan provinces.

The other place where the empire's frontiers required periodic attention was its desert borders. Egypt was a peculiar case, of course, for, despite being essentially immune to capture by regular military forces, its habitable and regularly administrable parts stretched in a more or less narrow strip for hundreds upon hundreds of kilometres up the Nile. The southernmost reaches of Upper Egypt were a very long way indeed from Alexandria and the Mediterranean core, and the Thebaid in particular was subject to raids by the Nobades and Blemmyes who lived in the neighbouring deserts. In order to deal with this problem in a more regularised way, and to insulate the more heavily civilian north of the province from the south, the Thebaid was broken into two provinces late in the reign, an arrangement that endured into the sixth century. The governor of the upper province was now given merged civilian and military jurisdiction, in an arrangement that oddly echoes the treatment of the Rhineland under the regime of Flavius Constantius in the West. This suggests that administrative solutions to manageable but insoluble problems were quite widely diffused as part of imperial policy.

The merging of offices in Upper Egypt seems clearly to have improved relations with the desert tribes, for, early in the reign of Theodosius' successor Marcian, the then *dux* in the Thebaid Florus concluded a long-term treaty with the Blemmyes that allowed them to worship periodically at a temple of Isis that they revered in the Roman city of Philae. We are, of course, used to looking at Persia and the Rhine–Danube frontier in Europe as the main objects of imperial policy, but minor episodes such as this one are a reminder of the sheer extent of the empire and the challenges faced on nearly every one of its frontiers – and also serve as a reminder that the day-to-day experience of frontier communities, the uncertainty they faced, the potential for violence, may have been experienced quite similarly whether they were in the Thebaid or in Gaul. It is we, with our retrospective knowledge and the burdens of our own history, who attribute the greater significance to Europe.

When it comes to the politics of Constantinople, as is so often the case everywhere in this period, we have spots and highlights of information to work with rather than a continuous narrative and, because the nature of our sources continues to vary while their number grows smaller, the possibility of triangulating the evidence is limited. We saw in the last chapter that the rioting in Ravenna between the supporters of Placidia and those of Honorius had led to such bloody street warfare that Placidia was forced to leave Italy with her children to seek support in Constantinople. It was there that she and the court of her niece and nephew received word of Honorius' death, and then, in December 423, further word that a palatine official named Iohannes had been declared emperor. He was *primicerius notariorum*, but nothing grander, and was thus presumably a stalking horse for others. It seems very likely that, on hearing of his uncle's death, Theodosius had initially intended to try to govern the empire as a whole from his palace in Constantinople, without troubling to appoint a western junior emperor, but that the usurpation of this non-entity altered the calculus dramatically. It became a matter of protecting not so much the dynasty, as the rights of the senior augustus – which Theodosius had become on the day of Honorius' death – to appoint junior emperors.

Placidia and her eastern relations suddenly had reason to make common cause. The eastern court retrospectively recognised the legitimacy of Constantius III's elevation to the rank of augustus, and also accepted Placidia as augusta and Valentinian as *nobilissimus puer* (which it had likewise declined to do earlier). Valentinian, though still a child, was betrothed to the still younger Licinia Eudoxia, the daughter of Theodosius II and Eudocia, and named for her grandmother who had been augusta during the later years of Arcadius. Licinia Eudoxia had been born in 422, just a year after Pulcheria had arranged the wedding between her brother and the then-Athenaïs. The betrothal would not, of course, be consummated for many years, but it marked out a clear and united path for both branches of the dynasty. The alliance secure, an eastern army and fleet were recruited to reinstall Placidia and her son in the court of Ravenna. Placidia and Valentinian were sent ahead to Thessalonica, and there Valentinian was proclaimed caesar by Theodosius' *magister officiorum* Helion on 23 October 424. The generals Ardaburius and Aspar, father and son and among the most powerful men in the East throughout the reign, commanded fleet and field army respectively – with great success, as we shall see in the next chapter.

In the long run, the Italian victory would raise the spectre of continuous civil war in the West, but in the short term there was much to celebrate. Valentinian was proclaimed augustus in 425, his sister Iusta Grata Honoria became an augusta like her mother Galla, and Theodosius – who had chosen not to go personally to Rome for the coronation after falling ill – led a spontaneous procession of thanksgiving through the streets of Constantinople to celebrate the victory. Ardaburius was honoured with the consulate of 427 for this success, alongside the praetorian prefect Hierius. He and his son Aspar, indeed, founded a military dynasty that would continue to exercise power through generations, marrying into the imperial family at several different times and coming close to seizing the purple itself on more than one occasion. In the East, the 420s remained a time of relative peace, not least in comparison to the troubles besetting the West that we will examine in the next chapter.

More troubling to the imperial court than frontier disturbances was the way the unstoppable rise of Constantinopolitan prestige was leading the episcopates of Antioch and Alexandria to clamour all the more loudly for their own positions – something made relatively easy for them by the longer and greater tradition of deep theological investigation on the part of their respective bishops. Theological controversies, which always began with genuine problems of belief whose correct answers were of pressing necessity to those who raised them, nearly always became embroiled in the personal politics of the episcopate and its ramifying allies and associates in government. By the 420s, the struggle between homoousians and homoians over the relationship of God the Father to God the Son had been going on for a full century. In north Africa, the endless wrangling of Caecilianists and Donatists that dated back to the 310s was still not wholly resolved a hundred years after Constantine first turned his attention to the issue. Exemplary as those controversies might be, there had been dozens of other theological disputes, of more interest to students of Christianity than to the historian of the Roman empire. The eastern controversies of the 420s and 430s cannot be set aside so easily, because they had momentous consequences for the way Christianity developed outside the Roman world, and the way the internal politics of the Greek church would, two centuries later, play a major role in the Islamic conquests.

As had happened with John Chrysostom two decades earlier, the problems of the 420s began with a celebrated Antiochene receiving the imperial summons to take up the bishopric of Constantinople, on 14 April 428. The preacher in question was Nestorius, and it is perhaps no coincidence that Chrysostom began to be honoured as a saint at precisely this time. Nestorius brought with him to Constantinople a strikingly Antiochene position on the relative role of the human and the divine in Christ – not, that is, the relationship of Christ to God the Father, but rather the manner of his incarnation. *How* was Christ human, if Nicaea had already established that he was one in substance (*ousia*) with the father?

Perhaps not surprisingly, given the misogyny of ancient societies in general and the bitterly anti-female strain of much early Christian thought, the problem came to centre on the relationship of Christ to his mother Mary – or rather, her relationship to him. Nestorius insisted – and did so presumably with imperial favour – that Mary was not *Theotokos*, the 'bearer of God', but rather *Christotokos*, the 'bearer of Christ'. Mary, and devotion to her, had been virtually unknown a hundred years earlier, when

Constantine converted to Christianity and made the imperial state responsible for enforcing orthodox belief. But in the century since then, she had become the focus of enormous devotional and intercessory power and it was the term *Theotokos* that had emerged as an honorific way of addressing her. The term *Christotokos*, by contrast, emphasised the humanity of Christ by focusing on the mortal and carnal nature of his birth to a human woman. Mary had given birth to Jesus, the anointed Christ, not to God the Son.

This Antiochene theology had always been opposed by Alexandria, and it was Alexandria that had emerged as the arbiter of true orthodoxy at the council of Constantinople that Theodosius I had called in 381. In the fifth century, the incompatibility of Nestorius' Antiochene position with that of the Alexandrians was badly exacerbated by the ongoing tenure of Cyril as patriarch of Alexandria (he had an astonishingly long episcopate, from 412 to 444). Earlier in the chapter we saw his propensity for violent action against those of whom he disapproved, and the relatively light punishment meted out to his *parabalani* for the murder of Hypatia and the public wounding of a *praefectus Augustalis*. An Antiochene whose views he disapproved sitting as patriarch of Constantinople – Cyril was not going to stand for that, any more than he truly believed in the primacy granted to the Constantinopolitan see by the council of 381. He accused Nestorius of heresy, arguing that the human and divine natures of Christ were indivisible, that they formed a personal 'hypostatic union' so that, while the human and the divine natures were different, they were also inseparable. This excluded Nestorius' contention that Mary bore only the human nature of Christ, and not the divine; she was, for Cyril, inalienably the Theotokos and no mere Christotokos. Both sides appealed to the western patriarch, Celestinus, bishop of Rome, who sided with Alexandria because he would never tolerate the claims of Constantinople to equality with Rome.

Theodosius celebrated his *tricennalia* on 10 January 430 with great pomp and circumstance, and a son named Arcadius was born to him and Eudocia either in the same year or in the year before. But the controversy between the patriarchs was already causing rioting in the streets of the imperial city. The emperor was convinced to call a council to adjudicate the problems caused by opposition to the theology of Nestorius. Conciliar decision remained the normal way to settle such disputes, but Theodosius had the sense to call for this one to be held not in Constantinople but in the Asian city of Ephesus. There, a greater degree of neutrality – and certainly, less threat of partisan violence – could be hoped for.

Shortly after Easter Sunday, which in 431 fell on 19 April, Nestorius set out for Ephesus, accompanied by a large force of palatine troops under the command of the *comes domesticorum* Candidianus. By June, Cyril and his partisans had begun to arrive from Alexandria, and the entire affair was conducted in an atmosphere of great violence. It took more than seven sessions, drawn out over many months, during which Cyril's supporters refused to communicate with those of Nestorius and held what was functionally their own separate council, before the matter was resolved: Nestorius was condemned, on the allegation that he was proposing to separate the natures of Christ into a human and a divine, but Cyril was briefly deposed as well.

Pulcheria, it seems, was instrumental in securing the condemnation of Nestorius' doctrine, having loathed the independence Theodosius had shown by calling to Constantinople a new bishop of whom she disapproved. Maximianus, a churchman more acceptable to Cyril, was made bishop of Constantinople on 25 October 431. Nestorius was briefly allowed to return to his monastery outside Antioch before going into exile in Upper Egypt, where he remained until his death in 450. Cyril was rapidly restored to power, after splashing out great sums in bribes to the churchmen and courtiers of Constantinople. Despite a partial reversal of the first council of Ephesus' decisions later in Theodosius' reign, Nestorius was never rehabilitated fully. His most devoted followers settled in Edessa, on the frontiers of Persia. His doctrines, which he refused throughout his life to accept as anything but fully orthodox, were formally endorsed by the church in the Persian empire at a council held in 486, and this formal break from the Roman church was solidified after the Edessene Nestorians were driven out by the emperor Zeno in 489. Very significantly for later central Asian history, it was a Nestorian theology that was exported by the Christians of Persia to the wider Eurasian landmass in centuries to come.

If the Nestorian controversy was one of the great events of the later 420s and 430s, another was the compilation of the Theodosian Code. It had been well over a hundred years since the imperial government had tried to deal with the massive accumulation of legal rulings and pronouncements that it generated. Under Diocletian, the jurists Gregorius and Hermogenianus had attempted to gather up imperial laws from the first three centuries of empire: they had hoped to introduce some systemisation into the administration of justice, and to help judges work out which law was appropriate for which case instead of relying upon whatever documentation happened to be available to them wherever they happened to be. Although laws continued to be issued in great profusion thereafter, there appear to have been no attempts to archive them, collate them, or maintain any corpus of those that did or did not retain their legal validity.

The era of Theodosius II had already witnessed other attempts at systematisation, at fixing the form of practical documents in a way that would simultaneously monumentalise them. We have already discussed the deluxe version of a rather mundane working document, the *Notitia Dignitatum*, which dates to this period, but so, too, do the illustrated road atlas (as close as we come to a surviving Roman map) known as the *Peutinger Table* and various technical treatises, on subjects ranging from equine medicine to military discipline. It is as if, conscious that the two halves of empire had at some level ceased to be one, a fixed version of an idealised past was being set down to assert that nothing had changed.

Thus, on 26 March 429, the emperor ordered that a commission headed by his prefect Antiochus Chuzon collect, edit and publish all the laws with general applicability up until his own day, which could then be supplemented by commentary from the writings of jurists. This fine intention did not survive its encounter with messy reality: archives suitable for so sweeping a purpose simply did not exist. Instead, the commissioners sought out imperial pronouncements as best they could, wherever they could find them – and a surprising number appear to have come from Carthage, perhaps from the archives of a series of proconsuls of Africa. In 435, the decision was taken to limit the exercise to collecting all the general laws from Constantine until the date of completion, which was, in the end, 438. Laws were arranged by topics, in sixteen books, these being divided into thematic 'titles', with the texts of original laws chopped up and placed in different titles depending on their content. Equally, most of the preambles and other supplementary verbiage of fourth-century law-making was excised, as we learn from the few surviving alternative sources that preserve laws intact and entire, as written. Still more confusingly, the compilers of Theodosius' Code worked from an authorised consular calendar, meaning that exactly which emperor issued a law might be disguised.

Yet, for all its evident flaws – and the many pitfalls those pose for unwary historians – the Code is not only our best source for the structure of the late Roman state, it is also our best source for the individuals who served that state, because it preserved the addressees of the laws and their positions, and usually when the law was issued and/or received and posted. The insights we still have into the political struggles of the fourth century and the early fifth century would be impossible without the Code. When it was issued in 438, and publicly acclaimed by the senates of Constantinople and Rome, it was meant to serve as the sole source of law that might be cited in litigation before imperial officials.

New laws, of course, continued to be issued, and many of these are preserved in the sixth-century legal compilations sponsored by the emperor Justinian. Justinian still found the legal landscape of his empire inadequate despite the efforts of Theodosius' commissioners, and it was Justinianic compilations of imperial legislation and juristic commentary that would change the history of western law when they were rediscovered in the high Middle Ages. Nevertheless, we must not underestimate the scale of the Theodosian project, and the importance it had in preserving and to some extent systematising the laws that could be cited or enforced. What is more, as an embodiment of imperial ideological unity, it preserved a sense of identity between eastern and western Romans that was rapidly slipping away in practice.

The 430s, which witnessed not just the great council of Ephesus and the publication of the Theodosian Code, but also the marriage of Valentinian and Licinia Eudoxia, was also the decade in which the empire really began to feel the impact of the Huns. Rua, as we have seen, was the first Hun leader of real consequence, having in 422 launched the raids that instigated the eastern Roman policy of paying off the Danubian threat at whatever cost seemed sustainable. That year, he had agreed to an annual sum of 350 pounds of gold as tribute, or what we might sensibly call protection money. Because of events in Africa – the Vandal invasion and conquest that we will examine in the next chapter – the year 434 gave the Hunnic chieftain an opportunity to increase the scope of his predation. The main praesental field armies had been despatched westwards to aid the Italian government in retaining control of the western Mediterranean, so Rua again threatened to invade the Balkans, this time attempting to extract a still larger sum and, more importantly, the return of those enemies who had fled his hegemony into the Roman empire. The court of Theodosius was disinclined to do this, no doubt needing the recruits these recalcitrant tribesmen provided for the imperial forces. Flavius Plintha led an embassy to negotiate terms with Rua, but the king's sudden death, and the succession of his nephews Bleda and Attila, offered temporary reprieve until they had established the same degree of authority over their barbarian subjects as their uncle had held. But when large eastern armies again travelled west to deal with the Vandals, the Huns would again intervene forcefully in the Balkans.

By then, the long-awaited marriage of Valentinian III to Licinia Eudoxia had taken place. In the summer of 437, the western emperor and his entourage had travelled to Constantinople, and on 29 October 437 the pair were married. This was celebrated by the striking of a special issue of *solidi* with the legend FELICITER NVBTIIS, or 'Happy Wedding'. After this, the couple returned to Valentinian's western residence at Ravenna. As a form of public thanksgiving for the marriage and the union of the two halves of the empire, the augusta Eudocia undertook a pilgrimage to Jerusalem to collect relics for the imperial churches of Constantinople. She went via Antioch, where she addressed the *boule* and the populace in a speech laced with Homeric echoes and was honoured with the presentation of a golden statue in the council chamber. She found herself similarly fêted upon her return to Constantinople, but then palace intrigue obtruded with painful effect.

Theodosius' *praepositus sacri cubiculi*, the eunuch Chrysaphius, had successfully inveigled himself further and further into the confidence of the emperor, as *praepositi* frequently did, but the return of the empress from Jerusalem could have given her a chance to reestablish her position. Chrysaphius therefore provoked a breach between the two augustae. First, he played on Eudocia's jealousy, pointing out that she did not have her own *praepositus* although the emperor's sister Pulcheria did: when she pressed Theodosius on this, she was told that, as Pulcheria had been born in the purple, the distinction was only right and good. Then Eudocia – perhaps again encouraged by Chrysaphius – suggested that her virgin rival should be ordained a deaconess, which would have got her out of the way for good. Pulcheria forestalled this with an ostentatious retirement to the Hebdomon palace a few miles outside the city walls, while keeping many of her own loyalists in the emperor's household.

With Pulcheria removed to a safe distance, Eudocia may have believed herself the victor. She was able to manoeuvre a long-standing ally, the Egyptian poet Flavius Taurus Seleucus Cyrus, urban prefect of Constantinople since 437, into simultaneous tenure of the praetorian prefecture of Oriens. This was a really unprecedented accumulation of power in a single individual, almost a veiled coup on the part of the empress. Cyrus was genuinely popular, however, and demonstrations in his favour are reported in the hippodrome. A district of the city that he rebuilt was referred to by his name, and it was there that he built a famous church of the Theotokos. He is also a very early example of the increasing Greekness of the culture of imperial administration in the East. The language of law and administration had throughout the Roman East always been Latin, however much Greek remained both the majority language of the average person and the high cultural language par excellence. Laws might be translated into Greek to be put up in public, but it was their Latin versions that had legal force. Cyrus, however, issued his decrees in Greek, as we are explicitly told by a reliable antiquarian writer a century later. It was an innovation that did not at the time find much traction, but it was also a sign of things to come: within a hundred years, the language of new law in the East would shift from Latin to Greek.

The preponderance of power accumulated by Cyrus – and his connections to Eudocia – undoubtedly mobilised opposition to him, and again it seems to have been Chrysaphius who made the running. Late in 441, Theodosius dismissed Cyrus from office, supposedly frightened by the prefect's great popularity. His property was confiscated and he was compelled to take holy orders – much to his distaste – following which he was made the bishop of the remote town of Cotyaeum in Phrygia. It was a deliberate punishment, for the townspeople were said to have killed no fewer than four previous bishops, probably for expressing Nestorian sympathies. Cyrus, however, made a timely show of his anti-Nestorian attitude, survived his episcopate and returned to public life after the death of Theodosius, living on late into the century.

But in 441 Cyrus just had to take his punishment, because Chrysaphius had already got his patron Eudocia out of the way. The stories we have are late and contain folkloric elements (the secret gift of an apple during the celebrations of Epiphany, for instance), which presumably indicates that contemporaries had little real idea of what went on in the cloistered atmosphere of the palace. Eudocia, it was insinuated, had taken up a congenial liaison with Paulinus, the *magister officiorum*, and it may be that the parentage of the young Arcadius was called into question. Whatever the truth of the matter – and it cannot be established – Theodosius came to find Eudocia's continued presence intolerable. She retired to Jerusalem, keeping the title of Augusta and living out the next sixteen years performing lavish works of charity and pious construction work in the city. Paulinus was executed. Arcadius, the potentially embarrassing heir, died naturally, probably in 439 or 440, never having been elevated to the rank of caesar, let alone augustus, and almost entirely suppressed from historical memory by contemporary cover-up.

Yet, despite the disappearance of her rival, Pulcheria did not return to power. On the contrary, the affairs of the palace seem now to have been entirely controlled by Chrysaphius. Indeed, a canard which is more reliable than many claims that Theodosius signed documents given to him in his last decade without so much as reading them. Perhaps it is true, but it is certain that we can detect no towering administrative figures in the court of the 440s in the same way we could in the first three decades of the emperor's reign. However, it is equally true that the *consistorium* continued to provide the same sort of consistency of governance, law and policy as it had in the 430s. Then, in 446 the Senate of Constantinople was brought into the formal process of making law for the first time, so that it was no longer just the consistory – in particular, the *quaestor* and his staff – who composed legal pronouncements and judgements, but rather there was a full consultative process that focused eastern senators on the imperial city in a way that had long since ceased to be true in the West.

The final years of the reign were shaken by new Hunnic invasions and by renewed ecclesiastical controversy, deriving ultimately from the unsatisfactory resolution of the Nestorian controversy. Back in 434, Plintha and his embassy had agreed with the brothers Bleda and Attila not to receive any more fugitive Huns, to ransom back Roman prisoners of war, and to double the annual protection money paid to the brothers to 700 pounds of gold – perhaps to reflect that there were now two, equal kings in place of one. That the eastern court could contemplate such numbers with equanimity is a sign of its overall economic security, by contrast with the floundering West.

During the later 430s, Bleda and Attila consolidated their hegemony over the various pastoralist and sedentary populations north and east of the Danube, though the full extent of that control is not at all clear. Then, in 439, the Vandal king Gaiseric succeeded in taking Carthage. The better part of the eastern campaign armies were despatched to Africa to deal with the threat in concert with the western regime of Valentinian. Almost at once, claiming that the empire had violated the terms of the 435 treaty,

Attila and Bleda seized several towns along the Danube frontier, including Viminacium, which was razed to the ground. Margus, Singidunum and the Transdanubian fortress of Constantia were all taken and badly damaged. In 441, Sirmium fell, and most of its inhabitants were enslaved. That was a staggering loss – Sirmium (now Sremska Mitrovica in Serbia) had been an imperial residence throughout the third and fourth centuries, and it was the hinge in the military defence of the Balkans, the main transfer point between east and west. The Danube had ceased to be a meaningful frontier and, practically speaking, the dioceses of Pannonia and Dacia were exposed to Hunnic assaults whenever Attila and Bleda chose. It is, in fact, very hard to determine the extent to which civilian imperial government continued to function in most of the Pannonian and many of the Dacian provinces during the rest of the century, even after the return of the praesental field army encouraged Attila and Bleda to retreat north of the Danube.

In 445, Bleda died, probably murdered on his brother's orders, and in 446 Attila claimed that the emperor was in arrears on his payments to the Huns and that an invasion would follow any failure to deliver 2,100 pounds of gold. The government of Theodosius refused the demand, since it was at peace on its eastern frontiers and could perhaps handle a Balkan war. Attila prepared an invasion for the campaigning season of 447. The imperial response was thrown into sudden disarray by a massive earthquake that brought down many of Constantinople's defences. Attila's forces supposedly sacked seventy cities, but declined to enter the parts of Thrace that the earthquake had devastated, and so turned north to Marcianopolis and then back up the Danube towards Pannonia. They were intercepted by an imperial field army and suffered heavy losses before ultimately routing their Roman opponents.

Forced into negotiations again, the imperial government agreed to pay 6,000 pounds of gold to compensate for its alleged arrears, and to increase the annual tribute to 2,100 pounds. The Hun king also demanded that a strip of frontier land, five days' ride in breadth and running hundreds of kilometres along the Danube, be evacuated to serve as a buffer zone. So far as we can tell, Theodosius' ministers acceded to this, and it may have meant the stripping of such garrisons – there cannot have been many – as were still present in the region; but there is no evidence for the wholesale transfer of a population that may well have been heavily depleted already by years of raiding and Hunnic extortion. Regardless, the peace seems to have held, though perhaps only because there was little more left on the bones of the Balkan provinces for Attila to pick off. After 447, he turned his attention to the West.

Devastating as the Hunnic impact on imperial authority in the Balkans must have been, the more impressive thing here is the East's capacity to pay out vast sums of gold for years on end without bankrupting itself or precipitating a crisis in government. Ecclesiastical controversy, by contrast, was a constant threat to imperial control, both in the capital and the great metropoles, and in the countryside of the richest provinces. Cyril of Alexandria had died in 444, after an episcopate of unprecedented length and barely precedented violence. His successor Dioscorus was unsatisfied that the Antiochene theology of Nestorius had been sufficiently extirpated and put forward an argument of extreme simplicity against the possibility of Christ having two natures (*physis*). In Constantinople, Dioscorus' position was taken up by Eutyches, the archimandrite of an urban monastery and an intimate of the eunuch Chrysaphius. He was opposed by Flavianus, the bishop of Constantinople, who supported the formula worked out after Ephesus that had, in theory, ended the Nestorian controversy. In 448, Flavianus condemned Eutyches as a heretic, but the latter sought the intervention of the bishop of Rome, Leo.

Leo's conception of the power of his office to judge the rights and wrongs of Christian belief far exceeded those of his predecessors, and it is with Leo that we can start to think about bishops of Rome in terms of their future status as 'popes', claiming a preponderance of spiritual authority in the church with others frequently accepting that claim. At the time, and as always, Rome preferred to side with Alexandria against Constantinople or Antioch, and so Leo intervened with alacrity. Upon examination, he decided that Flavianus of Constantinople was right, Eutyches was indeed the holder of heretical views, but that he, Leo, should alone be the judge of that. Dioscorus pushed for a general council to be called to vindicate his own and his protégé's perspective, but the fact that Eutyches had an ally in the *praepositus* Chrysaphius counted for a lot. Theodosius called a council for 449, again to be held in Ephesus.

The council convened in August, against the wishes of Leo, and with Dioscorus of Alexandria presiding. Leo's representative presented his *Tomus*, a theological work that, it must be said, continues to demonstrate the inferiority of Latin to Greek as a linguistic vehicle for philosophical or theological subtlety. Unsurprisingly, Greek bishops on both sides of the controversy regarded the Roman document as worthless. Dioscorus overwhelmed any potential opposition, gathering the support of over a hundred bishops who, carefully watched by imperial troops, determined that Eutyches was orthodox and that Flavianus should be deposed as bishop of Constantinople. This action was duly undertaken, and several other of the Antiochene supporters who refused to accede to his deposition were likewise exiled.

Back in Italy, a furious pope Leo persuaded the court at Ravenna to intervene with its senior partner in Constantinople. Valentinian III, as weak as his cousin and seemingly somewhat stupider, complied – to no effect. The Latins might denounce the second council of Ephesus as a 'robber council', but the senior emperor would uphold its decidedly Alexandrian formulation: the one nature of Christ incarnate in the single person of God and Christ. Dioscorus duly excommunicated Leo of Rome. Had this been the old days of the fourth century, one emperor might have tried to compel the other to bring his troublesome clerics to heel. Not so now, with the politics of the West in near total disarray, and neither side in the mood for civil war.

Indeed, matters might well have rested there, but for a series of odd historical accidents. Pulcheria – how, we do not know – secured the fall of Chrysaphius and returned to her brother's palace to reassert herself. Then, on 28 July 450, Theodosius fell from his horse, breaking his back and dying of the injury. This brought a new complexion to the politics of the eastern empire, for there was never any likelihood that the rights of Valentinian as senior emperor would be respected at Constantinople: the eastern court had come to regard the West as what we might now call a failed state, one to which it gave periodic aid while recognising that actual solutions would prove wholly elusive.

The sixth-century chronicle of Marcellinus *comes*, which preserves quantities of information derived from the official announcements of the Constantinopolitan regime, suggests that on his deathbed Theodosius indicated his successor. Probably Pulcheria and the magnates present when Theodosius received his mortal wound stitched up a plan to rescue the situation while he lay dying. Aspar, son of Ardaburius and the most senior military man at court, did not himself seek the throne, but instead procured it for his second-in-command, a Thracian officer named Marcianus (customarily referred to as Marcian in English). Pulcheria then married Marcian, though it is unlikely the marriage was consummated.

Valentinian's western court refused to recognise what they regarded as a usurpation, and the western laws issued in the early 450s omit the eastern emperor's name in their headings. Although Valentinian's attitude was technically quite correct, in terms of eastern public sentiment the marriage to Pulcheria legitimised Marcian as a member of the Theodosian house. The augusta herself crowned her consort on 25 August 450 – the marriage would follow on 25 November – and his reign opened with the execution of the disgraced Chrysaphius. A new dawn was thus proclaimed and its first measures would be ecclesiastical.

As we have seen, the second council of Ephesus had been denounced as a 'robber council' by Leo, the bishop of Rome, primarily because it ignored the theological formula (the 'Tome') which he had laid out. In the East, it was loathed by those bishops who, rightly, saw it as an imposition of Cyril of Alexandria's one-nature doctrine on the whole eastern church by Cyril's equally domineering successor Dioscorus. We need not detain ourselves here on the complex theological niceties it raises, but the dossier of the council that Marcian called is among our richest sources for fifth-century court practice and the conduct of ecclesiastical politics. Marcian, following his predecessor's policy, determined that the Tome of Leo should at least be discussed in another general council, to be held in the East and attended by the pope. In preparation for this, Anatolius of Constantinople – despite having been put on his patriarchal throne by the influence of Dioscorus and the Alexandrians – agreed to subscribe to the papal *tomus*. Leo chose again to resist the calling of a council, but Marcian ignored these protests and summoned one to meet at Constantinople in autumn of 451, though it was moved across the Bosporus to Chalcedon to reduce the risk of riots.

This council would later be accepted as the Fourth Ecumenical Council (after Nicaea, Constantinople and I Ephesus), that is, a council the rulings of which have general efficacy for the whole church – and it is to this day accepted as such by both the Catholic churches of the west and the Orthodox churches of the east. Fully 600 bishops attended Chalcedon and, after many months of wrangling, a compromise – and politically compromised – formula was reached that nearly every bishop subscribed to, even many of those who believed it to be fundamentally incorrect. Some writings of Cyril and the *tomus* of Leo were accepted as containing true doctrine, but the statement of belief would have satisfied neither man: there was just one Christ, but in two inseparable, indivisible and unchangeable natures, each nature preserved in their union as one person and one substance.

This will read as gobbledygook to many modern readers – including those religious ones in whose churches Chalcedon's canons remain orthodox doctrine. That is because at the time it was pure waffling: a form of expression that allowed considerable leeway for Antiochene views; that seemed to exclude the most extreme tenets of the Alexandrians while allowing those of them who so chose to believe that the formula merely brought out the subtleties of their point; and allowed the Latin supporters of papal primacy to declare a victory that easterners were free to ignore. Dioscorus was deposed by the council and his successor was imposed on a mutinous Alexandria by imperial troops. The lasting damage the council did to the loyalty of many Christians in Egypt and Palestine, who continued to hold to the one-nature theology of Cyril and Dioscorus (soon described as monophysitism by its foes), would prove a lasting scar on the religious life of the eastern empire. It committed the imperial government to enforcing a doctrine that many of its subjects could never accept, so Marcian's immediate successors would confront massive outbursts of violence in both Alexandria and Antioch, as well as in the holy city of Jerusalem, in protest against the Chalcedonian settlement. Resistance to the Chalcedonian formula in Syria, Palestine and Egypt continued more or less unabated for centuries and, in large parts of each region, opinion remained stubbornly and intractably monophysite. That fact would continue to have consequences for centuries, not least during and after the Arab conquests which removed most of the East from the control of the imperial capital two centuries later.

The council of Chalcedon also laid up further troubles for the future relationship of the Greek and Latin churches, for the twenty-eighth canon of the council formally confirmed that Constantinople had privileges and authority equal to those of Rome – meaning that the much older, and within the early church far more significant, churches of Antioch and Alexandria were now definitively subordinated to Constantinople in the formal authority they could claim. The equally upstart see of Jerusalem – not an ancient seat of the church, but one exalted far above its history by the boundless patronage of imperial pilgrims since the reign of Constantine – now also had its position defined as an independent foundation, and no longer a suffragan of Antioch. Eighty years later, this so-called 'autocephaly' would lead to Jersulaem being recognised as a 'patriarchate', along with Rome, Constantinople, Alexandria and Antioch, during the reign of the emperor Justinian.

The other great feature of Marcian's reign might well have had direr consequences than in the end it did: he determined to stop buying peace on the Danube frontier. He did this both as a signal of his own prestige, and also as an ostentatious measure of financial prudence, one that would add something tangible to the virtues of orthodoxy displayed by his predecessor: in the reign of the later emperor Justinian, he was still praised for the amount that he had left in the treasury. And, despite the affront, Attila chose not to react, having decided that the Balkans could no longer be profitably fleeced. Pulcheria died in 453, and the marriage to Marcian had, naturally enough given her age, been a childless one. She left all the wealth of her personal household to the poor of Constantinople. By the time Marcian followed her to the grave, in January 457, he was the last reigning member of the Theodosian dynasty. Pulcheria's nephew Valentinian had been killed in Italy in 455, the climax of a reign both less cloistered and less successful than that of Theodosius II.

In Constantinople, the military high command asserted itself in a manner that had been normal in the West for decades, and a junior officer, the *tribunus* Leo, was raised to the throne by his patron, Flavius Aspar. What precise manoeuvring had gone on at court to achieve this result is deeply unclear, for there was an in many ways superior candidate available in the shape of Anthemius: he was linked by descent to both the civilian and the military elites of the East, being the son of the general Procopius who had successfully prosecuted the Persian war of 421–2; he was also the maternal grandson of the great praetorian prefect Anthemius, the consul of 405. As the sons of senior officers almost always did, he progressed up the rungs of the junior officer class, and at some point was noticed by Marcian and married to his daughter Aelia Marcia Euphemia. The date of this marriage is unknown, but since Anthemius appears quite suddenly in the sources of 453 with a fairly senior command (*comes per Thracias*), it is likely that the promotion and the marriage were connected. He was honoured as consul posterior of 455 (with the emperor Valentinian as western consul prior), and was holding a praesental *magisterium* and had the honorific title of *patricius* when Marcian died.

The succession of Leo begins therefore to look like a palace coup by one of the great *magistri* to exclude the other from power, using the time-honoured method of filling the post with an officer junior enough to pose no threat. Or perhaps a deal had been reached between the *magistri* to precisely the same end. Aspar remained a dominant figure in the eastern military for another decade and a half, and Anthemius suffered no setback to his career after the new emperor took the throne. Later in the century, he would attempt to rule the shreds of the western empire. Those shreds were the leavings of the long, depressing reign of Valentinian III, which ended in the extinction of his dynasty in the West.

9

PLACIDIA, AËTIUS AND VALENTINIAN III

Honorius died, as we have seen, on 15 August 423. Placidia had been driven from Ravenna not long before. There was no one to pick up the mantle of Constantius and so the West experienced a de facto interregnum. Theodosius II, or those who claimed to speak for him, may well have hoped to rule the whole empire alone from Constantinople, but that was never a realistic possibility. By December, there was action, and the *primicerius notariorum* Iohannes was proclaimed augustus at Ravenna.

Who precisely lay behind this move is unclear: just two supporters of the coup are named in the extant sources. One was the *magister utriusque militiae* Castinus, whom we last saw failing in his campaign against the Spanish Vandals and driving Placidia's client Bonifatius out of Italy and into Africa, where he became *comes Africae*; the other was Flavius Aëtius, a junior officer of Moesian origin, born at Durostorum and by now about thirty years old. His father, Gaudentius, had served on Theodosius I's campaign against Eugenius but was later sidelined by Stilicho: while Gaudentius was still in favour, Aëtius had been a high-born hostage among the Huns and he still had good connections in the Hunnic polities beyond the Danube. Father and son seized the opportunity of Iohannes' usurpation to succeed where they had previously failed to prosper: Gaudentius was made *magister militum praesentalis* and Aëtius, who, despite having served as a *protector domesticus* for the better part of a decade, had not yet been promoted, now became *cura palatii*, a staff officer with rank equivalent to the tribune of a *schola*. The attitude of the Roman Senate is irrecoverable, but there must have been some bastions of support apart from the Ravennite courtiers whose cooperation with Castinus we must conjecture: all the *solidi* struck for Iohannes come from Ravenna, but there are many bronzes minted at Rome which demonstrate his recognition there.

The accession of a dynastic challenger, as we saw, mobilised the Constantinopolitan regime behind its exiled relatives: the ambassadors sent from Ravenna with Iohannes' imperial portraits were rebuffed and sent into exile. Theodosius finally acknowledged the late Constantius III as a legitimate emperor, along with Valentinian as *nobilissimus puer* and Galla Placidia as augusta. Theodosius' daughter Licinia Eudoxia was betrothed to Valentinian, eastern forces occupied Salona, and a base was established at Thessalonica, where Valentinian was raised to the rank of caesar by Theodosius' trusted *magister officiorum* Helion. Placidia and Valentinian accompanied the army as far as Salona, where a fleet took the larger part of it to Italy under the command of Ardaburius. The other section of the army, under Ardaburius' son Flavius Aspar, marched via Sirmium (then not yet a casualty of Attila's Huns) to Aquileia, encountering little organised resistance. Placidia and her son took up residence in Aquileia until the campaign was concluded. In 424, Castinus held the western consulate, but this was unrecognised in the East, where the *magister militum* Victor was recognised as sole consul. News of the coming eastern invasion sent Aëtius on a mission to Pannonia, where he planned to recruit an army of Huns, though whether these were mercenary freelancers or soldiers in the gift of king Rua we cannot know. He was making good progress in these negotiations when Ardaburius set sail from Salona.

Luck was with Iohannes, at least briefly, for a storm wrecked much of the fleet and Ardaburius was captured when he made shore. Iohannes now had in his hands an excellent bargaining chip, which he decided to retain until he had a proper army at his back – that is, until Aëtius returned with soldiers. Sound though that plan was, it foundered on the popularity of Ardaburius among the Italian troops and his capacity to suborn the garrison of Ravenna while sending messengers to Aquileia, encouraging Aspar to begin a full-scale invasion. Aspar's forces arrived outside Ravenna but, as they consisted mainly of cavalry rather than the infantry units dispersed by the shipwreck, they had little chance of either taking it by storm or drawing its defenders out into battle. However, a local shepherd

– so it was said – guided a force of Aspar's soldiers through the swamps that surrounded the city, which then opened its gates to them. Eastern propaganda claimed that this was thanks to the personal intervention of Theodosius and his prayers: God had sent one of His angels to guide the eastern army to its goal. Ardaburius' golden tongue and the promise of great rewards are a more likely diagnosis.

Be that as it may, Iohannes was captured in the palace and taken under guard to Aquileia, where the augusta had him put to death – though not before mutilating him and parading him round the circus on a donkey. Castinus, with too much of a following to dispose of, was sent into exile, where he soon died. But it was then that Aëtius arrived at the head, some claimed, of 60,000 Huns. A force even a tenth that size would have posed terrible problems for eastern forces that remained in disarray after their multiple shipwrecks. Aëtius recognised the strength of his position and refused to disarm, despite the defeat of the cause he had been supporting. Instead, he demanded a position of authority in the new regime – were he to be refused it, he would carry on the war in his own right. This was the model Alaric had pioneered two decades before, one that was becoming increasingly accepted in the West as the fastest route to power. Placidia acceded to his demands, gave Aëtius a *magisterium*, and paid the Huns off so they returned home without the pleasures of a battle; Aëtius' son Carpilio went with them as the empress's hostage to their good behaviour.

From Aquileia, this ill-assorted set of victors processed to Rome and, on 23 October 425, the caesar Valentinian was proclaimed augustus, crowned, as in Thessalonica, by the eastern *magister officiorum* Helion standing in as representative of Theodosius. Coins with the legend VICTORIA AVGG ('Victory of the Two Augusti', i.e. Theodosius and Valentinian) were issued, with a reverse image of the diademed emperor treading on a human-headed snake that represented the defeated usurper. Ardaburius, the ultimate architect of the victory despite his misfortunes at sea, was rewarded with the consulship, serving as consul posterior of 427 alongside Theodosius' powerful praetorian prefect for Oriens, Flavius Hierius.

This imperial proclamation at Rome formed the climax to the history of Olympiodorus of Egyptian Thebes. Olympiodorus had served as an ambassador and shared the traveller's curiosity that had characterised Ammianus in the previous generation. He wrote a history that covered the years 407–25 (or rather, what he called *Materials for History*, since he declined to give it the Thucydidean polish that would have rendered its prose both timeless and vague, preferring to use newfangled or technical Greek words where these conveyed his meaning better). He had completed this work by 427, which makes it as close to instant history as the ancient world tended to come, and the narrative arc that is readily enough discerned in its surviving fragments suggests that, for him, the East had consistently made the right sorts of choices that the West had not – dynastic continence; the responsible begetting of heirs; short, sharp shocks to the impertinence of barbarians – and thus the eastern branch of the family had needed to bail out the western. But his was not, as more than one scholar has imagined, an optimistic narrative: though he celebrates the benevolent care of Constantinople for its hapless Ravennite kinsmen, his final surviving fragment (preserved in a source too unimaginative to have rearranged things) is the arrival of Aëtius in Italy with his army of Huns, ready to prosecute a war – but willing not to, if paid off with high office. That was not casual; Olympiodorus was in Italy during its long time of troubles and he knew how intractable its problems were. He portrayed the menacing warlordism of Aëtius as a harbinger of future violence, such as would in fact engulf the West after the illusory triumph of Placidia and her son.

Though perhaps only partly illusory: Placidia would prove adept at harnessing the violence of potential opponents and potential supporters alike; Valentinian III would reign for thirty years without serious challenge of usurpation. It was simply that, by the end of his reign – indeed, by the time Galla retired from active politics in the earlier 440s – there was little about the imperial title worth usurping, so thoroughly had its power been gutted by the wrangling of generals, each of them willing to destroy some part of the imperial apparatus in order to claim his place in it. That hollowness of empire was an open secret by the time Valentinian died in 455, and there was no real chance that any of the multiple contenders for his position would make anything of it, after thirty years in which the legitimate dynasty had proved incapable of doing so.

For all that, and for all the depressingly elegiac musings that the last fifty years of the western empire inspire, it is worth remembering that there was nothing inevitable about imperial collapse and that those most responsible for bringing it about – the warlords and petty kings that dotted the western empire, with or without imperially sanctioned credentials – had no desire to destroy the political system over which they fought. Destruction was merely a byproduct of their wrangling. In 425, Placidia may have made brief peace with Aëtius, but she certainly did not trust him. When

the eastern field armies returned home shortly after the accession ceremonies of Valentinian, the *magisterium utriusque militiae* was in the hands
not of Aëtius but of Flavius Constantius Felix, a man whose background
we know nothing about, but who was presumably a senior officer trusted
by both the eastern high command and Placidia herself.

Aëtius was made *magister equitum* and sent to Gaul. His activities
there in the next few years are hard to disentangle in the contradictory
sources, but he came to blows with Theoderic over control of Arelate – it
is possible that the latter had initially tried to hold Gallia Narbonensis
against the forces of Iohannes and was unwilling to give up his control
of them after Placidia made her peace with Aëtius. In the later 420s, we
learn of campaigns in Belgica Secunda as far as the Somme, and along the
middle Rhine, probably near Moguntiacum, in both cases probably against
one or another Frankish warlord. At roughly the same time, the imperial
control restored to Spain in the 410s was challenged by the presence of
the Vandals in Baetica, whence various warbands launched piratical raids
in the western Mediterranean throughout the later 420s. Ongoing tension
between the Vandal king Gunderic and the Sueves in Gallaecia also led to
open fighting, and we know that the diocesan capital at Emerita Augusta
(Mérida) was threatened more than once. When Gunderic died in 428, his
brother Gaiseric took over the Vandal kingship and continued his brother's
hostilities. Meanwhile, in Africa, Bonifatius campaigned against various
Mauri, though we have no details of what that entailed.

Felix, probably with good reason, harboured intense suspicions of his
subordinates and their ambitions. Each of them was clearly plotting against
the other, and he could assume that both were plotting against him. We
cannot disentangle the court politics, but at a minimum it would appear
that, in 427 or so, Bonifatius was threatened with replacement, refused
to step down, and defeated the commanders sent by Felix to force him
to do so. In 428, one of Placidia's Gothic supporters, Flavius Sigisvultus,
was named *comes Africae* in Bonifatius' place and successfully occupied
major coastal cities like Carthage and Hippo, but Bonifatius continued to
defy orders to stand down. Then, in 429, seeing that Felix's energies were
occupied with Bonifatius, Aëtius provoked a mutiny against the *magister
militum*, and both Felix and his wife Padusia were killed.

With no reliable ally close to hand, Placidia and the palatine bureaus
had no choice but to accept Aëtius as Felix's successor to the highest *magisterium*. Sigisvultus was recalled to Italy, probably to counterbalance Aëtius

on Placidia's behalf, leaving Bonifatius in control of Africa once again. At the same time, though, the Vandal king Gaiseric decided to take advantage of the chaos and invade Africa. He and all his followers, including their women and children, embarked from Spain and proceeded by cabotage from Tingitania across to Mauretania Caesariensis and Sitifensis, where the real work of conquest began. A later source, written to commemorate the persecution of Nicenes by the homoian Vandals, claims that Gaiseric had taken a census of his people and found that there were 80,000 of them to trans-ship. The number is not in itself implausible, but it is the only testimony of its type we possess and we have no particular reason to think it correct. In response to this new danger, Bonifatius was brought back into the official military hierarchy, resuming the legitimate title of *comes Africae*, with a brief to fight Gaiseric.

The latter invaded Numidia, where Bonifatius was defeated in May or so of 430 before taking refuge with his forces in Hippo, which Gaiseric then besieged. The city held out for a year, during which the city's long-time bishop of Augustine finally died of old age, on 28 August. Gaiseric gave up in July 431, when forced to defend himself from an army sent by the eastern court. As we saw in the last chapter, the great general Ardaburius' son Flavius Aspar went west to try to rescue the flailing western regime for a second time. He and Bonifatius joined forces and met Gaiseric in a pitched battle, in which they were routed and dispersed. Quite what happened to the remnants of the eastern army is unclear, but Bonifatius withdrew to Italy, leaving Gaiseric to take Hippo and then begin to subdue the interior of Numidia before making an assault on the capital at Carthage.

Aëtius had taken the consulship of 432 – and the fact that he could afford to put on consular games suggests that he had managed to collect a good deal of booty from his campaigning in the Rhineland – but he and Placidia again promptly quarrelled. She deposed him and appointed her client Bonifatius to the *magisterium*. Given the latter's failures in Africa, all he had to recommend him was the fact that he was not Aëtius. The latter, of course, no more accepted this supersession than Bonifatius had his own five years before. It was just this sort of pointless rivalry that undermined the capacity of the western state to govern. In 432, Bonifatius and Aëtius went to war on Italian soil. At this point, the number of troops either had available without resort to mercenary warlords (or 'allies', the terms are elastic) was very small. The main battle, fought near Ariminum, went against Aëtius, who fled to Dalmatia, but Bonifatius had been wounded in the fighting and died of his injuries soon afterwards. His son-in-law, Flavius Sebastianus, was made *magister utriusque militiae* in turn, while Aëtius went back to the Huns to secure an army that would allow him to take back power.

This he did in 433, again reappearing in Italy with a force of Hun mercenaries, threatening the imperial court and demanding reinstatement. Clearly, he had allies as well as enemies in the palace and, though we once again do not know any details, Sebastianus was deposed and fled into exile, while Aëtius resumed his *magisterium*, took the honorific title of patrician, and married Bonifatius' widow Pelagia. Once again, the Huns were paid off and returned to Rua's territory. In 434, with his own power now secure, Aëtius determined to negotiate a settlement with Gaiseric, having decided that the latter was too powerful to destroy, and might also be an ally against other rivals. Trygetius, a member of the civilian administration who was formerly *comes rei privatae* but whose office at the time is unknown, was sent to negotiate with the Vandal king. In an agreement reached in mid February 435, the Vandals ceded Hippo back to the imperial government, but were permitted to remain in control of the Mauretanias and parts of Numidia. Neither side can have imagined the arrangement to be anything other than temporary, but it had the effect of leaving the all-important control of the grain fleets in imperial hands for the time being.

That in turn meant Aëtius remained securely in control of Italy, if not yet Gaul – to which he now turned his attention. In the same year that he settled the affairs of Africa, he again sought Hunnic aid, this time in dealing with the Burgundians on the upper Rhine. Their nascent kingdom had begun to extend from its centre in Borbetomagus (modern Worms) on the Rhine out into the Lugdunensis with the active collaboration of some of the local aristocracy, disaffected more than ever by the neglect of the Italian government and by what looked like the exclusion of Gauls from positions in the imperial hierarchy except in specifically Gallic offices. As we saw in the last chapter, Aëtius' old ally Rua had died in 434, and it was now his two nephews, Attila and Bleda, from whom the required troops came: the military power of the Burgundians was comprehensively smashed, in 436 or 437, and their king Gundahar and thousands of Burgundian soldiers killed in battle. In hugely distorted form, these events passed into legend, eventually finding classic expressions in the *Nibelungenlied*, a Middle High German epic of the twelfth century, and thereafter in the alternately sublime and gruelling hours of Wagner's *Ring Cycle*.

The year 437, the second consulship of Valentinian III, was of course the year he turned sixteen and was taken to Constantinople, there to celebrate his wedding to Licinia Eudoxia, the daughter of Theodosius and Eudocia. Within a year of their return to Ravenna, a daughter was born to them and named Eudocia after her grandmother, the eastern augusta. In the following year, a second daughter, Placidia, was born. A year or so after that, Aëtius' marriage produced a son, Gaudentius, and Aëtius was no doubt planning to dominate the imperial succession through a marriage arrangement – much as Stilicho had once done with Honorius – if only he could keep control of the politics spiralling around him. His difficulty was the forces that had been unleashed earlier in the century, and the enthusiasm with which he himself had prosecuted the politics of attacking and withdrawing from imperial power structures when it suited him. Nevertheless, as could have been predicted, the young Placidia was betrothed to Gaudentius by early in the 440s, setting the stage for the same sort of bitter resentment as Honorius had, in the end, felt towards Stilicho.

More immediately problematical for Aëtius were the ambitions of his junior officers. In the later 430s, while Aëtius remained patrician and the supreme *magister militum*, various other generals appear as *magistri militum*, and the old title of *magister equitum* for a subordinate general disappears. In Spain, the *magister militum* Asturius, perhaps a descendant of the Asterius whom we met suppressing the second usurpation of Maximus in Gallaecia, campaigned against the Suevi and an outbreak of provincial rebellion that the sources characterise as mere banditry. As in north-western Gaul (the region loosely designated as Armorica), and perhaps elsewhere, too, a substantial part of the local population preferred the governance of strongmen and warlords to that of the imperial centre – perhaps because, for want of funds and loyal personnel, that imperial centre no longer delivered much in the way of governance. Indeed, rather than government, the populace in places like Armorica and the north of Spain found themselves on the receiving end of punitive campaigns, ostensibly waged against barbarians, but equally against provincial populations that were starting to look to their own, local resources for leadership and the administration of justice. Forty years after 409, the Suevi had not become Hispano-Romans, but nor were they a foreign or alien element in the provincial landscape.

Something similar can be said of the Goths in the south-west of Gaul. We have seen that, over the previous fifty years, the Gallic aristocracy had been more than willing to defy the control of the Theodosian dynasty and, since the time of Placidia and Athaulf, they had done so with the help of a Gothic military. When Constantius, by then the husband of Placidia, had settled the Goths in Aquitania, they were meant to be a check on the potential of the Gauls for rebellion, and so they must have been, for there was no Gallic usurpation over the course of a full generation. But what Constantius could not have foreseen was the degree to which some parts of the Gallic aristocracy would find the presence of Theoderic and his Goths a congenial alternative to rule from Ravenna.

The situation was messy and ambiguous. There was no real precedent for a figure like Theoderic: clearly legitimately appointed to control the region over which he exercised power, but doing so without any formalised role that was recognisable within the imperial hierarchy. If he was a *magister militum*, he seems not to have been called one. At the same time, the title of *rex* (king) had only negative connotations when used inside the imperial frontiers and, though some of our sources refer to him as a king, Theoderic himself did not use that title in any context even remotely official. And yet, for all the ambiguity of his position, he was nearer and more responsive than any representative of the Italian regime, and certainly more reliable an interlocutor for the nobility of the Gallic south-west and the Spanish north than was Ravenna. What is more, he kept government going along traditional lines – taxation, the administration of justice, and so on – which could only have happened on a de facto understanding between Gallic senators and Gothic military elites. The scale of this social transformation was signalled by the fact that, at least in some circumstances, procedures of customary law (it goes too far to call it 'Germanic', but it is certainly not classical Roman law as a Roman jurist, even a provincial one, would recognise) were in use between those who identified as Goths, and may have intruded into relations between Goths and Romans who needed their disputes adjudicated. But it is all very murky, as are so many things in the more peripheral parts of the western empire in the fifth century. A hundred years earlier, and a hundred years later, the distinction between Goth or Frank or Roman could be measured – and still can be by the modern historian; in the middle fifth century, though contemporaries surely must have made such distinctions, their criteria seem to have been rapidly shifting. Because of that, any line we draw between 'Roman' and 'barbarian' will be both arbitrary and ahistorical.

Besides, when the central government decided to take a hostile stance to local accommodation with alternative sources of authority, fine distinctions did not matter much. We saw as much already with the punitive campaigns in Armorica, in parts of Spain, and in the middle Rhine of the Burgundian Gundahar. These struggles are coded in the sources as the forces of law suppressing the forces of banditry, or as Romans fighting barbarians, and that is only natural, since those are the intellectual categories within which Roman writers thought. But it is more realistic and useful to think in terms of a central government periodically attempting to reel in, and harness the tax base of, a periphery that was spiralling away from it and into local self-help because of the central power's own actions, or more frequently its inaction. The centre periodically lashed out at such local self-help: the more accessible (that is, closer to the *comitatenses* in north Italy), the more effectively centralised (that is, one warlord was clearly in control of a region) and the more attractive it was to the provincial Roman elites, the more likely it was that Aëtius would send in an army, as both Burgundians and Goths found out. Thus Aëtius' successful *magister militum per Gallias*, Litorius, commanded a few *comitatenses* and large numbers of Hunnic mercenaries against Theoderic in 436–7 and thereafter he 'subdued the Armoricans', which is to say the 'rebellious' provincials of Armorica. In 439, he again attacked the Goths, this time suffering a severe defeat near Theoderic's residence in Tolosa. Aëtius welcomed this humbling of an ambitious subordinate: he needed his commanders to be like Asturius and Merobaudes, successful but not too successful, if he was to hold on to his control at the centre.

It is vital for us to remember that, however much Aëtius might imagine himself as the successor of Stilicho and Constantius, he had also witnessed far more of what could go wrong for the regnant strongman, and he commanded vastly fewer resources than either of them had, in terms of men, materiel and ready cash to pay the troops. At the end of the day, his interests were better served by living with an ambiguous and liminal figure like Theoderic than with a rival within the military hierarchy whose role was fully legible to everyone – and who might well have his own independent arrangement with the Hunnic power now that Rua was dead and Aëtius could no longer take that long-standing relationship for granted.

And so Litorius was allowed to die in captivity at Tolosa and Theoderic was left unmolested, a reliable force for stability in south-western Gaul until Aëtius found himself calling upon Gothic aid to fight Attila a decade and more later.

If Theoderic was often quite tractable, Gaiseric was not, though he was by far the most adept of the fifth-century warlords. He kept on good terms with the most powerful potential rivals and allies – his son Huneric was married to an (unnamed) daughter of the Goth Theoderic – but his greatest advantage was to have a fleet and a part of Africa, both of which could challenge not just the western but also the eastern Roman empires. Piracy could be a threat anywhere in the Mediterranean, but, because the inland sea had been perfectly safe for commerce for five hundred years, coastal towns were unprepared for what the Vandals might be able to do. Gaiseric could also threaten the annual shipment of African grain to Rome, and thus had the potential to shut down the entire western empire. Finally, the fact that the revenues of so many Roman senators were vested in their African estates played into his hands, making them dependent on the imperial government's good relations with the Vandal king.

The ease with which Gaiseric had extorted the treaty of 435 that gave him the Mauretanias soon encouraged him to try for more, and he resumed campaigning to capture the other main towns of Numidia and Proconsularis. On 19 October 439 Carthage fell to his army, and with it an even greater supply of ships with which to threaten havoc. By October, the sea was closed – the Vandals proved no more willing to break the old tradition of *mare clausum* than were any other ancients – but the prospect of his launching an attack on Italy or some other vital location in the new year was terrifying. We have a law of Valentinian (his ninth *novella*, or 'new law', issued in June 440) that lists the preparations that were to be taken to defend Italy, including the repair of fortifications at Rome and patrols of the sea coasts under the *magister militum* Flavius Sigisvultus. Meanwhile, in Constantinople, the *magister militum* Aspar was tasked with organising an army and invasion fleet against the Vandal king. As we have seen, he used *comitatenses* from the Balkan dioceses which left them exposed to the attentions of Attila. In 440, Gaiseric sent his fleet against Sicily, besieging Panormus and capturing Lilybaeum. Nicene writers at the time blamed homoian bishops in Sicily (of whom we otherwise know little) for betraying their towns to the 'Arian' Vandals. This is the sort of canard that cannot be entirely ignored, as we have clear evidence from

Spain of bishops using rival warlords to prosecute disputes with their ecclesiastical foes.

The Italian government took no action to defend Sicily in 440, although an edict was issued on 24 June permitting Italian civilians to arm themselves against a Vandal invasion and again ordering the *magister militum* Sigisvultus to defend coastal towns. Aëtius returned from Gaul and held his *comitatenses* in readiness for a possible Vandal descent upon the mainland that never materialised. Meanwhile, the eastern assistance confidently predicted in the June edict took more than a year to arrive. By September, the government at Ravenna felt it necessary to lower the tax burden on Sicily to compensate for the damage Gaiseric had done. Indeed, it was not until 441 that West and East attempted to cooperate on a major venture to dislodge the Vandals. Aspar commanded an invasion force that made it as far as Sicily before acrimony between the eastern and western courts and the threat of a Hunnic invasion in the Balkans caused it to be recalled. Another treaty was negotiated, in 442, which returned the less important provinces of Tripolitania and the Mauretanias to imperial control, while giving most of Numidia and all of Byzacena and Proconsularis to Gaiseric.

It is not possible to exaggerate the importance of this move, which, despite one or two attempts, was never reversed. It was the first time that imperial provinces had been formally ceded to the control of any power other than the Persian shahanshah, to whom a parity of prestige had always been conceded. And this was not simply the acceptance of settlement and de facto autonomy in an imperial province – as with the Suevi in Gallaecia, the Goths in Aquitania and Gallia Narbonensis, or even, for a time, the Vandals themselves in Spain – but rather the cession of several rich provinces from which the emperor no longer hoped to receive revenues and to which he no longer aspired to appoint governors. The idea that the imperial government did not just cede territory but admitted to having done so was an ideological turning point of real significance. But even more significant were the dire financial implications of the move.

It has been said that the Vandal occupation of Byzacena, Proconsularis and the valuable parts of Numidia broke the 'tax spine' of the empire. So it did. The state-subsidised grain fleet was the link that held the imperial economy together, exporting both grain and the huge quantities of everyday pottery and tableware produced in Africa. Every other sort of commerce piggy-backed on the fleet. The senatorial estates of Proconsularis were the prime sources of the revenue that they in turn fed into imperial coffers. The Vandal settlement thus marked the point at which the western government ceased definitively to be able to finance itself. It also marked the beginning of the decline of an integrated Mediterranean economy, though it would take a hundred years for the full impact of the decline in trade to be felt.

While the workings of the imperial tax system is no one's idea of a riveting read, the importance of taxation to keeping the Roman (and *particularly* the late Roman) empire together should not be underestimated. The late Roman model was not just a matter of publicans and sinners, as the New Testament had it, in which the emperor set a tax rate on a given parcel of land, allowed potential tax and tribute collectors to bid on that sum, and left them to raise it according to whatever methods seemed indicated. On the contrary, the whole business of revenue collection was in the hands of imperial officials, be they in the employ of the emperor's private bureaucracy, the *res privata*, or the larger imperial budgetary department, the *sacrae largitiones*.

Because tax had to be paid in gold, but a relatively restricted portion of the provincial population had access to money coined in that metal, taxation was a permanent cycle of recycling gold into the system, which mattered particularly in the western empire where the emperors had access to no new source of gold with which to replenish whatever was sucked out of circulation by private interests. Access to the gold needed to pay tax was uneven, and imperial bureaucrats had privileged access to such coined gold as was available. This meant that the possibility of arbitrage between provinces, or perhaps even between regions within a province – and thus the toing and froing of various minor *rationales* and junior *apparitores* from the imperial bureaus – resulted in coins circulating alongside supplies for the army. The highways along which these officials circulated among provinces carried trade as well. Peripheral regions might fall away from this system with no visible loss to the central government, but the whole thing was predicated on the control of north Africa. That was where grain production took place on a scale large enough to feed the whole of Rome, allowing the other dioceses to feed their own provincial establishments, military and civilian. It was correspondingly the place with the most rapid circulation of specie through the tax system.

The loss of Africa to Gaiseric was thus a blow in two ways. It took a very substantial source of imperial revenue out of the system and it turned the African grain supply into a giant drain on the imperial coffers. Gaiseric had no interest in depriving Italy of north Africa's abundant grain; it is not as if his own needs were not being met. Rather, he was interested in selling it to the emperor at a profit, thereby in essence doubling the cost of the loss of Africa. The continuation of grain exports as a commercial venture on the part of the Vandal state explains why the trade that piggy-backed on the grain *annona* did not decline instantly at mid century, but only gradually as the fifth century changed to the sixth and an integrated West ceased to exist in economic as well as political terms.

The core of Gaiseric's new state was Proconsularis and he made Carthage his residence. Tripolitania and the Mauretanias remained theoretically subject to Ravenna, but their economic value was much less than the African heartland held by Gaiseric. In 445, to curry absentee landlords' favour, the imperial government granted a petition lowering the tax burden of the provinces it still controlled, thus depriving itself of still further revenue. Gaiseric, though, inherited an efficient and effective state. The vast majority of the former imperial governing apparatus was taken over by the new rulers, and the share of tax revenues that remained in the Vandal king's hands allowed him to build a much larger fleet that would challenge imperial control of the Mediterreanean – the first time such a thing had happened since Pompey the Great cleared the sea of pirates in the waning days of the Republic half a millennium before.

In the Vandal provinces there is widespread evidence of collaboration between local elites and the new rulers, who rapidly adopted the lifestyle of Roman aristocrats themselves. It is very striking how little archaeological evidence there is for the disruption of land holding patterns. There were refugees, to be sure, and we meet them all over the Roman East in particular: it seems that the senatorial and municipal elites who were unwilling to make their peace with the new order saw their chances in the East as substantially better than in the West. Likewise, it is quite unclear to what extent the absentee landholders in Italy retained control of their estates and the revenue to be generated from them, but there is no evidence for the widespread confiscation of lands. The one group that suffered quite substantial loss of status and authority was the African clergy, who were banished in large numbers by a Vandal ruler who was ideologically committed to his homoian creed. Exiles from the African settlement appear as far afield as Syria in this period, attested in the letters of eastern clerics.

The sense that this was an independent kingdom – that this was a cession of imperial territory, not a settlement of provisionally autonomous but ultimately dependent people – was enhanced by the adoption of a new calendar in Proconsularis, one that was certainly used by at least a part of the population and by Gaiseric's royal chancery. This dated from 19 October 439, the day Carthage was occupied by the king's army. Even more significant – and probably negotiated at the time of the treaty of 442 – was the betrothal of Valentinian and Licinia's elder daughter Eudocia to Gaiseric's son Huneric, who, as we have seen, was already married to a daughter of the Goth Theoderic. This first wife was now repudiated and returned to her father having suffered mutilation of her ears and nose – a deliberate insult that can only be explained by political motives now lost to us. Eudocia and Huneric were not to be married during Valentinian's lifetime, but the symbolic power of the betrothal was impossible to ignore.

What Aëtius' role in all these negotiations might have been remains far from clear and, if he was the moving force in them, it is even harder to understand what he was hoping to gain. Perhaps the answer lies in an attempt at balancing his fellow warlords, for that is all Aëtius actually was. He had perfected the method of hijacking the state for his own ends, using outside forces with no loyalties to the Roman state itself to fight his battles. Later legend – begun in the sixth century by the Greek writer Procopius and carried on by modern scholars who ought to know better – saw him as the 'last of the Romans', the bulwark against various barbarians and the hammer of their leaders. Really, though, he was himself just a warlord who often held a better hand than most of his rivals. That is the key to understanding the appeasement of Gaiseric, who, like Aëtius, Theoderic and Attila, had forces at his disposal with no loyalty to Rome.

The Gothic alliance had always been more in Placidia's interests than those of Aëtius, and the latter had always made a point of regarding Theoderic as a potential threat. The alliance with Gaiseric pushed the Gothic leader further into the political wilderness. It also created a political relationship that could be used against the Huns of Attila and Bleda, with whom Aëtius had nothing like the same privileged relationship he had once had with Rua. Since he lacked the ability to field decisive numbers of soldiers himself, balancing the risks and advantages of other warlords was the main tactic that remained to him. The fact that Gaiseric honoured the imperial peace from 442 until after the deaths of both Valentinian III and Aëtius attests to its success, even if it, like so much else Aëtius did, was geared solely towards his own short-term advantage.

One thing that makes that analysis more likely is the fate of Placidia at this time. In the early 440s, her influence at court seems to all but disappear. While Valentinian and Licinia Eudoxia were increasingly resident in Rome, Placidia remained in Ravenna, where the building now described as her mausoleum still stands. That city is still a magnet for tourists interested in late Roman and Byzantine art, because it preserves the sort of mosaic decorations, most of them made by Greek artists, that were destroyed in the eastern empire during the iconoclastic spasms of the seventh and eighth centuries. Ravenna seems to have achieved its really monumental form in precisely this period of Placidia's retirement, in much the same way that the exiled and then widowed eastern augusta Eudocia made Jerusalem her home and devoted herself to building up its treasures. At Ravenna, Galla was responsible for the construction of many churches, including that of the Holy Cross. A small cruciform building, once attached to that church, was known from at least the ninth century as the mausoleum of the empress. The legend was that she had her brother Honorius and her long-dead husband Constantius reinterred there, and some have even thought the chapel or 'mausoleum' was built to hold the remains of her first child, the infant Theodosius in whom Athaulf and she had reposed such high hopes. She herself died in 450, having been silent for many years, and was most probably buried in her brother's mausoleum at Rome. The 440s marked, therefore, the true ascendancy of Aëtius, in Italy and parts of Gaul, if nowhere else.

In Italy, Aëtius had no rivals to speak of, and Flavius Sigisvultus seems to have been a loyal subordinate rather than a rival, commanding the praesental forces around Valentinian while Aëtius managed affairs elsewhere. In the provinces, it was increasingly a matter of hoping that Gallic aristocrats could be induced to prefer imperial control and access to imperial honours over the less time-tested and less prestigious, but nearer and more powerful offices in the service of warlords and petty dynasts. The suspicion of parts of the Gallic aristocracy towards rule from Italy still lingered from the civil wars of Honorius' reign – many leading aristocrats had lost close ancestors in the purges. Similarly, the growing monopoly of Italians over the highest imperial honours (the consulship, the urban prefecture) drove a further wedge into the relationship between the two regions. That set up a dangerous formula, for when the imperial government offered little beyond the penumbra of its long history, every concession of land to a warlord outside direct imperial control was an encouragement to local self-help. Much of northern Gaul, save for the islands around Treveri and important Rhineland cities like Moguntiacum, was outside effective imperial governance, though whether it had actually fallen out of the hands of local elites seems less likely.

Given his intense hostility towards Theoderic – who was perhaps the only warlord apart from Gaiseric who might actually challenge him – Aëtius relied upon others to help him. In Spain, where Theoderic's influence was powerful, Aëtius sent campaigning armies in the early 440s, first under the *magister militum* Asturius, then under the latter's son-in-law Flavius Merobaudes. Merobaudes was not just *magister militum* but also a court poet who celebrated the major events in the supreme commander's life, including his three consulships and the birthdays of Gaudentius. Elsewhere, the survivors of the Burgundian kingdom – destroyed only a few years earlier in part because its ties to the Lugdunensian aristocracy had been so close – were settled in Sapaudia, the part of the old province of Maxima Sequanorum north of Lake Geneva, in 443 (though Sapaudia is the etymological root of Savoy, the modern county and duchy of Savoy lay south of the Roman region).

Our overall impression of the 440s is one of relative peace, though this is in some measure a result of the limited available evidence: most of the secular history recorded for this period comes from the sparse testimony of chronicles, many of them transmitted much later than events, while the richer and more contemporary witnesses are generally very localised in their outlook. Thus the Spanish bishop Hydatius tells us a great deal about regional affairs in the northern and western provinces of Spain, but precious little about events elsewhere; in his pages, we learn about the gradual disintegration of imperial authority in the peninsula, the succession of Suevic kings, the growing power of the Gothic king Theoderic over the roads and the main cities of the peninsula, and the rise of Spanish 'bagaudae' – often glossed as peasant rebels or bandits, but better understood as coalitions of local Hispano-Romans rejecting the demands of imperial government since it no longer brought them anything worth having. The Gallic cleric Prosper has a somewhat less limited geographical perspective, but he is far more interested in the ecclesiastical controversies of the period than in the politics of the court and great events of state. Along with such staples of ecclesiastical controversy as Manichaeism and

Arianism, the former once again condemned by imperial law in this period, new disputes over 'Pelagianism' – the extent to which free will plays a role in salvation – and the aftermath of Pope Leo's intervention in the eastern councils of Ephesus and Chalcedon are much better attested than almost anything else in the West of this period.

After spending several years in Ravenna, Valentinian and his wife Eudoxia journeyed to Rome early in 450. That was the year in which the emperor's mother Placidia died at Ravenna, and his cousin Theodosius II in Constantinople – Valentinian was not consulted about the succession there, though he was now senior augustus, and it would be two full years before the western court agreed to recognise Pulcheria's choice of Marcian.

The year 450 also saw the denouement of a grave scandal involving Valentinian's elder sister Justa Grata Honoria. She, like many of the Theodosian princesses, had remained unwed rather than risk the rise of cadet branches of the imperial line who might in turn develop ambitions that threatened the reigning emperor. The exception to this rule had been Galla Placidia, and her example was the opposite of reassuring, given her and Athaulf's attempt at setting up a rival Theodosian line in Gaul and then the unwelcome accession of her second husband to the purple. Honoria, then, had spent much of her life at her brother's court, invisible to us, if not necessarily to her contemporaries, bearing as she did the title of Augusta from shortly after 425.

In 449, she began to plot a coup. The details are sketchy, buried by later propaganda, but she is said to have taken up with one Eugenius, her *procurator*, which is to say one of her estate managers. Nothing else is known of the man, and the affair itself would not have caused the trouble it did without hints of much wider treachery. Valentinian discovered the affair, cut it off, executed Eugenius, and placed Honoria under house arrest. He then arranged her betrothal to Bassus Herculanus, a blameless though useless senator whom he designated consul for 452, two years hence. Casting around for allies, Honoria turned to a power that would certainly give her brother pause: the Hunnic king Attila. She sent him her ring, which may have been intended as an offer of marriage alliance, and was certainly portrayed as such by Attila.

The latter, as we have seen, had killed his brother Bleda and gained sole control of the Pannonian and Transdanubian Huns in the course of the 440s. While the protection racket he ran against the eastern empire had been successful for the better part of a decade, the accession of Marcian in

450 and the cutting-off of tribute was a diplomatic complication he had not foreseen. The overture from Honoria was thus a piece of luck – so much so that it confirms the wisdom of her choice; after all, Aëtius was unlikely to help her, and Theoderic's involvement would have provoked instant opposition from him, while Gaiseric already enjoyed a marriage alliance to the main branch of the dynasty. Among the great warlords able to command viable armies out of private resources, Attila was surely the most plausible prospect.

The plan might have worked. Attila demanded both his 'bride' and a portion of the western empire as her dowry. Valentinian was enraged, and only the intervention of Galla Placidia shortly before her death prevented him from executing his sister. She still might have had her coup, had Attila not staged a spectacularly incompetent response to Valentinian's intransigence. For, despite the 'leadership secrets' sometimes attributed to him, his later role as an all-purpose barbarian villain of historical memory, and the outsized significance which some otherwise sober historians accord him, Attila was a good politician but an indifferent general. Aëtius understood the threat Attila might have posed – he had, after all, relied time and again upon Hunnic mercenary support. Attila's capacity to field large armies, composed of units of his subject peoples, was probably greater than that of any contemporary ruler in the Roman world save the king of Persia. Intelligently deployed, their combined weight might be devastating; but, like the Persian army, the hard core of fighting men – Hunnic nobles, the retinues of subject princes and chieftains – was only a small fraction of the total number of indisciplined infantry whose value, such as it was, lay in mass alone. Numbers could be telling, and the effectiveness of the elite troops was never in doubt, but the risk of an army turning into a rabble was ever present.

Rather than threaten, or use, handpicked troops to turn up the pressure on the empire, Attila launched a massive invasion into Gaul in 451, with contingents of Gepids, Pannonian Goths, Rugi, Sciri, Heruls, and many more. Why he chose Gaul rather than Italy is unclear, though it was assumed at the time that he was trying to retain good relations with Gaiseric, whose enmity with Theoderic in Gaul was well known. Early in April, the army crossed into Belgica, taking Divodurum (Metz) shortly thereafter and moving south and west towards the Loire valley, picking up the support of some local warlords along the way.

Marching his own campaign army out of Italy and calling upon allied

1. The Notitia Dignitatum

2. Monastic Saints from Coptic Egypt

3. Mausoleum of Galla Placidia, Ravenna

4. Ivory Diptych of
Anicius Petronius
Probus

5. The Barberini Ivory

6. Mosaic of Ambrose of Milan

7. The Anthemian Wall of Constantinople

8. The Intaglio of Alaric II

9. An Eagle Brooch from the Domagnano Treasure

10. Christ Pantocrator from St Catherine's Monastery, Sinai

11. The Madaba Map – below, in situ, 1900

12. The Missorium *of Theodosius*

13. The Honorius Cameo

14. Throne of Maximianus

15. *The* Vergilius Vaticanus

16. The Sarcophagus of Junius Bassus

17. The Istanbul Evangelist

18. An Alkhan 'Hun'

19. A Tessera *of Basilius*

20. The Taq-e Kesra, Ctesiphon

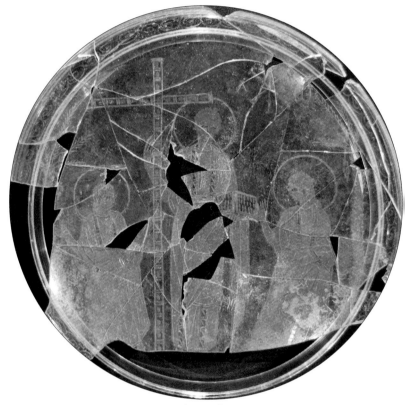

21. The Castulo Paten

22. *Szilágysomlyó Medallion*

23. *A Bracteate from Funen*

24. São Cucufate, Portugal

25. The Corbridge Lanx

princes among the Belgic Franks and the Burgundians in Sapaudia, Aëtius sent the Gallic senator Eparchius Avitus to Tolosa to recruit the aid of Theoderic, who was already mustering his own forces. The Gothic advance turned Attila away from Aurelianum (Orléans) early in June and back towards the Rhineland – presumably his coalition was already starting to crumble, the irresistible prospect of rich plunder limiting the possibilities of coordination. The combined forces of Aëtius and the Gothic king cornered Attila's retreating army at a place called by the ancient authors the Catalaunian plains, near Tricasses (modern Troyes). (This is the same battle occasionally still called the battle of Châlons.) The forces on the field were numerous – this may have been the largest engagement of the whole century – and the evidence suggests considerable casualties on both sides. The most prominent of these was king Theoderic himself, but the overall result was a Hunnic rout. Theoderic's son Thorismund was in a hurry to get back to Tolosa to ensure his own succession against his adult brothers Theoderic and Frederic, while Aëtius possessed too small an army to do more than mop up the remnants of the invading forces. He regrouped, as Attila retreated beyond the Danube, to what is now the Hungarian Puszta.

The year closed peacefully, the Italian clergy taken up with responses to the eastern controversies surrounding Ephesus and then Chalcedon. Ecclesiastical reconciliation would prove difficult when the imperial courts barely acknowledged each other – neither recognised the other's consuls at the start of 452. In that year, Honoria's intended spouse Flavius Bassus Herculanus took up the fasces as western consul, but Honoria herself disappears from view: it is quite possible that she was quietly executed, given the crisis she had intentionally provoked, and now that her mother Placidia was no longer alive to shield her. Attila, for his part, continued to claim his dowry, and in 452 invaded Italy. Again, there was little foresight – Aquileia was besieged and sacked, and Mediolanum was taken as well but, as so often, Italy's climate took its toll on the invaders. The Hun king's army was already beginning to fragment, and food was in short supply, when an embassy of Roman nobles, the consul Gennadius Avienus, the former prefect Trygetius and the bishop of Rome Leo among them, negotiated the terms of Attila's withdrawal. Perhaps the most significant effect of the invasion was to induce Valentinian's court to recognise the accession of Marcian, whose imperial images were solemnly accepted on 30 March 452.

Attila died in the next year, before he had determined what course of action to pursue next. Cavorting with his most recent bride, the daughter of a subject prince, he suffered a haemorrhage that killed him in the night. Rumours of murder of course spread (and have filtered into modern culture via the twelfth-century epic poem the *Nibelungenlied* and its Wagnerian descendant). Hunnic power disappeared almost instantly, a semi-legendary battle between Attila's sons and his subject peoples being fought in Pannonia near the river Nedao in 454. The aftermath of Hunnic collapse injected new instability into the politics of the eastern empire in particular, where a number of former Hunnic subjects sought refuge from the fracturing chaos north of the Danube. The West felt no such impact, but nor did it find any new stability. The Hunnic invasion had damaged Gaul, but worse, it had destabilised it. For many Gallo-Romans, it was irrefutable evidence that the Gothic kings at Tolosa were potentially more reliable and valuable than was the emperor in Italy and all his *magistri militum*. But Tolosa was not what it had been under Theoderic.

Thorismund and Aëtius had quarrelled, and there was a desultory campaign that pitted the damaged forces of both sides against one another, but the Gothic king had more to fear from his own brothers than he did from the imperial *magister*. In 453, he was murdered by Theoderic and Frederic, the former taking control of the Gothic *regnum* – which we must now begin to regard not as an imperial client of indeterminate status but as a separate political power on imperial soil. Theoderic II, as we shall call him, was a Gallic aristocrat as much as a Gothic warlord, and he was on good terms with many of the great senatorial houses of Gallia Narbonensis and Aquitania. A flattering letter by a contemporary, Sidonius Apollinaris, portrays the king as a consummate gentleman: he had some of the ill-humour and unpredictability that comes with great power, but he was certainly no rougher round the edges than any general might be. There may be quite a lot of truth in that portrait. Theoderic declined to perpetuate the rivalry with Aëtius that had consumed his father and elder brother, and he would succeed in ruling for more than a decade, in the meantime bringing stability to the Spanish provinces for the first time in many years.

But then Aëtius died on 21 September 454 – murdered by the emperor himself. Whether this came about as a result of Valentinian's immediate frustration, his fear of the great general, or maybe a long-harboured resentment that could finally vent itself as the patrician entered old age, it was a mistake. Aëtius had come to Rome to discuss imperial finances with the emperor – finances that were in an ever worse state as potential sources of taxation dried up one after the other. There, as the patrician handed over some documents for the emperor's inspection, the latter drew his sword, accused his general of treason, and cut him down with his own hand while the eunuch *primicerius sacri cubiculi* Heraclius held him down.

Whether, as later sources suggest, Heraclius had conceived of the plot along with Valentinian's eventual successor Petronius Maximus is open to doubt. What is not in doubt is that the murder of Aëtius did not have the shocking impact that had attended the execution of Stilicho fifty years earlier. Perhaps there was simply no longer a large enough field army in Italy for its response to the murder to matter. Perhaps the 36-year-old Valentinian had actually begun to win some respect back for the imperial person in the last years of the patrician's ascendancy. What is clear, though, is that Aëtius had successfully enough quelled the ambitions of his subordinates that there was no one able to step into his commanding place. Nor do we see the chaos of rival junior officers that characterised the 420s and the rise of Aëtius himself. Instead, a sort of silence descends on the sources, until spring of 455, when Valentinian was murdered on the parade ground. More than the death of Aëtius, the extinction of the Theodosian dynasty precipitated the final disintegration of the western Roman polity.

10

THE FALL THAT NO
ONE NOTICED

❧

On 16 March 455, the emperor Valentinian rode out to the Campus Martius (Field of Mars), just north of the Capitoline hill, to practise shooting with his bow. Among his guardsmen were two former body-guards of Aëtius, Optila and Thraustila. Optila struck down Valentinian and Thraustila killed his *primicerius*, Heraclius. It may have been a simple act of vengeance, or they may have been suborned by the senator Petronius Maximus, who would go on to claim the imperial diadem that Thraustila and Optila took with them when they left the Field of Mars. Rome fell into confusion. There was no obvious successor and, with Justa Grata Honoria dead, there was no senior princess to whom an ambitious general might attach himself, as Marcian had to Pulcheria five years before. There was no shortage of ambitious generals, including Majorian, Marcellinus, Ricimer, Gundobad and Syagrius – mainly relatively junior officers during the as-cendancy of Aëtius who would gradually emerge as serious contenders for power in the later 450s – but none of them was on the spot. Petronius Maximus was and, as a member of the great Roman family of the Anicii, his wealth was legendary. He could afford to buy himself the purple and so he did. Two days after Valentinian's murder, Maximus was proclaimed emperor and confirmed by a pliant Roman Senate on 17 March. He married Valentinian's widow Eudoxia, and betrothed his own son Palladius to the imperial daughter Eudocia, having elevated the former to the rank of caesar.

Eudocia, of course, had long since been betrothed to Huneric, son of the Vandal king Gaiseric, who could no more be expected to tolerate Maximus than could Marcian in Constantinople. Whether, as some sources suggest, Valentinian's widow Eudoxia appealed to Gaiseric, or whether he simply seized the opportunity presented to him, he launched a fleet against Italy as soon as he got word of events. Other Vandal fleets took control of Corsica, Sardinia and the Balearics, while the two Mauretanian provinces, returned to Ravenna under the terms of the 440 treaty, were now reoccupied as well. Gaiseric himself arrived in Italy less than two months after Valentinian's murder. Rome was in an uproar, rioting against the feeble emperor who had brought a Vandal fleet down upon the city. Maximus tried to escape, but was assaulted by the mob and killed by a hurled roof tile. His body was torn limb from limb in the streets on 31 May, the caesar Palladius was hunted down and killed, and on 3 June north African forces took control of the city.

We hear of palaces being stripped of their wealth, temple and church treasures seized and the imperial treasury denuded. Among the treasures famously carried off to Carthage was the great golden menorah looted from the Temple of Jerusalem by the conquering armies of Titus in AD 70. Unlike Alaric's haphazard and hurried sack in 410, Gaiseric's was systematic. This is unsurprising – the Goth was an itinerant general in desperate straits, the Vandal was king of a flourishing and sophisticated polity in what remained the richest part of the Roman West. The sack of 455 was effectively the organised coopting of one great city's wealth to the benefit of another. When Gaiseric left Italy two weeks later, he took with him Valentinian's widow Eudoxia, her daughters Eudocia and Placidia and Aëtius' son Gaudentius, who had survived the debacle of his father's death the year before. Soon enough, Gaiseric would try to place his own candidate on the imperial throne.

In Italy, the shock of the sack, the lingering presence of Vandal armies and the total failure of Maximus' regime paralysed what was left of the imperial government. None of the generals were present, and it may be that at this point the bureaucracy found it safer to await events – perhaps Marcian would intervene. As it happened, however, a new emperor arrived from Gaul. One of Maximus' *magistri militum* had been Eparchius Avitus, a Gallo-Roman aristocrat who had served as praetorian prefect of that diocese in 439 and then played an important role in gaining Theoderic I's support against Attila. Avitus had been charged by Maximus with announcing his acclamation to the allied court at Tolosa, and he arrived there in spring 455 just in time to avert a civil war between Theoderic II and his younger brother Frederic. He was still there, reconciling members of the Gothic royal family to one another, when news arrived of Maximus' death.

Urged on by Theoderic, Avitus seized the purple, with the full support of a Gallic aristocracy that had long since lost its affection for Italian rule. The Gallic provincial assembly at Arelate acclaimed him their emperor on 9 July. Avitus' ally Theoderic took his main army off to Spain to reestablish central control in that province; in just over a year he had completely destroyed the Suevic kingdom and brought most of the peninsula's main cities under his control in the name of Avitus. The Gallic emperor went rapidly to Italy, crossing the Alps late in September and finding a cautious welcome in Rome, where he entered his first imperial consulate on 1 January 456. The panegyric recited to him by his son-in-law Sidonius Apollinaris is both a bravura piece of triumphalism hearkening back to a happier age and a subtler warning to the Italian aristocracy not to underestimate its Gallic relations any longer: the Italians had had their chance and they had blown it; the Gauls would now set things right.

It was not to be. The Senate and the Italian court had accepted this interloper from beyond the Alps only for want of a better alternative and his failure to make any effort to reconcile them to him was both foolish and ultimately ruinous. Almost the whole of his high officialdom was appointed from men who had accompanied him to Rome from Arelate. The urban prefect, Vettius Iunius Valentinus, was presumably a Roman aristocrat, and he had his name inscribed all over the city for the restoration work he undertook, but he was a rare exception. It was the same with the military: junior military commands stayed in the hands of Italians like Ricimer, Remistus and Maiorianus, all of whom had served Aëtius, but the senior *magistri* came from Gaul and the emperor's personal troops were deputed from Theoderic's army. Other Aëtian generals – Marcellinus, for instance – had effectively ceased to serve anyone but themselves upon the death of Valentinian and had no incentive to cooperate with the new Gallic regime.

Early in 456, the *comes* Ricimer successfully drove part of Gaiseric's forces out of Sicily, for which Avitus felt compelled to promote him to a full *magisterium* as colleague to Remistus. That did nothing for the emperor's popularity, however, with either the army or the Roman populace. The deprivations of the previous year's sack were still being felt, food was scarce, and Avitus' Gallic troops were resented as an occupying army, especially after he insisted the Romans surrender bronze from their roofs to be turned into coinage. He wisely decided to return to Gaul for Easter, which he spent at Arelate. Rumours of treachery, though, must have reached him, for he returned to Italy to assert himself, this time at Ravenna.

Late in September, he had the *magister militum* Remistus executed in obscure circumstances, which in turn pushed Ricimer into open revolt, along with the emperor's *comes domesticorum* Maiorianus, whom we call Majorian. This was dangerous. It was hard to hold the throne with both the palatine troops and the field army openly defiant, however reduced in numbers they might be. Pursued by Ricimer's forces, Avitus was cornered at Placentia (modern Piacenza), deposed and ordained as bishop of the town. His children were sent back to Gaul, but he himself was soon executed, reputedly starved to death by order of Ricimer and Majorian.

Once again, a western interregnum loomed, and potentially more wars. The powerful Goth Theoderic had got news of his ally's death while he himself was suppressing the Suevic king Rechiar's last stand in Gallaecia. (He had taken the Suevic residence at Bracara Augusta (modern Braga in Portugal) in early December 456 and had caught and executed Rechiar by the end of the month.) How he would respond must have been much on the mind of Avitus' assassins. So, too, was the reaction of Gaiseric in Africa, given that he had legitimate princesses of the Theodosian line as guests of his court. In the East, Marcian was no better pleased with the latest turn of events than he had been with the accession of Avitus, whose legitimacy he never recognised. But then Marcian died, on 26 January 457, and for the first time since the death of Julian back in 363 there were no obvious and immediately legitimate successors to either the eastern or the western thrones.

Marcian had no sons, only a son-in-law, Anthemius. He had been honoured with the consulate of 455, alongside the western emperor Valentinian, in another token of the reconciliation between West and East that the invasions of Attila had forced upon the western court. But Anthemius was too dangerously prestigious for the court and the eastern high command; as was no longer the case in the West, the combined interests of palatine bureaucrats and the praesental *magistri* could, in the East, ensure that over-powerful figures would not impose themselves upon the court. And although Flavius Aspar, a dynast of imposing political skill, had become a leading figure in the regime of Marcian just as his father Flavius Ardaburius had been under Theodosius II, he fell back on Leo, a mere tribune of the Mattiarii, without a real power base of his own. It was the same sort of political calculus that had brought about the accession of Valentinian I a hundred years before: a cabal of senior officers chose a relatively junior officer (Valentinian had likewise been a tribune when he had been given the purple) to ensure a balance among rival factions – but, as with Valentinian, Leo would prove to have a mind and some skills of his own.

Insofar as there might remain some question of his legitimacy after the army and the Constantinopolitan Senate had acclaimed him emperor, Leo also sought the approval of the bishop of Constantinople, Anatolius – the first time the patriarch had been consulted in such matters. It was a sensible precaution in uncertain times, and one calculated to appeal to the sentiment of a large urban populace whose ritual calendar was now inextricably tied up in the ceremonies of the church. By acting sooner than his western counterparts, Leo acquired for himself the de facto position of senior emperor by simple virtue of the western interregnum. The ongoing ecclesiastical warfare in the East remained entirely unresolved at the time of Marcian's death and it was preoccupying enough for Leo to leave the West to its own, not very effective, devices.

Neither Majorian nor Ricimer was prepared to act decisively, and instead spent the last months of 456 and the first months of 457 reconciling with various potential challengers to their rule – the Vandal kingdom in north Africa, the Burgundian and Gothic states in Gaul, the bruised and betrayed aristocracy of southern Gaul, and the remaining strongmen and warlords of the Gallic north. The way was smoothed by a token of recognition from the eastern court: on 28 February Leo made Ricimer western *patricius*, thereby joining him to the eastern *patricii* Aspar and Anthemius, and made Majorian *magister militum*. That was enough for Majorian to take further liberties, arrogating to himself the title of Caesar on 1 April 457. This was a pregnant claim, and one that Leo would feel compelled to counter. In the end, Majorian would not feel strong enough in his own position to take the decisive action and make himself augustus until much later, on 28 December. We have evidence of retrospective retouching of narratives in the extant accounts, which tell us both that he was acclaimed by the army and raised up by Leo. Almost certainly, he

took the decision himself and at Ravenna, to make clear that he was suc-
ceeding as a legitimate augustus at the main centre of western government.

Leo was in no position to object, and the shape of Majorian's coalition
begins to emerge in the sources: the palatine bureaucracies of Ravenna;
Ricimer and the Italian army; the Gallo-Roman general Aegidius as
magister militum per Gallias (he had been a junior officer under Aëtius
just like Majorian); and the Goth Theoderic, representing the last of the
interest groups to be conciliated. Conspicuously absent were the Burgundians under Gundioc at Lugdunum, and Gaiseric in Africa. Early in 458,
a *magister epistularum* named Petrus led an army against Lugdunum – a
bizarre command for a poet and civilian palatine official, and yet another
sign of the fundamental breakdown of western governance. The siege
compelled Gundioc and the Lyonnais population to submit to the Italian
regime; a show of force between Majorian and Theoderic, each personally commanding his own troops, ended in their reconciliation late in
that year. Meanwhile, the situation around Lugdunum had been resolved
so that Gundioc and his family, already close allies of the central Gallic
aristocracy, would be accepted as officers in the Italian military. This left
only the Vandals, and here West and East might have hoped to collaborate,
for Leo had as much interest in securing the Mediterranean as Majorian
had in reestablishing control of the African grain supply.

Theoderic, who considered Spain very much his sphere of influence,
sent an army into Baetica and the western provinces under his general
Cyrila in advance of Majorian's planned attack on Africa. In Gallaecia and
the Spanish north-west, the crumbling remnants of the Suevic aristocracy
jockeyed for local power, fighting each other and the Gallaecian provincials, but were largely ignored by both the emperor and the Gothic king.
Majorian himself advanced from Gaul across the Pyrenees in 460, doing
some symbolic campaigning, but mainly overseeing the collection of an
invasion fleet with which to assault Gaiseric. How all of this worked on
the ground is very hard for us to reconstruct, for, though laws continued
to be issued, taxes seem to have been collected very rarely. For all we know,
the fleet was assembled largely through impressed labour, supplied by
the city councils of the Spanish provinces: these had by now got used to
acting on their own initiative much of the time, and not just in distant
Gallaecia where the imperial writ had ceased to run entirely and even
Gothic management was intermittent.

The western invasion fleet was gathered by May, but that had given

Gaiseric quite long enough to get wind of it and act: the king, who, unlike the emperor, had a standing navy of some quality, sent it out from Carthage to Carthago Nova ('New Carthage', Cartagena in south-eastern Spain) and burned the larger part of the emperor's boats at their moorings. Once again, Gaiseric had proved more than a match for the imperial establishments of both West and East. The disappointed emperor made his way back to Gaul, hoping to reestablish his authority there and in Italy after the Spanish fiasco. He lingered in Gaul well into 461, and then headed back to Italy. He had reached Dertona (modern Tortona in the Piedmont), the first major stopping point on the Italian side of the Ligurian Alps, when he was met by Ricimer.

At Dertona, on 2 August, the patrician deposed his long-time ally and fellow conspirator against Avitus. Five days later, Majorian was executed on the banks of the river Ira. Another interregnum began and only on 19 November was a new emperor, Libius Severus *signo* Serpentius, raised to the imperial purple. Severus was a Lucanian senator, and one of high enough status to follow the then-fashionable trend for taking on a *signum* or nickname (his means 'Snakey'). Apart from that, we know only that he was the choice of Ricimer, that Constantinople was not consulted in his acclamation and never recognised him, and that those marshals of the Aëtian period who survived at the heads of troops not only refused to recognise Severus but all now aimed at replacing Ricimer as the leading warlord of the West.

By early 462, Marcellinus had fled Sicily to the Dalmatian coast, where he began to prepare an invasion force against Italy. Aegidius, Majorian's *magister militum per Gallias*, did the same in Gaul, where the regular army units remained loyal to him rather than to the otherwise unknown general Agrippinus whom Ricimer sent to confront him. Theoderic bided his time at Tolosa, waiting to throw his considerable power behind the winner of this contest, and Gaiseric opened friendly overtures with the eastern court, exploiting Leo's open breach with a western administration that had failed to acknowledge his authority as senior emperor.

By early 462, the empress Eudoxia and her daughters Eudocia and Placidia were sent to Constantinople from Carthage, in a gesture of reconciliation that allowed Gaiseric to preserve the betrothal of Eudocia to his son Huneric. In Gaul, Theoderic allowed himself to be persuaded by Agrippinus to side with Severus and Ricimer, rather than Aegidius. Control of the port at Narbo was his asking price and, though Agrippinus was cashiered for his efforts, Theoderic led an army out to the Loire, where he was defeated by Aegidius at Aurelianum. The Gothic king's brother Frederic was killed in the battle, a fact that would have important consequences for the Gothic succession in the next couple of years.

This fighting also disrupted Aegidius' plan to invade Italy, and brought a new and more effective general on to the scene: Ricimer promoted his relation-by-marriage, the Burgundian prince Gundioc, to the position of *magister militum per Gallias* in 463. Gundioc continued to press the battle against Aegidius, who in turn sent an embassy to Gaiseric, seeking an alliance. Nothing came of that overture before Aegidius was murdered in obscure circumstances in either 464 or 465. The remainder of his forces – what had once been the Gallic *comitatenses* and were now to all intents and purposes a private army – split their loyalties between Aegidius' son Syagrius and one of Aegidius' fellow generals, the Frank Childeric. Syagrius withdrew north of the Loire, where he is sometimes imagined as ruling a 'Kingdom of Syagrius' that included some portion of the region's population of Franks. In fact, he became one of the many north Gallic strongmen whose hegemony never extended beyond a small and shifting territory, as predatory on the local rural population as they were protective; it would be five decades before any of these petty commanders could muster enough power and authority to bring a substantial piece of Gallic territory under his control and attempt to administer it. In the meantime, with the possible exception of Treveri and its immediate hinterland, Gaul north of the Loire valley had finally joined Britain as a place without any kind of government legitimately tied to the imperial state.

Southern Gaul and much of Spain had now, like Africa, become kingdoms on formerly imperial soil, their rulers exercising more authority, collecting more revenue, enforcing more of the rule of law than did the imperial government anywhere outside Italy and Provence. That is to say, the old Roman imperial rhetorics survive in the literature of the age, and the contrast between 'barbarian' and Roman remains the interpretative framework in many of our sources. But equally clearly, the majority of the elite population in the lands controlled by Theoderic, Gaiseric and Gundioc preferred the certainties and genuine efficacy of the local royal court to the vagaries and ineptitude of the would-be imperial government in Italy. Gaiseric, with his usual mix of skill and opportunism, took advantage of his alliance with Leo to harass Italy mercilessly with annual naval expeditions. Marcellinus, allied to neither imperial court though clearly in diplomatic contact with Constantinople through Leo's envoy Phylarchus, tried to carve out a kingdom of his own, sailing a fleet out to confront the Vandals' ships in Sicily in 464–5 and winning a victory over Gaiseric that confirmed the rogue admiral as a powerful player in the politics of the disintegrating West.

The degree of political chaos, and the opportunity it provided for potential gain as well as violence, is illustrated in trivial ways as well as large ones: one of the few securely dated events of the period is Ricimer's defeat of an otherwise unknown Alan 'king' named Beorgor near Bergamum in the foothills of the Alps. Who Beorgor was, whose cause he fought in, why he was fighting against Ricimer – we lack all evidence. But this incident illustrates how, at a very real level, the early 460s resembled a war of all against all. Ricimer, though he controlled a powerless emperor, controlled very little else.

Severus died unlamented on 14 November 465. Leo was again sole emperor de facto, though in the East he had always been sole emperor as far as political rhetoric went. The events of 466 are deeply obscure, indeed almost nothing in our sources for political history is securely dated to that year. But by the time of Severus' death, Ricimer was finally ready to take seriously the idea of working with the eastern emperor to impose some sort of stability: nothing else he had tried had worked, so rapprochement with the East was the last remaining option. More than a year passed during which Leo remained the sole augustus, and those months seem to have been taken up with negotiations between the eastern and western courts, the latter presumably made up of the remaining civilian bureaucrats at Ravenna. Leo had problems enough of his own in the East, and he was therefore willing to look more favourably on the western court in 466 than ever before.

As we saw, Leo's accession had depended upon his having been junior to the state's great men. One of these men was the patrician Anthemius, the son-in-law of the emperor Marcian, and thus an ever-present dynastic challenge to Leo. Honouring Anthemius' prominence, assuaging any pretensions he might harbour, and getting him out of the way would all be achieved by sending him west as junior augustus. Ricimer clearly took some convincing, but on 25 March 467 Anthemius was raised to the rank of caesar in Constantinople, before being sent to Italy at the head of a large eastern army. Then at an unknown location called Brontotae, 'at the third milestone' from Rome, Anthemius was acclaimed as augustus on 12 April.

Commanding one part of his army was the freebooting admiral Marcellinus, now raised to the rank of *patricius* on the authority of the eastern emperor. That promotion was surely meant, and was understood by Ricimer, as a challenge to his own authority and a sign that Anthemius would be no one's puppet. But something stronger than pedigree would be needed to cement Anthemius' place in the West's shifting politics, and a success against the Vandals was one thing that could unite the interests of Ricimer, Marcellinus, Anthemius and the eastern court. All agreed to cooperate in a massive combined assault on Gaiseric. And then there was a marriage alliance: Ricimer married Anthemius' daughter Alypia.

The next year opened with Anthemius celebrating his second consulate at Rome, which would serve as his main residence, while Ricimer preferred Ravenna. Sidonius Apollinaris, son-in-law of Avitus, had led a Gallic embassy to Italy to welcome the new emperor and he now delivered his third imperial panegyric, this time to Anthemius, and was rewarded for his efforts with the urban prefecture. Much of the Gallic establishment was less happy with the new emperor, whom they regarded as yet another disappointment coming out of Italy. The situation in Gaul had been complicated by the murder of Theoderic II at Tolosa in 466 by his younger brother Euric. Theoderic had not given Euric a share in monarchical government after Frederic died in battle against Aegidius, which fuelled Euric's resentment as well as his ambition. The new king was popular with some sections of the aristocracy, though not with those who, like Sidonius, nurtured a forlorn hope for an imperial revival and the restoration of harmonious parity between the aristocracies of Gaul and Italy.

But those who disliked Anthemius even more than they had Severus or Majorian saw in Euric an opportunity. In 468 the praetorian prefect of Gaul, Arvandus, who had already served two terms as prefect under several emperors, suggested that Euric seize control of Gaul from the 'Greek emperor'. This Arvandus was low-born but had succeeded on the basis of his administrative skills, in the meantime incurring the enmity of many local aristocrats. Among these were some of Sidonius' own close relatives, and they and others took the opportunity to accuse the prefect of peculation. In the evidence against Arvandus were his letters to Euric, the authorship of which he freely admitted – he had not been seeking the purple and therefore thought himself quite safe from accusations of treason. He was wrong.

Tried before the Senate at Rome, from which the urban prefect

Sidonius prudently absented himself, Arvandus was condemned to death for *maiestas*, treason. Sidonius and a few other senators intervened and secured a commutation of the sentence to exile, but the episode illustrates the extent of the century's confused loyalties. This was no longer the regional faction fighting of the previous century or even the tussles at the court of Honorius. This was a full-fledged crisis of political legitimacy in which everyone had a stake, in which no candidate for the throne was self-evidently more legitimate than any other, and where all the lines between what was and what was not a permissible part of the political game had disappeared – or seemed to have disappeared until you found yourself on the wrong side of one on which everyone agreed.

Euric would remain the preponderant military power in southern Gaul, and with a great deal of Gallic support. Our sources preserve the oppositional voices of men like Sidonius, but they were a minority of the Gallic aristocracy and very soon definitively on the losing side. It was men like Arvandus, their voices lost to posterity, who had a clearer vision of the future, and the coming break with Italy. Euric never did reconcile himself to Anthemius and the Italian regime, but in 468 he could still be ignored while everyone focused on the joint expedition against the Vandals.

As soon as the seas opened in March, the fleets sailed, two from Constantinople, one from Italy, bearing substantial parts of the standing armies of both *partes imperii*. The number of mercenaries must also have been huge, units of soldiers coming from as far afield as Öland in Sweden (where the gold coins they were paid in survive in large quantity) to fight for the imperial side. One of the eastern fleets, under the *comites rei militaris* Heraclius and Marsus, landed in Tripolitania, took the main cities and set off overland for Carthage. The larger eastern fleet, under Leo's brother-in-law Basiliscus, made for Sicily, where it was to rendezvous with the Italian fleet under Marcellinus, who had expelled Gaiseric's naval garrisons from Sardinia and Sicily. Marcellinus and Basiliscus consulted with each other in Sicily before the latter sailed for Cape Bon and weighed anchor near Carthage, demanding Gaiseric's surrender. The Vandal king played for time, entering negotiations and claiming to be at work on peace terms; he was instead preparing his own navy and a flotilla of fireships, which he launched at the eastern fleet, burning half of it entirely and forcing Basiliscus into ignominious flight.

The aftermath of this debacle in the East will occupy us in the next chapter. In the West, it poisoned the high hopes with which the new emperor's first consular year had begun. The only comfort it brought Ricimer, besides the discomfiture of Anthemius, was the death of Marcellinus, murdered in Sicily. Another rival out of the way. In the years that followed, the relationship between Anthemius and Ricimer grew steadily worse, though it is difficult to piece together the sparse and disparate evidence.

Ricimer's crony Romanus, made *patricius* at his instance, was tried and executed by Anthemius in 470 at Rome, in response to which Ricimer put himself on a war footing, raising an army at Mediolanum. The bishop of Ticinum, a charismatic holy man named Epiphanius, effected a reconciliation, but it did not last. In Gaul, all but a few aristocrats who retained a nostalgia for empire now threw in their lot with the most effective nearby authority, be that Euric, the Burgundian Gundobad – who was a relative of Ricimer and technically the legitimate *magister militum per Gallias* under the Italian regime – or the various warlords who populated the territory north of the Loire. Euric, confident now not just in his power but in his legitimacy in the eyes of many Gallo-Romans, besieged Arelate in 471. It was defended by a garrison loyal to the Italian government, and Anthemius sent a small army under his own son Anthemiolus to relieve the Gallic capital, but failed yet again. Anthemiolus died in battle, Euric took Arelate and Gaul remained a part of the 'legitimate' empire more in theory than in reality.

Goaded by the emperor's increasing powerlessness, but himself little more capable, Ricimer decided to do away with a Greek emperor whom he now dismissed as a 'hysterical Galatian', too frivolous to govern. Leaving any Gauls loyal to the central regime to their own devices and Euric's control, Gundobad joined his uncle Ricimer in Italy, and together they besieged Anthemius in Rome in February 472. Back in Constantinople, the Italian strife afforded Leo the chance to rid himself of another undesirable rival while still claiming to help his junior augustus in the West.

Anicius Olybrius was the husband of Valentinian III's daughter Placidia, a Roman senator of the city of Rome, and a member of the Anician clan. He had joined his wife in exile among the Vandals and had developed good relations with Gaiseric and Huneric, the husband of Valentinian's other daughter Eudocia, and thus Olybrius' brother-in-law. The moment Gaiseric sent the Theodosian princesses to Constantinople, their families became potential threats to Leo, in precisely the manner that Anthemius had been. Leo ostensibly sent Olybrius to Italy to help mediate between Ricimer and the western emperor, though getting him out of the way was surely just as important. Both plans backfired – instead of negotiating with Anthemius, Ricimer proclaimed Olybrius emperor in April 472 and carried on with his siege of Rome. When the city finally fell, Anthemius was taken prisoner and executed on 11 July. There was again only one claimant to the western throne, but Olybrius, like Ricimer's earlier protégés, went unrecognised in the East. That quickly became an irrelevance, however, for Ricimer died on 19 August, barely a month after his hated enemy Anthemius. Gundobad, then still in Italy, took Ricimer's place as patrician and senior *magister militum* in Italy, appointing his brother, the Burgundian prince Chilperic, as *magister militum per Gallias*. Whether he was recognised as such in Gaul outside Burgundian territory is unlikely – Euric was implacably hostile. Unfortunately for the princely brothers, their emperor Olybrius was also dead before the year was out, succumbing to dropsy on 2 November.

A by-now customary interregnum ensued: little value remained in a title that guaranteed only misery and an early, probably violent, death. The senior emperor Leo was not consulted, functionally irrelevant to western politics as he was, but there were negotiations between Gundobad's Italian army, the palatine establishment in Ravenna and the senatorial aristocracy in Rome. Finally, on 3 March 473, the *comes domesticorum* Glycerius, hitherto unknown to our sources, was proclaimed augustus. Almost immediately, Euric's *comes* Vincentius led an army into Italy, which Gundobad's generals Sindila and Alla defeated and destroyed, killing Vincentius at the same time; in the same year, an eastern Gothic army under one Vidimir attacked the north Italian plain from Pannonia, but was bought off by the Italian regime and moved on to Gaul, where it melted into the welter of competing warlords. The merest tenability of imperial government, even in Italy itself, was now unclear.

Leo died on 18 January 474 in Constantinople. His general Zeno, as we shall see, had married Leo's daughter Ariadne. Their child Leo, born in 467, had been made caesar in 472 and promoted to the rank of augustus on 17 November 473, after his grandfather fell seriously ill. When Leo died in January, the way was cleared for Zeno. On 9 February 474, the 7-year-old emperor made his father part of the imperial college, raising him to the rank of augustus. This meant Zeno was now the effective ruler in Constantinople. The boy emperor Leo II would die in November 474, ostensibly of natural causes, but Zeno's hold on the throne would be

PLATE CAPTIONS

1. The *Notitia Dignitatum*
In the fourth- and fifth-century empire, the *primicerius notariorum* was responsible for maintaining a master list, known as the *laterculum maius*, of every official in the imperial hierarchy. In the fifth century, perhaps in Italy in the 420s, two working copies of such a list – one eastern, one western, each of somewhat different date – were recopied as a deluxe, illustrated manuscript. We can only speculate about what commemorative purpose it might have served. However, because no examples of actual working copies survive, the deluxe version, known as the *Notitia Dignitatum* ('List of Offices'), is among the best evidence we possess for the military and civilian administrative organisation of the empire, in both east and west. The civilian establishment of each major bureau is listed, as are the units under each senior military commander, while the functions of the bureau or command is illustrated with representative objects or locations. In the example here, the page for the *dux Mesopotamiae*, we see thirteen of the forts or *castella* in which the region's garrison troops were quartered, while

the region itself is represented by the Tigris and Euphrates rivers that flow through the image. The original manuscript of our *Notitia Dignitatum* did not survive the Middle Ages but, as with many late antique Latin texts, its contents were saved from oblivion during the Carolingian renaissance of the ninth century. The ninth-century copy, known as the *Codex Spirensis*, was itself lost in the seventeenth century, but only after several copies had been made during the Renaissance. The Bodleian manuscript, shown here, was commissioned by the Venetian humanist Pietro Donato in 1436 and is thought to most closely reflect the images in the lost *Spirensis*.

2. Monastic Saints from Coptic Egypt
Saqqara, now in Egypt's Giza province, was the burial ground of Memphis, the capital of the Egyptian pharaohs from the third millennium BC. It continued to be used as a funerary precinct for thousands of years. In the late Roman period, thousands of Christian monks settled there and elsewhere on the edge of the Egyptian desert, alternating periods of prayer with the hard labour

needed to feed their communities. The monks, some of whom became celebrities, decorated their monasteries with religious themes of various sorts. The haloes on these two bearded figures, one raising his hands in prayer, the other holding a sacred book, mark them out as saints, possibly founder saints of the monastery of Saint Jeremiah. Discovered on the walls of a monk's cell early in the twentieth century, they are now in the Coptic Museum in Cairo. The dense, emphatic lines of the painting, and the rigid frontality of the saints, are characteristic of Egyptian painting in late antiquity, and are associated in particular with the rise of Coptic (written vernacular Egyptian) as a liturgical language alongside the official Greek.

3. Mausoleum of Galla Placidia, Ravenna

Galla Placidia, youngest daughter of the emperor Theodosius I, was a powerful figure in fifth-century politics from the early 400s until her death in 450. As the century progressed, the imperial court resided more and more frequently at Ravenna, rather than in Rome or Mediolanum (Milan), and the city was therefore filled with buildings for the use of the court and the imperial family. Galla commissioned many such buildings, certainly including the perfectly formed cruciform structure known as her mausoleum, if not necessarily designed for that purpose, or indeed the place she was actually buried (the evidence for her burial there is no

earlier than the ninth century). Built of brick, with a central dome enclosed in a square tower and barrel vaults over each of the four transepts, it was richly decorated with mosaics of Christ the Good Shepherd, the four evangelists, and various saints and martyrs. It was later said that when Galla retired from active political life in the early 440s, she had the remains of her brother, the emperor Honorius, and her husband, the emperor Constantius III, who had long since predeceased her, reinterred at Ravenna. Some have argued that her first child, with Athaulf, the infant Theodosius who had died at Barcino, was, or was meant to be, buried there. As with several other monuments in the city, the mausoleum is particularly important for students of late ancient and early Byzantine figural art, so much of which was destroyed across the eastern provinces of the empire – where it was once far more common than in Italy – during the iconoclastic era in the eighth and ninth centuries.

4. Ivory Diptych of Anicius Petronius Probus

The highest honour to which a Roman official could aspire was the consulship. Though it was purely symbolic – consuls had not had any special powers since the fall of the Roman republic – the consulship remained the apex of a career in public life, because there were only two ordinary consuls in any given year and the emperors very frequently monopolised the consular office for themselves. Romans did not number years sequentially as we do, but rather spoke of 'the year in which x and y were consul'; it was therefore a very great privilege to give one's name to the year that began on 1 January. Senators and officials of every rank might commemorate their entry into office, but in 384, the emperor Theodosius issued a law restricting the use of ivory commemorative diptychs to consuls alone. Two ivory plates, intricately carved on the exterior and blank or more simply engraved on the interior, were joined together by hinges. Although they took the form of wax tablets for writing, these deluxe ivory productions were meant for commemorative display and were given as gifts to a new consul's family members and closest allies. The diptych of Anicius Petronius Probus (consul of 406), preserved in Aosta, northern Italy, is the only surviving example to portray and identify the reigning emperor, in this case Honorius. The Anicii were one of the great aristocratic families of Rome: the consul of 406 was preceded in that honour by his father, and by his two elder brothers who had held the consulship jointly in 395. Here, Probus describes himself as the *famulus*, servant, of the emperor, who is depicted in full military panoply (ironically enough, given that Honorius never set foot on a battlefield). He carries a globe surmounted by the goddess of victory in one hand, while in the other he holds the *labarum*, the imperial standard crowned with the *chrismon* (the Greek letter chi superimposed on the Greek letter rho, a symbol of Christ) and bearing the legend *In nomine Christi*

vincas semper, 'In Christ's name may you always be victorious'.

5. The Barberini Ivory

Now in the Louvre, this ivory panel is composed of five plaques held together by interlocking tongue-and-groove joints (the right hand vertical plaque is lost) and dates to the fifth or sixth century. It was discovered in the seventeenth century and formed part of the collection of the papal legate Francesco Barberini. Unlike the consular diptychs, the purpose of this plaque is unknown, though it clearly depicts a mounted Roman emperor trampling a barbarian, a motif well-known from the imperial coinage. A winged victory hovers at his shoulder, and a personification of the earth offers up her fruits at his feet. The central panel is a masterpiece of late Roman art, with the horse in particular sculpted nearly in the round. The side panels are in bas-relief, and show, at top, Christ and his angels, at bottom, barbarian suppliants offering tribute, and at the side, an officer wearing the same sort of military cloak (the *paludamentum*) worn by the emperor himself. Although we are not able to identify the emperor depicted here, the ivory is a comprehensive catalogue of late antique imperial symbolism – universal rule, eternal victory, Christian piety and divine protection.

6. Mosaic of Ambrose of Milan

Ambrose was one of the two or three most influential Latin churchmen of the fourth century. An Italian aristocrat whose family had chosen the wrong side in the civil war between Constantine's sons, he nevertheless prospered in the imperial service, becoming a provincial governor before the people of Mediolanum acclaimed him bishop and he was rushed through all the lower clerical grades in order to take up that role. Classically educated and thoroughly at home in aristocratic politics, he was also a staunchly Nicene Christian who was able to naturalise complicated ideas from Greek theology in a Latin context. He was likewise a master of political manipulation and several times forced major concessions from emperors by threatening to refuse, or actually refusing, them communion. This depiction of Ambrose comes from the sixth-century church of San Vitale in Ravenna, which commemorates the legendary Milanese saint Vitalis, father of the (equally legendary) saints Gervasius and Protasius whose relics Ambrose discovered, gaining a great deal of popularity and power from the miracles they were said to perform.

7. The Anthemian Wall of Constantinople

Anthemius was praetorian prefect of the East from 405 (in which year he was consul) until 414, under both Arcadius and Theodosius II. As the politics of the western court became ever more fractious and unstable, the continuity of governance at Constantinople looks ever more remarkable. Among many other measures to shore up the stability of civilian governance in the eastern capital, Anthemius ordered the construction of a massive wall to cordon off the peninsula that housed the city centre. A single curtain wall stretched from the Propontis to the Golden Horn, punctuated by towers and a rampart. The wall was six metres thick and twelve high, made of bricks and mortar and faced with limestone ashlars, while ninety-six square or octagonal towers, one every sixty metres or so, stood as much as twenty metres tall depending on the topography. The walls were meant to render the city impenetrable to whatever violence was afflicting the rest of Thrace and the Balkans, and they did so, particularly after they were reinforced by a second curtain wall and moat in the late 440s.

8. The Intaglio of Alaric II

Alaric II ruled the Gothic kingdom of Tolosa, which controlled Aquitania, Narbonensis and parts of Hispania, until his death in battle at Vogladum (Vouillé) in 507. Now in the Kunsthistorisches Museum in Vienna, the sapphire ring stone was probably used as a seal, perhaps in the chancery of the kingdom. Sapphire is one of the hardest gemstones and particularly difficult to work with ancient technology, so it is impossible to overstate what a rare and precious item this was. The portrait is reminiscent of that of emperors as portrayed on the coinage, and the legend, ALARICVS REX GOTHORVM, is also in the style of *celatores* (coin die-engravers). The use of the ethnonym is very rare, however, as most fifth-century kings called themselves simply *rex*, 'king', in official contexts, without specifying what or who they were king of. It has been conjectured, on the basis of the Italian style of the lettering, that the seal was commissioned for Alaric by his father-in-law Theodoric, the Ostrogothic king of Italy. If true, the gift was perhaps meant to underscore the support of the much more powerful ruler for his weaker relation: Alaric was at the time locked in a tense diplomatic standoff with the Frankish king Clovis that would end with Alaric's death and the conquest of his kingdom.

9. An Eagle Brooch from the Domagnano Treasure

This twelve centimetre long brooch is in a style known as *cloisonné*, in which precious and semi-precious stones are laid artfully within a metal frame. Here, garnets are set in a finely designed frame of gold, which combines the eagle, a traditional symbol of nobility and military leadership, with a Christian cross. Portable metalwork of this sort was very much in vogue in late antiquity, both inside the Roman empire and among the barbarians of the frontier. Gold and garnet chip-carving is particularly characteristic of the so-called 'Danubian style', which emerged in the culturally mixed military zone of the Roman Balkans during the fifth century. This brooch forms part of a hoard, including earrings, necklace elements and several more brooches, discovered in the late nineteenth century at Domagnano (San Marino) and now dispersed among several museums. These probably represent the

grave goods of a Gothic noblewoman: although the types of object are typical of burial furnishing in sixth-century Italy, their quality is very much higher.

10. Christ Pantocrator from St Catherine's Monastery, Sinai

This icon, 84 x 46 cm, is painted in encaustic (hot coloured wax) on wood. It is the earliest known example of 'Christ Pantocrator' iconography, which is to say, Christ 'the All-Powerful' (literally, the 'ruler of everything'). It also carries an important theological message about Christ's nature. The left hand half of his face (the viewer's right) depicts his human nature, while the right hand half, more abstract and with a more piercing gaze, depicts his divinity. Preserved at the monastery of St Catherine's at the foot of Mount Sinai, which was founded by the emperor Justinian in 548, the icon was probably painted in Constantinople: some speculate that it is a copy of the miracle-working icon of Christ that stood over the imperial capital's Chalke Gate until its destruction by iconoclasts in the eighth century. While that cannot be confirmed, this iconography became canonical, reproduced down the centuries in the Greek orthodox world.

11. The Madaba Map

Part of the floor of the church of Saint George in Madaba, Jordan, this mosaic (a detail of which is reproduced here) is the earliest known cartographic representation of the Holy Land, probably dating to the third quarter of the sixth century. The walled city in the centre of the image bears the legend *hagia polis ierousa*[...], or 'the holy city of Jerusalem'. Situated in the apse of the church, the map is oriented east and thus depicts the actual compass points of its various cities and buildings. Scholars have identified many of the monuments shown on the map, including the church of the Holy Sepulchre and Justinian's church of the Theotokos. The map was rediscovered in the nineteenth century, preserved in the ruins of the old church which had collapsed in an earthquake in the eighth century. Though badly damaged in places, the accuracy of the map, where it can be checked, makes it a highly important source for the geography of the Byzantine empire from Lebanon to Egypt.

12. The *Missorium* of Theodosius
Missoria were large ceremonial silver plates given by the emperor to high officials on significant occasions, such as their *quinquennalia* or *decennalia* (the fifth and tenth anniversary of their accession). They were both a marker of the recipient's status and a means to store wealth – the silver used to make this example weighed more than fifteen kilos. It was found in 1848 buried in a field at Almendralejo, near Mérida (Emerita Augusta, the late imperial capital of the *diocesis Hispaniarum*), folded in half and accompanied with other silver items – it had clearly been buried as bullion, possibly in the disturbed conditions of the fifth century. Probably made in Constantinople, its date and

iconography are disputed. The most likely interpretation, reflected in its traditional name, is that the *missorium* depicts the emperor Theodosius I investing a high official with the diptych symbolising his office, flanked by the young emperors Valentinian II and Arcadius, and by members of the imperial guard with their spears and oval shields. The majesty of Theodosius is distinguished from that of all the other figures both by the halo and by his setting, framed in the central niche. Traditional symbols of bounty decorate the lower register. If that identification is correct, then the dish was probably made to celebrate Theodosius' *decennalia* in 388 and found its way to Spain in the baggage of a high imperial official serving there. It is one of just nineteen known ceremonial plates depicting the emperor, but massive gilt silver dishes of every sort were found throughout the empire as a useful and pragmatic way to keep a cash reserve on hand.

13. The Honorius Cameo
The Rothschild cameo, known for its first owner, is thought to represent the emperor Honorius and his first wife Maria, daughter of the great patrician Stilicho. It was perhaps a gift for a particularly favoured guest, or even from the western imperial court to the eastern. The carved sardonyx stone is now set in a later filigree frame. Based on the style of the clothing and the proportions of the two figures' heads, the cameo may be a late antique reworking of an early imperial (Julio-

Claudian) stone, or the composition may simply be deliberately classicising. Either way, the central gem on the emperor's laurel wreath prominently bears a cross, marking the scene as Christian. The imagery on this cameo (unlike that of the *missorium* of Honorius' father Theodosius) reflects the early imperial tradition of showing the emperor and his relatives as a real human family, rather than the late imperial preference for a strictly hierarchical presentation far removed from any sort of naturalism.

14. Throne of Maximianus
Maximianus was a native of Dalmatia and became bishop of Ravenna during the reign of Justinian, having previously been a deacon of that church. His episcopate is associated with the construction of several churches, including San Apollinare in Classe and San Vitale, which preserve some of the finest late antique mosaics known: one of them shows Maximianus himself standing at the left hand of the emperor. This ivory *cathedra*, or episcopal throne, is one of the most remarkable pieces of late antique carving to have survived, standing nearly five feet tall and two feet wide and richly decorated on all four sides. It was probably built in Constantinople, using some specially carved and some existing ivory panels, which are a mixture of Constantinopolitan and Alexandrian styles. Amid much vegetal decoration and vine scrolls, the five panels on the front of the seat depict the four evangelists and John the Baptist, while

the back of the seat is decorated with Gospel scenes. The side panels show scenes from the life of Joseph in the book of Genesis: Joseph's role as adviser to Pharaoh was sometimes used as a symbol of a bishop's role as adviser to the emperor.

15. The *Vergilius Vaticanus*
Two illustrated manuscripts of Vergil survive from late antiquity, the *Vergilius Vaticanus* (Vat. lat. 3225) and the *Vergilius Romanus* (Vat. lat. 3867), both now in the Vatican Library. Seventy-six parchment leaves of the *Vaticanus* survive, out of an original 440 or so, and contain fifty illustrations. They are much the most important evidence we have of late ancient manuscript illumination, very little of which has survived. The pictures of the *Vaticanus* are all framed in red and the figures are set in a well-populated and naturalistic landscape, with colours shading from grey to pink, purple and blue to give a sense of distance and open space. The script is a beautifully calligraphic rustic capital and was probably executed in Italy, perhaps at Rome. The illustration here shows part of folio 33 verso, and depicts queen Dido of Carthage making a sacrifice. She is attended by slaves, one of whom carries an axe, indicating that he is the *victimarius*, or ritual slaughterer. The iconography is based on that of Roman sacrifices, in which the magistrate conducted the ritual of sacrifice, but a specially trained slave actually killed the sacrificial animals. How the manuscript survived the Middle Ages is unclear, though it was

known in Carolingian Francia, and already back in Rome in the sixteenth century.

16. The Sarcophagus of Junius Bassus

This sarcophagus was made for the urban prefect of 359, Junius Bassus, who died that year while in office and received the rare honour of a public funeral. It is one of the most famous pieces of early Christian sculpture, highly naturalistic by the standards of the period, and quite large, at more than two metres long. Scenes from the New Testament, and Old Testament scenes prefiguring them, are portrayed in niches, between columns that are carved fully in the round. Many of the figures are likewise in extremely high relief or partly in the round. The scenes in the upper register are, from left to right, the sacrifice of Isaac (prefiguring the Crucifixion), the arrest of Peter, Christ enthroned between Saints Peter and Paul, the trial of Jesus and Pilate washing his hands. In the lower register we find Job on his dungheap (prefiguring martyrdom), Adam and Eve (prefiguring fallen man saved by Christ's suffering), Jesus' entry into Jerusalem, Daniel in the lions' den (prefiguring the Resurrection) and the arrest of Paul. The back of the sarcophagus is undecorated, allowing it to be placed against a wall or in a niche, while the sides have the kind of classical imagery long standard on sarcophagi. Although probably carved in Rome, scholars have long detected a Hellenistic element in the sculptors' preference for naturalistic drapery on the human

figures. The inscription along the top of the sarcophagus translates as 'Junius Bassus, *vir clarissimus*, who lived forty-two years and two months, went to God while holding the urban prefecture and newly baptised (*neofitus*), on the seventh kalends of September (= 25 August) in the year that Eusebius and Hypatius were consuls'. Although the sarcophagus was discovered in 1597, it was only in 1951 that a fragment of its lid resurfaced, inscribed with a poem in elegiac distichs on the funeral and memory of the deceased.

17. The Istanbul Evangelist

This finely sculpted tondo (that is, circular) portrait depicts one of the four evangelists, or perhaps an apostle. While it might have been carved as early as the middle of the fourth century, it is more likely a product of fifth-century Constantinople. The figure wears the standard dress of a Greek civilian, which is to say a mantle or *himation* over a tunic or *chiton*. His wavy hair is brushed forward and his beard is cut short in the manner of a Christian holy man, rather than worn long in the style affected by pagan philosophers (and by the emperor Julian). He holds a codex, which is what has led scholars to label him an evangelist. The sensitivity and human scale of the carving are unusually pronounced for a late imperial sculpture and in strong contrast to the highly stylised and static effect more normally achieved.

18. An Alkhan 'Hun'

In the fourth century, various steppe

nomads claimed the legacy and heritage of the ancient Xiongnu, whose empire had been destroyed by the Han Chinese several hundred years earlier. We find these peoples described as Hunnoi (Latin and Greek for their own steppe neighbours) or Chionitae (the Latin and Greek word for central Asian subjects of the Persian empire), Huna (Sanskrit) and Xwn (Sogdian), almost certainly different transcriptions of the same indigenous word. While the Huns who appeared in the European steppe left no records, and precious little material evidence of any sort, those Huns who occupied the eastern parts of the Sasanian empire and the old Kushan kingdom minted coins in great quantity. As a result, we know a great deal more about them. The first group of eastern Huns of whom we learn are the Kidarites, and the next, who challenged Kidarite control over Gandhara, were the Alkhan. The silver drachm shown here depicts the fifth-century Alkhan ruler Kinghila. The iconography of the reverse is largely Sasanian, with a prominent fire temple even though the legend is in Brahmi, while the ruler portrait has the distinctively elongated head (achieved by skull deformation) favoured by the nomadic elites of this period.

19. A *Tessera* of Basilius

In the fifth and sixth centuries, urban (and occasionally praetorian) prefects issued small, postage-stamp sized *tesserae*, invoking the health of the emperor(s) and referring to something the prefect had done or made. Bronze,

with letters inscribed on slightly raised bands and washed in silver, these *tesserae* are a great mystery, in that we have no true idea what they were for or why they were made. The style of the legends is consistent with that found on coins, but they cannot, as is often claimed, be *exagia* (coin-weights). Some twenty-five or so are extant or definitively attested and it may be that they were a sort of invitation or entrance-ticket to a major event sponsored by the prefect. The example here reads SALVIS DD/ NN ALBIN/VS FECIT // BASILI/ VS REPA/RAVIT, which means 'to the health of our lords the emperors, Albinus made [this], and Basilius repaired [it]'. The prefects in question are Albinus (consul of 493) and Basilius (consul of 541), the last *privatus* to hold the consulship.

20. The Taq-e Kesra, Ctesiphon

Now near the Iraqi town of Salman Pak, thirty-five kilometres south-east of Baghdad, the Taq-e Kesra is the only part of the Parthian and Sasanian city of Ctesiphon that survives above ground. Although the power-base of the Sasanian dynasty was Fars in Iran, Ctesiphon remained the main royal residence in Mesopotamia and thus the target of Roman invasions, like that of Julian in 353. The Taq-e Kesra was part of the royal palace complex, probably one of its grand audience chambers, with an arch fully thirty-seven metres high and walls almost seven metres thick at the base. Scholars debate the date at which it was built, some arguing for the third century, others the fifth or sixth, but regardless, it is the largest vaulted structure to have survived antiquity. While it also survived the past two decades of warfare in Iraq, part of it collapsed in 2019 after restoration work undertaken two years before.

21. The Castulo Paten

Only discovered in 2014, this clear greenish glass paten, 22 cm in diameter, is one of the oldest depictions of Christ yet discovered, showing him in majesty between Saints Peter and Paul. He holds a bejewelled cross in one hand and a Gospel book in the other. The figures are set within a frame of palm trees, representing heavenly immortality. In the upper field of the image, an alpha and an omega are set on either side of a chi-rho symbol. A paten for the consecrated host and a chalice for the consecrated wine were the essential furnishings for the Eucharistic rite (Holy Communion). This one was discovered in a house at the archaeological site of Castulo in southern Spain, in a building that the archaeologists interpret as an early church. Its incised decoration is reminiscent of examples known from fourth-century Italy and it was almost certainly made in a workshop in or near Rome.

22. Szilágysomlyó Medallion

Two parts of a massive hoard of gold and silver were discovered a century apart (in 1797 and 1889) in what was then Szilágysomlyó in Habsburg Hungary and is now Şimleul-Silvaniei, Romania. Seventy-three objects,

weighing more than eight kilos, are now divided between the Kunsthistorisches Museum in Vienna and the Hungarian National Museum in Budapest. This gold medallion of Valens was one of seven found in the first hoard to be discovered. It is a multiple of a *solidus* that was struck in Rome in 376, after Valens had successfully repaired relationships between the courts of his nephews Gratian and Valentinian II. Multiples of *solidi* were used to reward senior officials and generals, and also as payments to barbarian leaders on the frontiers. There, they were often fitted with a ring so they could be worn as a necklace, and were sometimes set in a golden frame, as here. These reworkings illustrate the way Roman objects could be repurposed as symbols of authority, as well as stores of wealth, and how the line between currency and bullion blurred along the edges of imperial society. Given the scale of the Szilágysomlyó hoard, scholars assume it was accumulated over one or two generations of a noble family in the region (speculatively identified as Gepids), and deposited in the fifth or the earlier sixth century during the endemic warfare of those years.

23. A Bracteate from Funen

Scandinavia was a long way from the empire, but for many centuries Roman luxury goods made their way there via the barbarian polities of continental Europe. Even though warriors from Sweden and Denmark served as mercenaries in the fifth-century imperial West, luxury imports of Roman goods into Scandinavia largely stopped. In their place, locally-designed prestige items (ultimately derived from Roman models) came into vogue, in particular the type of artefact known as a bracteate, shown here. Resembling gold *solidi*, these little discs are so thin as to be almost foil-like. Originally associated with the cult and palace site at Gudme on the Danish island of Funen, bracteates appear in great quantity in the fifth century, covered in mythological designs, stylised ruler portraits and intricate animal forms. Whether they served as a form of political display or were actually exchanged as currency has been debated, but this example is particularly fine. It shows a highly stylised human head, flanked by even more stylised animals, including a bird and a horse. The runic inscription has been variously transcribed, but many have seen in it an invocation of Odin.

24. São Cucufate, Portugal

These imposing brick vaults are part of the façade of the villa of São Cucufate, in the Roman province of Lusitania, now the Portuguese Alentejo. The region is noted for soaking winters, scorching summers and a harsh granitic soil that favours the olive and vine over other crops. In antiquity, unlike today, it was populous and rich, as exemplified by developments at São Cucufate. In the fourth century, a massive new villa was constructed on a property that had been occupied by modest agricultural structures since the first century. Rather than the one-storey peristyle villas

typical of the earlier period, the fourth-century villa was on two levels, the upper, residential floors supported on the massive barrel vaults. The western façade was flanked on each side by these two arched pendants, perpendicular to the main hall of the villa, and still preserved to a height of six metres. To ascend to the villa's entrance, one climbed a massive podium running the length of the façade. The total habitable space of the villa was more than 800 square metres, making it by far the largest villa complex in Lusitania even before one takes into account the baths and a huge reservoir or *natatorium*, also still extant. By contrast, only small traces of the villa's industrial sector, including the workers' quarters and the house of the *vilicus* or overseer, have been discovered. Undoubtedly the residence of a senatorial family, São Cucufate was probably abandoned by the sixth century, a small chapel occupying part of its ruins during the Middle Ages.

25. The Corbridge *Lanx*

Part of a hoard discovered in 1735 in Corbridge on the banks of the Tyne, this silver platter (known as a *lanx*) is the only piece still known to be extant. Weighing nearly five kilos, the *lanx* is among the finest pieces of fourth-century silver work known, matching the detail and subtlety of the best pieces in the equally famous Mildenhall Treasure, also in the British Museum. Stamps on some fourth-century vessels of this type show that *argentarii comitatenses*, officials in the bureau of the *comes sacrarum largitionum*, guaranted the quality of the silver after a vessel was formed but before it was decorated. Where the Corbridge *lanx* was made is unclear, but both Africa and Asia Minor have been suggested. From left to right, the main scene depicts two goddesses in conversation, Diana with her bow, Minerva with her helmet and spear; two other goddesses whose identity is disputed; and finally Apollo at the entrance of a temple, holding a bow and with his lyre at his feet. The lower register shows Diana's hound, a fallen stag, an altar and a griffin. Large works in silver were a favourite way to both store and display wealth among late imperial elites.

subject to constant challenge from Leo's widow Verina and his brother-in-law Basiliscus, as we shall see in the next chapter.

The consequences of this eastern regime change were rapidly felt in the West. Leo had died without ever recognising Glycerius, and his successor Zeno adhered to the growing eastern precedent of sending potential trouble westwards. Among the many possible challenges to Zeno was Julius Nepos, a nephew of the late mercenary leader Marcellinus and the husband of Leo's niece. It was said that Leo had already been planning to make Nepos western emperor, but Leo II and Zeno did so in fact. Seeing this, and recognising that the ephemeral imperial regime he was supporting had no future, Gundobad returned to Gaul to succeed his father as king of the Burgundians. That marks a significant milestone: for half a century, men who might have styled themselves king had preferred the title and the powers of a *magisterium militum*. Gundobad shows us that this was no longer the case, as decisive an illustration as one could find of the depth to which imperial prestige had fallen in the West.

Nepos launched his expedition from the Dalmatian coast and sailed around Italy, landing at Portus, where he was proclaimed augustus in June 474 before marching on Rome. Glycerius, most of whose army may have followed Gundobad to Gaul, surrendered without a struggle and was exiled to Salona in Dalmatia, there to serve as the city's bishop. Nepos attempted to replicate the strategy of his predecessors in marshalling varied western factions into some sort of coalition. He appointed Avitus' son Ecdicius, the brother-in-law of Sidonius Apollinaris, as *magister militum per Gallias* and also tried to negotiate peace with both Euric and Gaiseric, the latter in concert with Constantinople. The aged Vandal king was now more concerned with guarding his own succession plans than with tormenting the Italian regime, and peace was easily made. Nepos' treaty with Euric finally recognised the Gothic kingdom for what it had become: an independent polity on what had once been imperial soil. Euric's control over most of western and southern Gaul was accepted, in return for which he allowed forces loyal to Nepos to garrison Arelate and Massilia. Sidonius Apollinaris, who by now had been ordained bishop of Civitas Arvernorum (today Clermont-Ferrand in the Auvergne), experienced this as a bitter and treacherous reward for Gallic loyalty. He failed to notice how few of his fellow aristocrats shared his enthusiasm for a lost imperial ideal.

Nevertheless, the rivalry between Italians and Gauls for the scraps of imperial power continued, and, when the Italian government ceded

Arelate to Euric as well, Ecdicius moved to Italy, where he immediately found himself out of his depth. He withdrew to Gaul, and another *magister militum*, Orestes, replaced him. Just as swiftly, in August 475, this new *magister* fell out with his emperor. Nepos fled to Dalmatia, still the legitimate augustus as far as Constantinople was concerned, but never again to set foot in Italy. Orestes proclaimed his young son Romulus emperor at Ravenna on 31 October 475, but he found the task of actually governing to be impossible. It did not help that there was essentially no empire left to govern. Italy had precious little tax base, and Orestes' support rested on the few soldiers personally loyal to him. The remains of the standing army, which had refused to fight for either Glycerius or Nepos, now mutinied, demanding land on which to support their families because they were no longer being paid adequate salaries.

One Odoacer (or Odovacar, as he is sometimes known) led the revolt. Rather than putting up a pretender, or challenging Orestes for the *magisterium*, he declared himself king of Italy and marched on Ravenna from the north Italian garrison town of Ticinum. Orestes tried to counter him, and their armies met at Placentia, where Orestes was captured and killed on 28 August 476. Odoacer's army moved on to Ravenna, his original target, where Orestes' brother Paulus led the defence. On 4 September, the city fell, and Paulus joined his brother in meeting a violent end. Their notional emperor, the boy Romulus – known to history as Romulus Augustulus, 'Romulus, the Little Augustus' – was deposed. Instead of executing him, however, Odoacer sent him back to live on the family estates in Campania. Neither the family of Romulus nor the fugitive Nepos looked to be much of a threat.

In that calculus, Odoacer proved right. Zeno, as we shall see, had fought off a usurpation of his own in the same years during which Glycerius, Nepos, Orestes and Odoacer had in turn struggled for power. The eastern augustus had no interest whatsoever in further western entanglements. When Odoacer and the Roman Senate sent an embassy to Constantinople recognising his authority, they did so on their own behalf, not that of any emperor. They no longer needed one. Zeno continued to recognise Nepos in Dalmatia as the legitimate western augustus, but did nothing to restore him to power in Italy; nor did Nepos presume to try his luck on a solo venture. Hard as it might have been to believe, western aristocracies, up to and including the Roman Senate itself, had discovered that they no longer needed a Roman emperor. They could conduct their own affairs and function well enough with the surviving mechanisms of imperial government, to which the personal presence of an emperor had become irrelevant. Indeed, wrangling claimants to a vestigial imperial title were self-evidently more trouble than benefit. Perhaps even more remarkably, both Zeno and Nepos could perceive the wisdom of this new constitutional fiction. They recognised Odoacer's regime as legitimate, he in turn minted coins in the names of both Zeno and Nepos, but his de facto independence went unchallenged. The basic structure of imperial government survived in Italy: praetorian prefects continued to administer public and civil affairs with Odoacer in overall command, and the Roman Senate gained, if anything, more power than it had exercised for many centuries. That Odoacer was barely able to project his power outside Italy, however, illustrates just how comprehensively the superstructure of imperial government had disappeared between the 440s and the 470s.

In less than a generation, provinces had become kingdoms. Some of these were governed by stable coalitions of military elites and old Roman landed aristocracies, and in these regions – Italy, Vandal Africa, Gothic western Gaul and north-eastern Spain, Burgundian eastern Gaul – the machinery of Roman government continued to function quite effectively; it was simply no longer connected to the machinery of imperial government elsewhere. In other kingdoms, however, power devolved to the cities and municipal elites, as happened in much of Spain outside north-eastern Tarraconensis. Alternatively, it fell into the hands of extortionate warlords and landed aristocrats, whose government entailed as much protection racket as administration: in northern Gaul and Germania, whether under a Syagrius or a Frankish princeling, the structures of government disappeared and would have to be rebuilt from scrap over the coming centuries – only the surviving episcopal sees continued to maintain some semblance of Roman administrative habits. In Britain, even the church structure had disappeared by the later fifth century.

The contrast between regions that retained their imperial imprint, however locally, and those that did not can best be illustrated by toponymy. In Spain, Italy and most of southern Gaul, Roman city names have survived in their Romance form to this day, and would have done so in Africa but for the Arab conquests of the seventh century. All across Britain and Gaul north of Narbonensis and Aquitania, however, Roman city names disappeared. They were replaced either by the old pre-Roman tribal name (thus the capital of modern France, the Roman Lutetia Parisiorum, is now called Paris and not Lutèce) in a regional change that can already be seen in the fourth century, or by new, philologically Germanic names. It is a rough measurement, but a significant one. The post-Roman kingdoms of the western empire are a subject for a different book. Largely ignored in the press of events recounted in this and the previous chapter, however, is another story in which the western empire differed very distinctly from the eastern: that of the role of the Christian church. The reigns of Leo and Zeno in the East illustrate that distinction quite clearly.

11

AFTER THE
THEODOSIANS

M arcian died on 26 January 457, having never recognised the Gallic emperor Avitus. Though the latter had by now been deposed and murdered, no one else had yet claimed the western throne. But whereas the politics of succession in the West had begun to devolve into a free-for-all, the East was still operating within a recognisably fourth-century mode of governance: multi-sided debate among the army high command, the civilian administration and the palatine bureaucracy.

Under Arcadius and Theodosius II, far more of the machinery of government had become concentrated in the vast imperial palace complex at Constantinople, and that gave the civilian and palatine officials greater influence than they had enjoyed when emperors were regularly chosen in the field. This was one curb on the military men, but the rise of a single overmighty general was prevented by another built-in limitation on the power of the eastern army. Whereas in the West since the time of Stilicho, one general had tended to tower above all others, a cadre of canny subordinates scheming to take his place, in the East there had long been two *magistri militum praesentales*. Each commanded his own separate field army, garrisoned near the capital. This duplication of the praesental *magisterium* blunted the military's influence in politics, while the stationary court made for a civilian bureaucracy both more complex and more deeply rooted than in the West. Finally, the relative weakness of eastern aristocracies, and their dependence on the machinery of state rather than on vast landed wealth, was a powerful force for stability – whereas western grandees could, when it suited them, defy or ignore the government, aristocratic power in the East required ongoing participation in the governing bureaucracy. Eastern politics thus favoured compromise over violence, whereas in the West the best results were often obtained by violent confrontation.

And so, with Marcian dead, the palatine bureaucracy, the civil adminis-trators and the praesental high command found a compromise candidate: the Balkan officer Leo, a tribune in a unit of one of the praesental field armies, the Mattiarii. He was connected to Flavius Aspar, one of the two *magistri militum praesentales*, but he was not the great general's puppet. Had he been, he would not have enjoyed such wide consensus, and consensus there was: the generals, the imperial church in the person of the bishop Anatolius, the palatine bureaucracy led by the *magister officiorum* Martialis and the heads of the other bureaus were all in agreement. On 7 February 457, Leo was proclaimed emperor in the Hebdomon palace, after which he led a procession into the city. This looked rather like a Christian liturgical ritual and it marks another stage in the resacralisation of the imperial office. Leo, as yet, had no sons, which may have been one reason he was chosen, but he did have two daughters, the elder named Ariadne and the younger Leontia, born around the time Leo became emperor. Leo's wife Verina would prove another powerful figure at court, even into the next reign.

Leo inherited an ecclesiastical mess that went back to the days of Theo-dosius II, the utter failure of lasting consensus at the first and second councils of Ephesus, and thereafter also at Chalcedon in 451. The theological issues, as we may remind ourselves, were complex. The condemnation of Nestorius at Ephesus in 431 had not been enough for many Alexandrian churchmen, who continued to press for an extreme interpretation of their bishop Cyril's views on the single divine nature of Christ. Then, the total triumph of Alexandrian doctrine at the second council of Ephesus in 449 had alienated not just many eastern bishops but also the Latin churches and particularly Leo of Rome. Thereafter, at Chalcedon in 451, Marcian had pushed for and won a theological solution that actually solved very little. That is, many who found it politically convenient to support the Chalcedonian formula did not believe in its actual theological validity.

Staunch Alexandrians, who had come to be known by their opponents as monophysites for their belief in the single divine and human nature of Christ, rejected the views of Chalcedon as outrightly false. A majority of the Alexandrian population, and large numbers of violent Egyptian monks, favoured strict monophysite doctrine, and in 457, as soon as they learned that Marcian was dead, they set up a rival bishop at Alexandria to challenge the Chalcedonian patriarch Proterius. This was Timothy Aelurus (Timothy 'the Cat'), a true believer in the doctrine of Cyril and Dioscorus, and a conscientious imitator of their thuggery.

On Good Friday 457, Timothy's partisans murdered Proterius in his baptistery. This scandal was the first problem with which the new emperor Leo was confronted. The emperor was a Chalcedonian, but willing to listen when Timothy sent an embassy to Constantinople demanding that a new council be called to reopen doctrinal debate: Chalcedon, he argued, had demonstrably failed to resolve questions over the divinity's nature. Leo reserved his judgement and instead wrote to many leading bishops, including those of Rome, Antioch and Jerusalem, to consult them on the wisdom of holding another council. They were unanimously hostile to the idea and so Leo sent Timothy into exile in a distant imperial outpost on the Crimean Chersonese, from which he was allowed to return only after Leo's death. But the rift in the Greek church caused by Chalcedon would long outlast the century.

We know surprisingly little about the first years of Leo's reign beyond its ecclesiastical affairs, but we can see something of the structure of the court by looking at its office holders. The family of Aspar prospered, one son, Ardaburius, having followed his father into the high command as *magister militum per Orientem* and holding the consulate as early as 447. Another, Patricius, who held the consulate of 459, was promised marriage to the princess Leontia, and, in an extraordinary honour, would eventually be appointed caesar; the third, Hermeneric, would be made consul in 465. The empress Verina's family did well, too, her brother Basiliscus holding high command and eventually leading the disastrous invasion of Africa in 468. None the less, in the absence of narrative sources, it is difficult to make sense of the day-to-day rhythm of politics. Only in the 460s, when a surprising threat to the throne produced a flurry of evidence, can we begin to follow events at the imperial centre in any detail. On the frontiers, however, the start of Leo's reign was eventful, and remained so throughout its length.

The new emperor faced an increasingly restive eastern frontier after the long period of peace under Theodosius and Marcian, and it is time to return briefly to the wider Eurasian context. Fifth-century Persia had become a more stable, less aggressive imperial state. It had ceased its constant expansionism since the death of Shapur II in 379, and its stability rested on its strength. An entrenched Iranian aristocracy provided the core of large field armies that could project the shahanshah's authority far beyond the regions he actually administered. The Zoroastrian priesthood constituted a large administrative bureaucracy that oversaw the fiscal and legal operations of the empire, while the Mazdean fire temples managed the land and functioned as banking houses and treasuries. The Persian kings minted a very pure silver drachm, wider and thinner than any other coins, on which each reigning monarch was identified by his elaborate, distinctive headgear. This royal Sasanian currency had by the fifth century become the standard means of exchange throughout all of central Asia and much of south Asia as well, trusted and widely imitated by the more transitory polities that grew up on the frontiers of the Sasanian empire (its thin shape and pattern, though in gold, was ultimately adopted by the Byzantine rulers of the seventh century, and, in silver, by later medieval coin issuers across Europe).

By the fifth century, as recent archaeological work in Iran has begun to show, Mesopotamia and Khuzestan – the Iranian region at the head of the Persian Gulf – were more densely populated than at any other time before the modern era, thanks to state-sponsored irrigation on a huge scale. Meanwhile, construction on the north-western and north-eastern frontiers intensified, with the military sites supported by state-directed population transfers and the forced settlement of nomads to work the newly cleared arable land.

The level of economic stability that this resulted in meant that the dynastic stability of the Sasanian kings could be sustained without recourse to wars of conquest. For the most part, indeed, even succession crises could be avoided by the judicious assassination of rival heirs, although there were some exceptions, like the attempted rebellion against Peroz of his brother Ohrmazd. For the Roman world, this meant a general easing of tensions on the eastern frontier, which enjoyed extended periods of tranquillity in the first half of the fifth century. Indeed, we have already seen that relations between Yazdgerd I and Constantinople were so good that Arcadius may perhaps have asked the king to serve as guarantor for the succession of the imperial heir Theodosius II. A Greek church historian suggests that Yazdgerd was so impressed by bishop Marutha of Silvan in

Armenia that he contemplated converting to Christianity; while that is unlikely, the king did permit the first Christian church council ever to meet on Persian territory, at Ctesiphon in 410.

Only very late in the reign of Yazdgerd and at the start of Varahran V's reign was there renewed persecution of Christians in Persian territory, instigated by the Christian destruction of a fire temple, but even then the open warfare that threatened to break out was avoided by both sides. Real tensions between the two empires remained, of course, for instance over control of the Caucasus, and while these were sometimes aggravated by foreign events, they were also sometimes mitigated, as both sides dealt with their respective challenges. For in the same way that eastern emperors had constantly to reckon with the open wound of the fifth-century Balkans, Persian kings faced dramatic problems with the steppe nomads on their north-eastern frontier.

The brief subordination of the Kushanshahr to Shapur II in the 370s had not made Persia's eastern frontiers secure against a changing array of Hun polities – first the Kidarites and the Alkhan, and latterly the Hephthalites. These Hephthalites were one of the many clans who emerged from the fourth-century Hunnic dislocation into southern central Asia, and for a time they seem to have coexisted with their fellow 'Huns', sharing sovereignty over the different regions that had at one time or another made up the Kushanshahr. But by the 430s or 440s, the Hephthalites had either displaced or subordinated their various rivals and, for the better part of a hundred years, constituted a formidable and predatory state against which successive mid-fifth-century Persian kings had to range themselves: Yazdgerd II and, especially, Peroz I were consistently more focused on their eastern than on their western frontiers.

The single largest hoard of Sasanian coins from what was once Soviet central Asia, the Dushanbe Hoard in what is now Tajikistan, is composed entirely of homogeneous issues from between 399 and 457, all of them countermarked for local exchange. They can only be part of a tribute payment to a Hunnic group beyond the aspirational boundaries of Sasanian control – presumably to persuade some kinglet in the Dushanbe region to serve as a check on the Hephthalites nearer to the Sasanian frontier. Ironically, although Peroz had sought refuge among the Hephthalites during one of the Sasanian dynasty's many civil conflicts, it was also at the hands of the Hephthalites that he died in battle, at Herat in modern Afghanistan, during the third of three major wars he had fought on that frontier. In the first of them, in 469, Peroz's son Kavadh had been taken captive by the Hephthalites and was ransomed at great expense. More so even than the fourth-century Hunnic challenge, it was the consolidation of Hephthalite power at the fringes of eastern Iran that transformed Sasanian royal ideology permanently from a mix of Hellenistic, Mesopotamian and Iranian symbolism into an intensely Persian, and theologically Zoroastrian, mould, pitting the good and orderly world of Iran against the chaotic and evil void of Turan – the steppe empire now symbolised by the Hephthalite Huns.

The reconceptualisation of Sasanian identity as contrasting more starkly with the steppe world than with the Roman one made it easier for both empires to cooperate when necessary. One place this certainly mattered was Armenia, culturally as much Iranian as it was Hellenistic, and so often a bone of contention. Persian control of the kingdom, though it was now Christian, went more or less unchallenged by the Romans during the fifth century, while the northern Caucasus, over which Rome and Persia had long bickered, also fell increasingly under Persian influence.

The northern Caucasus was historically divided by the Surami ridge into the western region of Colchis, or Lazica, and the eastern region of Iberia. Because the western part abutted the Black Sea, it had for centuries interacted with the Hellenistic and Roman worlds as well as the Armenian and Persian. Iberia was more easily accessible from the south and east and, though it had been in the Roman orbit during the fourth century, by the early fifth century the kingdom was firmly a vassal of the Persian kings. In the 450s, the Lazican king Gubazes sought to follow the same path as Iberia, throwing off his alliance with Rome and seeking the patronage of Persia. Constantinople sent an army to prevent that, deposing Gubazes in favour of his son. This wrangling over client states did not prevent a more generalised spirit of cooperation on the thorny matter of mutual defence.

Guarding the Caucasus passes was a costly business, made more difficult by the break-up of Attila's empire after 453 and the dislocation it had caused on the steppe. In response, the Persians began to reshape the infrastructure of the Caucasus, with the Roman emperors helping to pay for the expense. Nomadism and transhumant pastoralism have been a consistent element in Iranian history over millennia, and recent scholarship has demonstrated long continuities in the way nomads coexisted with settled urban and agricultural communities in the more populous regions of the Iranian plateau. Iranian rulers, into the modern era, have periodically sought to sedentarise their nomadic populations and the fifth century was one such time.

Partly as a measure of defence, the early fifth-century kings began to resettle nomads from central Iran along the north-eastern and north-western frontiers, just as the first Parthian king Arsaces had resettled the nomadic Mardi for the same purpose hundreds of years earlier. New irrigation systems were paired with fortified urban centres at various sites, most importantly at Ultan Qalasi in the valley of the Araxes (the modern Aras) river, which flows through the Mughan steppe into the Caspian Sea in the far north-west of modern Iran. Likewise in the Mil steppe, nearby in Azerbaijan, the archaeological record reveals a population explosion in the reigns of Yazdgerd I and Varahran V. Under their successors Yazdgerd II and Peroz I, the fortifications guarding the passes into the Iranian steppes from the north were heavily reinforced, especially the Derbend wall, which may be where Yazdgerd I's new fortress of Biraparakh was built, assisted by a Roman subsidy. Though events north of the Caspian and south of the Urals are comprehensively lost to our view, it seems very likely that the intensive expansion of military infrastructure in the Caucasus was a byproduct of both the collapse of Attila's western Hunnic empire and the new dominance of the Hephthalites in the east: the steppe was restive in the mid fifth century, as both the winners and the losers sought new lands in which to establish themselves.

Direct evidence for cause and effect is available only where written sources survive, and these mostly concern the Balkans. They make clear just how damaging the destruction of Attila's European empire was to Roman interests. With Attila's sudden death in 453, and then the stunning defeat of his children at the river Nedao in the following year, his former subjects were suddenly liberated from their obligations to a violent and predatory hegemon. That left them free to fight among themselves, which they promptly did. Their struggles soon threw up entirely new political constellations in the *barbaricum*. In the course of the next hundred years, we first hear of such new barbarian groups as the Bulgars or Sclaveni (Slavs), and that must be in part a consequence of Hunnic collapse in Europe. How these new polities formed, and with what admixture of the local and the immigrant, will remain a perennial subject of scholarly controversy. That said, among the various groups whom we know to have been subjects of Attila, the Sciri and the Gepids seem to have done very well for themselves, retaining the choice Transdanubian lands in which

Attila had based his personal following. Several Gothic groups – one led by the brothers Valamir, Theodomir and Vidimer, and another led by Theoderic, son of Triarius, known as Strabo ('the Squinter') – did rather less well, driven by rival kinglets into parts of the Balkans still notionally controlled by Constantinople.

Attila had, of course, devastated huge swathes of the Balkans, denuding them of portable wealth, slaves included, and harrowing the imperial infrastructure. Precisely when different fourth-century provinces fell out of imperial control is a matter of debate: some scholars argue that we can assume the survival of the imperial administration until we have explicit evidence that a region was lost to the government; others think that, without explicit evidence of a continued imperial presence, we must assume that a given province had already been lost. On balance, the latter, minimalist approach seems the more probable. If we follow this line of thought, then the four provinces in the diocese of Pannonia (Pannonia Prima and Secunda, Valeria and Savia) were probably lost to both the western and the eastern empires during the 430s and Noricum Ripense (modern Austria between the Danube and Alps) by the 450s or so. From Sirmium on the border of the Pannonian and Dacian dioceses, all the way to the coast of the Black Sea in the diocese of Thrace, stretches of land south of the Danube remained a playground for barbarian warlords. The only Balkan territories firmly under the control of Constantinople were the Thracian provinces south of Moesia Secunda, along with the dioceses of Macedonia and Achaea.

In the mid 450s, both Valamir and Theoderic Strabo tried to find a place for themselves on Roman territory, since they and their followers could no longer rely on their former status as privileged infantry units of the Hun empire. Marcian granted Valamir and his brothers the right to settle in Pannonia and an annual subsidy for their troops, but when Leo discontinued this practice, they invaded the Balkan provinces still governed by Constantinople and seized some towns on the Adriatic coast, among them the important port of Dyrrachium (now Dürres in Albania). Valamir eventually accepted peace terms in 461: his nephew, Theodemir's son Theodoric, was sent to Constantinople as a hostage for his father's and uncles' good behaviour. There he acquired a taste for Graeco-Roman high culture that would make him the most polished diplomat among the kings of his generation. Leo agreed to pay Valamir an annual tribute of 300 pounds of gold – which was very little by eastern standards. Theoderic

Strabo, for his part, led a private army that was subsidised by the imperial government in parts of Thrace as a sort of balance to Valamir further north and west.

The arrangements with Valamir and Strabo demonstrate that the eastern empire's frontier policy now involved the same sort of balancing act that had become the chronic fate of the West, but with the essential distinction that it worked more sustainably. Not only could the eastern empire's finances weather a periodic soaking, but, unlike in the West, even upheaval among key generals and courtiers did not send its politics spiralling out of control. In 466, a devastating conflagration – rumoured to have been caused by a malignant demon in the shape of an elderly woman with a careless candle – burned whole sections of Constantinople, including the Senate House in the original forum and many other public buildings. The fire blazed for three days, and Aspar won great praise for his commanding leadership in a crisis, personally rushing about the city with pails of water and hurling them on the flames. He won particular praise for his actions by contrast with the emperor Leo, who retreated to an auxiliary palace across the Golden Horn.

Soon after these heroics, however, the great general suffered a major blow to his prestige. His son Ardaburius, by then the long-serving *magister militum per Orientem*, was accused of conspiring against Leo with the Persian king. Letters to that effect were discovered by an Isaurian officer, Flavius Zeno, who brought them to court and showed them to Leo. Rather than react with a bloodbath, as might have been expected, Leo summoned Ardaburius to court and had his case heard in a full meeting of the consistory, chaired by the *magister officiorum* Patricius, at which his father Aspar was present. Leo even allowed Aspar to have a say in the fate of his son. Faced with what must have been irrefutable evidence, Aspar had the good sense to acquiesce in Ardaburius' exile. He himself maintained his high position in the government, which would have been unthinkable if the same scenario had played out among the skirmishing generals of the West.

While Aspar suffered no immediate derogation from his authority, the man who had discovered his son's plot was rewarded for his efforts. Zeno was from the small mountain province of Isauria, which Diocletian had carved out of the early imperial province of Cilicia, in what is now south-eastern Turkey. The Isaurians had a partly deserved reputation for rampant banditry, which modern scholars have at times exaggerated to the point of calling them 'internal barbarians', aliens inside the imperial borders. That their home region posed challenges to law and order is not in doubt, however, and for an Isaurian to succeed in the capital required visible efforts at assimilation. Zeno, for instance, had Hellenised his name upon joining the army, discarding his native name of Tarasicodissa. After he exposed Ardaburius, he was appointed *comes domesticorum*, putting him in charge of the emperor's own guard units, among them a palatine corps known as the Excubitors, soon to become a powerful force in imperial politics for the next three hundred years.

With this promotion there also came an imperial marriage, to Leo's elder daughter Ariadne. We do not know whether Zeno was required to discard his first wife, Arcadia, with whom he had a son also named Zeno, or whether she was by now dead. Regardless, the marriage went ahead, and in 467 the imperial couple had a son, called Leo after his grandfather. A new *magister militum per Orientem*, Jordanes, succeeded the disgraced Ardaburius, and Zeno was rapidly promoted to *magister militum per Thracias* in succession to the emperor's brother-in-law Basiliscus. (The latter, it was intended, should take charge of the grand expedition against Gaiseric's Vandals then being planned in concert with the West.)

Zeno's time in Thrace was complicated by rivalry with supporters of Aspar, and by continued fighting among the would-be successors of Attila. This landscape of barbarian rivalry shifted constantly. In the later 460s, the Gothic brothers Valamer, Theodemir and Vidimer destroyed a large coalition of the Sciri, but Valamer was killed on the battlefield and primacy among the brothers now fell to Theodemir, who had cultivated a good relationship with Aspar. Theodemir's son Theodoric remained in the general's company in the imperial city. At roughly the same time, Attila's surviving son Dengizich, who had for a time fled to the northern coast of the Black Sea, began to see a chance of restoring his father's authority, and started raiding Thrace. When trying to counter these attacks, Zeno faced a mutiny threatening enough to force his flight to Chalcedon in Asia Minor. He was succeeded by another general, Flavius Anagastes, who would go on to play a fatal role in the downfall of Aspar and his dynasty.

That lay in the future, and Aspar's family had clearly come off lightly after the treachery of Ardaburius, perhaps because Leo needed all his best generals for his grand project and the East's last major intervention in western affairs: a triumphant Vandal expedition that would revive the western empire under a new augustus, Anthemius. We have already seen how badly this fared, after initial successes: Anthemius had been welcomed in Italy; the mercenary leader Marcellinus, to whom Leo had granted the patriciate, defeated Vandal garrisons in Sardinia and Sicily; and the eastern *comites* Heraclius and Marsus seized Tripolitania from Gaiseric's forces. But then Gaiseric destroyed the main imperial fleet, commanded by Verina's brother Basiliscus, ruining an expedition that had cost, it was said, a whopping 64,000 pounds of gold and a full 700,000 pounds of silver.

Disaster on such a scale was hard to accept, and there were inevitably rumours of treachery back in Constantinople, some directed against Basiliscus, others against Aspar. Amazingly, the latter emerged unscathed, as he had done from the debacle with his son two years previously, but Basiliscus was less lucky. He had to seek sanctuary in the church of St Sophia until Verina's petitions won him a public pardon. It is unclear whether he retained his *magisterium* after this, but there is no doubt that he was now sidelined by Aspar and Zeno. The latter was already a member of the imperial family, having married Ariadne, and Aspar was now granted the same privilege. His son Patricius, consul of 459, agreed to reject his homoian beliefs in favour of Chalcedonian orthodoxy after rioters in the Hippodrome demanded it, and was in 470 made caesar by Leo and married to Leontia, who had just reached marriageable age. It was canny politics, keeping Aspar and Zeno close, allowing their rivalry to play out at court, rather than on the battlefield, as would have happened in the West.

The Balkans were now a stage on which court rivalries could be prosecuted by proxy. In 469, Theodemir had come into conflict with Gepids and Rugi, who were worried by the fate that had befallen the Sciri. The *consistorium* was divided over which side to support. Aspar argued for his Gothic client, but his advice was not taken and the emperor threw his support behind Theodemir's enemies. Theodemir proved the better general, however, winning a battle over the Gepids and their allies at a site on the unidentified river Bolia, probably the Ipel' in what is now Hungary. After this success, he seized control of the old Balkan garrison towns, from Sirmium through Singidunum (now Belgrade) down to Naissus (Niš). Unwelcome as this was to the emperor, it had to be tolerated, and the hostage Theodoric was released to his father's care as a sign of imperial good will.

In the same year, a rare imperial success could be registered in the troubled region: Dengizich, whose attempt at reestablishing his father

Attila's old power had failed, now sought to enter service with the Romans after years spent raiding imperial territory. Instead, he was taken captive and executed, his head displayed publicly in Constantinople as evidence of Leo's power.

Dengizich's conqueror was the *magister militum per Thracias* Anagastes, who felt himself insufficiently rewarded for such signal a service. This professional grievance was exacerbated by what he took as a personal insult: the *magister militum per Orientem* Iordanes was not just a rival of Anagastes, but also a long-standing enemy (Anagastes' father Arnegisclus had killed Iordanes' father Ioannes some years before). The Thracian *magister* was bitterly resentful when his eastern rival was nominated for the consulate of 470. In response, late in 469, he rebelled, garrisoning several forts in Thrace against the central government. Envoys sent from court soon mollified the rebel, but in negotiating his own safe return to his office, he tried to shift the blame for his rebellion on to Aspar's disgraced son Ardaburius, whose blandishments, so Anagastes claimed, had suborned him into rebellion.

Whether there was anything in this charge or not, the rumour of a second conspiracy from that quarter was too much for Leo to tolerate. In 471, most of Aspar's family was murdered in the imperial palace at Constantinople, in a purge that engulfed Aspar himself, the caesar Patricius, Ardaburius and quite a few of their immediate supporters. The youngest brother Hermeneric fled eastward to Isauria, where he married the daughter of one of Zeno's many bastard sons, and eventually secured a new role at court after Leo's death. For the destruction of Aspar and his family, Leo earned the nickname Makelles, 'the Butcher'. Now Zeno, the emperor's surviving son-in-law, took Aspar's place at court. He had prudently absented himself from the palace during the furore over Aspar and his family and instead campaigned against Isaurian highwaymen in his own native countryside. He now became *magister militum praesentalis* in succession to Aspar, and his young son by Ariadne, Leo, was made caesar in 472.

In the Balkans, Theodemir died in about 471, to be succeeded by his ambitious son Theodoric, whom we shall refer to simply as Theodoric to distinguish him from Theoderic Strabo. The two Goths were related to each other, though precisely how is unclear, and they swiftly fell into a habitual rivalry. In the short term, it was Strabo who gave the government the most trouble, demanding the *magisterium* that Aspar had held and the place in the imperial consistory it would bring. Denied this, he assaulted some of the larger Thracian cities, among them Arcadiopolis and Philippopolis. Zeno and Basiliscus commanded the defence of Constantinople, however, and they forced Strabo to the negotiating table. Meanwhile, the emperor's health was failing more and more visibly. The onset of violent illness late in 473 suggested that he might not last much longer, and in October of that year he was persuaded to make his 6-year-old grandson Leo, the child of Ariadne and Zeno, his co-augustus. On 6 February of the following year, he died in the palace at Constantinople, which meant the child Leo II was now senior emperor (no western emperor save Anthemius had been accepted as a legitimate member of the imperial college since the death of Valentinian two decades earlier).

For three days, the palatine officials, the factions of Verina and Basiliscus, the great generals, and Zeno himself conferred and bargained and eventually reached an agreement, for which they sought the token consent of the Constantinopolitan Senate. Then, on 9 February 474, the young emperor crowned his father as his co-augustus before a massed public in the Hippodrome. The 7-year old emperor would die of illness before the year was out, and by 17 November Zeno was sole emperor.

ZENO AND
ANASTASIUS

Zeno faced considerable opposition, on many sides, from the very start of his reign. Almost immediately, Gaiseric sent a fleet to attack Greece, capturing the port city of Nicopolis in Epirus. An embassy led by the Constantinopolitan senator Severus, who was given the honorary title of *patricius* for the occasion, negotiated a peace with the ageing king. Roman hostages from Nicopolis who were in Gaiseric's personal possession were released free of charge, and other Vandals were encouraged to sell their hostages back to the ambassador. The king also now permitted some limited freedom of worship to the Nicenes of Carthage. This marked the end of the long conflict between Carthage and Constantinople. Severus' embassy concluded a 'perpetual' peace that would in fact last unbroken for more than half a century, until the eastern emperor Justinian seized on a flimsy pretext to destroy the Vandal kingdom in the 530s. In the Balkans, Theoderic Strabo again took up arms, but was defeated and paid off by Zeno's fellow Isaurian general Illus. Trouble with Persia, and on the desert frontiers of Syria, is also recorded by our sources, but in only the vaguest terms. It was intrigues at court that caused Zeno the greatest worry.

The dowager empress Verina, who retained her title of Augusta, organised a conspiracy against her son-in-law. She was joined by her brother Basiliscus, whose reputation had never recovered from the disastrous Vandal campaign of 468, and their nephew Armatus, the *magister militum per Thracias.* Basiliscus also secured the alliance of Zeno's Isaurian comrades Illus and his brother Trocondes, while the former *magister officiorum* Patricius (possibly also Verina's lover) was also involved in the conspiracy.

Zeno learned of the plot – quite how is unclear – and fled before it was too late. Sailing to Chalcedon with his bodyguard and close retainers, he made for Isauria in January 475. Though Verina had hoped to make Patricius emperor, Basiliscus bribed the palatine establishment into elevating him instead, and he was proclaimed emperor in the palace and then acclaimed by the Constantinopolitan Senate. Patricius was executed, Armatus was made one of the praesental *magistri militum*, while Illus and Trocondes set off for Isauria with a field army in pursuit of Zeno. For praetorian prefect, Basiliscus chose Epinicus, a Phrygian notary who had served as both *comes rei privatae* and *comes sacrarum largitionum* under Leo, thanks to the patronage of the *praepositus sacri cubiculi* Urbicius. Basiliscus made his own wife, Zenonis, augusta, and his son Marcus caesar, signalling to his dowager sister that she would not, in fact, be allowed to exercise the power she so clearly craved. Her ally Patricius dead, Verina retired to her palace and continued to intrigue fitfully, but now for the return of Zeno.

While the Isaurian brothers Illus and Trocondes campaigned against their former comrade Zeno, Basiliscus received an embassy from the monophysite bishop of Alexandria, Timothy Aelurus, who had returned from exile in the Crimea when he learned of Leo's death. He now persuaded the emperor to attack the Chalcedonian settlement that was so deeply hated by the Alexandrian monophysites. This, more than the fact of his coup, alienated Basiliscus from the staunchly Chalcedonian population of Constantinople, and he was forced to retire from the city when the patriarch Acacius draped the church of Saint Sophia in black and urged his congregation to mourn the profanation of their faith by a heretical emperor. Perhaps unsurprisingly, a substantial part of the population now began to agitate for Zeno's return.

Illus and Trocondes had fared well in their initial campaigns, and Zeno's brother Longinus fell prisoner to Illus, who kept him hostage on his Isaurian estates. But intrigue in the palace, probably led by Epinicus and Urbicius, persuaded Illus and Trocondes to reconcile with the legitimate emperor, return to the capital and depose Basiliscus. Basiliscus' praesental *magister* Armatus was sent to intercept them on their march back through Asia Minor, but was quickly suborned by the promise of pardon and perpetual tenure of his *magisterium*, as well as the promotion of his young son to the rank of caesar. Armatus chose not to make his betrayal public, but instead let Zeno and Illus pass by his own army along a different route, thus allowing Zeno to enter Constantinople unchallenged in August 476. Basiliscus, Zenonis, Marcus and their family were captured, sent to imperial estates in Cappadocia and there executed. As promised, Armatus' son was made caesar at Nicaea, but his father was almost at once accused of treason and executed, while the boy was ordained and immured in a monastery.

Then, shortly after his return to power, Zeno was confronted by the embassy from the Italian *magister militum* Odoacer, who returned to Zeno the symbols of western imperial office and offered to rule as king of Italy in Zeno's name. Zeno seems to have known and trusted Odoacer, perhaps because the latter's brother Onoulphus was serving in the eastern army and had been trusted with the execution of Armatus just months before. Zeno hit upon a perfect path of compromise: he continued to recognise Julius Nepos (then in exile in Dalmatia) as the legitimate western emperor, but made no effort to restore him to the actual governance of Italy, from which Orestes had driven him a year or so before. Instead, Nepos remained in Dalmatia and the fiction of his imperial rule was studiously maintained by all; by the time he died in 480, there remained no one who could wish to see the diadem bestowed on a western emperor.

Zeno could not have done much for Nepos even had he wanted to. Though the capital's populace had preferred him to Basiliscus, he was unpopular with the army and feared its mutiny. For that reason, he declined to lead it into battle against Theoderic Strabo in the years after 476. We have detailed, if rather confused, evidence for the goings-on in the Balkans in the later 470s, where a shifting set of alliances and betrayals unfolded among Constantinople, Strabo and Theodoric, the son of Theodemir. They are both too tangled and too arid to discuss here. At one time or another, each of the Theodorics was given the title of patrician and titular commands in the Roman hierarchy. Thus, when Strabo seemed the greater threat, Theodoric was made patrician and *magister militum*. Later – in 478 probably – there was a brief period in which the two were reconciled with one another and used their combined heft to extract more resources from Zeno. Not long thereafter, the positions were reversed and Theodoric had become an enemy and Strabo was given the titular *magisterium.* Imperial control over the Balkans had become more notional than real. Effectively, only a few cities in Thrace, the praetorian prefect of Illyricum's residence at Thessalonica, and peninsular Greece remained under imperial government. The rest of the Balkans were left to their own devices. In some places which had been denuded of their populations, ancient field systems ceased to be cultivated and the larger infrastructure of the region began to break down.

More strangely, after having played so dominant a role over Leo's court, Zeno seems not to have learned to avoid a similar overshadowing himself. No doubt the twenty months of exile in Isauria had weakened his authority, but it was now Illus as much as Zeno who dominated public affairs. His influence was balanced by the powerful *praepositus* Urbicius and the praetorian prefect Epinicus, but when Zeno made Illus *magister officiorum* in 478 (the year in which he was also consul), the latter played a direct role in every aspect of palace affairs. He used his new position to intrigue against Verina, who in turn plotted with Epinicus to have Illus murdered. When the plot was discovered, Illus forced the emperor to depose his prefect and hand him over to Illus as captive. Then, late in 479, Epinicus and Illus did a deal whereby the former was promised restoration in return for betraying Verina. Illus retired to Isauria and blackmailed Zeno, who needed him to command the Balkan armies against both Theodorics – he would not return unless Verina was surrendered to him.

Again, Zeno bowed to his minister's wishes; Verina was sent to Tarsus in Cilicia, where she was ordained as a nun and kept prisoner on the Isaurian properties of the *magister officiorum*. But the sheer perseverance of Leo's family becomes still more impressive: in 479, there was another coup against Zeno, this time led by Marcianus, the son of the late emperor Anthemius, and husband of Leo and Verina's youngest daughter Leontia, formerly the wife of Aspar's son Patricius. Marcianus and his brother Procopius rallied some of the praesental units to their cause and marched on the palace, seizing control of the city, though not yet of the emperor. Overnight, however, Illus summoned his large private army of Isaurian soldiers from Chalcedon, across the Bosporus, and the next day there was some confused fighting in the streets of Constantinople. Illus and his retainers prevailed, Marcianus and Leontia were captured, while Procopius fled to Theoderic Strabo and thence to Rome, from where he was recalled by the next emperor before going on to hold the consulship of 515. Both Leontia and Marcianus were ordained and banished to monasteries in remote Cappadocia, but the latter escaped in the next year, raised an army from disgruntled supporters of the previous dynasty and seized Ancyra, where he was besieged by Illus' brother Trocondes, captured again, and imprisoned.

It had taken Zeno several years, and domination by Illus, to secure some measure of safety on the throne, but he was left to pick up the debris of the ecclesiastical conflict that had erupted, as it was bound to do, after Leo's death in 475. The latter, as we have seen, was quite happy to throw his weight behind the Chalcedonian settlement but, as soon as Zeno fled from Constantinople, Basiliscus had recalled the monophysite exiles Timothy Aelurus of Alexandria, and Peter the Fuller of Antioch, restoring them to their sees. Rioting in Constantinople and the renewed threat of Zeno's restoration led Basiliscus to revoke the pro-monophysite policies he had initially enacted. However, once Basiliscus was deposed and executed, Zeno had to decide what to do about the monophysites whose hopes had been raised by their brief interlude of success under Basiliscus.

Timothy Aelurus died in 477, to be succeeded by the Chalcedonian Timothy Salophaciolus, but Aelurus' deputy Peter Mongus was one of Zeno's chief ecclesiastical advisers, along with the moderate Chalcedonian patriarch of Constantinople Acacius. In 482, they persuaded Zeno to issue an imperial letter to the Egyptian church, outlining a new policy. This text, the so-called *Henotikon* of Zeno, was probably written by Acacius or one of his clerics and was meant to conciliate opinion by condemning both Nestorians and the extreme monophysites and by affirming that the true doctrine was contained in the teachings of Nicaea and Constantinople. Chalcedon was thus to be written out of the record of orthodoxy, its memory condemned to oblivion. Monophysite bishops were pleased to endorse the *Henotikon*, but the Chalcedonians recognised its implicit condemnation of that council's theological formula.

For Acacius, this was quite a good result. Peter Mongus was now installed as bishop of Alexandria and the *Henotikon* provoked the first of many schisms between the Greek and Latin churches: Simplicius, at the time bishop of Rome, declined to acknowledge the right of the emperor to pronounce on matters of doctrine, holding that the bishop of Rome had primacy over questions of doctrinal truth. At a council of Roman bishops under Simplicius' presidency, both Acacius and Peter Mongus were excommunicated. This so-called Acacian schism (a very Latin way of conceptualising it, of course) demonstrates the increasing sense of profound differences between the eastern and western churches. It also demonstrates the increasing self-confidence with which the Roman see asserted itself, now that it no longer had to deal with a resident emperor or contend with an imperial bureaucracy.

The year 481 brought other news, too: the fortuitous death of Theoderic Strabo. Ever since he had planned to support the coup of Marcianus, Strabo's forces had remained dispersed in Thrace, periodically raiding its cities. In 481, he again marched on Constantinople and was either fought off or bought off. Returning to Thrace on the via Egnatia, he was thrown from his horse on to the spear of one of his men and died of his wounds soon after. Although his son Recitach inherited his following after murdering at least two of his uncles, he lacked his father's confidence or tactical skill and was much more easily contained. Theoderic, son of Theodemir, now became the sole threat of real stature in the Balkans, and a few years later he would kill Recitach and absorb the latter's following into his own.

Despite this easing of pressure in the Balkans, the overall position of the emperor remained weak. The augusta Ariadne, who had survived the disgrace and fall of her mother Verina and sister Leontia, now joined in the intrigues against Illus, persuading her husband to do away with him. Zeno would not take action himself, but condoned her doing so, and, in 481, an attempt was made on Illus' life in the Hippodrome. He evaded death but lost an ear to the sword of his would-be assassin Sporacius, a commander of the *scholae* whom Ariadne had bribed into acting. Sporacius was killed on the spot. The origins of the plot were suspected but never admitted: Illus resigned his palatine *magisterium*, instead demanding the *magisterium militum per Orientem*, which Zeno bestowed on him willingly, happy to get him away from the capital.

For several years thereafter, there was a cold war between the supporters of Zeno in Constantinople and those of Illus in Antioch, and open war seemed certain to break out at some point. In the end, it was Illus who instigated it. He released Marcianus from his Cappadocian prison and sent him to Italy to seek help from Odoacer. Illus also brought the old augusta Verina back from her monastic prison, and induced her to crown as emperor the patrician Leontius, a respected senator of Constantinople whom he had wooed away from Zeno. The rebellion was well received in the East, not least among Chalcedonians hostile to the *Henotikon* of Zeno. But the fighting did not go Illus' way. Zeno sent to Asia Minor the praesental armies under Ioannes the Scythian, along with large numbers of mercenaries recruited from the Balkan Goths and other barbarian groups, including one unit commanded by Aspar's youngest son Hermeneric. At the same time, Zeno's brother Longinus managed to escape from the prison in which Illus had kept him. Illus was comprehensively defeated and fled to one of his mountain castles, at Cherris, in the Isaurian mountains. There the old intriguer Verina finally died, while Illus and Leontius maintained the fiction of their usurpation for fully four years – only in 488 did supplies finally run out in Cherris, ending the siege. Illus, Leontius and their remaining supporters were immediately executed.

The year 488, then, was the first in which Zeno could to some degree rule undisturbed – Verina's faction and its many offshoots had finally been vanquished. The fighting in the Balkans was now also resolved. Theodoric's soldiers had acquitted themselves very well against Illus, and Zeno granted their leader permission to take his followers to Italy and make a home there, ruling in Odoacer's place until Zeno saw fit to come there himself. Zeno's actions were more than a little ungrateful, given that Odoacer had staunchly refused advances from Illus. But what Zeno needed most of all was peace, and if the two rival kings wished to fight it out over the remains of the western empire, that could only be to Zeno's advantage. That he had any intention of ever reoccupying the western empire may well be doubted, but the convenient fiction of eastern hegemony allowed all sides to save muchneeded face. Theodoric and his following, tens of thousands of soldiers, camp followers and their families, marched to Italy via Singidunum and Sirmium, where he defeated an army of Gepids that had installed itself in the city. In 489, his Goths invaded Italy and for the next four years control of the peninsula was contested between Theodoric and Odoacer.

The last few years of Zeno's reign were thus much less precarious than the first decades, though controversy over the *Henotikon* was still lingering when Zeno died on 9 April 491. There was no coup d'état. Instead, on 10 April, the widowed Ariadne donned the imperial cloak and addressed the assembled citizenry of Constantinople from the Kathisma (imperial box) of the Hippodrome. The *magister libellorum* read out her speech announcing the appointment of a new praetorian prefect and promising to announce the consensus of the Senate, the palatine bureau chiefs and the praesental high command after Zeno's obsequies had been performed. The choice fell on Anastasius, one of the leaders of the palace *silentiarii*, a man already in his sixties and not yet a senator, but a long-time favourite of the empress. He seems to have held unorthodox religious views (it is said, with little warrant, that his mother was a Manichee; more likely she was a homoian, since the family hailed from Dyrrachium in Epirus, a part of the Latin Balkans that had long been friendly to that theology), although he had once been considered a plausible candidate for the bishopric of Antioch. He had also tried his hand at preaching in Constantinople, but in so doing had infuriated the city's bishop, Euphemius, who now insisted on Anastasius signing a confession of orthodoxy before he would consent to the appointment.

On 11 April, Anastasius was dressed in the imperial garments, raised on a shield by the troops and crowned by the Constantinopolitan patriarch. He promised large donatives to both the plebs and the army. Then, on 20 May, he married Ariadne, thus accruing for himself some measure of dynastic legitimacy. All seemed happy save the Isaurian relatives of Zeno, who had expected Longinus, the late emperor's brother, to succeed him. A rebellion broke out in Isauria under Zeno's *comes Isauriae* Lilingis, the half-brother of Illus. It was reinforced by many high-ranking Isaurians whom Anastasius drove out of Constantinople, after blaming them for instigating a riot in the Hippodrome in favour of Zeno's brother Longinus. Many Isaurians were sent into exile, including Longinus of Kardala, Zeno's old *magister officiorum*, who would soon take leadership of the rebellion. Zeno's brother Longinus was ordained and exiled to the Thebaid, as far from Constantinople as one could go and still remain within the borders of the empire.

In 492, Anastasius sent an army against Lilingis, led by Ioannes Gibbus ('John the Hunchback'), who was one of the praesental *magistri militum*, and by Ioannes Scytha ('John the Scythian'), the *magister militum per Orientem* who had served in that role since the fall of Illus. Subordinate units were commanded by Ariadne's relative Diogenianus, Iustinus (the future emperor Justin) and some high-ranking Gothic and Hun allies. At Cotyaeum in Phrygia, they won a crushing victory over a large rebel army – the Isaurians were far better at guerrilla warfare in mountainous terrain than they were at pitched battles. Lilingis was killed at Cotyaeum, but the rebels fought on for six more years under other commanders, provisioned by sea by yet another Longinus ('of Selinus').

Longinus of Kardala held out until 497, when he was defeated and his severed head displayed on a pole at Constantinople, while Longinus of Selinus lasted until his capture at Cilician Antioch in 498. The victorious *magistri* were each rewarded with the consulate, the Scythian in 498 and the Hunchback in 499. The famous Isaurian mountain fortresses, which had provided protection for rebels in the region since the reign of Leo, were now levelled. Many rank and file Isaurians were disarmed and resettled in parts of Thrace that had been laid waste by years of fighting both among and between the Goths and the imperial forces, as were a new group of 'Scythian' barbarians, the Onogurs – one of several groups collectively known as Bulgars. An Onogur raid in 493 even led to the death in battle of the *magister militum per Thracias* Julian, while rioting in Constantinople was serious enough for the imperial statues to be thrown down and dragged through the streets.

As the fifth century turns into the sixth, the Onogurs, the Kutrigurs and the Utigurs became fearsome challengers to peace in the Balkans, dominating other barbarian groups in the grassland steppe from the Danube all the way to the Don, and inspiring the kind of military infrastructure building that the Persian kings had applied to the Caucasus a generation earlier. In particular, Anastasius financed the construction of the Long Walls (also known as the Anastasian Wall, after the emperor – though some of the individual installations probably date back to Leo's reign). Sixty or so kilometres west of Constantinople, these traced a 50-kilometre line from just beyond Selymbria on the Propontis to Podima on the Black Sea, closing off the Thracian peninsula from the dangers that constantly threatened the rest of Thrace.

Unlike most fortifications on such a scale, the Long Walls were meant to be defended, rather than to check and disperse enemy forces by their mere presence. The stone and brick ramparts were over three metres thick and nearly five metres high, with projecting polygonal towers and fortresses at intervals; the installation was also given its own military command, subordinate to the praesental *magistri*. In reality, it covered too long a distance to be properly defensible but, over the two hundred years during which it was maintained, it generally delayed invading forces long enough to keep the actual fighting away from Constantinople, even when the walls themselves were breached. Before the work was done, however, there had been other major incursions by the Onogurs: in 499, when the *magister militum per Illyricum*, Aristus, was killed along with a quarter of his *comitatenses*; and in 502, when the suburbs were again raided and looted, this time without opposition. However, it was a full fifteen years before raiders were next able to penetrate the Long Walls.

By that same time, new hostilities were opening up on the eastern frontier while, closer to home, Anastasius was experiencing very substantial opposition to his religious policies. Despite the cover initially bestowed on him by his marriage to Ariadne, the emperor was not popular. Rioting in 498 had led to the tearing down of the imperial statues in protest against the jailing of a popular charioteer, and the imperial excubitors shed blood in the Hippodrome, but it was a Christian controversy that really dragged the reign into a mire.

Anastasius' relationship with bishop Euphemius of Constantinople, poisoned from the start by the patriarch's suspicions over the emperor's orthodoxy, deteriorated rapidly. Euphemius was a Chalcedonian and deeply hostile to Zeno's *Henotikon* which Anastasius made a public show of upholding. Yet Anastasius himself was personally no more support-ive of the *Henotikon*, instead favouring monophysite views of Christ's nature, a preference that became more pronounced as he aged and he fell under the influence of the extreme monophysite patriarch Severus of Antioch. Beyond that, as was usual whenever there was a change of emperor, churchmen across the East competed to reopen closed theo-logical discussions and to do down their ecclesiastical enemies.

The Alexandrian bishops, first Peter and then Athanasius, began their usual scheming, knowing the emperor was sympathetic to their monophysitism. They accused Euphemius of being a Nestorian heretic and encouraged the emperor to hold a council, which he did at Constan-tinople in 496. There, Zeno's *Henotikon* was upheld as the theological law of the land, Euphemius was found guilty of Nestorianism and exiled to Euchaita. He was replaced by Macedonius – also a Chalcedonian, but one who was willing to accept the *Henotikon* for the sake of peace and power. Macedonius rubbed along with the emperor uneasily for about a decade, but there remained a seething intransigence on the part of all parties involved, and support of the *Henotikon* meant an ongoing schism with the Latin church. Macedonius found himself attacked on the one side by the intensely Chalcedonian monks of the Studion monastery, prone to religious violence in order to enforce their will, and irretriev-ably hostile to the bishop for his willingness to accept the *Henotikon*. On the other side, he was execrated by the monophysite episcopate in Alexandria and its many sympathisers throughout the empire (most importantly the charismatic bishop Philoxenus of Hierapolis, in Phrygia), who assumed – correctly – that Macedonius was far from agreeing with any part of their theology. The last years of the reign would bring these contests to a head.

Before then, however, troubles on the eastern front opened renewed trouble with Persia that it would take three decades to resolve. The Arabian frontier, though it did not march directly with Persia, was contested by proxies of both sides. In Arabia, as elsewhere, Roman and Persian power had galvanised tribal neighbours into forming larger and more complex polities, capable of a level of organisation that they would not have achieved without the motivation of an imperial challenger. The desert Arabs – or *Saraceni* ('Saracens'), as the Romans called them to distinguish them from the sedentary Arabs of the imperial provinces – were divided into several large coalitions or tribes. These included the Lakhmids of Hira, near Persian Mesopotamia and Khuzestan; the Salihids, long-time Roman allies who took responsibility for guarding the Diocletianic frontier lines that the imperial forces had by now abandoned; and the rising power of the Ghassanids of Jabiya in the Golan Heights. Further south, in central Arabia, was the enormous Kindite kingdom ruled by one al-Harith (Arethas, in Greek).

While the Ghassanids, or Banu Ghassan (already known to Ammianus Marcellinus as Assanitae), were generally Christians and clients of the emperor, the Lakhmids were more regularly clients of Persia. Those neat categories were frequently disrupted in practice, however, and so, while it was a Lakhmid force from Hira, commanded by al-Numan, that invaded the province of Euphratensis in 498 (it was defeated by Eugenius, *dux Euphratensis*), it was the Ghassanids on the imperial frontier who gave the most trouble for the next few years. A force led by Jabalah el-Harith (or Gabala son of Arethas, in the Greek) attacked Syria and Palaestina in 498 and made another major raid as far as Phoenicia in 502. In that year, Anastasius made peace with both the Kindite Arethas, whose son had been raiding the Roman provinces intermittently for several years, and the closer and more dangerous Ghassanid Arethas. Both the Kindites and the Ghassanids remained Roman allies thereafter, shoring up the desert frontier between Rome and Persia at a time of rising hostility – in 502, the two went to war for the first time in decades.

The dispute had been brewing since 483, when Zeno withheld the subsidies that the Romans had been paying to subvent the defence of the Caucasus passes, citing the Persian failure to return Nisibis to Roman control on the 120th anniversary of its cession by Jovian in 363. That the

363 treaty actually included any such provision seems unlikely – it was merely a pretext of Zeno's, but one that Anastasius maintained. Anastasius also went further, seizing control of the island of Iotabe in the gulf of Aqaba on the Red Sea, which had been a Roman customs post till its loss in the time of Leo. The seaborne Indian trade, on which both the Romans and the Persians relied, passed through Iotabe to Clysma on the mainland; the customs duties there were also very important for the defence budget of Mesopotamia. We possess fragments of a major customs decree from five different sites in Arabia, suggesting that this initiative in the Red Sea was regarded by Anastasius as a crucial part of his administrative plans. Certainly, renewed activity along the caravan routes and in the Arabian desert was a provocation of Persia as irritating as the cessation of contributions for the Caucasus. For a time, however, it was Persia's weakness that kept the peace.

This weakness was almost entirely caused by the threat from the Huns on Persia's eastern frontiers. We have seen that the shahanshah Peroz died in the battle of Herat against the Hephthalites in 484. After that, his brother Balash ruled insecurely for four years before his deposition and blinding by Peroz's son Kavadh. Kavadh I was, at least at the start of his reign in the late fifth century, almost as unpopular with his own nobility as Anastasius was with his. There are two possible ways to understand what was going on. As with Anastasius, Kavadh's unusual religious leanings may have been a cause of friction.

In fifth-century Iran, an ascetic reaction had emerged against the highly institutionalised, and very rich, Zoroastrian priests and their network of fire temples. One such priest, Mazdak, articulated a reformist theology that, while retaining the theological dualism of orthodox Mazdakism, shifted its social focus away from the priests and their correct performance of ritual and more towards the care of the common population. As with some forms of ascetic Christianity, Mazdakism concentrated on the importance of living a good and simple life, forbade killing, and insisted on vegetarianism as well as the redistribution of excessive wealth. What drew Kavadh to this new faith is unclear; indeed, some have suggested that the whole narrative of Mazdakism (the sources for which, it is true, are not contemporary) is a fiction designed to conceal Kavadh's campaign to redistribute wealth and undermine the independent power base of the nobility – sharing out the private properties of the great lords more broadly, the better to consolidate the power of the royal state. Either way, the priesthood and the nobility were deeply hostile to a king they thought was challenging their own authority and threatening their wealth, and they began to plot against him.

A coup by the great lords deposed Kavadh in 496 or 497, placing his younger brother Zamasp on the throne. Later stories explain how Kavadh escaped imprisonment and fled into exile among the Hephthalites, whom he had known since the days of his captivity among them decades before. Certainly, he returned to power at the head of a Hephthalite army in 499 and, after a purge of the nobles who had deposed him, he again turned to the Roman emperor to request the renewal of the subsidy to defend the Caucasian passes. When Anastasius refused, he launched an invasion, seizing Theodosiopolis on the edge of Roman Armenia in 502, moving past Martyropolis (which surrendered), and then heading south to besiege Amida, which fell to him in January 503. While the Hephthalite and Lakhmid contingents in Kavadh's army fanned out to loot the territories of Carrhae and Edessa, Eugenius, the *dux Armeniae*, retook Theodosiopolis from the skeletal garrison Kavadh had left behind and the war descended into a brief stalemate as winter encroached. Back in Persia, meanwhile, the outbreak of war had given cover to pogroms against Christians, many of whom fled to Syria, increasing the monophysite population and exacerbating the theological problems that would plague the latter parts of Anastasius' reign.

The emperor's *magister militum per Orientem* at this time was Flavius Dagalaiphus Areobindus, one of the most powerful men of his generation who was also the son and grandson of consuls. His father Dagalaiphus had held the consulship of 461, while his paternal grandfather, also named Flavius Areobindus, had held it in 434, sharing it with the great general Flavius Aspar. Aspar's granddaughter Godisthea, the daughter of Ardaburius (consul of 447), was the wife of Dagalaiphus, making our Areobindus part of a court and military dynasty of the highest status. His position was further enhanced by his marriage to Anicia Juliana, the daughter of the ephemeral western emperor Olybrius and the granddaughter of Valentinian III through her mother Placidia.

In 503, after the fall of Amida, Areobindus and his army were joined by the field armies of both the *magistri militum praesentales*, Patricius, and the emperor's nephew, Hypatius. These three combined to make a very large force that placed a heavy strain on the productive capacity of the Syrian provinces. It was also quite ineffectual, as the three commanders failed to cooperate, no doubt jealous lest one win a success that eclipsed those of the others – as Anastasius might have foreseen, had he had more experience of military matters. It required the secondment of the *magister officiorum*, Celer, to coordinate the armies, which then promptly retook Amida in 504, invaded Persian territory and ravaged it, slaughtering all the male population over the age of twelve.

Since Nisibis remained in Persian hands, the Romans decided to build a new fortress at nearby Dara (now renamed Anastasiopolis) to replace it as the easternmost outpost of empire. All that prevented a renewal of hostilities in 505 was yet another Hephthalite attack on Kavadh's north-eastern frontier, which encouraged him to sue for peace. The Romans responded positively, encouraged by an invasion of Roman Pontus by the Tzani (who came from what is now Georgia and who had been known to much earlier Greek authors as Macrones) exploiting the distraction of the two empires. In 506 a truce of seven years was arranged between the emperor and shahanshah, although it in fact endured for much longer than that.

The following half decade is poorly served by our sources, so it becomes difficult to write a narrative history, though there was certainly continued fighting in the Balkans, where a Gepid freebooter called Mundo ran a loot-fuelled protection racket over the inhabitants of Moesia Prima. Beyond that, we know about the administrative reforms of Anastasius, not least the creation of a new and viable bronze currency, and their major financial implications. The leading figures in these reforms appear to have been Anastasius' praetorian prefect of the East, Polycarp, formerly a *scriniarius* in the bureau of the praetorian prefect, whom the emperor had promoted not long after his accession; his *comes sacrarum largitionum*, Iohannes the Paphlagonian; and another *scriniarius* (promoted to the prefecture of Oriens late in the reign) called Marinus, who was said to be the most important of the emperor's advisers. Be that as it may, Anastasius was bent on economising, and he made a great effort to suppress the perfectly legal kickbacks, known as *sportulae*, that prospective officials expected to pay for the privilege of taking up their positions. In the army, he tried to stamp out unauthorised promotions secured by bribery as well as the practice by which commissaries sequestered supplies, creating false scarcity and forcing enlisted men to pay for items that should have been issued to them. Customs posts at Abydus on the Asian side of the Hellespont and Hieron in the Bosporus were meant not just to generate revenue but to prevent illegal cargoes (for instance, weapons and wine) being traded into the Black Sea and thence to the barbarians of the Ukrainian steppe. He likewise regularised and rearranged some elements of taxation, particularly by converting quite a lot of taxes in kind into payments of gold. This prevented waste, since taxation in kind was mainly useful where large armies were concentrated, and could not be transported efficiently from any distance away except by ship. In 498, the *collatio lustralis* (*chrysargyron* in Greek) was abolished, partly financed by the confiscation of the Isaurian rebels' property, and winning the emperor great praise.

Anastasius also revised the method by which the *annona* was collected, abolishing the rules by which city councillors, *curiales* or *bouletai*, were primarily responsible for the collection of the *annona* in their territory. The reason may have been a widespread displacement of the bouletic class by imperial officials who bought land once owned by curial families, who had less access to the gold currency than did bureaucrats and were forced to sell up. The curial oversight of the *annona* may actually have become impossible and, by handing the task to a new set of officials (called *vindices*), Anastasius was doing nothing more than acknowledge that the empire could no longer be governed in the manner of a hypertrophied ancient polis. At the same time, it also diminished the power of the Roman state, because the *vindices* were in fact simply tax farmers, who bid on contracts to deliver taxes in kind. Similar arrangements had not existed in Roman government for more than two hundred years; though the East saw nothing like the haemorrhage of imperial power that had destroyed the West, the new arrangements for the *annona* clearly signalled the declining capacity of the state to govern.

The Anastasian monetary reform, on the other hand, was something altogether different. The introduction of the gold *solidus* under Constantine had put the Roman state's economy on a solid and sustainable footing, but it had done nothing at all to make the economy of small-scale transactions better. On the contrary, the pegging of virtually everything to a very pure gold coin meant that any other type of currency was of fungible value, subject to instantaneous arbitrage from place to place, and doubly so when the time came to pay taxes to the government that could only be rendered in gold. What Anastasius did, at the instigation of his *comes sacrarum largitionum* Iohannes the Paphlagonian, was to introduce a stable bronze coinage. This was notionally pegged to the gold *solidus*, but was minted in such huge quantities that it could circulate without reference to the gold currency for small-scale transactions. A large base metal coin, denominated as forty nummi, circulated alongside three smaller coins, of twenty, ten and five sestertii respectively. All were marked with their nominal value, using a simple, legible numeral.

What this meant was that, from the year 498 until the very end of the seventh century, the empire had a viable form of small change for the first time in two hundred years, since the currency reforms of Aurelian, and then of Diocletian and the tetrarchs, had destroyed the early imperial coinage system. Likewise, because the basis of the monetary economy was now base metal rather than bullion, it was not subject to debasement, adulteration or clipping (by the state or anyone else), since it had no intrinsic value. Gold coins were still needed for taxation, and thus remained a burden on those without ready access to them, and a source of profit for the officials who did. But the restoration of a functioning monetary economy at the local level was none the less a significant achievement. Indeed, the sum total of the Anastasian economic reforms left the treasury with a substantial surplus at the time of the emperor's death in 518.

Before returning to the last years of the reign, and the renewed ecclesiastical struggles they brought with them, we will turn back to what had formerly been the western provinces of the empire, and was now a patchwork of kingdoms and chaos.

I 3

THE WESTERN
KINGDOMS

Pick a date for the fall of the Roman empire: 476, when Odoacer deposed Romulus and packed him off to comfortable retirement? 480, when Nepos, the last western emperor acknowledged by the legitimate senior eastern augustus, died? 568, when armies of Lombard client kings invaded Italy and shattered the eastern Roman hegemony briefly reinstalled, at huge economic and social cost, by the emperor Justinian after 535? 1204, when the Venetian doge bamboozled credulous and covetous Crusaders into sacking Constantinople? Or 1453, when the city fell to Mehmet the Conqueror, founder of what we now know as the Ottoman empire? It's a parlour game: good fun, but ultimately pointless.

By the 470s, it barely mattered whether there was anyone wearing the purple in Rome or Ravenna. And it certainly did not matter who that someone was. Aristocracies all across the Latin West had given up on imperial politics, those from the south of Gaul only recently, but everyone else for decades or more. Their prospects, so they had divined, were decidedly better in the local centres of power that had emerged over the five decades during which warlordism at court and in the provincial periphery had hollowed out the institutions of the state. That some of the warlords were first-, second- or third-generation immigrants to the empire matters a great deal to those modern historians who believe 'foreign barbarians' destroyed the Roman empire: ethnic essentialism, and sometimes borderline racist assumptions, are deeply enough rooted in both popular and academic culture that the search for the external bad guys never loses its appeal. But the sources show us that it made virtually no difference to fifth-century westerners whether the local big man who fought off bandits and enforced property rights was the grandson of a Spaniard, a Pannonian, a Frank or a Goth. Similarly, most fifth-century westerners believed that, at however many removes, they were still living under an emperor, and inside a Roman empire. It was only in the sixth century that the eastern regime of Justinian began to push the notion that the Roman West had fallen. Before that, the events of the 470s – and most especially those of 476 – were what the distinguished Italian historian Arnaldo Momigliano called a *caduta senza rumore*, 'a silent fall'.

The reign of Odoacer and then of Theodoric in Italy demonstrate this fact most clearly, but so, to varying degrees, does the history of Vandal Africa, Gothic Gaul and Spain, and the Frankish north of Gaul. The histories of these and other, smaller 'kingdoms of the empire' intersect and influence one another, but we can sketch their development by starting in Italy and working clockwise around the former western empire and beyond to the changing periphery. As we saw, it was the general Odoacer who led the coup against Orestes and his son Romulus. Odoacer had served in the Italian field army since the patriciate of Ricimer. His father Edeco had been a high-ranking courtier of Attila. Like many of those who lost out in the aftermath of the Hun collapse, he sought a position in the empire, taking with him some Scirians who were probably retainers of his wife's family.

Odoacer, who had been born around 430, would have been a young man when he entered imperial service, and both he and his brother Onoulphus must have prospered in the shade of the great generals Ricimer and Aspar (the notion that Odoacer commanded a band of Saxons in Gaul in the 460s, as is still sometimes asserted, is based on a misunderstanding of a much later source). When the pair emerge into the light of history, they are already in positions of power, Odoacer in the corps of the *domestici*, Onoulphus as *magister militum per Thracias*, first as the client, and then as the executioner of the rebel Armatus. When Odoacer overthrew Orestes in August 476, he decided to rule not as *magister militum* and *patricius* but as *rex*, 'king'. In this, he followed the recent example of Gundobad, Ricimer's successor as patrician: when he realised that the regime of Glycerius had absolutely no future – indeed, that a viable imperial regime was no longer possible – he returned to Gaul and contented himself with a royal title and a share in Burgundian rule. Office under a western emperor had become meaningless, better to rule as king, though one source says Odoacer was made king by the 'Heruli' (perhaps one of the barbarian units in the field army), he styled himself only as *rex*, without specifying just what or who he was king of.

Carrying the imperial insignia back to Constantinople, his ambassadors explained that one emperor, Zeno, was enough for the whole of the empire. The Senate in Rome had accepted Odoacer as a fit guardian of Italy, and so the ambassadors requested the emperor to name Odoacer *patricius*. This Zeno did, though reminding all concerned that Nepos was still western emperor. Odoacer was happy to accede to this fiction until Nepos' death in 480, and for much of his reign he minted coins in the name of Zeno. Even after he began to issue silver and bronze coins in his own name, and with his monogram on the reverse field, he never arrogated to himself the privilege of minting in gold.

The political history of Odoacer's reign, which lasted until 493, is virtually a blank. When Nepos was murdered in 480, he used the excuse to annex Dalmatia to Italy, but he generally tried to avoid conflict with the powerful kings ruling in Gaul and Africa and applied the same cautious diplomacy to his north-eastern frontiers – Noricum and Pannonia – where the landscape of barbarian warlords had not yet been consolidated under any single ruler. Late in his reign, however, he launched a war of conquest against the Rugian king Feletheus in Noricum, destroying a petty kingdom that had existed north of the Alps for about thirty years, during which we know very little about it save that it was there. Odoacer also cooperated closely with the senatorial aristocracy of Italy.

From late in the reign of Valentinian III and under the weak rulers that followed, the Roman Senate had enjoyed increasing independence from the throne and a corresponding cultural renaissance. This is the era of the one last great flowering of epigraphic commemoration at Rome; it is also the period in which cluster the surviving ivory diptychs – hinged panels of exquisitely sculpted ivory handed out by consuls as they inaugurated the year. Tiny postage-stamp size bronze plaques, which also cluster in this period, commemorated senators' urban prefectures in the same way, their names picked out in a silver wash. Under Odoacer, Anicii, Decii and the rest of the Senate's grandest names decorate the western consulship year after year, after decades in which ephemeral emperors squeezed senators out of the highest honour in the land and claimed the consulship for themselves. In another sign of senatorial self-confidence, bronze coinage was struck with the legend SC in the exergue of the reverse. That stood for *senatus consultum*, and thus restored the Senate's claim to mint in bronze after a lapse of more than two centuries. There is irony in the fact that both Italy and Rome itself prospered better without an emperor than with one.

This general peace and prosperity was not destroyed by the invasion of Theodoric's Ostrogoths in 489. On 30 August of that year, on the Soča river in modern Slovenia, Theodoric crushed Odoacer's field army, though the war between them dragged on for four years. Thanks to an accident of source survival, we can trace each year's serially indecisive fighting in a detail that need not detain us. In February 493, besieged in Ravenna, Odoacer accepted a truce negotiated by the city's bishop, Ioannes. On 5 March, Ravenna opened its gates to Theodoric. Ten days later, at a banquet meant to celebrate the conclusion of the peace, Theodoric personally murdered Odoacer. His wife Sunigilda and son Thela were massacred, as were hundreds of the late king's followers, among them his brother Onoulphus.

Now in control of Italy, Theodoric revealed himself as a master diplomat among rival western kings. Gaiseric's successors lacked the political aptitude of their father, and Theodoric had already driven king Gunthamund's small Vandal garrison out of Sicily before the death of Odoacer. Several years later, he imposed a tributary status on the African kingdom, while also honouring king Thrasamund with a marriage to his own sister Amalfrida. He himself married the Frankish princess Audofleda, sister of Clovis. Along with such marriage alliances, gift-giving established a far-flung network of client relationships: just as the emperors had given large multiples of the *solidus* to frontier chiefs and lords, fixing them with golden loops so they could be worn, so Theodoric distributed a new type of helmet (known as a *Spangenhelm*, German for 'clasp helmet', and manu-factured from iron plates clamped together with iron bands) across the length and breadth of central and northern Europe, even into the British Isles. Such gifts would have accompanied embassies bearing letters such as those preserved in one of the great monuments to late ancient govern-ment, the *Variae* of Cassiodorus.

Magnus Aurelius Cassiodorus Senator, born during the reign of Odoacer, came not from the senatorial aristocracy of Rome but from a family that had moved to Italy from the East, perhaps when Galla Placidia and Valentinian III were installed at Ravenna. His grandfather had been a *tribunus et notarius* under Valentinian III and had been part of an embassy to Attila led by Aëtius' son Carpilio; his father had been both *comes sacrarum largitionum* and *comes rei privatae* in the early years of Odoacer's reign, but switched sides early enough to enjoy a long career as a provincial governor and then praetorian prefect of Italy under Theodoric.

The son and grandson of these eponymous ancestors was born in Bruttium, where the family estates housed a stud farm famous for its warhorses. Traditionally educated, and naturally eloquent, he became *quaestor* while still quite young, probably in 507, drafting Theodoric's laws and public pronouncements during a tenure of five or six years which culminated in the consulship of 514. At some point, he was *corrector* of his home province of Lucania et Bruttii, and he became *magister officiorum* after his predecessor, the senator and philosopher Boethius, was imprisoned for treason late in Theodoric's reign. He continued in that role under Theodoric's grandson and successor, and then became praetorian prefect, a post he held until the Ostrogothic regime began to falter. He eventually sought exile in Constantinople where he carefully organised the letters he had drafted for the Gothic kings into a vast collection aimed both at justifying his own actions, painting the early years of Ostrogothic Italy as profoundly and respectably Roman, and laying the groundwork for a return to the West, perhaps under imperial patronage.

Even though Cassiodorus retrospectively shaped his *Variae* for a clear political end, they still reveal a great deal about the workings of Gothic diplomacy and, more importantly, the vision of rulership that Theodoric wanted to articulate. For the first couple of decades, the letters stress *civilitas* ('civility'), a good old Latin word with a huge semantic range. What it meant in the context of the *Variae* was the service of both Goths and Romans in an orderly, 'civil' state, Goths as soldiers and officers, Romans as magistrates and taxpayers. The lines between the two groups were somewhat fluid (Theodoric was claimed to have said 'the rich Goth acts like a Roman, the poor Roman apes the Goth', and it is clear that some 'Romans' could be accepted as 'Goths' through devoted military service). But the overall effect was to dull any sharp edges in the relationship, to remove the binary of conquerors and conquered, and to focus loyalties of Goth and Roman alike on the person of Theodoric. Doing so allowed Theodoric to marginalise rival Gothic clans who might have had equally good claims to royal authority, and to bring the local aristocracies of Italy into government alongside the senatorial dynasties of Rome. What is significant is the way Theodoric and his ministers had discovered a language of government that was definitely post-imperial, yet capable of satisfying those whose core identities still rested on being part – however distantly – of a Roman *imperium*.

The 500s and 510s were clearly the highpoint of Theodoric's power and authority, the era in which the general satisfaction with his rulership marched in step with the expansion of his kingdom's territories and the extension of its diplomatic influence far and wide. In 504 and 505, he campaigned in Pannonia Secunda, reestablishing this key to the land route through Illyricum as a buffer for Italy and inflicting a decisive defeat on the Gepids who had dominated the region around Sirmium since the fall of Attila's empire. He married one daughter, Theudegotho, to Alaric II of the Visigoths in Gaul and another, Ostrogotho (or Areagni), to the Burgundian prince Sigismund. Neither alliance saved Alaric II when the Frankish king Clovis decided to conquer southern Gaul in 507, but Theodoric secured the succession of his grandson Amalaric, son of Alaric and Theudegotho, to the rump of the Visigothic kingdom and himself annexed Provence to Italy. More successfully, the marriage of his niece Amalaberga to Hermanifred of the Thuringians kept the peace on the middle Elbe throughout the reign, and projected Ostrogothic power into a region that the Roman emperors had largely ignored. In 515, he married yet another daughter, Amalasuntha, to a Hispano-Gothic nobleman called Flavius Eutharicus Cilliga, intending thereby to bind the western and eastern Gothic kingdoms together. When the eastern emperor Anastasius died in extreme old age in 518, Theodoric was initially able to put himself on good terms with his successor Justin I: Eutharicus was symbolically adopted by the new emperor in Constantinople and shared the consulate of 519 with him. Relations with the Senate remained generally good and, despite himself being a homoian, Theodoric was trusted as an honest broker in the factional divisions of the Roman church.

Yet the reign did not end well. Flavius Eutharicus died in 522 or 523 and, as often happened when an heir apparent died, factions developed around potential alternatives. One was Theodoric's nephew Theodahad, son of his sister Amalfrida but born around 480, long before her marriage to the Vandal king Thrasamund. The other potential heir was Amalasuntha and Eutharicus' son Athalaric, obviously still a small child. Some of the senators at Rome attempted to get the eastern government involved in the succession plans on behalf of the highly erudite and genteel Theodahad.

This enraged the old king when he learned of it, and quite rightly so: as in every season of Roman government, speculating about the succession was treason. Senators unwise enough to defend this correspondence, among them the philosopher Anicius Manlius Boethius, found themselves jailed and then executed. (It was in his final and fatal imprisonment that Boethius wrote the *Consolation of Philosophy*, one of the few Latin philosophical works to have entered the canon of world literature.) Theodoric retained an iron grip on his court right until the end, in 526, and the succession of his grandson Athalaric, engineered by his mother Amalasuntha, who ruled as regent for fully eight years. Athalaric's death in 534 sparked a succession crisis, which led to the imperial invasion of Italy, the subject of our final chapter.

If we now turn from Odoacer and Theodoric's Italy to Africa, we can see a similar picture of very effective governance, though over a much smaller kingdom. The terrible reputation that the Vandals have in our most extensive sources (and in much of the modern literature) is largely based on their homoian Christianity and a royal willingness to exile captious Nicene churchmen. In reality, African elites got on very well with the new regime in Carthage, and Gaiseric had been the most successful politician in the fifth-century West. He, alone of the western warlords, felt no compulsion to join the imperial government, content to remain aloof and exploit the petty (and not so petty) rivalries of kings and generals to profit himself, his base of military retainers, and a remarkably loyal African populace. To recognise how unusual this was, we may remember that even the great bogeyman Attila very much wanted to be part of the empire: he would not have taken Honoria's overture to him so seriously had he not.

Gaiseric was as much of an opportunist as Attila, but his opportunism was far more creative. Feuds with resentful Nicene churchmen apart, the African populace reconciled itself to the Vandals very quickly, for two main reasons. The first was that there were a very small number of Vandals compared to the provincial population. While also the case in every other western kingdom, this fact was more significant in Africa because (outside the desert frontier zone and the mountains) it meant that there was no class of local big men in residence locally: the really rich African landowners all lived in Italy. A second explanation for Vandal success at coopting the provincials is a corollary of the first: because so much of Africa was owned by either Italian senators or by the *res privata* and *sacrae largitiones* of the emperor, there was plenty of land to give away without hurting the locals who did count for something. Did it matter to the peasant toiling in the olive groves if his sustenance was provided, and his performance evaluated, by a *rationalis* of the *res privata* or a bailiff of a Vandal general? Evidently not, and this meant that those Roman landlords who did reside in Africa could carry on without suffering the land confiscations that we find elsewere in the West.

Gaiseric ruled a mixed elite of Vandals, Alans, Goths and Romans (though the title *rex Vandalorum et Alanorum*, reflecting the absorption of the surviving Spanish Alans into his following after the Gothic campaigns of 415–18, was only adopted by his son Huneric), and the Vandal court was modelled on that of the emperor. Gaiseric and his successors governed from the old proconsular palace on the Byrsa hill in Carthage, as well as from estates scattered around Proconsularis and Numidia, where they enjoyed the riding and hunting lifestyle of a Roman senator. In administrative terms, many of the bureaus of the old proconsular and vicarial offices continued to function, though our evidence for the tax regime in the kingdom is poor. The kings did not mint in gold, and they allowed a new, small-denomination copper coinage to be minted at the municipal level, which kept the local economy monetised but also represented a retreat from centralised state control. A similar retrenchment is revealed by Gaiseric's reliance on ad hoc administration: he and later kings habitually sent *comites* and *domestici* (not in the old imperial sense of guardsmen, but rather 'household retainers') into the provinces to deal with problems on a case by case basis, rather than relying on regularised bureaucratic procedures. A new Vandal era dating from 19 October 439 (the date of the initial capture of Carthage) was promulgated and seems to have gained a modest purchase on the kingdom's social life.

In the heartland of the kingdom, royal control filtered down through landowners and estate managers, because, by contrast to those in Spain and southern Gaul, African cities lost most of their administrative function, surviving primarily as episcopal sees. Save at Carthage itself, public buildings and the habit of public inscription disappeared in less than a generation. There is evidence for the continued use of public baths, but very little else. Yet, quite oddly, Vandal Africa is the only corner of the Roman world in which priesthoods of the imperial cult survived, though they had atrophied in much of the West by the late fourth century. It may be that Gaiseric encouraged imperial cult as a way of stressing the legitimate linkage of his dynasty to the imperial dynasty of Theodosius through the marriage of his son to an imperial princess. Along with imperial cult, there survived a strong Latin literary culture: the poet Dracontius has left a substantial corpus of poetry from late in the fifth century, while the verse of Litorius, Felix and Florentinus is as fine as that of the much older poets whose work was anthologised at Carthage in the 530s and known as the *Anthologia Latina*.

Gaiseric died on 24 January 477, to be succeeded by his eldest son Huneric, a highly clubbable figure well known at the courts of Constantinople and Ravenna. He was already elderly at the time of his accession, and had once been married to the Theodosian princess Eudocia. Huneric is known for his persecution of Nicenes but, while violent, that was short-lived. More important for the future of the kingdom was his determined purge of collateral lineages, eliminating his brother Theuderic and all his descendants shortly after coming to the throne. Huneric was succeeded in 484 by his nephew Gunthamund, who was by then the eldest male descendant of Gaiseric available.

Whereas Gaiseric had needed to fight hard to establish himself and fend off imperial attempts at dislodging him, after Leo and Anthemius' attempted reconquest failed so spectacularly, the absence of any sustained external threat led to a decline in military preparedness in the kingdom. The notion that warrior peoples grow soft and decadent when exposed to luxury is a cliché we can find in the earliest of the world's literature, and sixth-century writers like Procopius certainly applied it to the Vandals. But here it contains a measure of truth. Not only did Theodoric drive the Vandal garrison out of Sicily in 491, but Vandal armies lost a whole series of engagements against unnamed Moorish leaders under both Huneric and Gunthamund. This led to a dynamic in which the Vandal kings controlled Carthage and the rich agricultural hinterland along the coast, but abandoned all but the pretence of governing the interior.

Military weakness is also visible in the reign of Thrasamund, who succeeded his elder brother in 496. He paid tribute to Theodoric in Italy, which both won him marriage to the Italian king's sister Amalafrida and allowed him to regain a foothold on Sicily as a way station en route to the Vandal satellite in Sardinia (since Gaiseric's time, Vandal kings had used Sardinia as a convenient dumping ground for exiled enemies and recalcitrant Nicene bishops). But the marriage also brought with it the new queen's Gothic bodyguard, said to have been 5,000 strong. Whatever else this meant – and perhaps Thrasamund thought its presence would help make him less reliant on his own nobility – it deprived him of a time-tested political weapon, the ability of Carthage to turn off the tap on Rome's grain supply, since he could never have done so with so large a Gothic force sitting on the royal doorstep.

The marriage alliance produced no male heir, so when Thrasamund died after a long reign, he was succeeded by the eldest surviving descendant of Gaiseric, his grandson Hilderic, born to Eudocia and Huneric at some point in the 460s. Brought up in the East, Hilderic had converted to the Nicene Christianity of his mother and, as soon as he returned to rule the Vandal kingdom in 523, he legalised Nicene Christianity. He also attempted to end his uncle's dependence on the Ostrogothic alliance, having Amalafrida executed and what remained of her Gothic bodyguard massacred. It was a mistake, alienating those who might have supported him and allowing the opposition to circle round a challenger. Hilderic's cousin Gelimer, put in charge of an army to drive out Moorish invaders, instead allied himself to the Moorish king Guenfan, marched on Carthage and deposed Hilderic, imprisoning him and thereby providing the eastern emperor Justinian with an excuse to invade in 533.

Justinian would intervene in Spain as well, this time exploiting a crisis among the Visigothic ruling elite who, early in the sixth century, had lost most of their former polity in Gaul. Before that, however, the history of the Iberian peninsula and of Gaul south of the Loire had been inextricably linked since the time of Athaulf and Galla Placidia. From the moment the Alans, Vandals and Suevi crossed the Pyrenees during the messy struggles of Honorius' reign, meaningful imperial control of the Spanish provinces would be sporadic at best. After 420 or so, the people in the far west and north-west went their own way and the sources begin to talk of Callaeci ('Gallaecians') rather than 'Hispani' or 'Romani'.

The chronicle of Hydatius, bishop of Aquae Flaviae (now Chaves in Portugal), shows us a world of intense competition among predatory strongmen (Suevic and otherwise), independent cities still governed by their old municipal councils, and bishops wrangling over both theology and politics. We can trace a series of Suevic kings, trying – and perpetually failing – to project their authority beyond Gallaecia into the richer, urban regions of southern Lusitania and Baetica. We can also see the faintest outlines of an independent Vasconia, from the eastern edge of Cantabria to the western Pyrenees, as well as a consistent displacement of people from sites in the lowlands on to defensible hilltops. But though we learn about this region in unusual detail thanks to Hydatius, his world of Callaeci and Suevi was of the most marginal interest to the larger world, left to its own, chaotic and microregional devices. The same is true of those parts of Spain for which we have no Hydatius to guide us: only when the Goths of southern Gaul impinged on Spanish history does it seem connected to the rest of the failing empire.

The ambitions of the Gothic kings based in Aquitania and Narbonensis have been subject to a great deal of exaggeration, driven by the search for the origin of modern nations, and by the false conviction that the Goths were 'Germanic' outsiders permanently at odds with everything Roman. Fifth-century events may have had a real, if tiny, connection to the later shape of France, but the notion that Athaulf and his successors were perpetually different from the Romans among whom they lived could not be more misguided. Many Gallic aristocrats were happy to cooperate in Athaulf and Placidia's dream of forming a new Theodosian dynasty to challenge the useless Honorius, while the first Theoderic was simultaneously the most powerful of the Gallic strongmen and the most secure in his own position. For the most part, Aëtius found Theoderic preferable to the many ambitious chancers among his own subordinates. Thereafter, Theoderic II was generally a reliable ally of the Italian court, and the sources (some of them deliberately meant to flatter) style him very much in the manner of a Roman nobleman. Having sponsored and then supported the regime of Eparchius Avitus, and having destroyed a Suevic dynasty in Spain in the name of imperial reconquest, he proved a cautious ally in the face of Majorian and Libius Severus' attempts to knit the western empire back together. (It is unclear what role the fact that he was probably a distant cousin of Ricimer played in his political calculus.) But throughout this entire period, pragmatism meant that the dichotomous binary of Roman and barbarian exists in the framing rhetoric of our sources rather than the practice of politics they reveal.

Theoderic's brother and assassin Euric has had much a worse press than the other Gothic kings and is sometimes portrayed as a ruthless expansionist bent on conquering all Gaul and overthrowing Roman rule in the West. But, as with the Vandal kings, the picture is coloured by theological partisanship, for the homoian Euric had exiled Nicene bishops whom he suspected of leading political opposition to his rule. Euric was also intensely disliked by Avitus' son-in-law Sidonius Apollinaris, Gallic man of letters and eventually bishop of *civitas Arvernorum*, and, thanks to Sidonius, some scholars still see the warfare between Euric and various enemies as a contest of Roman against Goth. In reality, Sidonius and his friends envied the aristocracy of Lugdunensis and its cosy relationship with the Burgundian dynasty of Gundioc and Gundobad. Since Gundioc and Gundobad were close allies of Ricimer and his string of imperial puppets, it makes perfect sense that some members of the western Gallic aristocracy should have sympathised with the Burgundian-Italian alliance rather than accepted Euric and the Goths. Equally, once Gundobad had given up on the viability of imperial politics and returned to Gaul, it made perfect sense for Orestes to cut a deal with Euric, ceding him the Massif Central and Provence, and thereby clip the wings of Gundobad and his Burgundian regime. This was all part of the last flailing decades of the western empire and, though Sidonius spent his declining years mourning the loss of the world into which he had been born, it had long since been rendered irrecoverable in the age of Aëtius and Attila. Euric and Gundobad were struggling to make their way in a new dispensation that they had not been responsible for creating.

Euric's later years were spent trying to maintain even tenuous control in Spain, although that was mainly confined to a handful of Gothic strongholds from Emerita Augusta through Toletum and up to Tarraco on the Mediterranean. Gothic armies might roam further afield than that, but, for the most part, the road axis between the old diocesan capital in Lusitania and the grand coastal capital of Tarraconensis anchored Gothic efforts at control. In Gaul, Gothic hegemony in the Loire valley was constantly contested, although Euric remained stronger than the haphazard armies of Franks, Saxons, Bretons and Romans squabbling to control the lands between the Loire, Seine and Scheldt (Escaut) rivers. With the Burgundians, Euric maintained a frigid neutrality, neither side wishing to confront the other in a way that exposed their northern flanks, and that dynamic was even more pronounced under Euric's son and successor Alaric II.

In the end, though, it was the rising power of the Franci north of the Loire that did Alaric in. The remnants of the north Gallic *comitatenses* were consolidated under the former lieutenants of Aëtius – first Aegidius, then Childeric, and finally the latter's son Clovis. Quite how it happened is unclear, but, by 490 or so, the northern Gallic territories from the North Sea to the Rhine experienced some sort of parlous unity, for the first time in three generations.

We will turn to Clovis, whose political skills rivalled those of Gaiseric and Theodoric the Ostrogoth, shortly. Here we may simply take note of the testing Frankish assaults on Alaric's kingdom. These began in the 490s and at times reached as far south as Burdigala (Bordeaux), one of the Gothic kingdom's key cities. Perhaps because Clovis had not yet consolidated his own power, he worked out a peace treaty with the Goths, probably in 503, that was concluded on an island in the Loire near Ambacia (now the tourist village of Amboise). But depite the efforts of Theodoric to keep the peace, the rival Gallic kings again came to blows in 507 and Alaric was killed on the battlefield of Vogladum (Vouillé). In the aftermath, the Goths lost almost all their Gallic kingdom save for a stretch of Gallia Narbonensis, from the eastern Pyrenees through to Narbo, that eventually became known as Septimania (and is now Languedoc). For more than half a century, Gothic kings and would-be kings attempted to recover a place in the politics of Gaul, but instead, by imperceptible steps, became more and more rooted in Spain.

After Alaric's death in battle, the rump of the Gothic kingdom was contested between his illegitimate adult son Gesalic and the child Amalaric, grandson of Theodoric the Ostrogoth, whose daughter Alaric had married. Theodoric's best general drove Gesalic into exile, first in Vandal Africa, then in Burgundian Gaul, and his Gallic host Gundobad eventually had him murdered. Amalaric, by contrast, was supported by his powerful grandfather Theodoric, who proved an effective regent for the young heir. Theodoric annexed Provence to Italy, thus securing the route into Liguria, but allowed Amalaric to reign in Gallia Narbonensis and Spain with the Ostrogothic general Theudis to watch over him. Theudis amassed so much power in Spain, where he married a Hispano-Roman aristocrat of great wealth, that he would eventually defy the ageing Theodoric and refuse to return to Italy when summoned. When Amalaric came of age and insisted on ruling in his own right, Theudis simply kept himself to his own territories and allowed Amalaric to alienate the Gothic nobility and, more dangerously, the Frankish kings.

In 511, Clovis had been succeeded by his four sons, who became Amalaric's brothers-in-law when he married an (unnamed) daughter of the late king. Seemingly mistreated by Amalaric, she summoned her brothers to her aid and in 531, almost twenty-five years after his father's death in battle against the Franks, Amalaric, too, was killed near Narbo. Thereafter, Theudis ruled central Spain without reference to Theodoric or his Italian successors. Political events are virtually a blank as far as our sources go, but when Theudis was murdered in 548, the Gothic kingdom was less a territorial state than a handful of noble lineages fighting over a diminished royal treasury and the symbols of royal office.

Before the 520s, however, in both Spain and Gaul, the Gothic kingdom looked very Roman. The mint at Arelate struck gold coins in the imperial name that circulated alongside official imperial issues. Euric's and Alaric's courts were staffed by Romans and Roman legal studies flourished. Lawyers at Alaric II's court edited and reworked the Theodosian Code, which is one of the main reasons the compilation has survived beyond antiquity. They also furnished it with a juristic commentary that shows an acute interest in maintaining Roman legal norms, but also recognises how much smaller the post-imperial state and its bureaucracy had become. A lively literary scene existed alongside this legal work, and it is ultimately through the Gothic kingdom in Spain that many ancient texts, both Christian and pre-Christian, were transmitted to the Middle Ages and the modern era. And yet, as elsewhere in the former western provinces, it is possible to exaggerate the Romanness of the kingdom.

A great deal of scholarly controversy centres on how the Gothic settlement worked in its early stages. Were Wallia and Theoderic I's followers billeted in cities and given salaries out of public revenues? Were they settled on land that had fallen out of use thanks to population loss and generalised disorder? Were there mass confiscations of Gallo-Roman estates? The answer is, we do not know. There is no evidence for mass confiscation, but alternative theories based on the redistribution of tax revenue do not stand up to scrutiny. Certainly by the later fifth century, Gothic elites owned a great deal of the kingdom's land, notionally two-thirds of it, regardless of how that redistribution came about. Royal laws also make clear the scope of institutional change. Until the last decades of the sixth century, Gothic kings legislated on two fronts, enacting and clarifying laws according to Roman traditions, but also overseeing the codification of what was once Gothic customary law: the *Lex Visigothorum* or *Forum Iudicum*, which was issued in multiple versions (but at uncertain dates) during the later fifth century (probably) and throughout the sixth century, contains a lot of material that resembles not Roman imperial law but rather the customary laws of other barbarian peoples. So Gothic Gaul and Spain were not simply Roman provinces under new management, but rather social worlds being transformed by outside practices that would have been utterly unfamiliar to the majority of the population. That was how the Latin Middle Ages began.

On one front, however, the majority population triumphed altogether: linguistically. Gothic was still spoken in the later fifth-century kingdom (Euric would occasionally insist on speaking in Gothic to bully Latin monoglots), but it was very soon confined to the liturgical language of the homoian rite. For everything else, Latin was victorious, and its spoken form began to evolve towards the regional dialects that became Portuguese and Gallego, Castilian and Catalan, Occitan and Provençal. Not unironically, the only Gothic word to survive into modern Castilian is *verdugo*, 'executioner'.

Similar language changes took place in the Frankish and Burgundian regions north of the Loire and east of the Rhône, which remained linguistically Latin except in the area just to the south of the Rhine–Meuse–Scheldt delta. Like the Gothic kingdom, and unlike the land of the Franks, the Burgundian lands preserved a good deal of the Roman administrative legacy and the habit of keeping written records. The Burgundian realm is too often treated as the poor relation of the other post-imperial kingdoms. That is in large part a result of only having a source base that is poor even by the standards of this period. We do not know the relationship among several of the Burgundian kings and in a couple of cases cannot even be sure whether we are dealing with one historical figure, or two different ones with the same name. None the less, it seems clear that by the mid fifth century the kings Gundioc and Chilperic (dates and relationship much disputed) had established a relatively secure presence in what had once been the Alpine province of Maxima Sequanorum, between Besançon in France and the Vaud in Switzerland. They were more or less tolerated by Aëtius and his successors, while the Gallo-Roman aristocracies of Lugdunensis Prima and Viennensis saw the Burgundians as useful allies, against both the imperial government in Italy and rivals in Aquitania and Narbonensis, where the Gothic kings were ascendant.

By the time the Italian government of Orestes permitted the partitioning of Gaul between Euric and Gundobad, Burgundian control centred on a line running through Augustodunum, Lugdunum, Vienna and Valentia (now Autun, Lyon, Vienne and Valence) but stopping short of Avaricum (Bourges) in the west and Nemausus–Arelate–Aquae Sextiae in the south (Nîmes, Arles and Aix-en-Provence). Gundobad had, as Ricimer's nephew, played a continuous role in Italian politics since the 460s, but when the regime of Glycerius faltered, he gave up trying to rescue anything from the dust heap of Italian politics. Returning to Burgundian territory in 473, he and three relations (Chilperic, Godemar and Godegisel – whether this Chilperic is the brother of Gundioc or a second king of the same name is disputed) shared power without any precise territorial division of the kingdom. Predictably, they came to blows: Godemar disappears from the record suddenly, Gundobad killed Chilperic, Godegisel fled to the Franks around the year 500 and returned at the head of a Frankish army which Gundobad paid off – and then executed Godegisel.

Gundobad proceeded to rule for a decade and a half. He conducted a great massacre of hostile nobles, both Roman and Burgundian, and eliminated collateral relations, in preparation for his own son, Sigismund, taking the throne. Like the Gothic kings, he issued many laws. These were collected by his son and promulgated as a code called *Liber Constitutionum* in 517. (This became known as *Lex Gundobada*, since its contents were indeed Gundobad's.) In these laws, Gundobad places himself in a line of kings going back five generations to a certain Gibich, which sets the limit of legal memory, while the defeat of Attila in 451 furnishes a statute of limitations for lawsuits. Thus the historical framework of Gallic politics was rewritten as a new, post-imperial world coming into being.

Like his Gothic contemporaries, Gundobad tried to legislate for the whole population of his kingdom, but was thwarted by persistent differences between his Roman and Burgundian subjects. Not only did he have to restrict Burgundians interfering in Roman lawsuits, but several laws regulated landed inheritance among Burgundians, reflecting the complications of land redistribution in the age of settlement. At times, one can almost sense the royal frustration: Burgundian indifference to the sanctity of sworn testimony under Roman law forced Gundobad to permit the old customary practice of trial by battle. By these sorts of small steps, the world and the worldview of antiquity slowly disappeared.

Gundobad had cultivated a cordial, long-distance relationship with the emperor at Constantinople and, when he died in 516, Sigismund was not just king, but also the *patricius* and *magister militum* of Anastasius. In a letter to the emperor, Sigismund calls himself *gentis regem sed militem vestrum* ('king of a nation, but your [the emperor's] soldier'). Despite strong beginnings, the reign of Sigismund was not a great success. He married a daughter of Theodoric, but then provoked a war by murdering his own son, who was, of course, the grandson of the Italian monarch. In

523, Gothic and Frankish armies caught Sigismund in a pincer movement, each seizing bits of Burgundian territory. Sigismund was captured and executed by the Frankish king Chlodomer (and is still, as a rare Nicene among the homoian western kings, honoured as a saint by the Catholic church). Sigismund's brother Godemar avenged him, defeating and killing Chlodomer in Frankish territory, but in 534 the remaining Frankish kings wiped out the Burgundian royal dynasty and turned its lands into a subordinate unit within the larger Frankish realm. The Frankish kingdom had a long posterity, unlike the Vandal, Gothic and Burgundian kingdoms whose history we have sketched, and the Franks ultimately reshaped the map of Europe, in ways we shall consider in the next chapter.

I4

THE FRANKS AND THE
IMPERIAL PERIPHERY

❧

The Franks had become the strongest power in Gallic politics by the 520s and they would be the main beneficiaries when Justinian launched his long war against the Ostrogothic kingdom. Frankish success, often treated as inevitable, is actually a historical paradox: the Gothic and Burgundian kings inherited the richest, least damaged and administratively soundest of the imperial provinces, but saw their *regna* collapse within a generation or two. Meanwhile, the Franks forged the northern provinces, already peripheral, badly damaged and marginally governed at the end of the fourth century, into the most successful of the post-imperial kingdoms. The traditional story has the Franks pushing southwards from what is now Belgium into the Seine and then into the Loire valley, but there was no such swift and steady Frankish conquest. The history of northern Gaul was messy.

Around the turn of the sixth century, a single Frankish warlord suppressed or coopted every one of his rivals north of the Loire river. This was Chlodovechus, known to Anglophones in its French form, Clovis, rather than the German, Chlodwig. Clovis was the son of another warlord, Childeric, whose richly furnished tomb was discovered near Tournai (Roman Turnacum) in 1653. Though its treasures are long since dispersed, they were central to much early modern French state-building – Napoleon's coronation robes were decorated with replicas of the golden bees that had adorned the caparison of Childeric's horse. We do not know why Childeric was buried as far north as Turnacum – perhaps it is the site of the battle in which he fell – but the centre of his power lay somewhere between the Seine and the Loire. He had probably become an officer in the Gallic field army during the ascendancy of Aëtius. After Majorian was executed in 461, the Gallic *comitatenses* utterly rejected Ricimer and his new emperor, Libius Severus, and fell into permanent rebellion under the command of Aegidius, *magister militum per Gallias*. A much later story claims that Aegidius was proclaimed king of the Franks, but it is more likely that his *comitatenses* were by now so heavily recruited from Franks that, in retrospect, he could be remembered as a king rather than the freebooting general he was. When Aegidius fell to an assassin, probably in 464, his soldiers appear to have splintered into at least two groups, one under the command of Childeric and one under Aegidius' son Syagrius.

Basing himself between the Loire and the Seine, Childeric spent many campaigning seasons besieging Lutetia and thus presumably trying to conquer and hold the Paris basin. Syagrius was based further north, at Noviodunum (modern Soissons) on the river Aisne. Some modern accounts still portray Syagrius as the 'Roman' defender and Childeric as the 'Frankish' attacker, but the ancient evidence proves that they were two among many warlords, each with his own private army and control over very little else. The *comes* Paulus, a former subordinate of Aegidius who joined Childeric in fending off Saxon pirates on the Loire, was another such figure, as was the *comes* Arbogastes, who commanded a small force at Treveri and kept up a friendly correspondence with the leading nobles of the Burgundian and Gothic kingdoms. A certain Riothamus entered this mix from Britain in the 470s. Whether he was a Celtic chieftain or the commander of a few surviving *comitatenses* is unclear, but he and his men were the losers in the gradual takeover of lowland Britain by Saxons from the continent (see below). All these competitors, too evenly matched to overpower one another, strove to present themselves as legitimate Roman officers, regardless of their parentage or earlier careers. The imperial framework to which they all still aspired is revealed when, after Childeric's death, bishop Remigius of Remi (Reims) congratulated his son and successor Clovis for becoming the ruler of Belgica Secunda, a Roman province whose existence was by now purely notional.

Our understanding of Clovis rests on the barest scraps of contemporary evidence along with the retrospective history by Gregory, bishop of

Tours, writing at the very end of the sixth century. His Clovis was already a legendary figure – a classical hero, an Old Testament patriarch and a new Constantine rolled into one, and the true founder of the Merovingian dynasty (named for a fictional ancestor, Merovech). Since the modern foundation myths of both France and Germany begin in Merovingian Gaul, scholars have spent centuries trying to untangle the true history of Clovis' reign, though it is practically irrecoverable and even a minimalist sketch may push the evidence too hard. None the less, at whatever date Clovis succeeded Childeric, he immediately went to war with Syagrius, each claiming to command the Frankish remnants of the old Gallic *comitatenses*. Clovis eventually won, and brought other Frankish kinglets into his following where he did not eliminate them. Syagrius fled to the Visigoths, who did Clovis the favour of executing him. The 490s are a blank (a victory over Alamanni, often placed in 496, is in fact undatable), though he probably married the Burgundian princess Clothilda in this period and intervened in a Burgundian civil war thereafter. His activities were not confined within the old imperial frontiers, however. As well as the Alamanni of the Black Forest, he attacked a powerful Thuringian kingdom that had flourished on the Elbe, away from the light of Roman sources, since the fall of Attila's empire.

In Clovis' wars, just as in Theodoric the Ostrogoth's far-flung diplomatic efforts, we can see the growth of a new European political landscape, its fulcrum north of the Alps and Pyrenees, away from the Mediterranean heartlands of antiquity. This emerging Europe cannot be explained by a binary of Roman south and Germanic north, nor by the evocation of some pan-Germanic spirit connecting migrating tribesmen back to ancestral homelands. Those ideas are deeply embedded in modern historical memory, but they are simply not true. The first kingdoms of the Roman empire – Vandal, Frankish, Burgundian, Gothic – were ethnically and linguistically hybrids, the product of the empire's ceaseless social churn. There was no sense of fellow feeling among them, no barbarian 'us' against an imperial 'them'. And yet. By the year 500, a significant portion of the ruling elite in the Vandal, Frankish, Burgundian and Gothic kingdoms had one or more immigrant ancestors who had entered the empire (peacefully or otherwise) from north of the Danube and east of the Rhine. Many had arrived two or three, and some as many as five, generations earlier. But not all of them. There were plenty of first-generation immigrants in every kingdom. The sudden absence of an imperial centre to anchor ambitions, or reshape identities, opened up space for more sustained links between the former imperial provinces and the old *barbaricum*. The post-Roman kingdoms were ethnically and socially heterogeneous, but they had reasons for renewing contacts with central and northern Europe that had not existed when the Roman empire was a going concern.

That said, for all that Clovis' aggressive campaigns beyond the Rhine reflected this new reality, the heartland of his kingdom lay firmly inside the old imperial frontier. We do not really know how Clovis governed his new kingdom. There is no evidence, such as we have for Theodoric's Italy, for a conscious ideology. One thing we do know is that Clovis' successors subscribed to the Nicene brand of Christianity, rather than the homoian theology of the Goths and Vandals. In the fifth century, most may have been pagans, if one can judge by the large number of horses sacrificed around Childeric's tomb. Indeed, the pious Gregory of Tours tells us that Clovis, unblemished by homoian error, converted to Nicene orthodoxy from the wickedness of paganism. Better, older evidence shows that Clovis' sister Lantechilda converted from homoian to Nicene Christianity and it is likely that the same was true of Clovis. We may speculate that he converted not long before 507, calculating that the Nicene episcopate of southern Gaul would support a co-religionist against the homoian Alaric II – as they did.

The destruction of Alaric's Gothic kingdom in Aquitania was the culmination of Clovis' career of conquest. He spent the last three or four years of his life eliminating rival claimants to the kingship among the Franks. He also called a church council to legislate for the lands between the Loire and the Meuse rivers and issued the first version of Frankish secular law known as the *Pactus Legis Salicae* (the 'Agreements' or 'Compact' of Salian Law: Clovis' Franks were referred to as Salian or 'salty' Franks to distinguish them from the Ripuarian or 'riverbank' Franks on the lower Rhine). This legislation, unlike Gothic and Burgundian legal texts, is thoroughly non-Roman, substituting a right to private vengeance for public prosecutions, and making the family and the clan responsible for many functions that belonged to the imperial state under Roman law. Clovis died in 511, having given his eldest son Theuderic control of a subordinate kingdom between the Meuse and the Rhine. Although Theuderic had a strong claim to succeed his father as sole ruler, his step-mother, the Burgundian Clothilda, had other ideas and insisted that Theuderic share the inheritance with her three sons, his half-brothers Chlodomer,

Childebert and Chlothar. Reluctantly, he did so, and this sort of divided inheritance became the Frankish norm. The Frankish subkingdoms shared out among royal heirs (*Teilreiche* is the evocative German word for it) came to have relatively stable territories, with lasting consequences for European geography. The region between the Loire and the Seine, with Paris and Soissons as its main cities, was known as Neustria. The core of Theuderic's kingdom, from the Ardennes and the Meuse to the Moselle and middle Rhine became Austrasia and, over the centuries, the centre of Frankish gravity. Aquitania retained much of its Roman shape, along the line of cities stretching from Toulouse to Bordeaux to Poitiers, with Tours on the Loire becoming effectively a border city between Aquitaine and Neustria. Finally, the former Burgundian kingdom – in the Middle Ages the duchy and county of Burgundy – kept its historical shape after the Frankish conquest of 534, with Lyon and Geneva as its main cities.

The reigns of Clovis' immediate successors are nearly as obscure as that of their father, and we will not trace the Merovingians' fratricidal squabbles here. When Gregory of Tours' narrative becomes more reliable, after the middle of the century and beyond the scope of this volume, Frankish power had grown dramatically in northern Europe. Theodoric the Ostrogoth's diplomatic mastery had died with him, leaving the Frankish kings with a much freer hand. They destroyed the Thuringian kingdom on the Elbe, annexing to Austrasia substantial territories east of the Rhine. When Justinian invaded Italy, the Franks seized Ostrogothic Provence. Later they made the Saxons of the North Sea coast tributaries, and also attacked the Danes – the first time these Scandinavians are named in the sources.

The horizons, and the habits, of this Frankish world were distinctly post-imperial. Nowhere is this clearer than in the spoken language and written word. We have seen how Latin remained the language of government and daily life in all of post-imperial Gaul (with the exception of the Meuse–Scheldt–Rhine delta), but just how early the line between Romance and Dutch/Flemish/German developed is unclear. (It had not hardened until the ninth century and remains fuzzy in Belgium, Alsace and Lorraine to this day.) It may very well be that, along with the disappearance of Roman infrastructure in the Low Countries, there was enough of a population shift for Germanic languages to displace spoken Latin, even while written Latin remained the language of government.

Once Frankish imperialism spread written Latin beyond the Rhine, it failed to displace spoken Germanic. Yet, even within those parts of the

Frankish kingdom where Latin continued to be spoken as well as written, there developed a striking cultural divide with great significance for the future. North of the Loire, the entire tradition of written administration atrophied and written legal instruments were very often replaced by oral and customary practice. The quality of the written Latin declined precipitously as well. A modern scholar can pick up Latin documents from Gothic Italy and Spain, read their script with reasonable ease and recognise the imperial template of their contents. Documents from the Merovingian north, by contrast, are written in a tortuous hand (one scholar has joked that scribes hid letters one under another) and in ungrammatical and phonetic Latin that unintentionally reveals how the spoken language was changing. Those same linguistic changes were taking place everywhere – for instance, all the Romance languages are uninflected, which is to say nouns are not declined according to grammatical function – but it was only south of the Loire that grammatical written Latin survived alongside evolving spoken Romance. This north–south division between the written and the customary, running roughly along the line of the Loire, would last well into the early modern period. As with the east–west divide in spoken language between Romance and Germanic, the outlines of a future Europe were beginning to take shape.

Justinian's western wars, which we will look at in the next chapter, accelerated these and other changes. Before turning back to Constantinople, however, I shall briefly sketch the world beyond the former imperial frontiers, which should give a better sense of how the ancient world came to an end. Parts of this world, like Britain or the Sahel, had once been integrated into the empire's frontier zones, while others, like Ireland, the Elbe and Scandinavia, had not.

We can start on the African frontier, where the small Vandal kingdom was surrounded by a new landscape of Moorish kings. The Mauri, ancestors of the medieval and modern Berbers, had been actors in Roman politics since the first century BC. Under the emperors, men who held positions of great power in the Roman state – most famously, Gildo and his family – were at the same time the lords of both settled and nomadic Moorish communities in the mountains and the deserts outside the cultivated coastal zone of imperial Africa. Even in the third and fourth centuries, it is hard for us to tell when things happened because of Roman territorial administration and when through the customary authority of a local chieftain. The line between the two was extremely hazy, at least outside the cities and the larger agricultural villages. Because the Vandal state was so much weaker than its imperial predecessor, the independent power of Moorish kings and big men is much clearer. Their kingdoms straddled the zone between fertile regions where Roman urbanism had flourished and the arid uplands which the Roman state had monitored but not governed.

One such kingdom is attested early in the sixth century by an inscription from Numidia, at Arris in the Aurès mountains (now in Batna province, eastern Algeria). This records the life of the *dux* and *imperator* Masties, who ruled over both Moors and Romans and never broke faith with either group. Scholars debate whether *imperator* should be read to mean 'augustus', which would imply some recognition that the Roman empire had fallen. More important, though, is the way an independent king lays claim to the rule of both Mauri and Romans (i.e., not just Moorish tribesmen), right on the edge of Roman Africa's old heartland. Procopius tells us of another such Moorish king, Antalas, who ruled in Byzacena, a day or two's ride from Carthage. But by far the most famous kingdom is attested by an inscription from Altava in Mauretania Caesariensis (now in western Algeria's Tlemcen province). In it, three named officials – a prefect and two procurators – are said to have built a fort on the orders of Masuna, *rex gentium Maurorum et Romanorum*, 'king of the Moorish and Roman peoples'. Because several of the westernmost cities of Africa were well-maintained in this period, including not just Altava but also Volubilis in distant Tingitania, some scholars have ascribed a very extensive kingdom to this *rex gentium* Masuna. More important than that is the way that all these Moorish examples represented a successful regional response to the end of empire: they provided reasonably stable governance and economic prosperity as the superstructure of empire withered away. In that, they provide a stark contrast to the instability and decline of a region like northern Gaul.

If we turn to a different imperial periphery, out beyond the English Channel, we catch tantalising glimpses of a social revolution that erased the heritage of the Roman province more thoroughly than anywhere else in the former empire. We also, for the first time in history, find tiny grains of genuine evidence for events across the Irish Sea. Written sources are virtually non-existent in the fifth and sixth centuries. We have a couple of treatises, in execrable Latin, from the pen of Saint Patrick, a handful of confused notices in Gallic chronicles, and the *De Excidio Britanniae* ('On the Ruin of Britain'), written at a disputed date by a monk named

Gildas. From these scraps, scholars have built whole palaces of speculation – this is the purported age of king Arthur – but a sober, minimalist
sketch reveals the limits of our knowledge.

As we have seen, it is likely that the fourth-century usurper Magnus
Maximus drew imperial administrators and soldiers back into the island's
lowland zone, along a line running from Dorset to Humberside. He was
probably also the first leader to recruit Saxon mercenaries into British
units. Constantine III then took most of the remaining *comitatenses*
with him to Gaul in 407 and, while the long civil war that he triggered
was in progress, the government of Honorius told an embassy of British
petitioners to look to their own devices. Around 430, bishop Germanus
of Autessiodorum (Auxerre in Burgundy) travelled to Britain to preach
against heresy and may have been caught up in a Pictish invasion into the
Midlands. One final provincial embassy may have petitioned Aëtius in
the 440s. Beyond that, there is nothing. Gildas names a number of petty
kings, but we can identify only the Constantinus who ruled in Dumnonia
(now Cornwall). Gildas' Ambrosius Aurelianus, frequently identified as
the historical king Arthur, cannot be dated if he in fact existed at all.
The homeland of Coroticus, who was certainly a genuine ruler to whom
Patrick addressed a letter, is unknown (Strathclyde is merely a guess).
Seventh- and eighth-century texts, like the so-called Tribal Hidage or
Bede's ecclesiastical history, are more or less imaginary for our period.

We have instead to rely upon archaeology, which suggests that Roman
administration in Britain had already begun contracting in the fourth
century, and continued to do so over many decades. Archaeology also
suggests a classic pattern of two-way migration between Britain and the
North Sea coast of modern Germany, which is to say the Saxon homeland.
Continental styles from there appear in Britain from the very late fourth
century, while distinctly British styles appear in Saxon lands almost immediately thereafter. That disproves the old-fashioned picture of a deliberate
Anglo-Saxon conquest, invaders driving the Romano-British and Celtic
populations into Wales, Cornwall and Cumbria. Yet it also indisputably
demonstrates a substantial movement of people from northern Germany
into Britain.

The best explanation of this evidence is that the imperial garrison in
Britain had come to be recruited overwhelmingly from Saxons, just as
the *comitatenses* in northern Gaul were recruited overwhelmingly from
Franci. Then, as imperial government crumbled and disappeared, some

of these soldiers decided to fill the power vacuum and expand their own control east and south from the frontier zone of the highland–lowland divide. Material evidence from northern Germany and the Netherlands – contraction of settlement, abandonment of coastal agricultural sites – suggests local political disruption in these years, which would help account for migration into Britain on a much larger scale than we find in Gaul or the Balkans.

Meanwhile, as this military population spread out into the British lowland zone, rivalry among surviving Roman aristocrats and migration from across the Irish Sea began to create what would become, after several centuries, the Celtic zone of western Britain. By the mid fifth century, three major archaeological regions can be identified, distinguished by the types of fancy metalwork their inhabitants preferred. One region, with fashions closely related to those across the North Sea in Germany, centred on East Anglia, the East Midlands, Lincolnshire and Yorkshire. Another region was characterised by local elaborations of old Roman military fashions and is concentrated south of the Thames, and in Essex. A third region centred on the Severn estuary ran from Devon and Somerset to South Wales.

If these three stylistic regions loosely reflect political and cultural zones, then they show us not an east–west divide between Saxon and Celt, but rather a north–south division along the Thames valley that lasted for more than half a century after the usurpation of Constantine III. In fact, right into the early sixth century, Mediterranean imports still reached southern and western Britain, but are exceedingly uncommon north of the Thames. Imports disappeared in the south-east before they did in the south-west, and the regional style of south-eastern Britain became increasingly absorbed into that of the East Midlands and the North at about the same time. That suggests that the two-way migration, and reasonably close connections, between eastern England and the North Sea coast of Germany continued, and indeed intensified, in the course of the sixth century.

Language, of course, is another indicator of what seems clearly to have been a massive social change: the total replacement of Romano-British Latin by Old English (Anglo-Saxon) is unparalleled anywhere else in the former western empire. Whether that reflects the weakness of Christianity and Roman urbanism in Britain or a disproportionately large number of English-speaking migrants is open to dispute. The scale and uniqueness of the change is not.

Whereas events in the southern and eastern parts of Great Britain seem to have played out chiefly in relationship to the continent, events in what is now North Wales, the West Midlands, the North-west and Scotland need to be understood in connection to developments across the Irish Sea. There, momentous social change had taken place in the fourth century, out of sight of Roman observers: a new script, Ogam, was invented to write the Irish language. Around the year 400, we start to find inscriptions (some bilingual in Latin and Ogam) bearing Irish names in South Wales and Cornwall. Further north, there is evidence of Irish migration from Ulster to Argyll, which would be ruled together as the kingdom of Dál Riata by the end of the sixth century. What sent these migrants from Ireland to Britain was probably the collapse of older, and larger, Irish kingdoms (still known to us through much later legends, but irrecoverable historically). The new, smaller territories into which Ireland was fragmenting are revealed by a proliferation of ring forts (known by various Gaelic names – *rath* if landlocked, *crannog* if built into a lake). Perhaps influenced by Irish immigrants, a similar multiplication of fortified sites is noticeable in Britain north of the Clyde–Forth line, while large Pictish polities, still active between the Solway and the Clyde in the fourth century, had disappeared by the end of the fifth. Clearly – and as we saw with the contemporaneous move to hilltop villages in north-western Spain – smaller and more localised power centres were safer.

Given the always marginal revelance of Ireland, and indeed much of Great Britain, to the Roman empire, scholars continue to dispute the degree to which the dramatic social changes visible there can possibly be an effect of the fall of the western empire. That is a fair point, but in many other regions beyond the old imperial periphery, events were clearly triggered by the implosion of the Roman state. Thus, in both Frisia and the Saxon lands in north-western Germany and south-western Denmark, the early fifth century saw the disappearance of Roman trade items, a major contraction of settlements and the abandonment of local cemeteries: suddenly lacking access to trade with, and predation on, an economically stable empire, the Saxon big men could no longer reward their followers and their power began to break down. Not until late in the sixth century, beyond the scope of this book, do we see a new material culture in the region, one influenced not just by two-way migration with Britain, but also by developments on the Elbe and in Scandinavia.

By contrast with these Saxon lands, northern Denmark, coastal Norway and southern Sweden were pulled into contact with former imperial provinces in ways they had not been before the break-up of the western empire. Scandinavian contact with the Roman empire had long been indirect, mediated through barbarian groups closer to the imperial *limes*. Even before that, Scandinavian rulers had relied upon high-value goods from the empire (especially metalwork, large multiples of gold *solidi* and weapons from the imperial *fabricae*) to demonstrate their own status and reward their followers.

That picture changed in the fourth century, as units of Scandinavian warriors from places like Öland, Scania and Jutland served as mercenaries in the imperial armies, before returning home with new riches. And yet at the same time that these Scandinavians were actually fighting for pay on imperial, or formerly imperial, soil, imports of luxury goods into Scandinavia largely dried up. Interestingly, they did so without producing the sort of crisis that affected the Saxon region when it was deprived of goods from the empire. Instead, new, locally designed (though derived from Roman models) prestige items came into vogue, in particular a type of artefact known as bracteate. These gold coin-like objects – little discs so thin as to be foil-like, first connected with the site at Gudme on the Danish island of Funen – appeared in great quantities in the fifth century, covered in mythological designs, stylised ruler portraits and intricate animal forms. Whether they served as a form of political display or were actually exchanged as currency has been debated, but they were clearly a successful response to the sudden disappearance of the Roman goods that had served as symbols of authority up to that point.

We cannot know whether this changed archaeological culture represents a single Danish kingdom or several, but it spread from the Danish islands to mainland Jutland where, by the sixth century, a Danish king is attested for the first time, fighting the Franks (he is also the Hygelac of *Beowulf*). This Danish expansion may have displaced earlier inhabitants of Jutland, because grave goods from just this time associated with northern Jutland begin to appear at coastal sites in south-west Norway, on the Jaeren shore of the North Sea in Rogaland. Changes in the material culture of Scania in southern Sweden suggest similar, though not identical, developments: an elite heavily influenced by the artistic and ritual customs of steppe nomad warriors seems to have asserted control, as illustrated by highly stylised burials of horse gear at Sösdala. On the island of Öland, hoards of Roman *solidi* suggest that rival groups of warlords, who had served in the imperial wars against the Vandals and in the civil wars of Ricimer and Anthemius, had returned home and fought each other to a standstill. The point here is neither to examine these changes in detail, nor to imply that any one such phenomenon is especially characteristic of the period as a whole, but rather to show that the collapse of the western empire was accompanied by, and helped to cause, social transformation hundreds of kilometres beyond the former frontier.

Another clear example of this comes from the Thuringian kingdom on the middle Elbe in Germany. Thuringians are first mentioned as subjects of Attila and their rise to power no doubt correlates with the rapid collapse of his empire. In the later fifth century, the near-contemporary *Life* of Saint Severinus of Noricum (generally regarded as quite accurate, though there are those who believe it to be a very clever fabrication) shows Thuringians and Rugi fighting for spoils in the former province of Noricum Ripense, north of the Alps. When the sixth-century kingdom on the Elbe came into being is harder to say. However, based on the archaeological evidence, it looks as if local rulers near the border of the emerging Frankish kingdom deliberately allied themselves to the Thuringians and began to adopt their material culture. The same thing seems to have happened further east, in Bohemia, where the Langobards played the same role as the Franks in the west. The marriage of the Thuringian king Hermanifred to Theodoric's niece Amalberga likewise demonstrates the importance of this ill-documented kingdom within the post-imperial scene.

The importance of Thuringian hegemony is actually demonstrated by the political upheaval its destruction by the Franks caused in central Europe. The Langobards (Lombards) had been clients as well as rivals of the Thuringians, but now, in the 530s, they invaded the former provinces of Pannonia, where they established themselves at the expense of Heruli and Gepids. Now, too, and for the first time, Bavarians appear in our sources. They were the people who had lived in the buffer zone between Thuringians to the north, Alamanni to the west and Ostrogothic Italy to the south. They emerge as a recognisable people with its own identity during the time when the Ostrogoths were busy fending off the imperial invasion of Italy but after the Franks had eliminated the power of the Alamanni and Thuringians.

When new people or 'peoples' come into being, the process is known as ethnogenesis, and early medievalist scholars have recently expended a great deal of energy thinking about how ethnic and political identities are merged and transformed, or sometimes re-emerge after decades or centuries. We need not spend time on theoretical issues here, but it is important to call attention to the historical impact of multiple ethnogeneses in Europe during the fifth and especially the sixth century: with the definitive disappearance of a western empire, the possibility of large-scale integration into an encompassing imperial identity disappeared, too. Nothing similarly universal existed or could take its place, because there was no power strong enough to make identification and assimilation attractive in the way the prospect of becoming a Roman had long done. Instead, people came to define themselves by reference to the neighbours – by who they were not. The bric-à-brac of the Roman past helped shape and reshape those self-perceptions, as did the military ideology of the successor kings. The emergence of new ways of communicating visually, the rise of customary law in place of Roman legal universalism, and most of all the displacement of Latin as a universal language all mark a meaningful cultural break that no ideological memory of a Roman past could disguise, whether inside or outside the old imperial frontier.

Perhaps surprisingly, the same dynamic holds true in regions that were still in close contact with Constantinople and its emperors. In fact, the Balkans and the Black Sea littoral became post-imperial, both culturally and economically, faster than any part of the empire save Britain. This has traditionally been associated with the ethnogenesis, or perhaps the migration, of the Slavs. 'Sclaveni', as the Greek and Latin sources call them, first appear around the year 500, sometimes in association with different groups of Bulgars – Onogurs, Kutrigurs, Utigurs – whom we meet beginning in 480 or so. Since the earliest Bulgar raids are attested in the easternmost Balkans, we can assume that they came from the steppes north of the Black Sea. And because they seem to have fought primarily as mounted horsemen, Roman authors quickly fitted them into the 'Scythian' stereotype that they had applied to steppe warriors since time immemorial. That makes it hard for us to distinguish what made Bulgars different from other horse nomads, save for their tribal names.

The Slavs are something else altogether. When we first hear of them, it is in the sixth-century pages of Procopius, who says that they lived on the left bank of the Danube, in what is now Romania. Philologists have never been satisfied with this account, arguing on linguistic grounds that the Slavonic languages originated in either Volhynia on the present Polish–Ukrainian frontier or in the Pripet marshes further east, on the border between Belarus and Ukraine – and therefore there must have been a Slavic migration to the Danube just before the Sclaveni appear in the late ancient sources. There is no good reason to accept this theory, since there is absolutely no literary or archaeological evidence for mass migration; only an argument that the oldest shared vocabulary of proto-Slavic reflects the flora, fauna and climate of Volhynia or the Pripet. The mechanics of language change are not in fact that straightforward. The ethnic group known as Sclaveni probably originated in the river valleys of Romania, Moldova and Ukraine, in the small family settlements that have been excavated in substantial numbers in all three countries. We do not know whether these people spoke Slavonic languages yet; that may have come later, in historical circumstances that are invisible to us (after all, the originally Germanic-speaking Franks gave their name to the Romance language we call French).

After devastating raids in the 540s that reached as far Thessalonica on the Aegean and Dyrrachium on the Adriatic, Justinian's armies seem to have fortified the Danube bank successfully enough to stop Sclaveni raids until the 570s, but for several hundred years Sclaveni appear as the foot soldiers and clients of a series of equine nomadic elites, the Avars and the Bulgars, the latter of whom were culturally and linguistically slavicised by the Middle Ages. It is probably best, then, to think of the Sclaveni in the same way we think about the Bavarians, as a regional agricultural population that developed a more conscious identity, and new, more assertive leaders when the old political landscape around them was disrupted. In the case of the Sclaveni, the trigger was probably the damage that the Bulgars, and even more so the Avars, did to Constantinople's position in the Balkans.

The Avars are a phenomenon of a much larger Eurasian history, just as the Huns had been in the fourth century. Though the main phase of their history falls beyond the scope of this book, they first came to the attention of the empire in the reign of Justinian, in a famous embassy to Constantinople in 558. They have been identified with the Rouran, known from Chinese sources as leaders of a steppe empire that stretched from Mongolia, around the Tian-shan and into central Asia, from the fourth to the sixth centuries. Before that, they had been a subordinate group within the steppe confederacy of the Xianbei. The Rouran maintained close connections with the Chinese dynasty of the northern Wei, which had itself been founded by the Tuoba Xianbei late in the fourth century, and they also kept up relations with the Hephthalite 'Huns' to their south and west. This meant that the Rouran were at the centre of the networks that connected the Chinese world with south Asia and Iran, as well as the various nomadic communities of the great Eurasian steppe. According to Chinese sources, the ruler of the Rouran was the first to adopt the title of *khagan* or 'khan', a move that distanced them from the Xiongnu heritage that had hitherto been the dominant marker of political prestige on the steppes (the Xiongnu leaders were called *chanyu*). In the 550s, one of the Rouran's tributary peoples rose up and inflicted a massive defeat on the *khagan*. These Türks (or Göktürks, 'Sky-Turks' as they are known in the modern Turkish version of their Chinese ethnonym) rapidly established themselves as the dominant power in the steppe world.

There has long been a tradition of connecting the defeat of the Rouran by the Göktürks with the sudden arrival of the Avars north of the Caucasus and Black Sea. That is not impossible. Certainly, a major disturbance to the balance of power in Mongolia and the Tian-shan might easily have caused ripples all the way to the Carpathian basin. These need not be understood as mass migrations, but rather as the rapid rearrangement of hierarchies within steppe coalitions, with some movement of population if it provided an opportunity for groups lower in the hierarchy to better their position. That the first ruler of the Avars of whom we have a record (Bayan) called himself khagan rather than chanyu certainly means he was claiming a Rouran rather than a Xiongnu tradition of steppe overlordship, though it does not necessarily make him a Rouran by descent. Justinian dealt with Bayan in time-honoured fashion: he bribed the khagan to attack and subdue the Utigurs and Kutrigurs, deflecting him away from the lower Danube and into the Carpathians. We need not concern ourselves with the future development of the Avar khaganate in central Europe, but two points about this earliest phase are important.

The first point is that stability at the crossroads between eastern and western Eurasia mattered a great deal to the way large-scale events might play out. Because, in the sixth century, the Hephthalites had a stable, hegemonic position in the Pamirs, the Hindu Kush and the former Kushanshahr, the disturbances triggered by the break-up of the Rouran confederation rippled westwards towards Europe rather than southwards into the Iranian borderlands. The second point is that the advent of the Rouran/Avars in the middle of the sixth century marked a major change in the way the Roman empire looked at the vast Eurasian interior. For three centuries, since at least the third century AD, developments there had made an impact on the empire, either directly from the steppe, or indirectly through the effect they had on Sasanian Iran. But whereas Roman emperors sometimes intervened in lands from the Caucasus and Crimea to Arabia, Himyar (Yemen) and Ethiopia, they had always waited for developments in the Eurasian steppe to come to them.

Justinian's direct negotiation with Avars based as far away as the Caspian marks the beginning of a new diplomatic outlook on the world, one that treated the steppe as a part of the Roman world that had to be managed with as much care as the settled cultures on the imperial periphery. Justinian's immediate successors sent embassies as far as the Tian-shan to meet with the khagan of the Türk and arrange an alliance, seeing in the new power a check on not just the steppe nomads but also the Persian empire of Khusrau I. As a result, when in the ninth century the northern periphery of Europe was drawn into contact with the steppe via the river systems of eastern Europe, it found there a long-standing network of Byzantine diplomacy that had grown directly out of the empire's sixth-century experience.

15

FROM ROME TO BYZANTIUM

❦

The long reign of Justinian, from 527 to 565, marked the final transition from antiquity to the Middle Ages in the Latin West, and the beginning of that same transition in the Greek East. The western kingdoms in the early sixth century already looked distinctly post-Roman, but the devastation wreaked by Justinian's wars, and the decisive boost to Frankish hegemony caused by the destruction of the Italian Ostrogoths, completed the transformation. The exhaustion of eastern manpower and the impoverishment of the eastern treasury, the failure to staunch the open wound of the Balkans, and the alienation of the huge monophysite populations of Egypt and Syria started the period of late Roman collapse in the East.

Within a hundred years of Justinian's accession to sole rule, the emperor Heraclius (who reigned from 610 to 641) can no longer be said to have ruled an imperial state. The machinery of government – already transformed and in part privatised by Justinian – had withered, and by the end of his reign, military threats could barely be countered, let alone suppressed. We may with some reason begin to call the Roman successor polity ruled by Heraclius and his successors a Byzantine empire (for Byzantium, the ancient city that lay beneath the new foundation of Constantinople). Although the term Byzantine was originally pejorative, the seventh-century Byzantine polity is sufficiently different from its sixth- (let alone its fourth- or fifth-) century predecessors to justify a distinctive name.

Its Greek-speaking inhabitants called themselves *Rhomaioi* ('Romans', in Greek), but they controlled only Asia Minor, the immediate Thracian hinterland of Constantinople and a few Mediterranean and Balkan outposts that could be supplied by ship. Justinian did not create this Byzantine empire, but he created the conditions in which it could emerge.

The sources for Justinian's reign are numerous, many more than for those of Anastasius or his uncle, Justin I, who directly preceded him. We know a vast amount about the theological conflicts of the reign, and some of that material may have come from the emperor's own hand. That and a copious outpouring of new laws allow us a rare insight into the emperor's mind: they draw a picture of a relentless, unsleeping fanatic for whom no detail was too small, an ancient analogue to Philip II of Spain, if without his spark of courtly wit. Along with doctrinal controversy, we can also trace the course of warfare on multiple fronts in minute, not to say excruciating, detail. Thanks to this bounty, there are scores of popular histories and purported biographies for those who want them, alongside dozens of military histories that clothe Procopius' *Wars* in modern dress. The following account will skirt all this detail, concentrating instead on the larger picture of imperial transformation, for better and mostly for worse, wrought by the dour ideologue over forty years in power. The focus will be on the Roman state: the fiscal, military and administrative outcomes, intended and otherwise, of sweeping change. There is another story to be told about Justinian's Greek Roman empire, about its cultural commonwealth of art and language and literature in a new era of abundant creativity; but outside the monumental architecture sponsored by the state, this efflorescence obeys a rhythm very different from the political narrative with which we have here been chiefly concerned.

There was general consensus in antiquity – as there has been ever since – that the reign of Justin I was merely a prelude to that of his nephew, and there can be little doubt of Justinian's wide-ranging influence on the politics of his uncle's reign. At the time of his accession, however, most of the problems Justin faced were prolongations of Anastasius' late reign. Religion was the main trigger. As we saw, the *Henotikon* of Zeno had been upheld at the council of Constantinople in 496, even as monophysites got their way and had the rigidly Chalcedonian Euphemius deposed in favour of Macedonius as bishop of the imperial see. Across the whole of the eastern provinces, monophysite prelates had been emboldened by Anastasius' obvious preference for their theology, despite the public show he made of accepting the *Henotikon*. In the 500s, led by Philoxenus, bishop of Hierapolis in Phrygia, and by the charismatic preacher Severus (later bishop of Antioch), monophysite clerics ceased working within the compromise framework that the *Henotikon* made possible, and instead began to demand that churchmen denounce a series of theologians and their works by name, deliberately advancing a position that would exclude even the most moderate Chalcedonians.

Anastasius found himself increasingly persuaded by their views and, in 509, he insisted that the Chalcedonian bishop Flavianus of Antioch convene a synod and defend his orthodoxy, with Philoxenus and other monophysites looking on. Despite his re-affirmation of the *Henotikon* and willingness to condemn by name some of the theologians abhorred by monophysites, it was not enough. Anastasius allowed Severus to draw up a creed that Macedonius would be obliged to sign, condemning Chalcedonian beliefs so explicitly that the monks and churchmen of Constantinople were outraged. Macedonius, long more willing to compromise than most Chalcedonians, agreed with his monastic counterparts that the monophysites had gone too far, but he was deposed in 511, arrested by the *magister officiorum* Celer and sent into exile. Timothy, a monophysite sympathiser, was put in his place, which further encouraged the Syrian extremists. Back in Antioch, in November 512, Philoxenus and others precipitated a riot that drove Flavianus out and allowed Severus to become bishop. At precisely the same time, Anastasius instructed Timothy to add a monophysite formula to the liturgy in Constantinople. He was rewarded by a riot in the church of Saint Sophia on Sunday, 4 November 512, in which several lives were lost.

The urban prefect Plato asked for troops to be seconded from the praesental army under the *magister militum* Patricius. The usual butchery of civilians ensued. The Chalcedonians remained defiant, however, and set up a makeshift rebel camp in the Forum of Constantine. There they attempted to provoke a usurpation, acclaiming the now elderly Flavius Areobindus emperor and tearing down the statues of Anastasius. Celer took the household guard out to join Patricius in suppressing the rioters, but the people fought them off and continued to demand the deposition of Anastasius. Areobindus, sensibly, kept well out of the way and, on the following day, Anastasius went to the Hippodrome and declared that he was willing to abdicate. In one of the reign's more mysterious episodes, this actually had the effect of calming the rioters, who dispersed after acclaiming him true emperor and begging him to replace the diadem on his head. In another mysterious turn, Areobindus was permitted to live on unmolested; though he died of old age soon afterwards, his children would prosper well into the next reign.

Problems mounted up all the same. Anastasius' Long Walls had been quite successful at keeping invaders out of Constantinople and its suburbs, but the rest of Thrace and the Balkans remained in bad shape. The region had lost enough of its population that it could not feed the forces needed to defend it, and it was the only part of the empire in which Anastasius had not abolished corvée labour and confiscatory taxes in kind. The region's problems were exacerbated by the virtual disappearance of *comitatenses* and their replacement by mercenary *foederati*, 'allies' under the notional command of a *comes foederatorum*, but more often loyal to their own chieftains than to the imperial state. Though Zeno had managed to get rid of Theodoric and send him off to Italy, the departure of that overmighty ally had not done anything to lessen imperial reliance on semi-independent warlords, such as the large group of Heruli settled in Illyricum in 512. Indeed, the degree of imperial control and administration throughout the Balkans is a matter of debate, and a lot of what passed for governance must actually have been local self-help, with imperial officials balancing rival strongmen against each other.

For reasons that are not entirely clear, but presumably to do with realising further economies, Anastasius withdrew eligibility for the *annona* from the Balkan *foederati* in 514, which led predictably to open revolt. This was led by the general Vitalianus, who was perhaps *comes foederatorum*, and supported not just by soldiers but by a substantial part of the agricultural population. Vitalianus murdered several of the colleagues who might have opposed him and formed an alliance with the *dux Moesiae* Maxentius. They seized the main cities on the Black Sea coast in Thrace and Scythia, protecting one potential avenue along which he could be attacked. Marching on Constantinople, he frightened one of the praesental *magistri militum*, Hypatius, into retreat, and also moved to give himself doctrinal cover, presenting his uprising as support for Chalcedonian orthodoxy against an emperor now so visibly sympathetic to monophysitism. Among his other demands was the reinstallation of Macedonius and Flavianus as bishops of Constantinople and Antioch respectively. Thinking his conditions would be met, he withdrew to Moesia, but did not otherwise back down. Anastasius took no action on the bishops, but deposed the failed *magister* Hypatius. His replacement as *magister militum praesentalis*, Cyrillus, then led some troops in pursuit of Vitalianus, but was captured at Odessus and murdered.

Only then did Anastasius begin to take seriously the scale of the threat. He placed his nephew, another Hypatius, in overall command and appointed one Alatharius *magister militum per Thracias*. Initial skirmishing seems to have gone their way, but Hypatius suffered a crippling defeat at Acrae near Odessus, where both he and Alatharius were captured. Ambassadors sent to negotiate a ransom also fell into Vitalianus' hands, allowing him to reward his followers handsomely and to pay a fleet to accompany him on his next attack on Constantinople, late in 514. Again, Anastasius negotiated, offering 900 pounds of gold for the ransom of Hypatius and agreeing to make Vitalianus *magister militum per Thracias* in place of Alatharius. Vitalianus agreed but continued to demand that Anastasius embrace Chalcedonian orthodoxy, and he tried to involve the bishop of Rome in the conflict. Angered, Anastasius withdrew the *magisterium* from Vitalianus, who promptly sailed on Constantinople again in 515. This time, his fleet was devastated by a fire that sent many of the ships to the bottom of the Propontis (although whether, as one rather folklorish text suggests, the fire was caused by an incendiary sulphur compound is open to question). Vitalianus and his land forces were then defeated at Sycae, and large numbers of them slaughtered by Anastasius' loyal troops, who were backed up by a large force of irregulars recruited from the circus factions of the imperial capital. Vitalianus went into hiding at Anchialus, where he remained until Anastasius' death. The engineer of these successes was Marinus, not a *magister militum* but rather the praetorian prefect. The military exploits of a civilian commander are an interesting indication that – as in many other corners of the government – the reign of Anastasius began the transformation of institutional norms that had been in place since at least the time of Constantine.

After the revolt of Vitalianus, events again become obscure. Alexandria experienced a destructive riot over olive oil shortages in 515 or 516. There were Onogur raids into Macedonia, Epirus and Thessaly in 517 that reached as far as Thermopylae, but there is little more to be said about the political events that preceded Anastasius' death on the night of 8 July 518, aged almost ninety, prodigiously old by ancient standards. He left no plans for the succession, only a clutch of nephews. The reputation of Anastasius' eldest nephew Hypatius, now *magister militum per Orientem*, had never recovered after his humiliation at the hands of Vitalianus, and his succession was not even considered by the palatine factions competing to place their own candidate on the imperial throne.

The long-serving *magister officiorum* Celer was pitted against the *comes* of the excubitors, Iustinus, as he was then called, who had risen from the ranks and served as an officer in the successful phase of Anastasius' Persian wars. Another contender was Theocritus, a *domesticus* of Amantius, the powerful *praepositus sacri cubiculi*, who wished to play kingmaker, whether or not he could install his own handpicked candidate. Everyone's hands were forced by the populace gathered in the Hippodrome, increasingly agitated and angry as no successor was announced. The Senate of Constantinople ultimately sided with Iustinus, who may have appropriated funds intended for Theocritus and splashed them around in bribes. Iustinus – or Justin, as we now know him – proved acceptable to the mob, in part because he was known to be Chalcedonian while the other contenders had supported Anastasius' shift to monophysitism, and so was duly made emperor.

The reign began well. Military threats were largely in abeyance, Anastasius' notorious thrift had left 320,000 pounds of gold in the treasury, and Justin moved immediately to restore Chalcedonian orthodoxy and heal the schism with Rome. He came from the remnant of Latin-speaking lands still inside the empire, having been born at Bederiana near Naissus (now Niš in Serbia). The humility of his background is played up in our sources – he is said to have been illiterate and to have married a slave woman whom he had bought, changing her name from Lupicina to Euphemia upon acceding to the purple. His favourite nephew and adopted son came with him to the imperial capital. This Iustinianus had been born Petrus Sabbatius, in a village (the present-day archaeological site of Caričin Grad in Serbia) that he later rebuilt as Iustiniana Prima. He changed his name to Justinian in the classical style after his adoption.

It seems likely, given the later evidence of his rigorous piety, that Justinian was responsible for much of his uncle's religious policy, which began with the almost instantaneous convocation of a council of those bishops who had happened to be in Constantinople when Anastasius died. Instructed to affirm their enthusiasm for the orthodoxy of Chalcedon, they did so and asked the bishop of the imperial see to begin whatever conversations were necessary to effect a reconciliation with the Latin church of Italy. A series of letters to Hormisdas, bishop of Rome, put an end to the Acacian schism between Rome and Constantinople that had lasted since 484. Only the church of Egypt, under the radical monophysite Timothy, refused communion with Rome. In another signal of Chalcedonian renaissance, Justin rehabilitated Vitalianus, who emerged from hiding and was rewarded with the praesental *magisterium* and the consulship of 520. Other potential rivals were removed – old Amantius was accused of fomenting a riot and put to death, as was his retainer Theocritus, while at the same time Justin placed another reliable nephew, Germanus, in command of the Thracian field army as *magister militum per Thracias*.

The emperor kept Justinian close by and the latter made sure to exploit his privilege to full advantage. He had Vitalianus murdered during his consular year of 520 and took for himself the position of *magister militum praesentalis*. He then took the consulship of 521, and some time after that year (perhaps 522, but certainly before 524), he contracted a marriage more scandalous than his uncle's had been: Theodora was the daughter of a bear-keeper employed by one of the circus factions and, after her father's death, became an actress (and thus a prostitute, for in Roman minds there was no distinction between the two). If we are to believe the narrative of Procopius' *Anecdota* (the 'Secret History' he wrote to record the dark side of the emperor he praised so lavishly in his public works), Theodora became a celebrity on account of her sexual appetites and her willingness to indulge specialist tastes.

When she returned to Constantinople after some years in Egypt as the concubine of a high imperial official, Justinian came under her spell. He got his uncle to issue a law making it possible for a senator such as himself to marry an actress – something Roman law had previously forbidden on the grounds that the social stain of her profession rendered an actress unfit to marry a well-born citizen. It is a sign of Justinian's influence with his uncle that he could engineer such transparently self-advantageous legislation, but there is no reason to accept hostile ancient reports of Theodora's secret power over her husband. She would go on to exercise influence in the palace until her death in 548, as strong augustae had done for centuries, but we should credit neither the vile misogyny of the *Anecdota* (and the winking innuendo too much modern scholarship derives from it), nor the implausibly large claims made by revisionist scholars for her pioneering feminism. That Justinian regarded her as his partner in empire would become clear in the preambles to some of his later legislation, but more than that we cannot say.

Apart from the renewed interest in Chalcedonian theology, the central concerns of Justin's reign seem to have been diplomacy with the western kingdoms and first diplomacy, and then accidental war, with Persia. Relations with the West were generally quite good. The Burgundian king Sigismund, as we have seen, ruled as both king and Roman *magister militum*. Ostrogothic embassies were a constant presence in Constantinople, and Justin not only shared the consulship with Flavius Eutharicus, Theodoric's heir apparent, but also ceremonially adopted him as his *filius per armas* ('son-in-arms', a recent innovation that acknowledged the autonomy of the western kings while preserving the fiction of their subordination to the imperial hegemon). As to the Vandals, the future king Hilderic, son of the Theodosian princess Eudocia, had resided in Constantinople for long stretches of his life, and shared with Justinian a taste for Chalcedonian orthodoxy and theological debate.

In the East, the truce arranged in 506 between Anastasius and the long-lived shahanshah Kavadh I, who reigned until 531, had lasted far longer than the seven years it had been designed to cover. Even when Kavadh faced a revolt in the Christian kingdom of Iberia, long a Persian client that now appealed to Rome, war between the two empires was avoided. But then diplomatic ineptitude altered that rosy picture. As he aged, Kavadh foresaw one of the perennial Persian crises of succession, since his state lacked any settled means of designating a royal heir. Kavadh wanted his third son, Khusrau, to succeed him, but the elder brothers had their partisans among the nobility, and the succession of a third son was certainly unusual. Kavadh was thus reluctant to attempt a wholesale purge. He instead took the unusual step of asking Justin to adopt Khusrau as his own son, thus securing either the support or the neutrality of the Romans in any ensuing civil war. Justin was in favour, but allowed himself to be persuaded that it was beneath the dignity of an emperor to adopt the son of a barbarian in this formal way – only the lesser adoption *per armas*, used with the princes of the western kingdoms, would do. Kavadh was, not unsurprisingly, outraged at this insult and promptly attacked the Roman client state of Lazica. Justin sent an army into Persian Armenia to retaliate, though, as usual in these perilous mountain regions, the weather placed limits on both sides' ambitions.

Early in 527, Justin fell seriously ill (he was in his seventies at this point, and thus old by ancient standards). At the request of the Senate, he made Justinian his co-emperor on 4 April, and so there was no awkward transfer of power when Justin died on 1 August of that year. The new sole ruler's first order of business was the Persian war, to which end he made sweeping changes to the command structure of the eastern frontier: military administration was devolved to local *duces*, instead of regional *comites*, and a new *magisterium militum per Armeniam* was created.

The first man to hold this post was an Armenian officer named Sittas who had served as a *protector* under Justinian in the early 520s; his colleague as *magister per Orientem* was Belisarius, another of the emperor's former bodyguards and the heroic central figure in Procopius' histories of Justinian's wars (Procopius served on Belisarius' staff and was an eyewitness to many of the various episodes on which he reports). The year 530 was a good one for Roman arms, Sittas winning a major victory at Theodosiopolis in Armenia, and Belisarius doing the same at Dara in Mesopotamia. But in 531 Kavadh inflicted a stunning defeat on Belisarius at Callinicum, and the general was summoned back to Constantinople, in great danger of being cashiered: Armenia had held, but the route through Mesopotamia, now threatened, led straight to the heartlands of Syria, and that was a far worse threat. The Romans were only granted a reprieve because Kavadh died in the autumn of 531. His favoured son Khusrau faced an inevitable civil war, for though he had the full support of the Zoroastrian priesthood (and thus of the rich resources of their temple lands), the Mazdakite clergy sided with his elder brother Kavus. Khusrau's first priority was thus to suppress the internal challenge and he sought a truce with Justinian.

In 532, the empires concluded an open-ended 'Eternal Peace', restoring the territorial status quo of Anastasian times, with Justinian paying out a lump sum to void any annual demands for subsidy of Persian garrisons in the Derbend and other Caucasus passes. Khusrau, his hands freed, brought his brother Kavus to battle and crushed him, massacring the Mazdakites where he could find them, and having every one of his male relatives executed. He would reign until 579, the most formidable Sasanian ruler since Shapur II, and known to posterity as Anushirvan, 'the Immortal Soul'.

If Khusrau had good reasons to make peace, so, too, did Justinian, who very nearly lost his throne in January 532. The circus factions of Constantinople were as riot-prone as ever in the early sixth century, but when, on 14 January, a disturbance between two sides was put down with exemplary severity by the *praefectus urbi* Eudaemon, they united and attacked the prefect's palace shouting *Nika*, 'victory'. They freed their imprisoned comrades and set fire to the palace and other buildings, then assembled in the Hippodrome and began shouting out their demands: not only should Eudaemon be sacked, but along with him the praetorian prefect Ioannes (known to modern scholarship as John the Cappadocian) and the *quaestor* Tribonianus, who was closely associated with Justinian's recent codification of imperial law. Justinian assented, but the mob was unappeased: they tried to find Anastasius' nephew Probus to proclaim him emperor, and then burned his house to the ground when they found he had gone into hiding.

Despite Justinian's offering a general amnesty in exchange for peace, the mob next turned to another nephew of Anastasius, the unlucky former *magister militum* Hypatius, and proclaimed him emperor. He seems to have assented in this dubious honour, for he and a group of senators joined the mob in the Hippodrome. That suggests that a faction of the city's aristocracy had become fed up with Justinian, and in particular with the reforming zeal and fiscal rigour of the officials he had appointed, and were seizing on the opportunity of the circus riots to press their case and perhaps depose the emperor. We are told that Justinian was already preparing to flee when Theodora stiffened his spine: 'The purple makes a fine winding sheet,' she is reported to have said. But, be that as it may, the emperor now decided to fight.

Belisarius was still in the palace, disgrace looming over him, along with his *bucellarii* (semi-private soldiers that most senior generals maintained at their own expense in this period). So, too, was Mundo, a Gepid prince who had formerly served with Theodoric in Italy and then joined the imperial army as *magister militum per Illyricum* after the old king's death in 526. At the head of their own retainers and some Herulian mercenaries, the two commanders stormed the Hippodrome, with predictable results. Crowded into a small space, armed with makeshift weapons, even the most resolute of rioters were no match for hardened soldiers – the massacre was fearsome, and if the figure from contemporary sources of 30–35,000 citizens killed is an exaggeration, there can be no doubt that they died in their thousands not their hundreds. Hypatius and his brother Pompeius were seized and executed and their senatorial supporters exiled. Never again would the emperor face so severe a threat to his personal hold on the throne.

In many narratives, the story of the Nika riots is followed by a long (often very long) account of Justinian's western wars, a lightning Vandal campaign and then an endless battle for Italy. Before turning briefly to those matters, though, we should look at something of much greater significance, the long-term changes Justinian and his ministers worked on the structure of empire, because these really did create a framework of governance that no longer obeyed the principles of Diocletian and Constantine's far-reaching reforms.

Indisputably the most enduring of Justinian's initiatives was the codification of Roman law. Within a year of his accession, on 28 February 528, the emperor had appointed a commission to replace all official and unofficial compilations of imperial constitutions with an up-to-date collection that would contain only valid law. Obsolete laws were to be omitted and those still in force emended and edited down to only those sections of them that were still in force. The commission's work took just under a year, and the first Justinianic Code was published on 7 April 529.

In December 530, under the presidency of the same Tribonianus who would be *quaestor* at the time of the Nika riots, a second commission was appointed to gather, review and compile the juristic writings which bore on the civil law. This was an even larger task, for the juristic commentary that had for centuries accumulated around the legislation of Roman emperors had never before been treated as a single object of study, capable of being reduced to a system. Thousands of pages of text were to be manhandled into a useable corpus in which only valid law should remain, divided up into titles by subject and edited accordingly. Improbable as it seems, the commission achieved its aims and three years later, this *Digest* of Roman law was published, on 16 December 533. A textbook, called the *Institutes* and based on an earlier work of that name by the Severan jurist Gaius, was issued with imperial sanction as a concise introduction for students of Roman law, a purpose for which it remains very well suited to this day. Then, in the following November, the revised Justinianic Code that we still possess was issued, further emending the texts of older laws and compiling the vast number of constitutions Justinian had himself issued in the previous half decade.

The historical significance of these legal compilations cannot be overstated. In use in the eastern Roman empire for a couple of hundred years, the Greek translations of the Code and the *Digest* were abridged in the eighth century and then superseded in the tenth by compilations (the *Ekloga* and the *Basilika* respectively) better suited to the reduced circumstances of the middle Byzantine period. In the West, the Justinianic compilations were introduced after Africa and Italy had been conquered, but the Islamic conquest of Africa in the seventh century ended the Roman legal regime there for ever. In Italy, too, the compilations were effectively lost for centuries after the last imperial governors were evicted from Ravenna in the middle of the eighth century. And yet, when rediscovered in eleventh-century Bologna, they swiftly became the focus of a vast legal industry. Ultimately, the Code, the *Digest*, the *Institutes*, and the *Novellae* ('new laws') of Justinian that had circulated in private collections came to be known as the Corpus Iuris Civilis ('body of civil law', a collective title canonised by the greatest of early modern legal scholars, Denis Godefroy, or Gothofredus as he was known in Latin).

The astonishingly sweeping authority that imperial Roman law had given the emperor made it very attractive to rulers for whom such power could hardly be imagined. Medieval monarchs, trying to build state structures in a world largely governed by custom while suppressing a welter of incompatible jurisdictions, welcomed Roman law and jurisprudence as an unassailably prestigious foundation for their new claims, and it would be adopted as the legal foundations of the nation states emerging during early modernity. To this day, the Justinianic compilations are an important stratum, quite near the surface, of continental Europe's national legal regimes, as well as of their former colonies.

Just as important at the time, however, were Justinian's other reforms, which continued and accelerated those of the Anastasian period. They came in different phases, at different moments in the reign, but their cumulative effect was to do away with most of what remained of the tetrarchic and Constantinian systems. The eastern praetorian prefect John the Cappadocian (in power until 541, save for his very brief deposition at the time of the Nika riots) was the man responsible for most of these changes, but his eventual successor, Peter Barsymes, was no less active a reformer, whether as prefect or *comes sacrarum largitionum*. The overall trend was to scale back and scale down, and to privatise certain aspects of government formerly undertaken by the state. The local officials known as *defensores civitatis* ('city advocates'), for instance, were given inappellable jurisdiction in cases worth less than 300 solidi, which kept the more expensive provincial jurisdictions for larger cases. Similarly, provincial governors were given inappellable jurisdiction in cases worth less than 750 solidi, with a similar aim of reducing expenses (and restricting opportunities for corruption).

The provinces themselves were drastically reorganised, and the vicariates abolished altogether. In the former vicariates of Asiana and Pontica, several pairs of provinces were joined together as one, and the governors of provinces at one remove from frontier zones were given military as well as civil authority (the frontier provinces retained civilian administrators separate from the new and complicated military network of *duces* serving under the *magistri militum per Orientem* and *per Armeniam*). The frontier provinces in Armenia and the Caucasus were completely reshaped as well, their number multiplied and their cities transferred among the different new provinces. Then, during the 540s, the interior provinces of the former vicariates were given new officials to manage policing duties that had to cross provincial boundaries, presumably to stop bandits from exploiting gaps in jurisdiction. The vicariate of Oriens (where the *vicarius* had long been known as the *comes Orientis*) was abolished as well, its functions assigned to the governor of Syria. The Egyptian vicariate also disappeared, though the *praefectus Augustalis* (as the Egyptian *vicarius* had been called) was retained and given military as well as civilian command, while a second *Augustalis* was created for the Thebaid and southern Egypt. In both Oriens and Egypt, there was a renumbering of some provinces, changes to the status of their governors and some redistribution of jurisdiction among them. Nearer the capital, the suburban region that was protected by the Long Walls from disruption in the rest of Thrace was placed under a *praetor per Thracias* with both civil and military authority.

The point of these changes was to maximise oversight while restricting costs to the central government, because Justinian found himself in perpetual economic crisis. Anastasius might have left the treasury full, but the Persian war had been costly and (as even Anastasius had found) there were parts of the empire – the Balkans in particular – from which it was virtually impossible to raise revenue. More damagingly, the invasion of first Africa and then Italy proved incalculably expensive. At first, that might not have seemed the case and Justinian's intervention in Africa, at least, seemed eminently sensible at the time. The Vandal king Hilderic, as we have seen, was already old when he came to the throne and he had nothing in the way of military ambition. He was, however, an old acquaintance of Justinian's and a Nicene Christian who ended his homoian predecessors' oppression of Nicene bishops. When his cousin Gelimer deposed him in 530, Justinian was outraged. He used it as an excuse to invade Africa, despite a track record of imperial failure in such expeditions going back to the 440s and also despite his officials objecting to the plan on those very grounds.

In 533, Belisarius landed in Africa unopposed. Gelimer had sent some of his best troops to suppress a rebellion in Sardinia, but that is not enough to account for the scale of Belisarius' victory at the head of no more than 20,000 troops in total – the Vandal state had apparently found no mechanism by which to sustain its nobility's warrior traditions, nor come up with any viable alternative. After only two pitched battles, the Vandal kingdom collapsed and the kings of the Mauri formally accepted the reimposition of imperial rule. Gelimer, having fled, soon surrendered to Belisarius in March 534. Along with several thousand Vandal noblemen, he accompanied the conquering general back to Constantinople, before retiring to expansive estates in Galatia where he lived out his life as a distinguished private citizen. His former soldiers were enrolled as units of the regular army on the eastern frontier and Belisarius was granted the right to celebrate a triumph, the first time a *privatus* had done so since the reign of Augustus more than five hundred years before.

And yet Africa was hardly at peace – the Moorish kings' acquiescence in the imperial conquest was more notional than real, and several attacked imperial territory almost as soon as Belisarius left. Then, in 536, the Roman garrison mutinied. Many of them had married Vandal women and they resented imperial encroachments on African estates they now saw as their own. All the same, swift success had left Justinian emboldened. Italy offered a target. The short reign of Theodoric's grandson Athalaric had seen a renaissance of senatorial authority after the scratchy interlude of Theodoric's later years. The young man's mother Amalasuntha proved an effective regent and, with Cassiodorus as *magister officiorum* and then praetorian prefect, the kingdom looks both high-functioning and very Roman to our retrospective eyes. Athalaric, however, became the tool of a faction of the Gothic nobility that (so we are told) looked askance at both the rule of a woman and the excessively Roman education to which the king was being exposed. Faced with these intolerable conflicts, Athalaric escaped into alcohol and drank himself to death late in 534.

Amalasuntha took the royal title for herself, after murdering the nobles most hostile to her, and made her cousin Theodahad her king and consort. The son of Theodoric's sister Amalafrida and her (otherwise unrecorded) first husband, Theodahad had grown up as a great landowner in his uncle's Italian kingdom. He cultivated the habits of a Roman senator, editing Plato and generally embracing the dignified leisure to which a politically unambitious nobleman would aspire. Married to the new, and unpopular, queen, he evinced a sudden taste for intrigue hitherto unsuspected. Siding with the Gothic courtiers most hostile to Amalasuntha, he confined her to an island prison and had her executed in secret in April 535. Royal officials like Cassiodorus were still just about ready to accept the dynastic dysfunction, but to Justinian's eyes, a fratricidal royal family had again handed him the opportunity for glory.

Vigorously deploring Theodahad's iniquity, the emperor sent Mundo, his *magister militum per Illyricum*, to seize Dalmatia from its Gothic garrison. He did so with ease, although the withdrawal of Gothic forces soon gave a Gepid king the opportunity to seize Sirmium and make it his headquarters for the next quarter century. Belisarius, meanwhile, seized Sicily with next to no opposition. Theodahad dithered between surrender and defiance, so Belisarius launched an invasion up Italy's Tyrrhenian coast. He met little opposition, but neither did he find much welcome. If Justinian expected his men to be greeted as liberators, he had misjudged the local mood, as would-be liberators so often do. The half century of post-imperial rule had been quite good to an Italian population among whom folk memories of the chaos of the fifth century remained vivid. At Naples, Belisarius discovered what this meant, as the urban populace joined the Gothic garrison in defending the city against the emperor's troops. They held out for several weeks and, in years to come, many more Italians would demonstrate just how ambivalent they were about the 'freedom' the emperor's soldiers was bringing them.

Confronted with this fast-moving assault, Theodahad sat paralysed at Ravenna. With the consensus of both civilian and military leadership, the king was deposed and replaced by the general Vitigis, who withdrew north of the Apennines to regroup, summoning garrisons from around the peninsula to join him. This meant that Belisarius was able to take Rome without opposition. From February 537 to late in the following winter, Vitigis besieged the imperial forces in Rome, both sides suffering badly from lack of provisions, until the arrival of re-enforcements carrying supplies for the imperial army forced Vitigis to retreat. It may be around now that Cassiodorus and other prominent Italians gave up on the Gothic cause and fled into exile in Constantinople, polishing their résumés for their eventual return. Though no longer confined within Rome's walls, Belisarius was soon confounded by the ambitions of several subordinates, including the eunuch general Narses, Justinian's *sacellarius*.

The position of *sacellarius*, first attested under Zeno, seems to have belonged to the imperial bedchamber and it may simply be a late synonym for *cubicularius*. Regardless, Narses could rely on his close personal relationship with the emperor to defy his commander-in-chief. Infighting among the officer corps led to inefficiency and a failure to coordinate, so that in 538 Vitigis was able to take Mediolanum, one of the great cities of the north Italian plain. He sacked it, massacring the men and giving the women as slaves to Burgundian contingents that had assisted the Gothic campaign. That brutal coda marked the temporary exhaustion of all involved. Both sides began to seek a truce and, in 540, Belisarius returned to Constantinople with the Gothic royal treasury. Vitigis accompanied Belisarius and was honoured as *patricius* by the emperor, who gave him estates on which to live, though he died of natural causes in about the year 542. The noble retainers who had joined him would soon find themselves accompanying Belisarius to fight a new war against Persia.

Back in Italy, imperial successes proved even more ephemeral than they had in Africa, where the mutiny of 536 had become so severe that Justinian had sent his cousin Germanus to suppress it, only recalling him in 539, at the same time that Belisarius seems to have finished off the Gothic campaign. Yet before Belisarius and Vitigis had even left Ravenna, some of the Goths who stayed behind in Italy elected a new king, Hildebad, and war broke out again. It would take twenty years to finish. Hildebad fell to an assassin, as did a short-lived successor named Eraric, but in 541 the highly competent nobleman Totila (sometimes called Baduila) was proclaimed king and began to eliminate imperial garrisons around the peninsula. His army swollen with runaway slaves, he retook fortified cities and razed their walls, leaving many of the most important Italian towns without any practical defences. Even though Belisarius himself returned in 544, the war dragged on and on, Rome changing hands more than once, and Totila even contriving to invade Sicily in 550. Finally, in the summer of 552, Narses defeated Totila at the battle of Busta Gallorum, where the Gothic king died on the battlefield. His successor Teias was routed in the following year, at the battle of Mons Lactarius, and the main Gothic forces surrendered, but though Justinian felt able to declare his Italian conquests at peace and issue new laws to govern them, Gothic garrisons at Verona and Brixia (Brescia) would actually hold out until 561.

By then, however, the empire had suffered many more years of crippling warfare on every front. In 540, a vast Bulgar raid had penetrated the Long Walls and carried off wagonloads of treasure. Then, in 540, Khusrau decided to break the Eternal Peace and invade the eastern provinces. His motive was purely financial. Although he had begun a process of land registration and survey that would finally bring a functional bureaucracy to Sasanian administration and increase royal revenues substantially, Khusrau did not yet enjoy the entrenched traditions of taxation on which Roman emperors could rely even in lean times. Rome's eastern provinces were therefore a tempting source of plunder to the shahanshah, and he led a massive invasion through Mesopotamia, extracting huge bribes from cities as he passed and marching as far as Antioch, which he put to the sack. Having met no effective opposition, he returned home with his booty, including many citizens of Antioch whom he settled in Khuzestan to farm the land. In the following years, fighting alternated between the Caucasus (especially the kingdom of Lazica) and Mesopotamia, and a five-year truce agreed in 545 on terms disadvantageous to Rome failed to address the disputed client states in the northern mountains.

By the time that truce was arranged, both sides had a more implacable enemy to deal with: plague. The ancient sources are universally agreed on the horrors of the disease that struck in 542, but scholars failed for years to agree about which pathogen was responsible. There is now a general consensus that – unlike the Antonine plague, whose identity remains disputed, or the third-century 'Cyprianic' plague that can be identified as haemorrhagic fever – the Justinianic pandemic was caused by Yersinia pestis, the bacterium that causes bubonic plague. The globe has three great reservoirs (in central Asia, east Africa and the North American south-west) from which the plague bacillus periodically jumps to new hosts from the rodent population in which it, and the fleas who harbour it, are endemic. With a very high morbidity and rapid incubation, plague can infect concentrated populations with great speed. Its mortality depends on whether the bacillus attacks the lymphatic system, the bloodstream or the lungs, which latter transmission is almost invariably fatal.

First recorded at Pelusium in Egypt, the plague began to ravage Syria and the eastern provinces before spreading both eastwards into Mesopotamia and Persia, and westwards, through the Balkans, Italy and Africa, to reach Gaul, Spain and perhaps even Ireland. As plague does, it recurred repeatedly for the next couple of decades, before reappearing approximately once in a generation (with decreasing virulence and more scattered distribution) until the year 750. We cannot accurately assess its effect on the size of the imperial population, but it must have been substantial. Moreover, the sudden impact of its mass mortality was undoubtedly compounded by the deteriorating climatic conditions of this period. Palaeoclimatology is a very young science, and a sound method by which to link its findings to historical events has yet to be generally agreed upon. We nevertheless know that, around 540, Europe entered a little ice age, probably brought on by a massive volcanic event in the Pacific, having already suffered several decades of highly erratic weather. Without positing a determinist link between climate, catastrophe and disease, we can be sure that environmental conditions militated against rapid demographic recovery, and that is before one even takes account of Justinian's ceaseless wars.

These continued – in Italy, as we have seen, till 554 if not 561, while in Africa a series of commanders continued to fight campaigns of varying intensity and little permanent success against various groups of Mauri. In 551, moreover, Justinian sent an invasion force to Spain. Theudis, once Theodoric's regent in the rump of the Visigothic kingdom, had for almost two decades ruled an independent Spanish kingdom, though of limited size and power, in his own right. He was assassinated in 548, as was his successor the year after. The next claimant to the Gothic crown, Agila, alienated potential allies among the Hispano-Roman cities of the south, and was challenged by one Athanagild, who invited Justinian to support him. An imperial army landed at Carthago Nova to find Agila dead, Athanagild's accession accepted by a majority of the Spanish Goths, and not one element among the Iberian population ready to welcome the intervention. Carving out a foothold along the coasts of south-eastern Carthaginiensis and Baetica, a small imperial territory centred on Carthago Nova and Malaca would survive until the 620s, by which point the vestigial Gothic state of the 550s had been restored as one of the richest and culturally most significant kingdoms of the early Middle Ages.

Back in the East, Justinian and Khusrau had renewed the peace of 545 in 551, though they continued to launch offensives against each other in the Caucasus. Even there, they patched up a permanent settlement over Lazica in 561, the same year the last Gothic hold-outs were finally suppressed in Italy. They agreed likewise to discipline their Arab clients and cease using Ghassanids and Lakhmids to fight proxy wars. In the Balkans, Justinian spent huge amounts of money on fortifications, but his manpower reserves were too small to sustain a proper field army – the result was that the impressive defensive sites that we know archaeologically, and that are praised with lickspittle gusto in Procopius' monographic *Aedificia* ('*Buildings*'), were not enough to prevent devastating raids of Bulgars and Sclaveni. The Avars, whom we met at the end of the last chapter, were persuaded by massive bribes to displace Langobards and Gepids from the Carpathian basin rather than invade the imperial Balkans – and as a result, shortly after Justinian's death, most of his Italian conquests were lost to Langobardic invaders unable to weather the Avar threat. All told, the many individual episodes of imperial success proved transitory, each in its turn. The cost to the imperial finances was devastating, especially when added to so much manpower wasted and now irreplaceable thanks to plague. Reforming conqueror he might have been, but Justinian left the empire weaker and poorer than he had found it.

He also left it more divided in religious terms, a topic from which we have so far refrained in this chapter. He, like his uncle Justin and most of the empire's Latin-speaking subjects, was a convinced Chalcedonian. He took very firm measures against the remaining pagans of Constantinople and sponsored campaigns to proselytise rural pagans in Asia Minor and elsewhere. While relatively cautious in attempting to convert Jews, he enacted anti-Jewish laws that reached the medieval West by way of Gothic Spain, and created a legal basis for the anti-Judaism that would, by the later Middle Ages, feed into the anti-Semitic strain in western societies that persists to this day. Against the Samaritan neighbours of the Jews, Justinian launched a quite merciless persecution, one that sparked a dangerous rebellion before effectively wiping the followers of this ancient religion from the face of the map.

Unsurprisingly, however, it was in theological disputes among Christians that the emperor's interventions were most intense. Montanist heretics in Phrygia were persecuted with such vigour that they committed suicide en masse, but his real target was necessarily the monophysites of the eastern provinces. The rapprochement with Rome at the start of Justin's reign had only been the beginning. Although he and his uncle had left the powerful Timothy of Alexandria alone, fearing the long-standing capacity of Alexandrian bishops to create violent disturbances, Justinian installed a moderate monophysite from Antioch after Timothy's death in 535. This bishop, Theodosius, had been willing to accept a compromise formula that ruled out Nestorianism, and allowed for a monophysite intepretation of Christ's nature, but did not insist on the explicit language about Christ's nature which so exercised extremists like Timothy. So hostile was the monophysite clergy of Egypt that Theodosius could only hold on to his see by force of arms. Justinian kept him there with an imperial garrison at his back until 538, by which point the emperor had given up on compromise with the monophysites and begun an all-out persecution, first in Syria and eventually in Egypt as well.

This did no more than entrench resistance and, in 544, Justinian again sought a path of compromise, accepting some monophysite demands: namely, that several works (by Ibbas of Edessa, Theoderet of Cyrrhus and Theodore of Mopsuestia), accepted at Chalcedon but absolutely inimical to the monophysites as Nestorian, should be condemned. He issued an edict in three chapters condemning them (hence the whole affair is known as the Three Chapters controversy) and eventually called a council in 548 to win the assent of eastern and western clerics. The bishop of Rome was forced to comply, but soon retracted his consent when he realised that western resistance to the imperial edict was insurmountable. A much larger council, called the Second Council of Constantinople and still regarded as an ecumenical ('universal') council by the modern Orthodox churches, ratified the condemnation of the Three Chapters in 553. In the West, this hollow victory meant Justinian had to enforce a new orthodoxy that virtually no Latin bishop would accept. The schism thus provoked lasted well beyond the emperor's own death. In the East, the monophysites were no more persuaded by this attempt at compromise than they had been by Zeno's *Henotikon*, or indeed by any other formula that would not affirm them as completely in the right. A clandestine movement in Syria and Egypt began to consecrate a separate hierarchy of monophysite bishops, ceasing so much as to engage with the Chalcedonians supported by the emperor. This monophysite church of Syria and Egypt would, so it happened, outlast Roman imperial rule in those provinces.

Justinian died in 565. His last decade had, by the standards of the early part of his reign, been peaceful. Diplomacy had kept the peace with Khusrau and the consolidation of the Göktürk empire in the steppes of central Asia provided a check on any major disruptions in Eurasia after the Avars had settled in the Carpathian basin. Much of western Europe had by now gone its own way, disconnected from the Mediterranean core but not yet reconnected by the new Eurasian networks that would arise in the eighth and ninth centuries, under the influence of Frankish imperialism in Europe and the vast Islamic cultural zone of the Abbasid caliphate in Asia and Africa. Justinian's Africa enjoyed a fragile prosperity

– the monumental centres of some cities were restored, inscriptions reappear for a brief time, the grain of Carthage could supplement that of Egypt to supply Constantinople, and the relationship between empire and Moorish kings settled into a stable pattern of trading, raiding and police action.

The Balkan interior was a lost cause, despite all Justinian's new fortifications, while the installation of the Avars provided a respite in Illyricum that proved short-lived: the Avar ability to mobilise Slavic and other subject populations so effectively meant the threat their khagans posed to the seventh-century empire was greater even than Attila's had been. The peace of 'reconquered' Italy was even more deceptive. Twenty years of war, and especially Totila's destruction of city walls, aqueducts and other infrastructure, had devastated the productive capacity of the whole peninsula. Rome itself had ceased to be a city, large parts of its townscape given over to ruin or to market gardens, its population reduced to that of a small town. When the Langobards of king Audoin invaded the north Italian plain in 568, there was very little the imperial troops could do to stop them. What remained of imperial Italy thereafter – in Sicily and the Mezzogiorno, with a chunk of Adriatic territory around Ravenna – proved to be a resource sink for successive imperial regimes. Like all Justinian's ('re-')conquests, Italy had failed utterly to pay for itself.

* * *

It is, of course, possible to accommodate all these events within quite an upbeat narrative about the 'birth of Europe': the Mediterranean culture of the ancient world gradually replaced by the young and dynamic kingdoms of northern Europe that preserved all that was best in antiquity for the modern West's triumphant future. And it is true that the roots of medieval culture, with its cathedrals and its castles, are dimly visible in the courts and churches of the post-Roman Latin kingdoms. But that cheerful picture overlooks the degree to which the years between 550 and 750 most often resemble not the creative transformation of an antique world but a war of all against all. The real brilliance of 'later late antiquity' is to be found in regions that cannot be slotted into a narrative of the 'rise of the West'.

We have drawn a bleak picture of Justinian's reign. Politically, financially and militarily, that is a perfectly reasonable thing to have done. The Roman imperial state left by Justinian was a diminished one, poorer and less efficacious than ever before, if still able to more or less contain the many threats that faced it. But there is another side to that coin, for the reigns of Justinian and his successors saw the undiminished flourishing of a rich literary and artistic culture that they would bequeath not just within the shrunken frontiers of the Byzantine empire but to the great Arabic and Persian empires of the Middle Ages.

This 'late late antique' culture flourished in many places, and not only at Constantinople, where Hagia Sophia still stands as the apex of ancient Christian architecture. Throughout the cities of the eastern provinces, a new piety, whatever its theological flavour, rebuilt the public face of urbanism and provided models for the brilliant domestic architecture of the early Islamic centuries. In Egypt, a Coptic vernacular canon developed side by side with the Greek one, creating a world of high vernacular writing revealed to us by the ever-growing store of papyri. Syriac became a common medium for Christian piety across the Near East, under Persian and Roman rule both.

Between the two empires, Arabic confederations developed into more and more sophisticated polities, responding both to the imperial hegemons that flanked them and to the Jewish and Christian communities of southern Arabia, Yemen and Ethiopia. It was among these Arabs that the last great ancient monotheism arose, following on the Jewish, Christian and Manichaean revelations of earlier centuries. The followers and successors of Muhammad would, in the seventh century, comprehensively transform the political landscape of the ancient world, conquering the Persian empire, bringing all of Constantinople's lands east and south of the Taurus under their control, and rapidly capturing Egypt and the fragile coastal strip that was Byzantine north Africa.

It is too easy to see the rise of Islam as part of an alien story, somehow antithetical to the Perso-Graeco-Roman world with which we have been chiefly concerned. But Islam grew in the cultural ferment of an eastern world that knew many cultures, many faiths, and had only two political models for empire: that of Rome and that of Persia. The Umayyad dynasty that finally stabilised Islamic government after its initial burst of conquest based itself at Damascus in Syria, a town with very ancient roots, Semitic, Persian, Greek and Roman. Like the Greek Roman empire forged by political and military trauma in the seventh century and better known to us as Byzantine – and indeed like the fractious and impoverished kingdoms of the Latin West – the early Islamic state was a product of the latest phase of antiquity. Yet each of these worlds is also recognisably new, their distance from the empires of Constantine and Shapur truly unbridgeable. The cultural and political legacies of ancient empires – several thousand years of ancient empires – remain visible, sometimes clearly and sometimes only dimly, throughout the latter half of the first millennium AD. But they no longer belong to that ancient world and they must await a different book.

ROMAN EMPERORS

FROM CONSTANTINE I TO JUSTINIAN I
(OMITTING CLEAR USURPERS)

Constantine I, r. 306–37
Licinius, r. 308–24
Constantinus (Constantine II), r. 337–40
Constantius II, r. 337–61
Constans, r. 337–50
Julian, r. 361–3
Jovian, r. 363–4

Western Emperors
Valentinian I, r. 364–75
Gratian. r. 367–83
Valentinian II, r. 375–92
Theodosius I, r. 379–95
Honorius, r. 393–423
Constantius III, r. 421
Valentinian III, r. 425–55
Petronius Maximus, r. 455
Avitus, r. 455–6
Majorian, r. 457–61
Libius Severus, r. 461–5
Anthemius, r. 467–72
Olybrius, r. 472
Glycerius, r. 473–4
Julius Nepos, r. 474–80
Romulus, r. 475–6

Eastern Emperors
Valens, r. 364–78
Theodosius I, r. 379–95
Arcadius, r. 383–408
Theodosius II, r. 402–50
Marcian, r. 450–57
Leo I, r. 457–74
Leo II, r. 474
Zeno, r. 474–91
Basiliscus, r. 475–6
Anastasius, r. 491–518
Justin I, r. 518–27
Justinian I, r. 527–65

PERSIAN KINGS

FROM SHAPUR II TO KHUSRAU I

Shapur II, r. 309–79
Adrashir II, r. 379–83
Shapur III, r. 383–8
Varahran IV r. 388–99
Yazdgerd I, r. 399–420
Varahran V, r. 420–38

Yazdgerd II, r. 438–57
Peroz, r. 457–84
Valazh, r. 484–8
Kavad I, r. 488–96; 499–531
Jamasp, r. 496–9
Khusrau I, r. 531–78

FURTHER READING

❧❧❧

Original Literary Sources

Almost the whole canon of Graeco-Roman authors up to the third century is available in the Loeb Classical Library, with facing page English translations, and recent editions have frequently improved those produced in the early twentieth century. The Loeb series serves late antiquity less well, although that is beginning to change. Liverpool University Press' Translated Texts for Historians series fills many of those gaps with excellent annotated translations. Two other series, Fathers of the Church and Ancient Christian Writers, can also be consulted: translations in the latter series are almost uniformly good, while those in the former are more variable. Coins are an essential primary source for Roman imperial history, and the basic reference remains the ten volumes of the Roman Imperial Coinage (London, 1923–94). Alternatively, the research page of the Classical Numismatic Group's website (http://www.cngcoins.com) has colour illustrations of all but the very rarest coin types from antiquity.

Reference

There are two basic reference works that anyone really interested in Roman history should have to hand: the third and best edition of *The Oxford Classical Dictionary* (Oxford, 1996) and *The Barrington Atlas of the Greek and Roman World* (Princeton, NJ, 2000), edited by Richard Talbert and breathtaking in its coverage, its detail and the beauty of its maps.

General Histories

Few introductory textbooks cover this period, and fewer do so well. J. B. Bury's long-standard *History of the Later Roman Empire from the Death of Theodosius* (London,

1923) can no longer disguise its age. Stephen Mitchell's *A History of the Later Roman Empire, AD 284–641* (London, 2006) is comprehensive but lacks a strong narrative. Hugh Elton's, *The Roman Empire in Late Antiquity: A Political and Military History* (Cambridge, 2018) is a much more compelling read. Mitchell and Elton, like the present author, remain in debt to the foundational work of A. H. M. Jones' *The Later Roman Empire, 284–602*, 4 vols. (Oxford, 1964) and its analogues in other languages, especially Ernst Stein's *Histoire du Bas-Empire* (Paris, 1949). Scott Johnson, ed., *The Oxford Handbook of Late Antiquity* (Oxford, 2012) is less uneven than most multi-author handbooks. W. V. Harris' *Roman Power: A Thousand Years of Empire* (Cambridge, 2016) is a brilliantly polemical attempt to assess the scale and nature of Roman power at three different stages of development: the late Republic; the Constantinian empire; and the seventh century. An inspired approach.

There are countless books on the fall of the western Roman empire, and more appear annually, with variable scholarly trappings but nearly all quite conventional. Still, ripping yarns and neo-Victorian analyses can be found in any bookshop. So, for those so inclined, can thinly disguised nativist tracts on how immigration (and 'immigrant violence') brought down the empire. To name names would be invidious.

That said, the western empire really did collapse in the fifth century, as the eastern would in the seventh, and the present volume covers the 'fall of Rome' not the 'transformation of the ancient world'. I would, however, argue that the unpleasant, violent and irremediable fact of imperial collapse needs to be explained by more than just good guys losing to bad guys. Three recent treatments, which favour the complex over the simplistic and from which I have learned the most, are: Guy Halsall, *Barbarian Migrations and the Roman West, 376–568* (Cambridge, 2007); Henning Börm, *Westrom von Honorius bis Justinian* (Stuttgart, 2013); and Christine Delaplace, *La fin de l'Empire romain de Occident* (Rennes, 2015). All are heartily recommended. The impact of climate change and epidemics is a fairly new horizon for historical studies, at present suggestive and often persuasive, but not yet probative. That said, everyone should read Kyle Harper, *The Fate of Rome* (Princeton, NJ, 2017).

On many topics covered by this book – religion, imperial administration, the military – the best studies span the whole period. Anyone who wishes to really understand the ideology of emperorship, and the way it was presented and consumed, should consult the German language works of Andreas Alföldi and Johannes Straub listed in the bibliography (and also perhaps contemplate the fact that the best, most insightful work on late Roman government mentalities was produced by men of the right, in Straub's case the far right). More accessible to most readers, Christopher Kelly's *Ruling the Later Roman Empire* (Cambridge, MA, 2004) ranges widely and provocatively from the fourth century to the sixth century.

For the integration of Christianity into Roman life, the best introduction is Gillian Clark, *Christianity and Roman Society* (Cambridge, 2004). Though traditionally patristic in its approach to the early church, Henry Chadwick's *The Church in*

Ancient Society from Galilee to Gregory the Great (Oxford, 2002) is the comprehensive summation of a lifetime's deep study. Since then, Brent D. Shaw's *Sacred Violence* (Cambridge, 2011) has revolutionised our understanding of religious thuggery, while the recently collected essays of G. E. M. de Ste Croix on *Christian Persecution, Martyrdom and Orthodoxy* (Oxford, 2006) reveal their author to have been ahead of his time.

Gunnar Mickwitz's *Geld und Wirtschaft im römischen Reich des vierten Jahrhunderts n. Chr.* (Helsinki, 1932) inferred what has now been proved – the existence of a new source of gold available to the eastern but not the western empire beginning in the fourth century. More recently, economic change has been provocatively discussed in a very difficult book by Jairus Banaji, *Agrarian Change in Late Antiquity*, revised edn (Oxford, 2007), which can be paired with the prescient *The Class Struggle in the Ancient Greek World from the Archaic Age to the Arab Conquests* (Ithaca, NY, 1983) by the aforementioned de Ste Croix. Banaji's essays, collected in *Exploring the Economy of Late Antiquity* (Cambridge, 2016), are also essential. Chris Wickham's *Framing the Early Middle Ages* (Oxford, 2005) is equally good on the documentary and the archaeological evidence and shows how the imperial *annona*, especially its African 'tax spine', was the engine without which the ancient economy eventually failed and gave way to the small worlds of the Middle Ages. Exhaustive when it appeared, Wickham's conclusions are not contradicted by more recent archaeological evidence discoveries.

On the late Roman army, there is a dull but worthy introduction in Martijn Nicasie, *Twilight of Empire* (Amsterdam, 1998), though the relevant chapter in A. H. M. Jones' *The Later Roman Empire* (see introduction, above) is still essentially unsurpassed. Hugh Elton's evocative *Warfare in Roman Europe, AD 350–425* (Oxford, 1996) is relevant for a much longer period than its title suggests, while A. D. Lee's *Information and Frontiers* (Cambridge, 1993) covers the intersection of military activity and foreign policy with great care. The title of John Matthews' *Western Aristocracies and Imperial Court, AD 364–425* (Oxford, 1975) belies the richness of its contents, which inspire new reflections on each re-reading.

As with those of Ronald Syme, Arnaldo Momigliano and Louis Robert in an earlier generation, the works of Glen W. Bowersock, Peter Brown and Sabine MacCormack are so many and so varied – and have had such a profound impact on how we understand late antiquity – that one could fill an entire essay with recommendations. Start anywhere that strikes your fancy, but then read the entire *oeuvres*.

Primary and Secondary Reading by Period

From Constantine to the Death of Theodosius I

The primary source evidence for the reigns of Constantine and his sons is scrappy. The last great Latin historian of antiquity, Ammianus Marcellinus, only picks up in

353 – the first thirteen (or perhaps eighteen) books of his *Res Gestae* are lost. The Loeb translation of Ammianus is neither readable nor particularly reliable, while the good Penguin translation can mislead through abridgements. My colleague Gavin Kelly (author of the best study of Ammianus as author, *Ammianus Marcellinus: The Allusive Historian* (Cambridge, 2008)) and I are currently at work on a new and fully annotated translation of the complete text, to be published by Oxford University Press as *The Landmark Ammianus Marcellinus*. For those wanting to know more about Ammianus, his life and his milieu, three English language studies are essential: E. A. Thompson, *The Historical Work of Ammianus Marcellinus* (Cambridge, 1947); John Matthews, *The Roman Empire of Ammianus* (Baltimore, MD, 1989); and T. D. Barnes, *Ammianus Marcellinus and the Representation of Historical Reality* (Ithaca, NY, 1998). And though they will be too much for the non-specialist, the 18-volume *Philological and Historical Commentary on Ammianus Marcellinus* (Leiden and Boston, 1934–2018) begun before the Second World War by P. de Jonge, has just been brought to a magnificent conclusion by J. den Boeft, J. W. Drijvers, D. den Hengst and H. C. Teitler. It is impossible to overstate the value of what this 'quadriga Batavorum' has done for our understanding of the fourth century.

In the absence of Ammianus, fourth-century abbreviated histories fill some gaps in our knowledge (the *Breviarium* of Eutropius and the *Caesares* of Aurelius Victor are translated in the Liverpool series). A handful of twelfth- and thirteenth-century Byzantine histories have recently been shown to preserve some good information on the third and fourth centuries, probably transmitted ultimately from a fourth-century Greek historian now lost. The relevant parts of one such Byzantine history are translated in Thomas M. Banchich and Eugene Lane, *The History of Zonaras* (London, 2009). The sixth-century Greek author Zosimus, who depends heavily on the fourth-century Eunapius, is translated by Ronald T. Ridley in *Zosimus: New History* (Canberra, 1982), while the fragments of Eunapius and three of his fifth-century successors are translated by R. C. Blockley in *The Fragmentary Classicising Historians of the Later Roman Empire II: Text, Translation and Historiographical Notes* (Liverpool, 1983). The chronicle of Theophanes, translated by Cyril Mango and Roger Scott with a fine commentary, preserves a few fourth-century details not found elsewhere. The deeply tendentious life of Constantine by Eusebius of Caesarea is expertly annotated in Averil Cameron and Stuart G. Hall, eds., *Eusebius: Life of Constantine* (Oxford, 1999), while shifting ancient views of Constantine can be traced in Samuel N. C. Lieu and Dominic Montserrat, eds., *From Constantine to Julian* (London, 1996). Laws are among the most important witnesses we have to the fourth century and most of them are transmitted by the Theodosian Code, the translation of which by Clyde Pharr (Princeton, NJ, 1952) is solid.

The vast bibliography on Constantine grows annually in every language. Paul Stephenson, *Constantine: Unconquered Emperor, Christian Victor* (London, 2009) is a rare biographical treatment worth reading. T. D. Barnes, *Constantine and Eusebius* (Cambridge, MA, 1980) was groundbreaking, and is now complemented but not superseded by his aggressively polemical *Constantine: Dynasty, Religion and Power in the Later Roman Empire* (Maldon, MA, 2011). Noel Lenski, ed., *The Cambridge Companion to the Age of Constantine* (Cambridge, 2005) includes a number of significant essays and is perhaps the best introduction to the period. Constantius' reign is rarely treated on its own, but see T. D. Barnes, *Athanasius and Constantius* (Cambridge, MA, 1993). By contrast, shelves groan under the weight of books on Julian. The emperor's intellectual world is well captured by Polymnia Athanassiadi-Fowden, *Julian and Hellenism* (Oxford, 1981) and his life by G. W. Bowersock, *Julian the Apostate* (Cambridge, MA, 1978). J. E. Lendon's *Soldiers & Ghosts* (New Haven, CT, 1985) has some shrewd observations on Julian's military motivation, while Shaun Tougher's *Julian the Apostate* (Edinburgh, 2007) is a useful assemblage of sources and comment. Matthews' *The Roman Empire of Ammianus* (above) is essential for the reigns of Julian, Valentinian I and Valens. Noel Lenski's *Failure of Empire* (Berkeley, CA, 2002) is an important treatment of Valens, though perhaps rather too positive about the emperor. There is no good study of Valentinian I in English, nor of Theodosius I – the general histories noted above should be preferred.

For the fourth-century empire, Matthews' *Ammianus* has an excellent chapter on the confusing world of Roman Africa. My own *Late Roman Spain and Its Cities* (Baltimore, MD, 2004) covers the Iberian peninsula. Damián Fernández's *Aristocrats and Statehood in Western Iberia, 200–600 CE* (Berkeley, CA, 2017) adds new insights. On Britain, David Mattingly, *An Imperial Possession* (London, 2008) is highly readable; more technical, though essential, is Anthony R. Birley, *The Roman Government of Britain* (Oxford, 2005). Up-to-date studies of Gaul and the Balkans are lacking for this period, while good treatments of the Roman East (e.g. Warwick Ball, *Rome in the East: The Transformation of an Empire* (London, 2000)) peter out in late antiquity. The best treatment by far of fourth-century European barbarians is John F. Drinkwater's *The Alamanni and Rome, 213–496* (Oxford, 2007), well complemented by Elton's *Warfare in Roman Europe* (above). On Persia, one should consult Matthew P. Canepa, *The Two Eyes of the Earth* (Berkeley, CA, 2009) and Richard Payne, *A State of Mixture* (Berkeley, CA, 2015), two of the most sophisticated treatments of the Sasanians ever written in any language. D. T. Potts, *Nomadism in Iran from Antiquity to the Modern Era* (Oxford, 2014) is a groundbreaking study, with much of value on our period. Finally, R. Malcolm Errington, *Roman Imperial Policy from Julian to Theodosius* (Chapel Hill, NC, 2006) is hard-going at times but worth the effort.

There is a superabundance of books on fourth-century Christianity, not least studies of individual churchmen. Among the best of these latter are: Peter Brown's *Augustine of Hippo* (London, 1967); Clare Stancliffe, *St Martin and His Hagiographer* (Oxford, 1983); Neil McLynn, *Ambrose of Milan* (Berkeley, CA, 1994); and Philip Rousseau, *Basil of Caesarea* (Berkeley, CA, 1994). For Antioch, the site of much Christian controversy in a highly contentious civic environment, see: J. H. W. G. Liebeschuetz, *Antioch* (Oxford, 1972); Isabella Sandwell, *Religious Identity in Late Antiquity* (Cambridge,

2007); and Christine Shepardson, *Controlling Contested Places* (Berkeley, CA, 2014). The differently problematical history of Alexandria is best approached through Edward J. Watts, *City and School in Late Antique Athens and Alexandria* (Berkeley, CA, 2006). Alan Cameron's magnum opus, *The Last Pagans of Rome* (Oxford, 2010), demolishes decades of tendentious – at times fantasist – writing on paganism in the Roman West. Long, and at times highly technical, it is one of the greatest books ever written on late antiquity.

The Fifth Century

The primary sources for the fifth century are very unevenly distributed, with short bursts of intense documentation and long stretches of near silence. Zosimus (see above) ends in 410, but is a valuable witness for the first decade of the century. The extant fragments of Olympiodorus, Priscus and Malchus are collected in Blockley's *Fragmentary Classicising Historians* (above). The only English translations of the three key church historians, Socrates, Sozomen and Theoderet, are extremely antiquated. There are, however, excellent translations of Evagrius Scholasticus' church history, and the tendentious *History against the Pagans* by Augustine groupie Orosius (both in the Liverpool Translated Texts). The brief but informative chronicle of Marcellinus *comes* is translated by Brian Croke (Canberra, 1995), while Sergei Mariev's edition of the fragments of John of Antioch (Berlin, 2008) includes an English translation. Two pseudonymous texts that are essential for eastern history in this period are Pseudo-Zachariah Rhetor and Pseudo-Joshua the Stylite, both translated in the Liverpool series. So, too, are the voluminous Acts of the Council of Chalcedon. For the sculpture and decorative arts that shed so much light on the aristocrats of Rome in the fifth and sixth centuries, see R. R. R. Smith and Bryan Ward-Perkins, eds., *The Last Statues of Antiquity* (Oxford, 2016) and Richard Delbrueck's classic *Die Consulardiptychen* (Berlin, 1929), with its lifesize photos of the diptychs.

Biographies of fifth-century emperors should be treated with suspicion. We know too little about their lives for the genre to be tenable. That said, F. K. Haarer's *Anastasius I: Politics and Empire in the Late Roman World* (Liverpool, 2006) is a fine study of the reign, while at the opposite end of the century, Alan Cameron and Jacqueline Long's *Barbarians and Politics at the Court of Arcadius* (Berkeley, CA, 1993) goes some distance towards clarifying the murky politics of Constantinople around the year 400. It follows in the footsteps of Cameron's pioneering *Claudian: Poetry and Propaganda at the Court of Honorius* (Oxford, 1970), which successfully extracted meaningful historical data from Claudian's recherché verse. Kenneth G. Holum's *Theodosian Empresses* (Berkeley, CA, 1982) is deeply insightful despite occasional inaccuracies, and preferable to several full-length studies of Galla Placidia; I owe my own reading of that remarkable augusta to conversation with Chris Lawrence about his as yet unpublished research. There are no English language equivalents to the fine German studies of Constantius III and Aëtius by Werner Lütkenhaus and Timo Stickler, respectively (see bibliography). With the exception of Fergus Millar's *A Greek Roman Empire* (Berkeley, CA, 2006), the reign of Theodosius II is rarely taken as a subject in its own right, but the Theodosian Code most certainly is: the essential work in English is, and will long remain, John F. Matthews' *Laying Down the Law* (New Haven, CT, 2000), though see also the essays in Jill Harries and Ian Wood's *The Theodosian Code*, 2nd edn (Bristol, 2010) and Tony Honoré's controversial *Law in the Crisis of Empire* (Oxford, 1998). Christopher Kelly, ed., *Theodosius II* (Cambridge, 2013) is uneven but has several excellent essays.

On the western empire, one should consult the general histories noted at the beginning of these pages. Treatments centred on one or another of the barbarian kingdoms (or 'kingdoms') are in constant danger of slipping into teleology. Ian Wood's *Merovingian Kingdoms* (London, 1993) escapes that trap. There is nothing as good in English for the Goths or Vandals, but Roland Steinacher's *Die Vandalen* (Stuttgart, 2016) cries out for translation and will long remain the standard account. Yves Modéran's *Les Maures et l'Afrique romaine* (Rome, 2003) is a brilliant monument to the best traditions of Francophone scholarship. For the end of Roman Britain, see the last chapter of Birley's *The Roman Government of Britain* (above) and for Gaul the unusually coherent multi-author collection edited by John Drinkwater and Hugh Elton, *Fifth-century Gaul: A Crisis of Identity?* (Cambridge, 1992). Though framed through the biography of Sidonius Apollinaris, Jill Harries' *Sidonius Apollinaris and the Fall of Rome* (Oxford, 1994) is actually a subtle reading of fifth-century western history.

Too much has been written about Alaric and the sack of Rome. My own views, much abbreviated in the present volume, can be found in *Rome's Gothic Wars* (Cambridge, 2006). Johannes Lipps, et al., *The Sack of Rome in 410 AD* (Rome, 2014) has the latest research, though much of it is not in English, and, for those who can read it, Mischa Meier and Stefan Patzold's *August 410 – Ein Kampf um Rom* (Stuttgart, 2010) is a model historiographic essay.

As with the sack of Rome, there is far too much out there on Attila and the Huns, and most of it is rubbish. One can still do a lot worse than E. A. Thompson's *A History of Attila and the Huns* (Oxford, 1948). The rest of the vast bibliography is surveyed in Hyun Jin Kim, *The Huns, Rome and the Birth of Europe* (Cambridge, 2013), worth reading if only to see just how far ostensibly sober scholarship can veer into fantasy. For the wider Eurasian context, Nicola di Cosmo and Michael Maas, eds., *Empires and Exchanges in Eurasian Late Antiquity* (Cambridge, 2018) breaks entirely new ground and, unusually, gives equal weight to the Chinese and the western perspectives on the steppe world. For China in our period, see Mark Edward Lewis, *China between Empires: The Northern and Southern Dynasties* (Cambridge, MA, 2009). An essential work of reference is Hermann Parzinger, *Die frühen Völker Eurasiens vom Neolithikum bis zum Mittelalter*, 2nd edn (Munich, 2011). The primarily numismatic works of Alram, Bopearachchi and Göbl (see bibliography) are all extremely important.

The fifth and sixth centuries are when the linguistic map of Europe began to take on the shape it has to this day. For developments in Greek, see the exhaustive collective volume, A. F. Christidis, ed., *A History of Ancient Greek from the Beginnings to Late Antiquity* (Cambridge, 2007); for Latin, see James Clackson and Geoffrey Horrocks, eds., *The Blackwell History of the Latin Language* (Oxford, 2007) and J. N. Adams, *The Regional Diversification of Latin* (Cambridge, 2007). Roger Wright's *Late Latin and Early Romance in Spain and Carolingian France* (Liverpool, 1982) has not convinced everyone, but seems to me more right than not in most of its conclusions. Finally, for a methodologically risky, philological approach to historical change, see D. H. Green, *Language and History in the Early Germanic World* (Cambridge, 1998).

The Sixth Century

The reign of Justinian is lavishly documented by comparison with earlier periods. All of Procopius is available in the Loeb series, and the Loeb translation of *The Wars of Justinian* has been updated and corrected by Anthony Kaldellis in an inexpensive paperback (Cambridge, MA, 2014). Agathias, who continues where Procopius leaves off, is available in a scarce translation by Joseph D. Frendo (Berlin, 1975), while Agathias' successor Menander can be found in R. C. Blockley's *The History of Menander the Guardsman* (Liverpool, 1985). Evagrius, Pseudo-Zachariah Rhetor, Pseudo-Joshua the Stylite, John of Antioch and Theophanes (see above) continue to be important. Several contemporary pamphlets are collected in Peter N. Bell's *Three Political Voices from the Age of Justinian* (Liverpool, 2009), while Sebastian Brock and Brian Fitzgerald translate *Two Early Lives of Severos, Patriarch of Antioch* (Liverpool, 2013). Finally, the great Justinianic legal codification, the *Digest*, is available in a 4-volume translation overseen by Alan Watson, the *Code* in a 3-volume set overseen by Bruce Frier, and the *Novels* in a 2-volume set by David Miller and Peter Sarris.

Works on Justinian and Theodora are legion. More than one cares to name are just Procopius rewritten in the modern style. Two very good orientations are John Moorhead, *Justinian* (London, 1994) and J. A. S. Evans, *The Age of Justinian* (London, 1996). Michael Maas, ed., *The Cambridge Companion to the Age of Justinian* (Cambridge, 2005) has a few weak contributions, but is generally very reliable. Geoffrey Greatrex, *Rome and Persia at War, 502–532* (Leeds, 1998) is a comprehensive treatment of a subject usually ignored in favour of the African and Italian campaigns, while Alexander Sarantis, *Justinian's Balkan Wars* (Liverpool, 2016) performs a similar feat in the Balkans. On the economics of the reign, Peter Sarris, *Economy and Society in the Age of Justinian* (Cambridge, 2006) is a useful supplement to the works of Banaji, noted above. Two very different treatments of Procopius are Averil Cameron, *Procopius and the Sixth Century* (Berkley, CA, 1985) and Anthony Kaldellis, *Procopius: Tyranny, History and Philosophy at the End of Antiquity* (Philadelphia, PA, 2004). The

Ostrogothic kingdom has seen a flurry of excellent recent work, which can be surveyed in J. Arnold, M. Shane Bjornlie and K. Sessa, eds., *A Companion to Ostrogothic Italy* (Leiden, 2016), as well as in M. Shane Bjornlie's *Politics and Tradition between Rome, Ravenna and Constantinople* (Cambridge, 2013) and Kristina Sessa's *The Formation of Papal Authority in Late Antique Italy* (Cambridge, 2012). Massimiliano Vitiello has produced excellent, fine-grained studies of both Amalasuintha (Philadelphia, PA, 2017) and Theodahad (Toronto, 2014), though they are probably too dense for the casual reader. These books join the seminal work of John Moorhead, *Theodoric in Italy* (Oxford, 1992), which remains particularly good on the ideology of the new kingdom. For the reign's most famous casualty, Henry Chadwick's *Boethius* (Oxford, 1980) has not been improved upon.

Into the Middle Ages

The barbarian kingdoms are the subject of many, many books, not least because of the part they have played in the foundation myths of European nations. Much European, and some Anglophone, scholarship on the early Middle Ages has centred on texts, identities and ethnicity for the better part of the past three decades. For a taste of this dominant strand in recent scholarship, consult the bibliography for the many volumes edited or co-edited by Walter Pohl, in particular *Strategies of Distinction* (Leiden, 1998) and *Kingdoms of the Empire* (Leiden, 1997), *Die Suche nach den Ursprüngen* (Vienna, 2004) and *Post-Roman Transitions* (Turnhout, 2013) – many contributions are in English, regardless of the book's title. From a very different perspective, Magali Coumert's *Origines des peuples* (Paris, 2007) is illuminating. Guy Halsall has written some of the most penetrating and historiographically informed recent work on the early Middle Ages. His *Warfare and Society in the Barbarian West, 450–900* (London, 2003) comprehensively shatters the illusion, cultivated by a number of prolific medievalists, that the barbarian kingdoms could function in the same fashion as the Roman empire once had; the essays collected in his *Cemeteries and Society in Merovingian Gaul* (Leiden, 2009) possess a similarly salutary iconoclasm. The modern history that has made this period so significant is explored in Bonnie Effros' *Merovingian Mortuary Archaeology and the Making of the Early Middle Ages* (Berkeley, CA, 2003) and *Uncovering the Germanic Past* (Oxford, 2012).

Spain and Africa are sideshows in these debates, which focus on the future Francia. My *Late Roman Spain* (above) carries the provincial narrative – such as it is – into the late sixth century. Roger Collins' *Early Medieval Spain* is better consulted in its original edition (London, 1983) than a later revision. Steinacher's *Die Vandalen* remains the key treatment of Africa.

Britain, thanks to the King Arthur industry (and, of course, the absence of a language barrier), bulks disproportionately large among early medieval histories. There is, frankly, more historical value in the Arthurian novels of Mary Stewart than there is in much of the purportedly academic scholarship. John Morris' *The Age of Arthur* (London, 1973), which remains a beguiling exercise in making sources say things that they don't, has inspired many scholars (and many more cranks). For a modern attempt to take the legends seriously, consult Christopher Gidlow, *The Reign of Arthur* (Stroud, 2004). For one that takes history seriously, see Guy Halsall, *Worlds of Arthur* (Oxford, 2013).

Early medieval Ireland elicits nearly as much crankery as King Arthur. Dáibhí Ó Cróinín's *Early Medieval Ireland, 400–1200* (London, 1995) is the least injudicious account. For the Low Countries and the North Sea coasts, as for Scandinavia and the Baltic world, there is no up-to-date synthesis to replace Lotte Hedeager's *Iron-Age Societies* (Oxford, 1992). Were Svante Fischer's *Roman Imperialism and Runic Literacy* (Uppsala, 2005) not so resolutely speculative, it would fill part of that gap, but it remains worth reading all the same.

Moving eastwards, English language work on the Slavic and Balkan worlds is dominated by the writings of Florin Curta. Much of it is quite technical, but see his more accessible survey, *Southeastern Europe in the Middle Ages, 500–1250* (Cambridge, 2006). For the transition from antiquity to the Middle Ages in the eastern Roman empire, see Mark Whittow's *The Making of Orthodox Byzantium, 600–1025* (London, 1996) and John Haldon's *The Empire That Would Not Die* (Cambridge, MA, 2016). The rump state of Byzantine Italy is brought to life in T. S. Brown, *Gentlemen and Officers* (Rome, 1984).

On religion and the church, the scintillating tableau of Judith Herrin's *The Formation of Christendom* (Princeton, NJ, 1987) belies its uninspiring title. The same can also be said of Robert Markus' *The End of Ancient Christianity* (Cambridge, 1990) and *Gregory the Great and His World* (Cambridge, 1997).

For the history of early Islam, Hugh Kennedy's *The Prophet and the Age of the Caliphates* (London, 1986) remains a safe option, while Aziz Al-Azmeh's *The Emergence of Islam in Late Antiquity* (Cambridge, 2014) shows how far the scholarly conversation has progressed. The many works of Patricia Crone and Michael Cook, writing both together and separately, can be read with profit by any historian regardless of field, even when too technical for the non-specialist to follow. The breathtaking iconoclasm of their – admittedly difficult – *Hagarism* (Cambridge, 1977) remains inspirational, even if both authors moderated their views considerably in later work. Less radical, but equally inspired, are Garth Fowden's *Empire to Commonwealth: Consequences of Monotheism in Late Antiquity* (Princeton, NJ, 1993) and *Before and after Muhammad* (Princeton, NJ, 2013). Finally, G. W. Bowersock's engrossing *The Throne of Adulis* (Oxford, 2013) takes readers into a world few will have known existed, and make them want to know much, much more.

BIBLIOGRAPHY

⬥⬥⬥⬥⬥

The works below are the secondary literature (in book form – journal articles would treble the already excessive length) of which I made most use while writing. The relevant primary sources are discussed in further reading with suggested translations; scholars will already know which critical editions are best consulted, and *The Oxford Classical Dictionary* or *The Oxford Dictionary of Byzantium* should point the way on more obscure texts. As I wrote the book, in stages and over several years, a lifetime's reading will have been brought to bear. I apologise to anyone whose ideas I have absorbed and used without being conscious of it, anyone whose work I have inadvertently omitted, and particularly those scholars whose work has influenced me deeply, but is acknowledged only here, rather than in further reading, because written in a language other than English.

Adams, J. N. *The Regional Diversification of Latin, 200 BC–AD 600*. Cambridge, 2007.

Agusta-Boularot, Sandrine, Joëlle Beaucamp, et al., eds. *Recherches sur la chronique de Jean Malalas II*. Paris, 2006.

Al-Azmeh, Aziz. *The Emergence of Islam in Late Antiquity: Allah and His People*. Cambridge, 2014.

Albert, Gerhard. *Goten in Konstantinopel. Untersuchungen zur oströmischen Geschichte um das Jahr 400 n. Chr*. Paderborn, 1984.

Alföldi, Andreas. *Der Untergang der Römerherrschaft in Pannonien*. 2 vols. Berlin, 1924–6.

Alföldi, Andrew. *A Conflict of Ideas in the Late Roman Empire*. H. Mattingly, trans. Oxford, 1952.

Alföldi, Andreas. *Die monarchische Repräsentation im römischen Kaiserreiche*. E. Alföldi-Rosenbaum, ed. Darmstadt, 1970.

Alföldy, Géza. *Noricum*. London, 1974.

Allen, Pauline and Elizabeth M. Jeffreys, eds. *The Sixth Century: End or Beginning?* Canberra, 1996.

Alram, Michael. *Das Antlitz des Fremden: Die Münzprägung der Hunnen und Westtürken in Zentralasien und Indien.* Vienna, 2016.

Alram, Michael and Deborah E. Klimburg-Salter, eds. *Coins, Art and Chronology: Essays on the Pre-Islamic History of the Indo-Iranian Borderlands.* Vienna, 1999.

Alram, Michael, Deborah E. Klimburg-Salter, Minoru Inaba and Matthias Pfisterer, eds. *Coins, Art and Chronology II: The First Millennium* CE *in the Indo-Iranian Borderlands.* Vienna, 2010.

Amitai, Reuven and Michal Biran, eds. *Nomads as Agents of Cultural Change: The Mongols and Their Eurasian Predecessors.* Honolulu, HI, 2015.

Amory, Patrick. *People and Identity in Ostrogothic Italy, 489–554.* Cambridge, 1997.

Ando, Clifford and Seth Richardson, eds. *Ancient States and Infrastructural Power: Europe, Asia, America.* Philadelphia, PA, 2017.

Antela-Bernárdez, Borja and Jordi Vidal, eds. *Central Asia in Antiquity: Interdisciplinary Perspectives,* British Archaeological Reports International Series 2665. Oxford, 2014.

Arce, Javier. *Scripta varia. Estudios de Historia y Arqueología sobre la Antigüedad Tardía.* Madrid, 2018.

Arnheim, M. T. W. *The Senatorial Aristocracy in the Later Roman Empire.* Oxford, 1972.

Arnold, Jonathan J., M. Shane Bjornlie and Kristina Sessa, eds. *A Companion to Ostrogothic Italy.* Leiden, 2016.

Athanassiadi-Fowden, Polymnia. *Julian and Hellenism: An Intellectual Biography.* Oxford, 1981.

Athanassiadi, Polymnia and Michael Frede, eds. *Pagan Monotheism in Late Antiquity.* Oxford, 1999.

Ausenda, Giorgio, ed. *After Empire: Towards an Ethnology of Europe's Barbarians.* Woodbridge, 1995.

Austin, N. J. E. *Ammianus on Warfare. An Investigation into Ammianus' Military Knowledge.* Brussels, 1979.

Austin, N. J. E. and N. B. Rankov. *Exploratio: Military and Political Intelligence in the Roman World from the Second Punic War to the Battle of Adrianople.* London, 1995.

Axboe, Morten. *Die Goldbrakteaten der Völkerwanderungszeit.* Ergänzungsbande zum Reallexikon der Germanischen Altertumskunde 38. Berlin, 2004.

Babut, E.-Ch. *Priscillien et le Priscillianisme.* Paris, 1909.

Bagnall, Roger S. *Egypt in Late Antiquity.* Princeton, NJ, 1993.

Bagnall, Roger S., ed. *Egypt in the Byzantine World, 200–700.* Cambridge, 2007.

Bagnall, Roger S., Alan Cameron, Seth R. Schwartz and K. A. Worp. *Consuls of the Later Roman Empire.* APA Philological Monographs. Atlanta, GA, 1987.

Balmelle, Catherine. *Les demeures aristocratiques d'Aquitaine.* Supplément Aquitania 10. Bordeaux, 2001.

Banaji, Jairus. *Agrarian Change in Late Antiquity*, revised edn. Oxford, 2007.

Banaji, Jairus. *Exploring the Economy of Late Antiquity: Selected Essays*. Cambridge, 2016.

Banchich, Thomas M. *The Lost History of Peter the Patrician: An Account of Rome's Imperial Past from the Age of Justinian*. London, 2015.

Banchich, Thomas M. and Eugene N. Lane. *The History of Zonaras: From Alexander Severus to the Death of Theodosius the Great*. London, 2009.

Barceló, Pedro A. *Roms auswärtige Beziehungen unter den Constantinischen Dynastie (306–363)*. Regensburg, 1981.

Barnes, T. D. *Constantine and Eusebius*. Cambridge, MA, 1980.

Barnes, T. D. *The New Empire of Diocletian and Constantine*. Cambridge, MA, 1982.

Barnes, T. D. *Athanasius and Constantius*. Cambridge, MA, 1993.

Barnes, T. D. *From Eusebius to Augustine: Selected Papers, 1982–1993*. Aldershot, 1994.

Barnes, T. D. *Ammianus Marcellinus and the Representation of Historical Reality*. Ithaca, NY, 1998.

Barnes, T. D. *Constantine: Dynasty, Religion and Power in the Later Roman Empire*. Maldon, MA, 2011.

Barrow, R. H. *Prefect and Emperor: The Relationes of Symmachus, AD 384*. Oxford, 1972.

Barthold, W. *Turkestan down to the Mongol Invasion*. H. A. R. Gibb, ed. 2nd edn. London, 1958.

Bastien, Pierre. *Le monnayage de Magnence (350–353)*. 2nd edn. Wetteren, 1983.

Bastien, Pierre. *Le buste monétaire des empereurs romains*. 3 vols. Wetteren, 1992–4.

Batty, Roger. *Rome and the Nomads: The Pontic-Danubian Realm in Antiquity*. Oxford, 2007.

Baumgart, Susanne. *Die Bischofsherrschaft im Gallien des 5. Jahrhunderts*. Munich, 1995.

Beaucamp, Joëlle, ed. *Recherches sur la chronique de Jean Malalas*. Paris, 2004.

Becker, Audrey. *Les relations diplomatiques romano-barbares en Occident au Ve siècle: Acteurs, fonctions, modalités*. Paris, 2013.

Becker, Audrey and Nicolas Drocourt, eds. *Ambassadeurs et ambassades au coeur des relations diplomatique. Rome–Occident Médiéval–Byzance (VIII-e avant J.-C.–XII-e après J.-C.)*. Centre de Recherche Universitaire Lorrain d'Histoire; Université de Lorraine – Site de Metz 47. Metz, 2012.

Behrwald, Ralf and Christian Witschel, eds. *Rom in der Spätantike: Historische Erinnerung im städtischen Raum*. Habes 51. Stuttgart, 2012.

Bell, H. I., et al., eds. *The Abinnaeus Archive: Papers of a Roman Officer in the Reign of Constantius II*. Oxford, 1962.

Bell, Peter N. *Three Political Voices from the Age of Justinian*. Translated Texts for Historians 52. Liverpool, 2009.

Bell-Fialkoff, Andrew, ed. *The Role of Migration in the History of the Eurasian Steppe: Sedentary Civilization vs. 'Barbarian' and Nomad*. London, 2000.

Bemmann, Jan and Michael Schmauder, eds. *Complexity of Interaction along the Eurasian Steppe Zone in the First Millennium CE*. Bonn Contributions to Asian Archaeology 7. Bonn, 2015.

Ben-Eliyahu, Eyal, Yehudah Cohn and Fergus Millar. *Handbook of Jewish Literature from Late Antiquity, 135–700 CE*. Oxford, 2012.

Berndt, Guido M. and Roland Steinacher, eds. *Das Reich der Vandalen und seine (Vor-) Geschichten*. Forschungen zur Geschichte des Mittelalters 13. Vienna, 2008.

Bidez, J. *La vie de l'empereur Julien*. Paris, 1930.

Birley, Anthony R. *The Roman Government of Britain*. Oxford, 2005.

Bjornlie, M. Shane. *Politics and Tradition between Rome, Ravenna and Constantinople*. Cambridge, 2013.

Bland, Roger and Xavier Loriot. *Roman and Early Byzantine Gold Coins Found in Britain and Ireland with an Appendix of New Finds from Gaul*. Royal Numismatic Society Special Publication 46. London, 2010.

Blockley, R. C. *The Fragmentary Classicising Historians of the Later Roman Empire I: Eunapius, Olympiodorus, Priscus and Malchus*. Liverpool, 1981.

Blockley, R. C. *The Fragmentary Classicising Historians of the Later Roman Empire II: Text, Translation and Historiographical Notes*. Liverpool, 1983.

Blockley, R. C. *The History of Menander the Guardsman: Introductory Essay, Text, Translation and Historiographical Notes*. Liverpool, 1985.

Blockley, R. C. *East Roman Foreign Policy: Formation and Conduct from Diocletian to Anastasius*. Liverpool, 1992.

Bolle, Katharina, Carlos Machado and Christian Witschel, eds. *The Epigraphic Cultures of Late Antiquity*. Heidelberger Althistorische Beiträge und Epigraphische Studien 60. Stuttgart, 2017.

Bóna, István. *Das Hunnenreich*. Stuttgart, 1991.

Bonamente, Giorgio, Noel Lenski and Rita Lizzi Testa, eds. *Costantino prima e dopo Costantino*. Bari, 2012.

Bopearachchi, Osmund. *Indo-Greek, Indo-Scythian and Indo-Parthian Coins in the Smithsonian Institution*. Washington DC, 1993.

Börm, Henning. *Westrom von Honorius bis Justinian*. Stuttgart, 2013.

Bourgeois, Luc, ed. *Wisigoths et Francs autour de la bataille de Vouillé (507)*. Saint-Germain-en-Laye, 2010.

Bowersock, G. W. *Julian the Apostate*. Cambridge, MA, 1978.

Bowersock, G. W. *Hellenism in Late Antiquity*. Ann Arbor, MI, 1990.

Bowersock, G. W. *Selected Papers on Late Antiquity*. Bari, 2000.

Bowersock, G. W. *The Throne of Adulis: Red Sea Wars on the Eve of Islam*. Oxford, 2013.

Bowman, Alan K. and Andrew Wilson, eds. *The Roman Agricultural Economy: Organization, Investment and Production*. Oxford, 2013.

Bratoz, Rajko, ed. *Westillyricum und Nordostitalien in der spätrömischen Zeit*. Ljubljana, 1996.

Braund, David. *Georgia in Antiquity: A History of Colchis and Transcaucasian Iberia, 550 BC–AD 562*. Oxford, 1994.

Brenot, Claude and Xavier Loriot, eds. *L'Or monnayé: Cahiers Ernest-Babelon*. Paris, 1992.

Brock, Sebastian and Brian Fitzgerald. *Two Early Lives of Severos, Patriarch of Antioch*. Translated Texts for Historians 59. Liverpool, 2013.

Brown, Peter. *Augustine of Hippo: A Biography*. London, 1967.

Brown, Peter. *The World of Late Antiquity*. London, 1971.

Brown, Peter. *Religion and Society in the Age of St Augustine*. London, 1972.

Brown, Peter. *Power and Persuasion in Late Antiquity: Towards a Christian Empire*. Madison, WI, 1992.

Brown, T. S. *Gentlemen and Officers: Imperial Administration and Aristocratic Power in Byzantine Italy, AD 554–800*. Rome, 1984.

Burgess, R. W. *The Chronicle of Hydatius and the Consularia Constantinopolitana*. Oxford, 1993.

Burgess, R. W. *Studies in Eusebian and Post-Eusebian Chronography*. Historia Einzelschriften 135. Stuttgart, 1999.

Burgess, R. W. *Chronicles, Consuls and Coins: Historiography and History in the Later Roman Empire*. Variorum Collected Studies 984. Burlington, VT, 2011.

Burrus, Virginia. *The Making of a Heretic: Gender, Authority and the Priscillianist Controversy*. Berkeley, CA, 1995.

Bursche, Aleksander. *Later Roman-Barbarian Contacts in Central Europe: Numismatic Evidence*. Berlin, 1996.

Bury, J. B. *History of the Later Roman Empire from the Death of Theodosius I to the Death of Justinian*. 2 vols. London, 1923.

Callu, J.-P. *La monnaie dans l'antiquité tardive: Trente-quatre études de 1972 à 2002*. Bari, 2010.

Cameron, Alan. *Claudian: Poetry and Propaganda at the Court of Honorius*. Oxford, 1970.

Cameron, Alan. *Circus Factions: Blues and Greens at Rome and Byzantium*. Oxford, 1975.

Cameron, Alan. *The Last Pagans of Rome*. Oxford, 2010.

Cameron, Alan. *Wandering Poets and Other Essays on Late Greek Literature and Philosophy*. Oxford, 2015.

Cameron, Alan and Jacqueline Long. *Barbarians and Politics at the Court of Arcadius*. Berkeley, CA, 1993.

Cameron, Averil. *Procopius and the Sixth Century*. Berkeley, CA, 1985.

Cameron, Averil. *Christianity and the Rhetoric of Empire*. Berkeley, CA, 1991.

Cameron, Averil, ed. *The Byzantine and Early Islamic Near East III: States, Resources and Armies*. Princeton, NJ, 1995.

Cameron, Averil and Lawrence I. Conrad, eds. *The Byzantine and Early Islamic Near East I: Problems in the Literary Source Material*. Princeton, NJ, 1992.

Canepa, Matthew P. *The Two Eyes of the Earth: Art and Ritual of Kingship between Rome and Sasanian Iran*. Berkeley, CA, 2009.

Capizzi, Carmelo. *L'imperatore Anastasio I (491–518)*. Rome, 1969.

Carlà, Filippo. *L'oro nella tarda antichità: aspetti economici e sociali*. Turin, 2009.

Cerati, André. *Caractère annonaire et assiette de l'impôt foncier au Bas-Empire*. Paris, 1975.

Cesa, Maria. *Impero tardoantico e barbari: la crisi militare da Adrianopoli al 418*. Como, 1994.

Chadwick, Henry. *Priscillian of Avila: The Occult and the Charismatic in the Early Church*. Oxford, 1976.

Chadwick, Henry. *Boethius: The Consolations of Music, Logic, Theology and Philosophy*. Oxford, 1980.

Chadwick, Henry. *Augustine*. Oxford Past Masters. Oxford, 1986.

Chadwick, Henry. *The Church in Ancient Society from Galilee to Gregory the Great*. Oxford, 2002.

Chastagnol, André. *La préfecture urbaine à Rome sous le Bas-Empire*. Paris, 1960.

Chastagnol, André. *Les fastes de la préfecture de Rome au Bas-Empire*. Paris, 1962.

Chastagnol, André. *Le sénat romain sous le règne d'Odoacre*. Bonn, 1966.

Chaumont, Marie-Louise. *Recherches sur l'histoire d'Arménie de l'avènement des Sassanides à la conversion du royaume*. Paris, 1969.

Chaumont, Marie-Louise. *La Christianisation de l'empire iranien des origines aux grandes persécutions du IVe siècle*. Louvain, 1988.

Chauvot, Alain. *Opinions romaines face aux barbares au IVe siècle ap. J.-C.* Paris, 1998.

Chin, Catherine M. *Grammar and Christianity in the Late Roman World*. Philadelphia, PA, 2008.

Christensen, Arthur. *L'Iran sous les Sassanides*. 2nd edn. Copenhagen, 1944.

Christidis, A. F., ed. *A History of Ancient Greek from the Beginnings to Late Antiquity*. Cambridge, 2007.

Christie, Neil. *The Fall of the Western Roman Empire: An Archaeological and Historical Perspective*. London, 2012.

Clackson, James and Geoffrey Horrocks, eds. *The Blackwell History of the Latin Language*. Oxford, 2007.

Clark, Gillian. *Iamblichus: On the Pythagorean Life*. Translated Texts for Historians 8. Liverpool, 1989.

Classen, Peter. *Kaiserreskript und Königsurkunde: Diplomatische Studien zum Problem der Kontinuität zwischen Altertum und Mittelalter.* Thessaloniki, 1977.

Clauss, Manfred. *Der magister officiorum in der Spätantike (4.-6. Jahrhundert).* Munich, 1981.

Clover, Frank M. *The Late Roman West and the Vandals.* Variorum Collected Studies 401. Aldershot, 1993.

Collins, Roger. *Early Medieval Spain: Unity in Diversity, 400-1000.* London, 1983.

Cooper, Kate and Julia Hillner, eds. *Religion, Dynasty and Patronage in Early Christian Rome, 300-900.* Cambridge, 2008.

Coumert, Magali. *Origines des peuples: Le récits du Haut Moyen Âge occidental (550-850).* Paris, 2007.

Courcelle, Pierre. *Les lettres grecques en Occident de Macrobe à Cassiodore.* Paris, 1948.

Courcelle, Pierre. *Histoire littéraire des grandes invasions germaniques.* 3rd edn. Paris, 1964.

Courtois, Christian et al., eds. *Tablettes Albertini: Actes privés de l'époque vandale (fin du Ve siècle).* Paris, 1952.

Courtois, Christian. *Les Vandales et l'Afrique.* Paris, 1955.

Coville, Alfred. *Recherches sur l'histoire de Lyon du V-me au IX-me siècle (450-800).* Paris, 1928.

Cracco Ruggini, Lellia. *Gli ebrei in età tardoantica: Presenze, intolleranze, incontri.* Rome, 2011.

Cribiore, Raffaela. *The School of Libanius in Late Antique Antioch.* Princeton, NJ, 2007.

Cribiore, Raffaela. *Between City and School: Selected Orations of Libanius.* Translated Texts for Historians 65. Liverpool, 2016.

Croke, Brian. *Christian Chronicles and Byzantine History, 5th-6th Centuries.* Variorum Collected Studies 386. Aldershot, 1992.

Croke, Brian. *The Chronicle of Marcellinus, Translation and Commentary.* Canberra, 1995.

Croke, Brian. *Count Marcellinus and His Chronicle.* Oxford, 2001.

Crone, Patricia and Michael Cook. *Hagarism: The Making of the Islamic World.* Cambridge, 1977.

Crone, Patricia. *Meccan Trade and the Rise of Islam.* Princeton, 1987.

Curran, John. *Pagan City and Christian Capital: Rome in the Fourth Century.* Oxford, 2000.

Curta, Florin. *The Making of the Slavs: History and Archaeology of the Lower Danube Region, c. 500-700.* Cambridge, 2001.

Curta, Florin. *Southeastern Europe in the Middle Ages, 500-1250.* Cambridge, 2006.

Curta, Florin, ed. *Neglected Barbarians.* Turnhout, 2010.

Dagron, Gilbert. *Naissance d'une capitale: Constantinople et ses institutions de 330 à 451.* Paris, 1974.

Deichmann, Friedrich Wilhelm. *Ravenna, Hauptstadt des spätantiken Abendlandes.* 5 vols. Wiesbaden, 1958–89.

Delaplace, Christine. *La fin de l'Empire romain d'Occident: Rome et les Wisigoths de 382 à 531.* Rennes, 2015.

Delbrueck, Richard. *Die Consulardiptychen.* Berlin, 1929.

Delbrueck, Richard. *Spätantike Kaiserporträts von Constantinus Magnus bis zum Ende des Westreichs.* 2 vols. Berlin, 1933.

Delbrueck, Richard. *Dittici consolari tardoantichi.* Marilena Abbatepaolo, ed. Bari, 2009.

Déleage, André. *La capitation du Bas-Empire.* Mâcon, 1945.

De Lepper, J. L. M. *De rebus gestis Bonifatii comitis Africae et magistri militum.* Breda, 1941.

Delmaire, Roland. *Largesses sacrées et Res Privata: L'aerarium impérial et son administration du IVe au VIe siècle.* Rome, 1989.

Delmaire, Roland. *Les responsables des finances impériales au Bas-Empire romain (IVe–VIe s.).* Collection Latomus 203. Brussels, 1989.

Delmaire, Roland. *Les institutions du Bas-Empire romain de Constantin à Justinien: Les institutions civiles palatines.* Paris, 1995.

Demandt, Alexander. *Die Spätantike: Römische Geschichte von Diocletian bis Justinian 284–565 n. Chr.* Handbuch der Altertumswissenschaft III.6. Munich, 1989.

Demougeot, Émilienne. *De l'unité à la division de l'empire romain, 395–410.* Paris, 1951.

Demougeot, Émilienne. *L'Empire romain et les barbares d'Occident (IV-e–VI-e siècles). Scripta Varia.* Paris, 1988.

Den Boeft, J., J. W. Drijvers, D. den Hengst and H. C. Teitler, eds. *Ammianus After Julian: The Reign of Valentinian and Valens in Books 26–31 of the Res Gestae.* Leiden, 2007.

Den Hengst, Daniel. *Emperors and Historiography: Collected Essays on the Literature of the Roman Empire.* D. W. P. Burgersdijk and J. A. van Waarden, eds. Mnemosyne Supplements. Leiden, 2010.

Dey, Hendrik W. *The Afterlife of the Roman City: Architecture and Ceremony in Late Antiquity and the Early Middle Ages.* Cambridge, 2015.

Di Cosmo, Nicola and Michael Maas, eds. *Empires and Exchanges in Eurasian Late Antiquity: Rome, China, Iran, and the Steppe, ca. 250–750.* Cambridge, 2018.

Diefenbach, Steffen and Gernot Michael Müller, eds. *Gallien in Spätantike und Frühmittelalter: Kulturgeschichte einer Region.* Millennium Studien 43. Berlin, 2013.

Diesner, Hans-Joachim. *Der Untergang der römischen Herrschaft in Nordafrika.* Weimar, 1964.

Diesner, Hans-Joachim. *Das Vandalenreich: Aufstieg und Untergang.* Stuttgart, 1966.

Dittrich, Ursula-Barbara. *Die Beziehungen Roms zu den Sarmaten und Quaden im vierten Jahrhundert n. Chr.* Bonn, 1984.

Downey, Glanville. *A History of Antioch in Syria from Seleucus to the Arab Conquest.* Princeton, NJ, 1961.

Drijvers, Jan Willem and David Hunt, eds. *The Late Roman World and Its Historian: Interpreting Ammianus Marcellinus.* London, 1999.

Drinkwater, John. *The Alamanni and Rome, 213–496.* Oxford, 2007.

Drinkwater, John and Hugh Elton, eds. *Fifth-century Gaul: A Crisis of Identity?* Cambridge, 1992.

Duncan, G. L. *Coin Circulation in the Danubian and Balkan Provinces of the Roman Empire, AD 294–578.* London, 1993.

Duval, Yves-Marie. *L'extirpation de l'Arianisme en Italie du Nord et en Occident.* Variorum Collected Studies Series 611. Brookfield, VT, 1998.

Ebert, Max. *Sudrussland im Altertum.* Bonn, 1921.

Edwards, Mark. *Optatus: Against the Donatists.* Translated Texts for Historians 27. Liverpool, 1997.

Effros, Bonnie. *Merovingian Mortuary Archaeology and the Making of the Early Middle Ages.* Berkeley, CA, 2003.

Effros, Bonnie. *Uncovering the Germanic Past: Merovingian Archaeology in France, 1830–1914.* Oxford, 2012.

Ellegard, Alvar and Gunilla Akerström-Hougen, eds. *Rome and the North.* Jonsered, 1993.

Elton, Hugh. *Warfare in Roman Europe, AD 350–425.* Oxford, 1996.

Ensslin, Wilhelm. *Theoderich der Grosse.* Munich, 1947.

Errington, R. Malcolm. *Roman Imperial Policy from Julian to Theodosius.* Chapel Hill, NC, 2006.

Esmonde Cleary, Simon. *The Roman West, AD 200–500: An Archaeological Study.* Cambridge, 2013.

Evans, J. A. S. *The Age of Justinian.* London, 1996.

Ewig, Eugen. *Spätantikes und fränkisches Gallien I–II.* Beihefte der Francia, Band 3/1–3/2. Munich, 1976–9.

Fabech, Charlotte and Ulf Näsman, eds. *The Sösdala Horsemen and the Equestrian Elite of Fifth-century Europe.* Moesgard, 2017.

Fagerlie, Joan M. *Late Roman and Byzantine Solidi Found in Sweden and Denmark.* New York, NY, 1967.

Favrod, Justin. *Histoire politique du royaume burgonde (443–534).* Lausanne, 1997.

Fehr, Hubert. *Germanen und Romanen im Merowingerreich.* Ergänzungsbande zum Reallexikon der Germanischen Altertumskunde 68. Berlin, 2010.

Fehr, Hubert and Philipp von Rummel. *Die Völkerwanderung*. Stuttgart, 2011.

Fernández, Damián. *Aristocrats and Statehood in Western Iberia, 200–600 CE*. Berkeley, CA, 2017.

Ferris, I. M. *Enemies of Rome: Barbarians through Roman Eyes*. Stroud, 2000.

Festugière, A. J. *Antioche païenne et chrétienne: Libanius, Chrysostome et les moines de Syrie*. Paris, 1959.

Fischer, Svante. *Roman Imperialism and Runic Literacy: The Westernization of Northern Europe (150–800 AD)*. Uppsala, 2005.

Fisher, Greg. *Between Empires: Arabs, Romans and Sasanians in Late Antiquity*. Oxford, 2011.

Fisher, Greg, ed. *Arabs and Empires before Islam*. Oxford, 2015.

Fornasier, Jochen and Burkhard Böttger, eds. *Das Bosporanische Reich*. Mainz, 2002.

Foss, Clive. *Ephesus after Antiquity: A Late Antique, Byzantine and Turkish City*. Cambridge, 1979.

Frend, W. H. C. *The Rise of the Monophysite Movement*. Cambridge, 1972.

Friedländer, Julius. *Die Münzen der Vandalen: Nachträge zu den Münzen der Ostgothen*. Leipzig, 1849.

Frolova, Nina A. *Essays on the Northern Black Sea Region Numismatics*. Odessa, 1995.

Frye, Richard N. *The History of Ancient Iran*. Handbuch der Altertumswissenschaft 3.7. Munich, 1984.

Gamillscheg, Ernst. *Romania Germanica: Sprach- und Siedlungsgeschichte der Germanen auf den Boden des alten Römerreiches*, 3 vols. Berlin, 1935–70.

García-Gasco, Rosa, Sergio González Sánchez and David Hernández de la Fuente, eds. *The Theodosian Age (AD 379–455): Power, Place, Belief and Learning at the End of the Western Empire*. British Archaeological Reports International Series 2493. Oxford, 2013.

Gariboldi, Andrea. *Sylloge Nummorum Sasanidarum, Tajikistan: Sasanian Coins and Their Imitations from Sogdiana and Tocharistan*. Veröffentlichen der numismatischen Kommission der Österreichischen Akademie der Wissenschaft 61. Vienna, 2017.

Garzya, Antonio. *Il mandarino e il quotidiano: Saggi sulla letteratura tardoantica e bizantina*. Naples, 1983.

Gaupp, Ernst Theodor. *Die germanischen Ansiedlungen und Landtheilungen in den Provinzen des römischen Westreiches*. Breslau, 1844.

Gazeau, Véronique, Pierre Bauduin and Yves Moderan, eds. *Identité et Ethnicité. Concepts, débats historiographiques, exemples (III-e–XII-e siècle)*. Caen, 2008.

Geuenich, Dieter. *Geschichte der Alemannen*. Stuttgart, 1997.

Gheller, Viola. *'Identità' e 'arianesimo gotico': genesi di un topos storiografico*. Bologna, 2017.

Giardina, Andrea. *Aspetti della burocrazia nel basso imperio*. Urbino, 1977.

Gidlow, Christopher. *The Reign of Arthur: From History to Legend*. Stroud, 2004.

Göbl, Robert. *Dokumente zur Geschichte der iranischen Hunnen in Baktrien und Indien*. 4 vols. Wiesbaden, 1967.

Göbl, Robert. *Sasanidische Numismatik*. Braunschweig, 1968.

Goetz, Hans-Werner, Jörg Jarnut and Walter Pohl, eds. *Regna and Gentes: The Relationship between Late Antique and Early Medieval Peoples and Kingdoms in the Transformation of the Roman World*. Leiden, 2001.

Goffart, Walter. *Barbarians and Romans: The Techniques of Accommodation, AD 418–584*. Princeton, NJ, 1980.

Goffart, Walter. *Rome's Fall and After*. London, 1989.

Goffart, Walter. *Barbarian Tides: The Migration Age and the Later Roman Empire*. Philadelphia, PA, 2006.

Greatrex, Geoffrey, *Rome and Persia at War, 502–532*. Leeds, 1998.

Greatrex, Geoffrey and Samuel N. C. Lieu. *The Roman Eastern Frontier and the Persian Wars, Part II: AD 363–630*. London, 2002.

Green, D. H. *Language and History in the Early Germanic World*. Cambridge, 1998.

Grey, Cam. *Constructing Communities in the Late Roman Countryside*. Cambridge, 2011.

Grierson, Philip and Mark Blackburn, *Medieval European Coinage with a Catalogue of the Coins in the Fitzwilliam Museum, Cambridge, Volume I: The Early Middle Ages (5th–10th Centuries)*. Cambridge, 1986.

Griffe, Élie. *La Gaule chrétienne à l'époque romain*. 3 vols. Paris, 1964–6.

Grig, Lucy and Gavin Kelly, eds. *Two Romes: Rome and Constantinople in Late Antiquity*. New York, NY, 2012.

Grosse, Robert. *Römische Militärgeschichte von Gallienus bis zum Beginn der byzantinischen Themenverfassung*. Berlin, 1920.

Guilland, Rodolphe. *Titres et fonctions de l'Empire byzantin*. Variorum Collected Studies 50. London, 1976.

Güldenpenning, Albert. *Geschichte des oströmischen Reiches unter den Kaisern Arcadius und Theodosius II*. Halle, 1885.

Haarer, F. K. *Anastasius I: Politics and Empire in the Late Roman World*. Liverpool, 2006.

Hachmann, Rolf. *Die Goten und Skandinavien*. Berlin, 1970.

Halsall, Guy. *Warfare and Society in the Barbarian West, 450–900*. London, 2003.

Halsall, Guy. *Barbarian Migrations and the Roman West, 376–568*. Cambridge, 2007.

Halsall, Guy. *Cemeteries and Society in Merovingian Gaul: Selected Studies in History and Archaeology*. Leiden, 2009.

Halsall, Guy. *Worlds of Arthur: Facts and Fictions of the Dark Ages*. Oxford, 2013.

Handley, Mark A. *Death, Society and Culture: Inscriptions and Epitaphs in Gaul and Spain, AD 300–750*. British Archaeological Reports International Series 1135. Oxford, 2003.

Hanson, R. P. C. *Saint Patrick: His Origins and Career*. Oxford, 1968.

Harl, Kenneth W. *Coinage in the Roman Economy, 300 BC to AD 700*. Baltimore, MD, 1996.

Harper, Kyle. *Slavery in the Late Roman World, AD 275–425*. Cambridge, 2011.

Harper, Kyle. *The Fate of Rome: Climate, Disease, and the End of an Empire*. Princeton, NJ, 2017.

Harries, Jill. *Sidonius Apollinaris and the Fall of Rome*. Oxford, 1994.

Harries, Jill. *Law and Empire in Late Antiquity*. Cambridge, 1999.

Harries, Jill and Ian Wood, eds. *The Theodosian Code*. 2nd edn. Bristol, 2010.

Harris, William V. *Rome's Imperial Economy: Twelve Essays*. New York, NY, 2011.

Harris, William V. *Roman Power: A Thousand Years of Empire*. Cambridge, 2016.

Harris, William V., ed. *The Transformations of Urbs Roma in Late Antiquity*, Journal of Roman Archaeology Supplementary Series 33. Portsmouth, RI, 1999.

Harris, William V., ed. *The Spread of Christianity in the First Four Centuries: Essays in Explanation*. Leiden, 2005.

Hartmann, Ludo Moritz. *Untersuchungen zur Geschichte der byzantinischen Verwaltung in Italien (540–750)*. Leipzig, 1889.

Heather, Peter. *Goths and Romans, 332–489*. Oxford, 1991.

Heather, Peter. *The Fall of the Roman Empire: A New History of Rome and the Barbarians*. New York, NY, 2005.

Heather, Peter J. and John Matthews. *The Goths in the Fourth Century*. Translated Texts for Historians. Liverpool, 1991.

Hedeager, Lotte. *Iron-Age Societies: From Tribe to State in Northern Europe, 500 BC–700 AD*, John Hines, trans. Oxford, 1992.

Hendy, Michael. *Studies in the Byzantine Monetary Economy c. 350–1450*. Cambridge, 1985.

Herrin, Judith. *The Formation of Christendom*. Princeton, NJ, 1987.

Herrin, Judith and Jinty Nelson, eds. *Ravenna: Its Role in Earlier Medieval Change and Exchange*. London, 2016.

Hodgkin, Thomas. *Italy and Her Invaders*. 8 vols. Oxford, 1880–99.

Hoffmann, Dietrich. *Das spätrömische Bewegungsheer und die Notitia Dignitatum*. Epigraphische Studien 7/1–2. 2 vols. Düsseldorf, 1969–70.

Holum, Kenneth G. *Theodosian Empresses: Women and Imperial Dominion in Late Antiquity*. Berkeley, CA, 1982.

Honoré, Tony. *Law in the Crisis of Empire: The Theodosian Dynasty and Its Quaestors*. Oxford, 1998.

Horsnaes, Helle W. *Crossing Boundaries: An Analysis of Roman Coins in Danish Contexts, Volume 1: Finds from Sealand, Funen and Jutland*. Aarhus, 2010.

Howard-Johnston, James. *East Rome, Sasanian Persia and the End of Antiquity*. Variorum Collected Studies. London, 2006.

Hübener, Wolfgang, ed. *Die Alemannen in der Frühzeit*. Bühl, 1974.

Hudson, Benjamin. *The Picts*. Chichester, 2014.

Humphrey, J. H., ed. *The Roman and Byzantine Near East: Some Recent Archaeological Research*. Journal of Roman Archaeology Supplement 14. Portsmouth, RI, 1995.

Humphrey, J. H., ed. *The Roman and Byzantine Near East Volume 2: Some Recent Archaeological Research*. Journal of Roman Archaeology Supplement 31. Portsmouth, RI, 1999.

Ivanišević, Vujadin and Michel Kazanski, eds. *The Pontic-Danubian Realm in the Period of the Great Migration*. Paris, 2010.

James, Edward. *The Franks*. Oxford, 1988.

James, Edward. *Europe's Barbarians, AD 200–600*. London, 2009.

Janiszewski, Paweł. *The Missing Link: Greek Pagan Historiography in the Second Half of the Third Century and in the Fourth Century AD*. Warsaw, 2006.

Jeffreys, Elizabeth, Brian Croke and Roger Scott, eds. *Studies in John Malalas*. Byzantina Australiensia 6. Sydney, 1990.

Johnson, Mark J. *The Roman Imperial Mausoleum in Late Antiquity*. Cambridge, 2009.

Johnson, Scott Fitzgerald, ed. *The Oxford Handbook of Late Antiquity*. New York, NY, 2012.

Johnson, Stephen. *Late Roman Fortifications*. New York, NY, 1983.

Jones, A. H. M. *The Later Roman Empire, 284–602*. 4 vols. Oxford, 1964.

Jones, A. H. M. *The Roman Economy*. P. A. Brunt, ed. Oxford, 1975.

Jones, Christopher P. *Between Pagan and Christian*. Cambridge, MA, 2014.

Jongeward, David and Joe Cribb. *Kushan, Kushano-Sasanian and Kidarite Coins: A Catalogue of the Coins from the American Numismatic Society*. New York, NY, 2014.

Jullian, Camille. *Histoire de la Gaule*. 8 vols. Paris, 1909–26.

Kahlos, Maijastina. *Vettius Agorius Praetextatus*. Rome, 2002.

Kaldellis, Anthony. *Procopius: Tyranny, History and Philosophy at the End of Antiquity*. Philadelphia, PA, 2004.

Kazanski, Michel. *Les Goths (Ier–VIIe après J.-C.)*. Paris, 1993.

Kazanski, Michel. *Les Slaves: Les origines I-er–VII-e siècle après J.-C.* Paris, 1999.

Kelly, Christopher. *Ruling the Later Roman Empire*. Cambridge, MA, 2004.

Kelly, Christopher, ed. *Theodosius II: Rethinking the Roman Empire in Late Antiquity*. Cambridge, 2013.

Kelly, Gavin. *Ammianus Marcellinus: The Allusive Historian*. Cambridge, 2008.

Kennedy, David and Derrick Riley. *Rome's Desert Frontier from the Air*. London, 1990.

Kennedy, Hugh. *The Prophet and the Age of the Caliphates: The Islamic Near East from the Sixth to the Eleventh Century*. London, 1986.

Kim, Hyun Jin. *The Huns, Rome and the Birth of Europe*. Cambridge, 2013.

Kim, Hyun Jin. *The Huns*. London, 2015.

Kraus, F. F. *Die Münzen Odovacars und des Ostgotenreiches in Italien*. Halle, 1928.

Krause, Jens-Uwe and Christian Witschel, eds. *Die Stadt in der Spätantike – Niedergang oder Wandel?* Historia Einzelschriften 190. Stuttgart, 2006.

Krieger, Rommel. *Untersuchungen und Hypothesen zur Ansiedlung der Westgoten, Burgunder und Ostgoten*. Bern, 1992.

Kuhoff, Wolfgang. *Studien zur zivilen senatorischen Laufbahn im 4. Jhr. n. Chr.* Bern, 1983.

Kulikowski, Michael. *Late Roman Spain and Its Cities*. Baltimore, MD, 2004.

Kulikowski, Michael. *Rome's Gothic Wars: From the Third Century to Alaric*. Cambridge, 2006.

Lammers, Walther, ed. *Entstehung und Verfassung des Sachsenstammes*. Darmstadt, 1967.

Langgärtner, Georg. *Die Gallienpolitik der Päpste im 5. und 6. Jahrhundert*. Theophaneia 16. Bonn, 1964.

Laniado, Avshalom. *Ethnos et droit dans le monde protobyzantin, v-e–vi-e siècle*. Paris, 2015.

Lapidge, Michael and David Dumville, eds. *Gildas: New Approaches*. Woodbridge, 1984.

Lebedynsky, Iaroslav. *Sur les traces des Alains et Sarmates en Gaule: Du Caucase à la Gaule, IVe–Ve siècle*. Paris, 2011.

Lebedynsky, Iaroslav. *Les Nomades: Les peuples nomades de la steppe des origines aux invasions mongoles (IXe siècle av. J.-C.–XIIIe siècle apr. J.-C.)*. Paris, 2017.

Le Bohec, Yann and Catherine Wolff, eds. *L'Armée romaine de Dioclétien à Valentinien Ier*. Paris, 2004.

Lee, A. D. *Information and Frontiers: Roman Foreign Relations in Late Antiquity*. Cambridge, 1993.

Lendon, J. E. *Soldiers & Ghosts: A History of Battle in Classical Antiquity*. New Haven, CT, 2005.

Lenski, Noel. *Failure of Empire: Valens and the Roman State in the Fourth Century AD*. Berkeley, CA, 2002.

Lenski, Noel. *Constantine and the Cities: Imperial Authority and Civic Politics*. Philadelphia, PA, 2016.

Léotard, E. *Essai sur la condition des barbares établis dans l'empire romain au quatrième siècle*. Paris, 1873.

Lepelley, Claude. *Les cités de l'Afrique romaine au Bas-Empire*. 2 vols. Paris, 1979–81.

Leppin, Hartmut. *Von Constantin dem Grossen zu Theodosius II: Das christliche Kaisertum bei den Kirchenhistorikern Socrates, Sozomenus und Theoderet*. Göttingen, 1995.

Lerner, Judith A. and N. Sims-Williams, eds. *Seals, Sealings and Tokens from Bactria to Gandhara (4th to 8th century CE)*. Vienna, 2011.

Lewin, Ariel S. and Pietrina Pellegrini, eds. *The Late Roman Army in the Near East from Diocletian to the Arab Conquest: Proceedings of a Colloquium Held at Potenza, Acerenza and Matera, Italy (May 2005).* British Archaeological Reports International Series 1717. Oxford, 2007.

Lewis, Mark Edward. *China between Empires: The Northern and Southern Dynasties.* Cambridge, MA, 2009.

Liebeschuetz, J. H. W. G. *Antioch: City and Imperial Administration in the Later Roman Empire.* Oxford, 1972.

Liebeschuetz, J. H. W. G. *From Diocletian to the Arab Conquest.* Variorum Collected Studies 310. Aldershot, 1990.

Liebeschuetz, J. H. W. G. *Barbarians and Bishops: Army, Church, and State in the Age of Arcadius and Chrysostom.* Oxford, 1991.

Liebs, Detlef. *Die Jurisprudenz im spätantiken Italien (260–640 n. Chr.).* Berlin, 1987.

Liebs, Detlef. *Römische Jurisprudenz in Gallien (2. bis 8. Jahrhundert).* Berlin, 2002.

Lieu, Samuel N. C. *Manichaeism in the Later Roman Empire and Medieval China: A Historical Survey.* Manchester, 1985.

Lipps, Johannes, Carlos Machado and Philipp von Rummel, eds. *The Sack of Rome in 410 AD: The Event, Its Context and Its Impact.* Rome, 2014.

Little, Lester K. *Plague and the End of Antiquity: The Pandemic of 541–750.* Cambridge, 2007.

Lizzi Testa, Rita. *Senatori, popolo, papi: Il governo di Roma al tempo dei Valentiniani.* Bari, 2004.

Löfstedt, Einar. *Late Latin.* Oslo, 1959.

Löhken, Henrik. *Ordines dignitatum: Untersuchungen zur formalen Konstituierung der spätantiken Führungsschicht.* Cologne, 1982.

L'Orange, H. P. *Studien zur Geschichte des spätantiken Porträts.* Oslo, 1933.

Lounghis, T. C., B. Blysidu and St Lampakes. *Regesten der Kaiserurkunden des oströmischen Reiches von 476 bis 565.* Quellen und Studien zur Geschichte Zyperns 52. Nicosia, 2005.

Loyen, André. *Recherches historiques sur les panégyriques de Sidoine Apollinaire.* Paris, 1942.

Loyen, André. *Sidoine Apollinaire et l'esprit précieux en Gaule aux derniers jours de l'Empire.* Paris, 1943.

Lütkenhaus, Werner. *Constantius III: Studien zu seiner Tätigkeit und Stellung im Westreich 411–421.* Bonn, 1998.

Maas, Michael. *John Lydus and the Roman Past: Antiquarianism and Politics in the Age of Justinian.* London, 1992.

Maas, Michael, ed. *The Cambridge Companion to the Age of Justinian.* Cambridge, 2005.

MacMullen, Ramsay. *Corruption and the Decline of Rome.* New Haven, CT, 1988.

MacMullen, Ramsay. *Changes in the Roman Empire: Essays in the Ordinary.* Princeton, NJ, 1990.

Maenchen-Helfen, Otto J. *The World of the Huns: Studies in Their History and Culture.* Berkeley, CA, 1970.

Mango, Cyril and Roger Scott. *The Chronicle of Theophanes Confessor: Byzantine and Near Eastern History, AD 284–813.* Oxford, 1997.

Marchetta, Antonio. *Orosio e Ataulfo nell'ideologia dei rapporti romano-barbarici.* Rome, 1987.

Markus, Robert. *The End of Ancient Christianity.* Cambridge, 1990.

Marrou, H.-I. *Saint Augustin et la fin de la culture antique.* 4th edn. Paris, 1958.

Marrou, H.-I. *Christiana Tempora: Mélanges d'histoire, d'archéologie, d'épigraphie et de patristique.* Rome, 1978.

Mathisen, Ralph Whitney. *Ecclesiastical Factionalism and Religious Controversy in Fifth-century Gaul.* Washington, DC, 1989.

Mathisen, Ralph W., ed. *Law, Society, and Authority in Late Antiquity.* Oxford, 2001.

Mathisen, Ralph W. and Danuta Shanzer, eds. *Society and Culture in Late Antiquity: Revisiting the Sources.* Aldershot, 2001.

Mathisen, R. W. and Hagith S. Sivan, eds. *Shifting Frontiers in Late Antiquity.* Aldershot, 1996.

Matthews, John. *Western Aristocracies and Imperial Court, AD 364–425.* Oxford, 1975.

Matthews, John. *The Roman Empire of Ammianus.* Baltimore, MD, 1989.

Matthews, John. *Laying down the Law: A Study of the Theodosian Code.* New Haven, CT, 2000.

Matthews, John. *Roman Perspectives.* Lampeter, 2010.

Mattingly, David. *An Imperial Possession: Britain in the Roman Empire, 54BC–AD409.* London, 2008.

Mazzarino, Santo. *Stilicone: La crisi imperiale dopo Teodosio.* Rome, 1942.

Mazzarino, Santo. *Aspetti sociali del quarto secolo.* Rome, 1951.

Mazzarino, Santo. *Il basso impero: Antico, tardoantico ed èra costantiniana.* 2 vols. Bari, 1974.

McCormick, Michael. *Eternal Victory: Triumphal Rulership in Late Antiquity, Byzantium and the Early Medieval West.* Cambridge, 1986.

McCormick, Michael. *Origins of the European Economy: Communications and Commerce, AD 300–900.* Cambridge, 2001.

McEvoy, Meaghan A. *Child Emperor Rule in the Late Roman West, AD 367–455.* Oxford, 2013.

McGill, Scott, Cristiana Sogno and Edward Watts, eds. *From the Tetrarchs to the Theodosians: Later Roman History and Culture, 284–450 CE.* Yale Classical Studies 34. Cambridge, 2010.

McLynn, Neil. *Ambrose of Milan: Church and Court in a Christian Capital.* Berkeley, CA, 1994.

Meier, Mischa. *Der Völkerwanderung ins Auge blicken: Individuelle Handlungsspielräume im 5. Jahrhundert n. Chr.* Karl-Christ Preis für Alte Geschichte Band 2. Heidelberg, 2016.

Meier, Mischa and Steffen Patzold. *August 410 – Ein Kampf um Rom.* Stuttgart, 2010.

Meier, Mischa, Christine Radtki and Fabian Schulz, eds. *Die Weltchronik des Johannes Malalas: Autor – Werk – Überliefrung.* Stuttgart, 2016.

Menze, Volker L. *Justinian and the Making of the Syrian Orthodox Church.* Oxford, 2008.

Merrills, A. H., ed. *Vandals, Romans and Berbers: New Perspectives on Late Antique North Africa.* Aldershot, 2004.

Meslin, Michel. *Les Ariens d'Occident, 335–430.* Paris, 1967.

Mickwitz, Gunnar. *Geld und Wirtschaft im römischen Reich des vierten Jahrhunderts n. Chr.* Helsinki, 1932.

Millar, Fergus. *A Greek Roman Empire: Power and Belief under Theodosius II (408–450).* Berkeley, CA, 2006.

Minns, Ellis H. *Scythians and Greeks: A Survey of Ancient History and Archaeology on the North Coast of the Euxine from the Danube to the Caucasus.* Cambridge, 1913.

Mitchell, Stephen. *Anatolia: Land, Men and Gods in Asia Minor. Volume II: The Rise of the Church.* Oxford, 1993.

Mócsy, András. *Pannonia and Upper Moesia.* Sheppard Frere, trans. London, 1974.

Mócsy, András. *Pannonien und das römische Heer: Ausgewählte Aufsätze.* Mavors 7. Stuttgart, 1992.

Modéran, Yves. *Les Maures et l'Afrique romaine (iv-e–vii-e siècle).* Rome, 2003.

Modéran, Yves. *Les Vandales et l'Empire romaine.* Paris, 2014.

Mohl, F. George. *Introduction à la chronologie du latin vulgaire.* Paris, 1899.

Moorhead, John. *Theodoric in Italy.* Oxford, 1992.

Moorhead, John. *Justinian.* London, 1994.

Moravcsik, Gyula. *Byzantinoturcica I–II.* Budapest, 1942–3.

Moravcsik, Gyula. *Studia Byzantina.* Budapest, 1967.

Mühlberger, Steven. *The Fifth-century Chroniclers: Prosper, Hydatius, and the Gallic Chronicler of 452.* Leeds, 1989.

Müller, Wolfgang, ed. *Zur Geschichte der Alemannen.* Darmstadt, 1975.

Murray, Alexander C., ed. *After Rome's Fall: Narrators and Sources of Early Medieval History.* Toronto, 1998.

Nechaeva, Ekaterina. *Embassies–Negotiations–Gifts: Systems of East Roman Diplomacy in Late Antiquity.* Geographica Historica 30. Stuttgart, 2014.

Nelson, Bradley R. *Numismatic Art of Persia: The Sunrise Collection Part I: Ancient – 650 BC–AD 650.* Lancaster, PA, 2011.

Nicolet, Claude, ed. *Les littératures techniques dans l'Antiquité romaine: Statut, public et destination, tradition.* Entretiens de la Fondation Hardt XLII. Vandoeuvres-Geneva, 1996.

Nixon, C. E. V. and Barbara Saylor Rodgers. *In Praise of Later Roman Emperors: The Panegyrici Latini.* Berkeley, CA, 1994.

Nock, Arthur Darby. *Essays on Religion and the Ancient World.* 2 vols. Cambridge, MA, 1972.

Norberg, Dag. *Beiträge zur spätlateinischen Syntax.* Uppsala, 1944.

Norberg, Dag. *Au seuil du Moyen Age: Études linguistiques, métriques et littéraires.* Padua, 1974.

Ó Cróinín, Dáibhí. *Early Medieval Ireland, 400–1200.* London, 1995.

O'Donnell, J. J. *Cassiodorus.* Berkeley, CA, 1979.

O'Flynn, John Michael. *Generalissimos of the Western Roman Empire.* Calgary, 1983.

Oost, S. I. *Galla Placidia Augusta.* Chicago, IL, 1968.

Orlandi, Silvia. *Epigrafia anfitreale dell'Occidente Romano VI. Roma: Anfiteatri e strutture annesse con un nuova edizione e commento delle iscrizioni del Colosseo.* Rome, 2004.

Palanque, J. R. *Essai sur la préfecture du prétoire du Bas-Empire.* Paris, 1933.

Palanque, J. R. *Saint Ambroise et l'empire romain.* Paris, 1933.

Parzinger, Hermann. *Die frühen Völker Eurasiens vom Neolithikum bis zum Mittelalter.* 2nd edn. Munich, 2011.

Paschoud, François. *Roma Aeterna.* Neuchâtel, 1967.

Paschoud, François. *Eunape, Olympiodore, Zosime. Scripta Minora.* Bari, 2006.

Paschoud, François and Joachim Szidat, eds. *Usurpationen in der Spätantike.* Historia Einzelschriften 111. Stuttgart, 1997.

Payne, Richard E. *A State of Mixture: Christians, Zoroastrians, and Iranian Political Culture in Late Antiquity.* Berkeley, CA, 2015.

Pelka, Wilhelm. *Studien zur Geschichte des Untergangs des alten Thüringischen Königreichs im Jahre 531 n. Chr.* Jena, 1903.

Peregrinatio Gothica I, Polonia 84/85. Archaeologica Baltica VII. Łodz, 1986.

Peregrinatio Gothica III, Frederikstad, Norway, 1991. Oslo, 1992.

Perin, Patrick, ed. *Gallo-Romains, Wisigoths et Francs en Aquitaine, Septimanie et Espagne.* Paris, 1991.

Perrin, Odet. *Les Burgondes: Leur histoire, des origines à la fin du premier Royaume 534, contribution à l'histoire des invasions.* Neuchâtel, 1968.

Petit, Paul. *Libanius et la vie municipale à Antioche au IV-e siècle après J.C.* Paris, 1955.

Petit, Paul. *Les étudiants de Libanius.* Paris, 1957.

Pfisterer, Matthias. *Hunnen in Indien: Die Münzen der Kidariten und Alchan aus dem Bernischen Historischen Museum und der Sammlung Jean-Pierre Righetti.* Vienna, 2012.

Pietri, Charles. *Roma Christiana.* 2 vols. Rome, 1976.

Pietri, Charles. *Christiana Respublica: Éléments d'une enquête sur le christianisme antique.* 3 vols. Collection de l'École Française de Rome 234. Rome, 1997.

Piganiol, André. *L'Impôt de capitation sous le Bas-Empire romain.* Chambéry, 1916.

Piganiol, André. *L'Empire chrétien.* 2nd edn. Paris, 1972.

Pohl, Walter. *Die Awaren: Ein Steppenvolk in Mitteleuropa 567–822 N. Chr.* Munich, 1988.

Pohl, Walter, ed. *Kingdoms of the Empire: The Integration of Barbarians in Late Antiquity.* Leiden, 1998.

Pohl, Walter, ed. *Die Suche nach den Ursprüngen: Von der Bedeutung des frühen Mittelalters.* Forschungen zur Geschichte des Mittelalters 8. Vienna, 2004.

Pohl, Walter and Max Diesenberger, eds. *Eugippius und Severin.* Forschungen zur Geschichte des Mittelaters 2. Vienna, 2001.

Pohl, Walter and Max Diesenberger, eds. *Integration und Herrschaft: Ethnische Identitäten und soziale Organisation im Frühmittelalter.* Forschungen zur Geschichte des Mittelalters 3. Vienna, 2002.

Pohl, Walter and Gerda Heydemann, eds. *Post-Roman Transitions: Christian and Barbarian Identities in the Early Medieval West.* Turnhout, 2013.

Pohl, Walter and Gerda Heydemann, eds. *Strategies of Identification: Ethnicity and Religion in Early Medieval Europe.* Turnhout, 2013.

Pohl, Walter and Mathias Mehofer, eds. *Archaeology of Identity – Archäologie der Identität.* Forschungen zur Geschichte des Mittelalters 17. Vienna, 2010.

Pohl, Walter and Helmut Reimitz, eds. *Strategies of Distinction: The Construction of Ethnic Communities, 300–800.* Leiden, 1998.

Porena, Pierfrancesco. *L'insediamento degli Ostrogoti in Italia.* Rome, 2012.

Porena, Pierfrancesco and Yann Rivière, eds. *Expropriations et confiscations dans les royaumes barbare: Une approche régionale.* Rome, 2012.

Potts, D. T. *Mesopotamia, Iran and Arabia from the Seleucids to the Sasanians.* Variorum Collected Studies 962. Burlington, VT, 2010.

Potts, D. T. *Nomadism in Iran from Antiquity to the Modern Era.* Oxford, 2014.

Price, Richard and Michael Gaddis. *The Acts of the Council of Chalcedon.* 3 vols. Translated Texts for Historians 45. Liverpool, 2005.

Price, Richard and Mary Whitby, eds. *Chalcedon in Context: Church Councils 400–700.* Translated Texts for Historians Supplemental Volume. Liverpool, 2009.

Prostko-Prostynski, Jan. *Utraeque res publicae: The Emperor Anastasius I's Gothic Policy (491–518).* Poznan, 1994.

Reddé, Michel. *Mare Nostrum: Les infrastructures, le dispositif et l'histoire de la marine militaire sous l'empire romain*. Rome, 1986.

Rezakhani, Khodadad. *ReOrienting the Sasanians: East Iran in Late Antiquity*. Edinburgh, 2017.

Rich, John, ed. *The City in Late Antiquity*. London, 1992.

Rouche, Michel. *L'Aquitaine des Wisigoths aux Arabes, 418–781: Naissance d'une région*. Paris, 1979.

Rousseau, Philip. *Basil of Caesarea*. Berkeley, CA, 1994.

Rubin, Berthold. *Das Zeitalter Iustinians I*. Berlin, 1960.

Ruggini, Lellia. *Economia e società nell'Italia Annonaria: Rapporti fra agricoltura e commercio dal IV al VI secolo d.C.* 2nd edn. Bari, 1995.

Sabbah, Guy. *La méthode d'Ammien Marcellin*. Paris, 1978.

Sabin, Philip, Hans van Wees and Michael Whitby, eds. *The Cambridge History of Greek and Roman Warfare*. 2 vols. Cambridge, 2007.

Salzman, Michele Renee. *The Making of a Christian Aristocracy*. Cambridge, MA, 2002.

Sandwell, Isabella. *Religious Identity in Late Antiquity: Greeks, Jews and Christians in Antioch*. Cambridge, 2007.

Sarantis, Alexander. *Justinian's Balkan Wars: Campaigning, Diplomacy and Development in Illyricum, Thrace and the Northern World, AD 527–65*. Liverpool, 2016.

Sarris, Peter. *Economy and Society in the Age of Justinian*. Cambridge, 2006.

Šašel, Jaroslav. *Opera Selecta*. Situla 30. Ljubljana, 1992.

Sauer, Eberhard W., ed. *Sasanian Persia: Between Rome and the Steppes of Eurasia*. Edinburgh, 2017.

Sauer, Eberhard W., Hamid Omrani Rekavandi, Tony J. Wilkinson and Jebrael Nokandeh. *Persia's Imperial Power in Late Antiquity: The Great Wall of Gorgan and Frontier Landscapes of Sasanian Iran*. British Institute of Persian Studies Archaeological Monographs Series II. Oxford, 2013.

Schäfer, Tibor. *Untersuchungen zur Gesellschaft des Hunnenreiches auf kulturanthropologischer Grundlage*. Hamburg, 1998.

Scharf, Ralf. *Der Dux Mogontiacensis und die Notitia Dignitatum*. Ergänzungsbande zum Reallexikon der Germanischen Altertumskunde 50. Berlin, 2005.

Scheidel, Walter, Ian Morris and Richard Saller, eds. *The Cambridge Economic History of the Greco-Roman World*. Cambridge, 2007.

Schenk von Stauffenberg and Alexander Graf. *Das Imperium und die Völkerwanderung*. Munich, 1947.

Schlinkert, Dirk. *Ordo Senatorius und nobilitas: Die Konstitution des Senatsadels in der Spätantike*. Stuttgart, 1996.

Schmidt, Ludwig. *Geschichte der deutschen Stämme: Die Ostgermanen*. 2nd edn. Munich, 1938.

Schmidt, Ludwig. *Geschichte der deutschen Stämme: Die Westgermanen.* 2nd edn. Munich, 1940.

Schmidt, Ludwig. *Geschichte der Wandalen.* 2nd edn. Munich, 1942.

Scott, Roger. *Byzantine Chronicles and the Sixth Century.* Variorum Collected Studies 1004. Farnham, 2012.

Seeck, Otto. *Die Briefe des Libanius zeitlich geordnet.* Leipzig, 1906.

Seeck, Otto. *Geschichte des Untergangs der antiken Welt.* 6 vols. Berlin, 1910–21.

Seeck, Otto. *Regesten der Kaiser und Päpste für die Jahre 311 bis 476 n. Chr.* Stuttgart, 1919.

Seibt, Werner, ed. *Die Christianisierung des Kaukasus/The Christianization of the Caucasus (Armenia, Georgia, Albania).* Vienna, 2002.

Sergeev, Andrei. *Barbarian Coins on the Territory between the Balkans and Central Asia: Catalog of Andrei Sergeev's Collection at the State Historical Museum (Moscow).* Moscow, 2012.

Sessa, Kristina. *The Formation of Papal Authority in Late Antique Italy: Roman Bishops and the Domestic Sphere.* Cambridge, 2012.

Shahid, Irfan. *Rome and the Arabs: A Prolegomenon to the Study of Byzantium and the Arabs.* Washington, DC, 1984.

Shaw, Brent D. *Rulers, Nomads and Christians in Roman North Africa.* Variorum Collected Studies. Aldershot, 1995.

Shaw, Brent D. *Sacred Violence: African Christians and Sectarian Hatred in the Age of Augustine.* Cambridge, 2011.

Shepardson, Christine. *Controlling Contested Spaces: Late Antique Antioch and the Spatial Politics of Religious Controversy.* Berkeley, 2014.

Sinnigen, William Gurnee. *The Officium of the Urban Prefecture during the Later Roman Empire.* Papers and Monographs of the American Academy in Rome 17. Rome, 1957.

Sinor, David, ed. *The Cambridge History of Early Inner Asia.* Cambridge, 1990.

Sivan, Hagith. *Ausonius of Bordeaux and the Genesis of a Gallic Aristocracy.* London, 1993.

Sivan, Hagith. *Galla Placidia: The Last Roman Empress.* Oxford, 2011.

Smith, R. R. R. and Bryan Ward-Perkins, eds. *The Last Statues of Antiquity.* Oxford, 2016.

Sneath, David. *The Headless State: Aristocratic Orders, Kinship Society, and Misrepresentations of Nomadic Inner Asia.* New York, NY, 2007.

Sogno, Cristiana, *Q. Aurelius Symmachus.* Ann Arbor, MI, 2006.

Sogno, Cristiana, Bradley K. Storin and Edward J. Watts, eds. *Late Antique Letter Collections: A Critical Introduction and Reference Guide.* Berkeley, CA, 2017.

Soproni, Sándor. *Die letzten Jahrzehnte des pannonischen Limes.* Munich, 1985.

Stallknecht, Bernt. *Untersuchungen zur römischen Aussenpolitik in der Spätantike (306–395 n. Chr.).* Bonn, 1967.

Stancliffe, Clare. *St Martin and His Hagiographer: History and Miracle in Sulpicius Severus*. Oxford, 1983.

Ste Croix, G. E. M. de. *The Class Struggle in the Ancient Greek World from the Archaic Age to the Arab Conquests*. Ithaca, NY, 1983.

Ste Croix, G. E. M. de. *Christian Persecution, Martyrdom and Orthodoxy*. Oxford, 2006.

Stein, Ernst. *Geschichte des spätrömischen Reiches I: Vom römischen zum byzantinischen Staate (204–476 n. Chr.)*. Vienna, 1928.

Stein, Ernst. *Histoire du Bas-Empire 1: De l'état romain à l'état byzantin*. Paris, 1949.

Stein, Ernst. *Histoire du Bas-Empire 2: De la disparition de l'Empire d'Occident à la mort de Justinien (475–565)*. Paris, 1949.

Steinacher, Roland. *Die Vandalen. Aufstieg und Fall eines Barbarenreiches*. Stuttgart, 2016.

Steinacher, Roland. *Rom und die Barbaren: Völker im Alpen- und Donauraum (300–600)*. Stuttgart, 2017.

Stevens, C. E. *Sidonius Apollinaris and His Age*. Oxford, 1933.

Stickler, Timo. *Aëtius: Gestaltungsspielräume eines Heermeisters im ausgehenden Weströmischen Reich*. Vestigia 54. Munich, 2002.

Storgaard, Birger, ed. *Military Aspects of the Aristocracy in the Barbaricum in the Roman and Early Migration Periods*. Publications of the National Museum Studies in Archaeology and History, vol. 5. Copenhagen, 2001.

Straub, Johannes. *Vom Herrscherideal in der Spätantike*. Stuttgart, 1939.

Straub, Johannes. *Regeneratio Imperii: Aufsätze über Roms Kaisertum und Reich im Spiegel der heidnischen und christlichen Publiztik*. 2 vols. Darmstadt, 1972–86.

Stroheker, Karl Friedrich. *Der senatorische Adel im spätantiken Gallien*. Tübingen, 1948.

Stroheker, Karl Friedrich. *Germanentum und Spätantike*. Stuttgart, 1966.

Strootman, Rolf and Miguel John Veluys, eds. *Persianism in Antiquity*. Oriens et Occidens 25. Stuttgart, 2015.

Suerbaum, Werner. *Vom antiken zum frühmittelalterlichen Staatsbegriff*. Münster, 1970.

Sundwall, Johannes. *Weströmische Studien*. Berlin, 1915.

Sundwall, Johannes. *Abhandlungen zur ausgehenden Römertums*. Helsinki, 1919.

Swain, Simon and Mark Edwards, eds. *Approaching Late Antiquity: The Transformation from Early to Late Empire*. Oxford, 2004.

Szidat, Joachim. *Usurpator tanti nominis. Kaiser und Usurpator in der Spätantike (337–476 n. Chr.)*. Historia Einzelschriften 210. Stuttgart, 2010.

Teillet, Suzanne. *Des Goths à la nation gothique*. Paris, 1984.

Thompson, E. A. *A History of Attila and the Huns*. Oxford, 1948.

Thompson, E. A. *Romans and Barbarians: The Decline of the Western Empire*. Madison, WI, 1980.

Thompson, E. A. *The Visigoths in the Time of Ulfila*, 2nd edn. with a foreword by Michael Kulikowski. London, 2008.

Tougher, Shaun. *Julian the Apostate*. Edinburgh, 2007.

Tseng, Chin-Yin. *The Making of the Tuoba Northern Wei: Constructing Material Cultural Expressions in the Northern Wei Pingcheng Period (398–494 CE)*. British Archaeological Reports International Series 2567. Oxford, 2013.

Tsetskhladze, Gocha R., ed. *New Studies on the Black Sea Littoral*. Oxford, 1996.

Ulrich-Bansa, Oscar. *Moneta Mediolanensis (352–498)*. Venice, 1949.

Vallet, Françoise and Michel Kazanski, eds. *L'armée romaine et les barbares du III-e au VII-e siècle*. Paris, 1993.

Vallet, Françoise and Michel Kazanski, eds. *La noblesse romaine et les barbares du IIIe au VIIe siècle*. Paris, 1995.

Van Dam, Raymond. *Leadership and Community in Late Antique Gaul*. Berkeley, CA, 1985.

Vanderspoel, John. *Themistius and the Imperial Court: Oratory, Civic Duty and Paideia from Constantius to Theodosius*. Ann Arbor, MI, 1995.

Van Hoof, Lieve, ed. *Libanius: A Critical Introduction*. Cambridge, 2014.

Vannesse, Michaël. *La défense de l'Occident romain pendant l'Antiquité tardive*. Collection Latomus 326. Brussels, 2010.

Varady, László. *Das letzte Jahrhundert Pannoniens, 376–476*. Amsterdam, 1969.

Varady, László. *Die Auflösung des Altertums. Beiträge zu einer Umdeutung der Alten Geschichte*. Budapest, 1978.

Vasiliev, A. A. *Justin the First: An Introduction to the Epoch of Justinian the Great*. Cambridge, MA, 1950.

Vitiello, Massimiliano. *Theodahad: A Platonic King at the Collapse of Ostrogothic Italy*. Toronto, 2014.

Vitiello, Massimiliano. *Amalasuintha: The Transformation of Kingship in the Post-Roman World*. Philadelphia, PA, 2017.

Vogler, Chantal. *Constance II et l'administration impériale*. Strasbourg, 1979.

Vondrovec, Klaus. *Coinage of the Iranian Huns and Their Successors from Bactria to Gandhara (4th to 8th century CE)*. 2 vols. Vienna, 2014.

von Haehling, Raban. *Die Religionszugehörigkeit der hohen Amtsträger des römischen Reiches seit Constantins I: Alleinherrschaft bis zum Ende der Theodosianischen Dynastie*. Bonn, 1978.

von Rummel, Philipp. *Habitus barbarus: Kleidung und Repräsentation spätantiker Eliten im 4. und 5. Jahrhundert*. Ergänzungsbände zum Reallexicon der Germanischen Altertumskunde, Band 55. Berlin, 2007.

von Simson, Otto G. *Sacred Fortress: Byzantine Art and Statecraft in Ravenna*. Chicago, IL, 1948.

von Wartburg, Walther. *Die Ausgliederung der romanischen Sprachräume*. Bern, 1950.

Waas, Manfred. *Germanen im römischen Dienst im 4. Jahrhundert nach Christus.* Bonn, 1965.

Wallace-Hadrill, J. M. *The Long-haired Kings and Other Studies in Frankish History.* London, 1962.

Watts, Edward J. *City and School in Late Antique Athens and Alexandria.* Berkeley, CA, 2006.

Wenskus, Reinhard. *Stammesbildung und Verfassung: Das Werden der frühmittelalterlichen gentes.* Cologne and Vienna, 1961.

Whelan, Robin. *Being Christian in Vandal Africa: The Politics of Orthodoxy in the Post-Imperial West.* Berkeley, CA, 2018.

Whitby, Mary, ed. *The Propaganda of Power: The Role of Panegyric in Late Antiquity.* Leiden, 1998.

Whittaker, C. R. *Rome and Its Frontiers: The Dynamics of Empire.* London, 2004.

Wibszycka, Ewa. *The Alexandrian Church: People and Institutions.* Warsaw, 2015.

Wickham, Chris. *Early Medieval Italy: Central Power and Local Society, 400–1000.* Ann Arbor, MI, 1990.

Wickham, Chris. *Framing the Early Middle Ages: Europe and the Mediterranean, 400–800.* Oxford, 2005.

Wienand, Johannes, ed. *Contested Monarchy: Integrating the Roman Empire in the Fourth Century AD.* New York, NY, 2015.

Wijnendaele, Jeroen W. P. *The Last of the Romans: Bonifatius – Warlord and Comes Africae.* London, 2015.

Winkelmann, Friedhelm. *Ausgewählte Aufsätze. Studien zu Konstantin dem Grossen und zur byzantinischen Kirchengeschichte.* Wolfram Brandes and John Haldon, eds. Birmingham, 1993.

Winkler, Gerhard. *Die Reichsbeamten von Noricum und ihr Personal bis zum Ende der römischen Herrschaft.* Sitzungsberichte der Österreichische Akademie der Wissenschaften, Philosophisch-Historische Klasse, Band 261. Vienna, 1969.

Wolfram, Herwig. *Intitulatio I: Lateinische Königs- und Fürstentitel bis zum Ende des 8. Jahrhunderts.* Mitteilungen des Instituts für Österreichische Geschichtsforschung Ergänzungsband 21. Graz, 1967.

Wolfram, Herwig. *Gotische Studien: Volk und Herrschaft im frühen Mittelalter.* Munich, 2005.

Wolfram, Herwig. *Die Goten: Von den Anfängen bis zur Mitte des sechsten Jahrhunderts. Entwurf einer historischen Ethnographie.* 5th edn. Munich, 2009.

Wolfram, Herwig and Andreas Schwarcz, eds. *Anerkennung und Integration.* Vienna, 1989.

Wolfram, Herwig and Walter Pohl, eds. *Typen der Ethnogeses unter besonderer Berücksichtigung der Bayern.* 2 vols. Vienna, 1989.

Woloszyn, Marcin, ed. *Byzantine Coins in Central Europe between the 5th and 10th Century.* Krakow, 2008.

Wood, Ian. *The Merovingian Kingdoms, 450–751.* London, 1993.

Wood, Ian, ed. *Franks and Alamanni in the Merovingian Period: An Ethnographic Perspective.* Woodbridge, 1993.

Wright, Roger. *Late Latin and Early Romance in Spain and Carolingian France.* Liverpool, 1982.

Zabiela, Gintautas, Zenonas Baubonis and Egle Marcinkeviciute, eds. *Archaeological Investigations in Independent Lithuania 1990–2010.* Vilnius, 2012.

Zazzaro, Chiara. *The Ancient Red Sea Port of Adulis and the Eritrean Coastal Region: Previous Investigations and Museum Collections.* British Archaeological Reports International Series 2569. Oxford, 2013.

Zecchini, Giuseppe. *Aezio: L'ultima difesa dell'Occidente romano.* Rome, 1983.

Zecchini, Giuseppe. *Ricerche di storiografia latina tardoantica.* Rome, 1993.

Ziegler, Joachim. *Zur religiösen Haltung der Gegenkaiser im 4. Jh. n. Chr.* Kallmünz, 1970.

Zöllner, Erich. *Geschichte der Franken bis zur Mitte des 6. Jahrhunderts.* Munich, 1970.

INDEX

❦

During the early and high empire, the nomenclature of Roman citizens generally, if not invariably, was the *tria nomina*, or three names (*praenomen*, *nomen* and *cognomen*), which are traditionally indexed under the *nomen* or family name. These naming habits began to change during the third century and fell apart completely in the fourth. At the lower end of the social scale, single names became commonplace. In the middle, after Constantine, the *nomen* Flavius tended to be taken by the men of highly variable backgrounds who had entered imperial service; it became the equivalent not so much of our 'Mr' but of the Spanish 'Don' or the Polish 'Pan', and is not used as a head-word in indexing. At the highest end of the social scale, however, aristocrats across the empire, and especially in Italy and the city of Rome, began to distinguish themselves from the mass of imperial servants by adopting an extravagant number of names (so-called polyonymous nomenclature). These names could be used in multiple different combinations of two or three name-elements in various social contexts, but in formal contexts, when only one name-element could be used, that single name-element never varied in the course of an individual's life (scholars call this the diacritical name). In the standard work of scholarly reference, *The Prosopography of the Roman Empire* (in three volumes covering the years 260–641), individuals are filed under their diacritical name, a practice followed in this index. Where there is possibility of confusion, e.g. a standard English form, or an individual commonly referred to by modern scholars by a name other than the diacritic, cross-references are given (hence Majorian rather than Maiorianus, or Magnus Maximus as well as Maximus, Magnus). 'St' is filed as spelt out in full. Plate captions are not indexed.

Cyril, Bishop of Alexandria 168–70, 186
  and Council of Ephesus 178–9
Cyrillus, *magister militum* under
  Anastasius 297
Cyrus, Flavius Taurus Seleucus, urban
  prefect under Theodosius II 182–3

D

Dacia (diocese) 98, 118, 185
Dadastana (near Karahisar, Turkey),
  Jovian dies at 35
Dadisho, Bishop of Seleucia-Ctesiphon
  173
Dagalaifus, Fl., *magister militum* under
  Julian 31, 32
  and Valentinian I 36, 40
Dagalaiphus, Flavius, father of
  Areobindus, 256
Dál Riata, kingdom of 286
Damascus, Umayyad capital 314
Damasus, Bishop of Rome 49, 100, 106,
  108
  and Ambrose of Mediolanum 94,
  114
Daphne, suburb of Antioch 29, 56
Dara (Anastasiopolis), Roman fortress
  257, 301
De Excidio Britanniae, *see* Gildas
De Providentia, *see* Synesius
De Regno, *see* Synesius
Demophilus, Bishop of Constantinople
  100–101
Dengizich, son of Attila 240, 241–2
Denmark 286–7
Derbend wall 237
Dertona (Tortona, Italy), deposition of
  Majorian at 220
Dexippus, Greek historian 83
Didymus, Spanish relative of Honorius
  145
Digest of Justinian 303–4

Diocletian 6, 7, 32, 56
  administrative reforms 9–14
  and 'Great Persecution' 17
  law codes 179–80
Diogenianus, general under Anastasius
  251
Dioscorus, Bishop of Alexandria 186–7,
  189
Divitenses, unit of the *comitatenses* 38
Divodurum (Metz, Germany), captured
  by Attila 210
Domnica, wife of Valens 91
Donatist schism 19, 21, 65–6, 81, 177
  circumcellions and 47, 168
Donatus, African bishop 19, 65
Doryphorianus, *vicarius* of Rome under
  Valentinian I 70–71
Dracontius, Latin poet in Vandal Africa
  268
Drepanius Pacatus, Latinius, Latin
  panegyrist 99, 111
Dura Europus, Julian at 31
Durocortorum (Reims, France) 41, 47
  mutiny at 34
Durostorum (Silistra, Bulgaria) 192
  and Valens' Gothic wars 56, 85
Dushanbe Hoard 235
Dyrrachium (Dürres, Albania) 238,
  251

E

Ecdicius, Gallic nobleman 150
Ecdicius, brother-in-law of Sidonius
  Apollinaris 227–8
Edeco, father of Odoacer 261
Edessa, Nestorians in 179
Edobich, *magister militum* under
  Constantine 'III' 139, 148, 150
Egypt (diocese) 10–11, 12, 174–5
  abolished 305
  see also Coptic language

Olybrius, Anicius Hermogenianus,
consul of 395 121
Olybrius, Q. Clodius Hermogenianus,
praetorian prefect under Gratian 91
Olympiodorus, Greek historian 142,
194–5
Olympius, *magister officiorum* under
Honorius 143–5, 148
enemy of Stilicho 141, 154
Onogurs (Bulgars) 252, 289, 297
Onoulphus, brother of Odoacer 246,
261, 263
Optila, assassin of Valentinian III
214
Ordos, Xiongnu origins and 174
Orestes, *magister militum* under Julius
Nepos 228, 246
and Visigoths 271, 274
father of Romulus, usurper 228, 261
Orestes, *praefectus Augustalis* under
Theodosius II 169
Oriens (diocese) 10–11, 12, 27, 36, 91, 157,
305
Orientius, Gallic poet 146
Ossius, Bishop of Corduba *see* Hosius of
Corduba
Ostia, port of Rome 117
Ostrogothic kingdom in Italy 263–5,
269, 288, 300
Ostrogotho, daughter of Theodoric I
265
Our Island Story (H. E. Marshall) 152

P

Pacatus, *see* Drepanius
Pactus Legis Salicae, Frankish law code
280
Padusia, wife of Felix 196
Palladas, Greek poet 24
Palladius, son of Petronius Maximus
214, 215

Pamir mountains 73, 171, 291
Pannonia (diocese) 12, 135, 185, 238
part of western empire 109, 118
Pannonia Prima (province) 68–9, 238
Pannonia Secunda (province) 265
Pannoniaca, unit of the *comitatenses*
Panormus (Palermo, Italy) 202
Pap, Armenian king 58, 82–3
parabalani, Egyptian monks, 168–9,
170, 178
Parthian empire 8, 72, 237
Patricius, father of St Augustine 116
Patricius, son of Aspar and caesar under
Leo 233, 241, 242
Patricius, *magister officiorum* under Leo
239, 245
Patricius, *magister militum* under
Anastasius 256–7, 295
Patricius, *see also* St Patrick
Patruinus, *comes sacrarum largitionum*
under Honorius 142
Paulinus, *magister officiorum* under
Theodosius II 183, 184
Paulinus, Nicene Bishop of Antioch 60,
101, 102
Paulus, brother of Orestes 228
Paulus, *comes* in Gaul 278
Paulus Catena, 'the Chain', *agens in
rebus* under Constantius II 28
pedites Constantiani, unit of *limitanei* 66
Pelagia, widow of Bonifatius, wife of
Aëtius 198
Pelagian heresy 209
Peroz, as Kidarite name 78
Peroz I, Persian shah 234–7, 255
Pessinus 40
temple of Magna Mater 29
Peter, Bishop of Alexandria 100
Peter, reader at Alexandria 169
Peter Barsymes, praetorian prefect
under Justinian 304